LOST
COUNTRY
LIFE

LOST COUNTRY LIFE

DOROTHY HARTLEY

PANTHEON BOOKS, NEW YORK

Whan no man had craft in minde
Then of craft had God and Kynde.
When no techer was in Londe
Men had craft by Goddes hande.
They that had craft so He thenne
Taught forth craft to othir menne.
Some craft that yet comes not in place
Some man shall have by God's grace.

Walter Mapes (*c.* 1140–*c.* 1209)

All rights reserved under International and Pan-American Copyright Conventions. Published in the United States by Pantheon Books, a division of Random House, Inc., New York. Originally published in Great Britain by Macdonald & Janes Publishers Ltd.

LIBRARY OF CONGRESS CATALOGING IN PUBLICATION DATA
Hartley, Dorothy.
Lost country life.

Includes index.
1. England—Social life and customs.   2. Folk-lore—
England.   3. Country life—England.   I. Title.
DA110.H36   942   79-3320
ISBN 0-304-51036-4

Manufactured in the United States of America

24689753

CONTENTS

INTRODUCTION

THIS book sets out to be a down-to-earth study of people, their animals, plants, and jobs, in the days when almost all of them lived on and from the land. It is not a history, being agricultural rather than academic. The term 'mediaeval', where it appears, is used loosely; for the most part, the life and work described pre-dated the early enclosures of common land and ended in the sixteenth century. A man of that century, one Thomas Tusser, published a farming calendar in rhyming verse, extracts from which are used here to introduce each month's activities.

Tusser was born at Rivenhall in Essex, and educated in London and Cambridge. He left his own farm on the Stour estuary to become the estate agent at Brantham Hall in Suffolk. His first *Hundred Points of Husbandry* were printed in 1557 from the old black-letter wooden type. The many subsequent and enlarged editions (*Five Hundred Points ...*) were printed from the new metal type. He died and was buried in Poultry, London, like a good Cockney.

Tusser knew his work people; he knew the land, and the grain and animals best suited to it. Understanding the way a farm operated, he could sympathise with honest poachers and condemn loiterers. At the same time, his familiarity with classical writers allowed him to show how early English living and working practices were part of a continuous stream of custom in the countryside. His verses were used as teaching devices in schools as late as the nineteenth century, and his observations still serve us well.

The feudal system under which most worked in these days hampered some men and supported others; a few were free entirely. There were early dealings in towns with busy traffic, but in general the country people preferred to buy and sell in markets where they could barter without the need of money. Most of the workers in this book spent their whole lifetime on the land where they were born. Even those who moved, a few to go overseas to the new colonies, tended to look for land such as they had left, the new land becoming their new home.

Throughout the period we study, any strong, healthy person could obtain the basic necessities from whatever land he chose, even wild, untameable fen or marsh. Though we live today in a much different world than the people in this book, we are still their direct descendants. Our bodily instincts still earth-instructed, we react to the reek of peat, sense the blue of woodsmoke, rejoice in clear running water.

I wish to thank all those who have contributed to the making of this book. First, my publishers for shaping such a complicated documentary on which both Susan Rea and Paul Minns have done hard work; my typist, Miss Etheridge, herself a writer, who can sort my bad spelling from even earlier English; the experts for their specialised contributions; the workmen, who on some pages speak for themselves; and my trusted friend and proof-reader, Fred Littman, for all his help. We all do hope you enjoy — and perhaps even learn from — our work.

Dorothy Hartley
Froncysyllte, 1979

A Note for American Readers

America begins where this book ends. The stern religious rebels in black felt hats and buckle shoes who were among the Founding Fathers were men bred largely from a farming community. The Puritan Bible itself is full of farming: sheep marking, flocks grazing contemplatively by rivers, settlements where grain was sown. Saxon Englishmen used oxen much like the biblical beast 'that treadeth out the corn,' and the thread is continuous: the Norman English bred horses that came to be the main power of American transportation.

Many homely survivals from the life in this book can still be found in America. Baked beans were winter food for Piers Plowman's 'little ones' centuries ago. Elizabeth I ruled that all her sailors were to wear the thick Appledore jersey and adaptable Monmouth cap still copied today. New England sugar-cured hams are the descendants of the mediaeval honey-cured bacon, and sweet-and-sour pickles derive from the two old English ways of pickling fruits and vegetables.

When Tusser wrote,

> *Wife, make us a feast, spare fleshe neither corne,*
> *make wafers and cakes, for our shepe must be shorne...*

his 'wafers' had been known since the twelfth century; they are mentioned in Chaucer. These oatcakes were originally baked, one side at a time, on flat iron pans until double plates hinged like a pair of tongs enabled both sides to be cooked at once on the open fire. The wafer irons, used for pre-Reformation holy bread, were later banned by the Protestant regime (and often buried, to be dug up and exhibited in our museums today). But Puritan settlers took them freely across the Atlantic, altered their size and shape to suit their finer maize flour, and eventually produced what we know today as the waffle-iron.

Many a sea-sick emigrant probably carried Tusser's lore in his head on the long voyage over. Do you recognise 'It's an ill wind that blows none to good'? That's Tusser.

D.H.

ACKNOWLEDGEMENTS

The author and publishers would like to thank the following for permission to reproduce illustrations: Aerofilms Ltd. for 58; the Bodleian Library, Oxford, for 1 and 15; the British Library for 7, 8, 10, 12, 14, 16, 24, 27, 28, 30, 33, 37, 39, 44, 53; Neil Chadwick for 50; *Farmers Weekly* for 13 and 34; John R. Freeman & Co. for 5, 11, 18, 19; the Museum of Rural Life, University of Reading, for 31, 40, 41, 42; Ripon City Tourist Association for 3 and 4; the Science Museum for the models shown in 54–57; John Tarlton for 20, 25, 32, 35, 36, 45, 46; the Welsh Folk Museum for 17; the Dean and Chapter of York Minster for 2.

BACKGROUND

THE MAN IN HISTORY

To DIVIDE HISTORY into periods is misleading. The river of history flows fast, or slow, in different places, and always it is the surface that moves most swiftly. In the hills the turbulent waters of history either foam in spate, or run dry; where a river passes over lowland it becomes clogged and slow. In places, where the land curves, the current circles round and round upon itself, or where the current is held behind a boulder, in that deep pool the dead water stays, unstirred. There the slow slugs slide through the slime, and blind fish sleep; there mud-dwellers move, in water so thick it does not even stir the trailing feelers of the tench floating above. Thus, in a backwater of history, man may exist unmoved for centuries.

Basically, the Man we are studying was an individual shaped by the earth itself. He might be a wizened brown gnome, or a golden giant, or anything between the two, according to his country of origin and adaptation to his living conditions. What he had in common with other men, however different they might appear, was the land itself. For on it they all depended completely; it had to supply their food, shelter, clothing, everything. As it supplied their bodies, so it occupied their thoughts: the land was the basis of their existence.

Physical Characteristics

Although the intellectual powers and social habits of man are of paramount importance, we must not underrate the importance of his bodily structure. This Man was intensely alive. The land shaped him physically producing hillman, lowlander, river- or sea-man. As work began early in youth, and was frequently continued for life, that work would develop him physically. He walked his flat earth barefoot, or on flat leather, so had the slightly backward stance of those who have never used a heeled shoe. In age, his strong feet appear flat and splayed and his legs sinewy and thin with horny knees. But he moved freely, and his clothing did not impede movement. He probably wore a breech clout, and loose shirt, often a hood, or cap, and (noteworthy) used working gloves. His skin was weather-beaten; in winter lightly smoke-tanned or chapped; in summer, sunburnt. His teeth were either good, or gone, depending on his diet, for he lacked all dental attention. His Woman worked beside him on many jobs, and the household work was definitely strenuous. Her hair was tied up with a strip of cloth, woven to the required width, and even by these simple means she could achieve much complicated variety with it.

While he remained healthy, his senses were probably more freely developed than our own, even to keeping some of the old animal instincts. Walking barefoot or on silent leather, he would hear many sounds we miss; the sounds of the streams, which were his guides, their ripple over pebbles directing him to a shallow ford; the thunder of a distant waterfall, broken water echoing from high rocks; the purr of a bog; the sound made by wind passing from short grass to high reeds.

It is familiar to everyone that watchmakers and engravers are liable to be short-sighted, whilst men living much out of doors, and especially savages, are generally long-sighted. Short sight and long sight certainly tend to be inherited. The inferiority of Europeans, in comparison with savages, in eyesight, is no doubt the accumulated and transmitted effect of lessened use during many generations.

Charles Darwin (1809–92)

Eyesight differed according to physique, but the eye musculature (aptly termed 'accommodation' which means 'focus from distance to near sight'), was probably better developed than ours is; for today, reading and reckoning keep many eyes for long hours on the same short focus. Even ordinary indoor occupations enforce fixed focus for long periods. (Short of a monk's cell, or a prisoner's dungeon, mediaeval environments were wide, and labourers used their huts more for sleeping purposes than indoor occupations.) He probably had better night sight for he was accustomed to the dim light of his hut and artificial lighting was little used.

His sense of smell seems to have been curiously selective (which by our reckoning must have been a merciful dispensation!) Yet he was susceptible to animal aromas, selective of plant flavours and had a reasonably appreciative taste.

Personalities varied, but all had the same basic training in material things. He learnt of water by using it, watched it change into ice and snow, learnt to heat it and, possibly by explosive accident, found out its power as steam! Earth taught him fire, and his hunger taught him the value of food. Languages and dialects were as varied as his gods, but basically lord and labourer were at one in that both relied *on* the earth for everything, for both shared the same earthly materials (and the same unreliable climate). The great lord in a draughty castle shivered in linen under a fur-trimmed robe; the peasant in a stuffy hut wore wool-next-the-skin – and the same fleas bit both. The land and the seasons ruled everybody. The king himself could not have spring chicken and green peas earlier than his lowest feudal dependant, who probably got his duck and green beans before the king did, depending on how skilfully he caught the one and grew the other. In all things, including acute discomfort, the land is a great leveller.

Mental Characteristics

The mental strength of this Man was his earth-inspired common sense. Much of our knowledge is second-hand and our very speech betrays us when we say 'I know for a fact', by which we mean a small definite piece of knowledge. In contrast, all our basic man did know was as 'fact', and this material knowledge went deeper than ours. A modern woman sees a piece of linen, but the mediaeval woman saw through it to the flax fields, she smelt the reek of the retting ponds, she felt the hard rasp of the hackling, and she saw the soft sheen of the glossy flax. Man did not just see 'leather', he saw the beast – perhaps one of his own – and knew the effort of slaughtering, liming and curing.

Communities were smaller and whether our Man lived on the outskirts of some feudal system, had escaped from it, or was entirely isolated, he would work alone, or daily with the same few fellow-workers – conversation would soon languish. But *think* he must. The clodhopper with his heavy wood mallet, working his slow way for hours as he broke up the clods of earth, must have thought that however small he broke the clods it would always be possible to divide them again, and yet again, until they were the very dust from which all began. Or, walking alone, perhaps stopping to water his nag, lying down to rest by a pool, he would let the weight of his conscious thought slide away, even as he let the heavy pack slide down his nag's sweating side. Almost mindlessly, looking into the water, seeing the reflection of his own face, and the fish swimming below, and hearing birds passing overhead, he saw separate worlds, each unconscious of the other. Small wonder if his thought reached as far as any man's may reach, and far beyond his simple speech. He realised his static earth held the elements of air and water; and air presumably held life, as life depended on air and water in order to live. Life from the earth used rain to push up the corn in order for it to live in the air. That this 'life' was invisible did not worry him: wind was invisible, but could fell trees. Our Man accepted invisibility quite naturally: he saw a coloured moth settle upon a tree and vanish, he saw a hare spring up from where it had crouched invisible in its form. If insects and animals had this skill, then people could develop it. Changing people into animals was a fact accepted not only by the unlettered labourer: Giraldus Cambrensis, of Norman-Saxon parentage, a travelled and erudite man, states cheerfully that Appuleius was turned into an ass and was cured by taking rose leaves. This whole idea carried on well into the sixteenth century – we should realise that Shakespeare's Bottom's head would still be a lively possibility to some of the audience. Possibly because this trick of invisibility was so much used by small wild things, wild fern seed – which does not exist – was long considered the dietetic vehicle for invisibility. (Fern plants, *pteridophyta*, have no seeds; they form a dust-like body of spores, for sporophyte generation.)

Our Man accepted life as a material force, saw it force its way into the rebellious babe at the first moment of birth. He saw life force the growth of its containing body. He watched it leave that body in death. Sometimes he watched life rend and struggle with the body, as if unable to get free. Another time, life slid out so quietly he could not see its passing. He could drive life out with a blow, or let it out slowly, as blood ran. But life and blood were not identical (though some thought so). The distinction between them may have been based on the difference between veinous blood and the spurting blood from a cut artery, for wars would give examples of both (though the circulation of the blood was not yet discovered).

But on the whole, life to material man seemed more like an invisible force in the air. As a materialist, a lot of his thought was occupied by life: he knew what happened to his body when life went out of it (unpleasant, but the way of all material earth), but it puzzled him where his life itself went to. Would it still go on knowing it was his? Obviously life was pressed into things, thrusting, as it were, to get itself into another body. His observations of family likeness, and the power of heredity (in breeds of cattle for instance) made it a reasonable belief that life would hang about the place it came from, like a lost animal wanting to get home into its old lair.

Any reasonable man (and our man was reasonable) would try to catch this life: it was a primitive hunter's instinct. Air could be seen playing on water, could be watched as it ran over grass; wind could be trapped in a box or a pipe. If life was in the air, might it too be trapped, or its escape delayed? Perhaps entangled in a very fine web as thick mist was caught when passing over bushes. Our Man saw the dew, caught by myriads of tiny cobwebs, which covered the grass like a net, and quivered with the life that was apparently rising from the earth. Again; when there was no breath of wind, he saw river mists stirred and moving, as if life passed through. Unseen things moved all round him: some he could see were caused by the forces of heat or cold; for others there was no cause. Because life was in everything it might be ensconced in some strangely formed root or rock, or even coerced to move into a specially carved receptacle; it could reside in wood or stone. To think of this as idolatry is to put our own modern condemnation on to his reasoning. The concept of something being 'supernatural' was meaningless to him.

Life was obviously there, and powerful, so that it was reasonable for him

The stones of this shrine were recovered from mended walls and sheep pens. The carving was done about 1180, when the Church employed skilled Italian craftsmen, yet the stone mason lived within sound of his waterfall and watched the fern fronds unfolding. The whole shrine was probably brightly painted and gilt.

The shrine was that of St Melangell, who settled in Pennant in Powys, a narrow valley winding between high hills, and blocked at the end by a rocky waterfall. Brochwel, a princeling, was galloping after a hare pursued by his hounds; he came upon the maiden suddenly, and saw his hare sheltering under her cloak. The hounds recoiled, his horn froze to his lips, and 'his heart refuged for ever with that lovely lady'. Even now, no one in that valley will harm a hare (known as 'wyn Melangell': Melangell's lambs). Her shrine has been restored and the waterfall still runs.

to try to obtain the power for himself. He probably thought of it as some imprisoned force that if caught he could make use of – as a modern woman uses electricity to boil a kettle. (If the kettle does not boil, her thought can go back as far as the fuse box before helplessly accepting 'a power cut', but she does not think past inexplicable convertors to a far-off unknown waterfall in a distant mountain.) Thus it was, that earth-taught man accepted the power of life as part of the earth but without knowing its source. To trap it was a natural desire. (The hope of catching it in quantity as it was forcibly driven from the body perhaps lay behind some human sacrifices.)

Thoughts weaving intricate patterns are normal, and as his fingers passed through wet weed strands, plaited straw or wove sibilant rush, he conceived the thoughts which, we dare to believe, are caught for ever in the unearthly intricacies of the Celtic scroll. There we see patterns of pliant wood, strands seeming unable to restrain their own creation of curious animal forms. He saw the wet wave-woven sea tangle teeming with imprisoned life, rounded straws cracked to calculated angles, smooth reeds bent to plaited patterns, the witch knots in the mane of a horse; and his own intricate designs are his thought made visible.

We have treated body and mind under separate headings, but the two are inextricably involved, for the brain retained primitive fears and warnings of danger in the same way that the body retains muscles and nerves, though the actions for which they originally developed are no longer needed. (Some people can still waggle their ears!) These animal instincts, that remain so strongly in use among primitive peoples, probably account for the second sight prevalent in the Outer Hebrides and other remote western islands. We have now the man himself, with all his faculties, his earth-taught common sense, his ability to think for himself. What his thoughts were we cannot know.

The Phoenix

Truth lives of itself. Man is but its crucible of clay. The clay can be burnt, but from the ashes, that instant – or in a thousand years – truth will rise again. Some men expend their strength in a search and fail, yet some helpless terrified wight will be invaded by inescapable truth and that bird of flame will live with him, till he dies. The phoenix must be accepted with its impact on the defenceless mediaeval labourer. For the fire of the phoenix is lit by no earthly flame, and the charred nest of that golden bird may have blown to dust in many a mediaeval furrow.

THE COMING OF CHRISTIANITY

The same high mental faculties which first led man to believe in unseen spiritual agencies, then in fetishism, polytheism, and ultimately in monotheism, would infallibly lead him, as long as his reasoning powers remained poorly developed, to various strange superstitions and customs.

Charles Darwin (1809–92)

'Such,' he said, 'O King, seems to me the present life of men on earth in comparison with that time which is unknown to us, as when you are sitting at supper with your warriors and counsellors in the season of winter, the hall being warmed by a fire blazing on the hearth in the centre, the storms of the wintry rains or snow raging without; and then a sparrow, entering the house should swiftly flit across the hall, entering at one door, and quickly disappearing at the other. The time that it is within, it is safe from the wintry blast, but the narrow bounds of warmth and shelter are passed in a little moment, and then the bird vanishes out of sight, returning again into the winter's night from which it has just emerged. So this life of man appears for a short interval; but of what went before, or what is to follow, we are utterly ignorant. If, therefore, this new doctrine conveys to us any more assured promise, it has just claims that we should embrace it.'

Ecclesiastical History, Bede (673–735)

In our study of the mind of our labourer we tried to show that in his long, laborious life, the earth had shown him Life as a powerful intrusive spirit, which eluded his capture, and most of his idols represented his attempts to control or propitiate this mysterious power. This earth-evolved, instinctive belief fitted well with simple monotheistic Christianity as it reached him. The idea of Christianity first reached him as one of the many speculations held by the varied nationalities who brought their beliefs to the island. There was no reason why this new possibility would alter his acceptance of all his lesser spirits which existed in trees, in rocks and streams, or maliciously as lights bouncing over the marshes to mislead on a dark night.

If the foreigner was a materially-minded man like themselves, his report would be on material matters. As any other stranger, he might join the men waiting by the quay for the return of the fishing boats, mending nets, or sorting bait. Or, sheltering in a warm stable, he would tell of a man who had been born in just such a stable 'some shepherds found him one night'. 'Why out at night?' 'Lambing time, maybe?' 'Were there wolves in those parts?' 'We don't get many wolves here now. We used to get well paid for a wolf head' . . . and the talk would change.

To our labourer it could be no more than another traveller's tale, and of no great importance. The character of the locality, receptive or antagonistic to new ideas, was probably of more importance than the skill of the reporter.

Celtic Christianity

In a still of the sea, so clear the sea they found
Below they saw on either side, clearly to the ground.
They saw the ground deep covered, with fishes in a heap
His monks bid St Brendan that he softe speak –
(So that we wake not the fishes, lest they the ship break,
For all the fishes layen still, as if they were asleep)
'Be ye afeard?' quoth St Brendan. 'Wherof be ye a-dread?
Upon the master of all fish back, I have walked glad!
And a fire maked on his back, and do from year to year!'
And the Holy man the louder sang, the fishes for to hear.

Then the Fishes starten up as though awoke from sleep
And comen about the monks ship, all in a heap,
So thick they floated about the ship they even inclosed it so
The while St Brendan his mass sang, for to hear was all their do,
And when the Mass was all done, each fish wend to his end.
Such wonders a man may see, that through the world will wend.

from *The Navigation of St Brendan*

Christianity seems to have reached Ireland and the western seaboard very early, probably in the fifth century, seaborne from Brittany. Ireland was an intellectual influence in Europe. Irish scholars passing to and from Ireland acquired mental flexibility and great physical stamina. Some suggest they showed the remains of a Greek tradition. They lacked the dominant drive of the Romans, or the acquisitiveness of the later Normans. Their forcefulness was induced by their environment. Their land was at the end of the known world; in the west the sea swept onwards to eternity. From St Brendan's Point, where still lie the stones of his small cell, they could see far out the Isles of the Blessed and watch the sun go down to the abyss of the 'waters under the earth'. Did they catch that instant flash of green as the sun sinks through the water? If so, what did it mean to them?

The Celtic missionaries were some of the best brains of their period, with the urge for exploration. Every voyage was perilous, which made them inter-dependent with their pagan fellows. (They were so often in the same boat.) Material matters preceded the spiritual. Two men in a leaky boat on the teeth of a reef do not discuss theology, they bail, while the strength and skill of the pagan as much as of the Christian is needed to save their lives. The halo of sanctity has obscured the strength and stamina of the early Irish saints – they had the gentleness that so often accompanies great physical strength. Though their life was of stern danger, they knew joy also. After the storm, a rift of sunlight on a shingle beach, the aroma of smoke where fresh-caught fish grilled on a little fire of driftwood, luscious, succulent shellfish, fresh crusted bread, and, with luck, butter. Inland, they knew the shelter of small, low cabins, cave-like among the rocks; and the sudden peace of utter weariness.

Monks lived monastically where possible, and St Columba founded on the flat island of Iona a flourishing settlement in about 565. He made it far more comfortable than most contemporary holy islands (though it was many times invaded by the pirate Picts).

Their sympathy and understanding extended to their people's devils, who were not derided, but domesticated, so that in the monastic manuscripts their strange half-animal forms (now safely controlled in strong strap-work coils) still keep their live eyes and ferociously engaging grins. This trapping of devils was ancient pagan usage, so that when the peasants saw the wonderful Lindisfarne and Kells illuminations, they believed they were done by the direct help of heaven (in which they were perfectly correct). In the quotation from the *Navigation of St Brendan* you can trace this skill of the Celtic church. 'Wherof be ye a-dread?' is gentle acknowledgment that they had the right to dread the power of spirits, but devils should be kept in their place and not imputed to the fish. The sailors who landed on a sleeping whale believed it an island – only when they started to make a fire on the 'island' did the whale object. (The story was reassuring; and this competent dealing with spirits did not necessarily disrupt all their previous ideas.)

The Peripatetic Missionary

hic habundant Lupi
Script from Gough map (*c.*1360)

We have noted Celtic Christianity, seaborne from Britanny, and explained its almost imperceptible percolation through travellers' tales; and so can account for small Christian families isolated on trade routes who developed their own ideas from random hearsay. This would go on for some time, for in the north many of the first missionaries were peripatetic people, pausing only as they travelled on elsewhere. Their talk would be earnest, but it might be a year before their return journey brought them that way again. This was providential, because it gave time to think, while previous ideas and instincts were still in full working order.

Our man, entirely earth-educated, thought slowly and still trusted to many of his natural animal instincts. Early Christianity was blessedly simple. It asserted that all life on earth belonged to one great God who was the spirit of Life. He had made the earth and had good will towards it, and man had that spirit within himself, so he could reach God direct. Our earth-educated man felt instinctively that this explained his own previous speculations. It turned his own nebulous ideas into a firm conviction, until gradually in his mind he felt as if it was something he had always known, for Christianity in its *simple* form appealed to his reason rather than his emotion. He knew his body was made of the earth, came from the earth and would return to the earth. Christianity taught him his spirit was of God and would return to God. Instinctively he felt this was right; it was the instinct by which animals hibernate or migrate. The earth's changing seasons transform the bodies of earth's creatures: the dormouse stores fat in his tail. Study their instinctive behaviour and see what they *do* – but what they *think* of, only God knows. ('Dear God, where gat these wild things wit?', as Langland exclaimed in *Piers Plowman*.)

The Missionary on the Job

We select Mael Rubbias at random. He was a monk from Iona a generation after Colomba, and has left his mark all over northern Scotland, probably arriving, with an experienced boatman, in a small boat with a square sail.

Mediaeval Scotland was more varied than England – in the south the Picts swarmed as fiercely as wild bees in heather, further north were mountains of snow and streams in spate. During the long twilight the northern sky flickered with coloured lights from beyond the known world's end. Routes along river valleys, or along lochs, were the only travellers' tracks. In those days people did not climb mountains for fun: when they needed to cross the end of a valley, they picked out the best pass. Mael Rubbias' journey began at the entrance of a long sea loch, with landings overnight. He would be reasonably young, tough, with a good head and, let's hope, a sound digestion. He probably had an interpreter with him. They would take with them dried grain, one iron cooking pot, knives, food bags and fishing tackle. A couple of deer skins could serve as waterproof groundsheets or windbreaks. Their landing places depended on fresh water, wind shelter, or their sheer inability to go any farther. They'd up-end the boat for shelter, or cut river willows to form a windbreak. There are so many stories of a saint's staff taking root at the place of his preaching, one suspects they used willows.

They might find some small settlement, or the smoke from their camp fire would attract curious locals. Friendly talk, or hostilities, might delay departure, but the missionary would more likely struggle for words productive of food, or travelling directions, than start theological discussion. Next day, a further journey, and next year he might be followed by others, tracing his route by the fire-split stones of his camp, or a clearing in the stream. Later, small chapels, and finally churches and cathedrals, traced the journey of many missionaries, but at first, to our labourer, he was just a travelling stranger. In the wilds he might be conspicuous, but there could be less variation in appearance when all clothing had to be either wool or leather (because there was nothing else to make it of). Later, a monk's robe, travel-stained and kilted up, might be recognised. The first Christian living among them would cause interest by his lack of fear; his disregard of awful warnings would be impressive; nor did he trust to special amulets, or fear local devils. A Christian hoping to convert others would not willingly insult another man's relatives, nor his gods. Compared with these adventures in the wilds, the report of St Augustine's visit is ceremonious:

> King Ethelbert, whose wife Bertha was a Christian, met them on Thanet where the King gave them fair and courteous hearing. After St Augustine had preached the word of Life [note the phrase] the King spoke: 'Your words and promises are fair, but they are new and strange to us and I cannot accept them and abandon the age-old beliefs of the English peoples. But since you have travelled so far and I can see that you are sincere, we will receive you hospitably, nor will we forbid you to preach and win any people you can to your religion.' The King then granted them accommodation in the city of Canterbury with a supply of provisions.

A fair and courteous greeting in 597, which proves that there had been infiltration of Christianity for some time; we know that Bertha, the queen, already Christian, had brought her own bishop with her, and there would be household talk. The King's servants would talk to their relatives among the outside workers, who would be most interested to know all about 'the new foreign Queen'. As feudal lord the King's greeting is sensible, for he had a legal control over his people, but did not rule their thoughts. This decorous English official opening was a result of St Gregory having earlier seen the golden-haired, blue-eyed slaves sold in the market at Rome, and made the well-known comment 'not Angles, but angels'; and so he despatched official Christianity to England as soon as possible. By Chaucer's time, there were definite churches in most of the towns.

The Parish Priest

Wyd was his parisshe and houses far asonder
But he ne lefte nat, for reyn ne thonder
In siknesse nor in meschief, to visite

The ferreste in his parisshe, muche and lite,
Upon his feet, and in his hand a staf.

                    The Prologue, Geoffrey Chaucer (1340?–1400)

Chaucer's parish priest bridges the gap between the early Christian missionary and the mediaeval church, which grew fast in village, town and city. But still away in the remote wild lands, mountains, islands or swamps, remained the simple, instinctive labourer, untouched by centuries of theological development. (The earth continued around him; the years came and passed, as his life would pass.) He believed his spirit would return to the God who gave it, all else was vanity. The earliest church buildings were simple. A few remain.

Long grooves are sometimes found in the stonework of old churches, caused by wooden arrows being sharpened there. Churchyards were the customary place for weekly archery practice at the butts; this was encouraged by law in order to preserve England's military monopoly of archery with the long-bow. An Englishman handled his bow differently from others: he did not keep the left hand steady and draw the bow with the right, but keeping his right in position he pressed the whole weight of his body into the horns of his bow. (The French spoke of 'drawing' a bow, but the English of 'bending' one.) Hugh Latimer, in Henry VIII's reign, described how he was taught 'not to draw with strength of arms, as divers other nations do, but with the strength of the body'. It was because this was a difficult art to learn that there were laws to ensure that people did practise it.

The Snowdon eagle, who wore a groove in the stone by sharpening his beak 'ready for the coming battle'.

THE MEDIAEVAL
WORLD

THE FEUDAL SYSTEM

CRYSTALS of different substances vary in shape according to their proportional contents, but each crystal of the same substance is constant to its type. However broken, that type of crystal breaks with the same fracture, because of its axial ratio. Even if pounded to dust and that dust scattered over the land, under the microscope each particle will hold the same crystalline facet. For centuries this peculiarity was also apparent in the feudal system, for every one belonged, by cohesive attraction, to his own system: all admired the same ideals, and resented the same foes – in fact every portion showed the same formation. The systems found in fen country, in a lake district or in dales and plains were separate and different but within each system, every man knew where he belonged; knew who had the right to oppress him; and who must defend him. The individuality of the different systems was intensified during the long French wars and through centuries of political confusion, when feudal armies recruited for home defence worked overseas.

That was the coherent strength of the feudal system. From the highest noble lord to the lowest dusty labourer, all were part of their own distinct feudal system. One factor was the land itself (whether it was mountain district, scattered hill, fenland or swamp), another was the character of the original leaders, and a further was their previous nationality: whether they had come as aggressors or refugees. Feudal systems were formed according to the proportional quantities of the substances of which they were comprised.

The Estate

Anyone who has known the Pennines during winter and deep snow wonders at the complete isolation in which some of the moorland households still hibernate and contrive to survive. In an eleventh-century low rock-built hut in gilsland, there would be a turf fire, a frozen deer, or a bacon rasher hacked off and thawed overnight. The loss of bread corn would be the worst disaster, and wolves the worst fear.

The early estates and farmsteads were comparatively small, and of varied nationalities; their old national usage determined their administration. The Norman Conquest tended to flatten these out, either by a complete takeover by Normans, or by forcing the original owners to combine in defence. William's later destruction of systems in the north had unexpected repercussions of interest to the historians, but to the small labourer dependent on the land, the break-up meant either death by starvation or curiously unexpected freedom as his owners were killed off or burnt out, so that he won freedom from them and swelled the number of 'escapists'. The north was a hard, wild, mountainous country on which the labourer had existed all his life. He would be inconspicuous and had a better chance to escape in the hills than in the valley.

Household serfs, protectors gone, would be slain or taken as slaves and cottars or bordars had small chance of escape, but the labourer, living remote on the moors, perhaps paying fee to the owner of the estate with wild heather honey, or bog myrtle for brewing, would be less likely to be taken alive as a slave, being untrained in the ways of the manor, and feeding extra slaves was a difficulty. In the same way live cattle were not wanted unless enough hay to feed them was also available; they were slaughtered and their skins, in which the meat was seethed to feed the soldiers, made use of later.

The newly-killed animal was skinned, and the skin tied to stakes by the four legs, fur-side down. The container thus formed was filled with water in which the pieces of meat were stewed; subcutaneous fat left on the skin enriched the broth. The fire, kept low, might singe some hair but would not burn through the skin. Bones might be used in the fire.

In both small and large feudal estates, every man knew his employer, or, in the case of a slave, who owned him. In general, barons and lords belonged to the king, villeins belonged to the lords, slaves belonged to anyone who could get them, and mercenaries fought for anyone who would pay them. Cottars, bordars, and others (the names are numerous) were semi-independent. They lived and died by their own efforts, though frequently within the jurisdiction of a feudal estate. Every feudal system entailed complicated layers of service, had its own household churls, its own household army and every department was managed by overseers. The owners were despots, feared, loved or hated as they deserved.

They might also be knowledgeable people. Some families would be skilled in languages, able to write, and be the proud owners of manuscripts worth gold untold. Others invested their money in the gold and silver tableware which was used for ceremonial dinners. Rich lords employed artists to design the elaborate salt cellars, ewers and wash-hand basins shown in the manuscripts. Other feudal lords might be more proud of their statesmanship, or be great warriors, with the man of action's slight disdain for the man of letters. Andrew Borde, the fourteenth-century butler, instructs his page 'to grip his table knife as a knight grips his sword' not, contemptuously, 'as a clerk holds his pen'. In most cases a feudal lord or owner of a manor would employ a cleric to keep accounts, act as secretary and perhaps as tutor to his children.

The feudal family had its own apartments and personal servants, but once a day, by custom, the lord came to dinner in the great hall where, from his dais, he could see his people at their lower tables and show a friendly or frowning countenance. At this time he would be available to hear any complaints or requests from his people. He might send down some special dish as a compliment to his game-keeper, or to his bee-ward or, when the children were of age to come to the lord's table, commend the nurse or rebuke the groom for their behaviour. At dinner in hall a good feudal lord learnt to know his people. Nearest to the high table was the 'best end'; set about half-way down, below the salt cellar, sat lesser folk. Those seated at the lower tables had some freedom, though they were expected to wash, and behave reasonably well. In the open space between the tables they might put on rustic amusements, and the lord could enjoy some jest, approve a song or a diversion the shepherds had invented.

Perhaps the best part of the feudal usage was this communal meeting in hall, when all workers and guests relaxed. It gave a personal contact which the labourer lost when, as the ploughman lamented, the rich had 'a rule to dine by themselves in a separate room, because of the noise [of their people] in the hall'.

The detailed employment and responsibilities of everyone working on a feudal estate were understood, disputed and firmly claimed by the workers themselves. On a mediaeval estate the rushes that were strewn over many of the floors had to be cut from definite places on the estate water, at definite dates, and in definite lengths, by special rush cutters, using special boats and a special knife. The rushes were collected on to the banks to drain, a job dependent upon the weather and the cutters of the rush. The rushes were then loaded into deep baskets, carried slung between two carriers. Details of the size of the basket, and the weight of the load were disputable, and there was provision of a cowstall.

Cowl staff (Latin: cupella; Norman French: cuvell 'tub'). The tub used for water, wet rush, or heavy loads, was carried slung on a strong pole between two men. This pole was the *cowl's staff*. As they carried it shoulder-high each man carried a forked stick upon which to rest his end of the pole when they had to change shoulders or rest. In the usual degeneration of words this hand staff became the 'cowls staff' (cowstall). So, in the *Merry Wives* (III, iii), the washing carriers ordered to take up the basket are told 'There is the cowl staff' and 'away to Datchett Meads'.

Any men toting weights daily develop their own methods, shown in contemporary representations. Most four-footed animals walk front and back legs out of step. On the authority of St John's of Jerusalem the six bearers at a funeral move their six inside legs forward together, and the outside legs together, to carry the corpse more respectfully. They assure me this goes for any number of bearers.

The social positions among household workers were most exact, and firmly insisted upon among themselves. Marshals and bailiffs managed indoor and outdoor departments with the servers or grooms under them; there were scribes and account keepers. There would be cooks, who superintended food supply, scullions, waiters (that was one part of a page's training), groundsmen, stablemen, women of the bedchamber, embroiderers, bedmakers, nurses (and the women who waited on the nurses), watchmen, messengers, pages resident in training, and perhaps a few hostages. All these people, from the Wardcorne on the roof to women strewing rushes on the lowest floor, had their definite jobs and unassailable rights, even before we consider the outside tenants, freemen, and assorted bondmen, down to the slaves, who had very few rights at all.

Through music an isolated independent worker might join a ruling-class community, for large feudal halls had a music gallery and usually a household orchestra to play at meal times. Smaller households employed a handy harpist who, besides preserving ancient legends, was expected to celebrate his patron's successes, and to provide music for the ladies spinning and weaving.

A household musician was not expensive to run, being a resident, though a skilled musician would certainly be rewarded for special efforts. (Today the Poet Laureate has somewhat the same responsibility.)

Monastic Estates

In agriculture, they (the monasteries) accepted and transmitted the Roman tradition of great landlordism. During the Dark Ages their estates resisted the forces of disorder better than the ordinary lay estate. They were more systematically managed and with a better system of accounts . . . There is no reason to doubt the traditions that certain varieties of pear, apple, and other fruits were popularised by the exchange of grafts between monasteries.

G. G. Coulton

By the fourteenth century the mediaeval church had some six hundred or more monastic institutions widely spread over Britain. Starting as religious foundations, many of them developed massive trading estates. Among the monks appeared some of the best brains of the period, often with a genius for finance. Their estates tended to expand by acquisitions from postulants and from death-bed legacies for men's souls, and in the process of managing they became agricultural educators and innovators.

Diplomatic and lavish hospitality to travellers helped the monasteries to keep in contact with the large feudal estates, and with important political people and events. Through talk with those of the travellers who were traders by land or sea, they learned of current market trends, both at home and abroad. Some had their own shipping and transport. Meticulous trading accounts still exist.

One entry in these accounts reads: 'Item – ready-cut millstone, by stone boat from Caen'. Here is evidence of long-term investment in water mills. (The term 'stone boat' is analogous to our 'cattle boat', and refers only to the boat's cargo.) Pressure to use – and pay for – the monastery's water mill, on those in the district who grew their own corn, was often resented and resisted (see also p. 187). But, in the long run, its builders gained a lucrative insight into local agriculture. They came to know which corn best suited local soils. Corn with too many weeds could be tracked down to its growers, who could be firmly rebuked and perhaps, where the monastery was a pious institution, provided with better seed.

Good prices were given for fine fleeces, but those of poor quality were usually rejected: the lesson was plain. In a Cistercian monastery's accounts appears: 'Item – a fine woolled foreign ram, landed at Hull'. Some Cistercians would be skilled shepherds, keeping breeding hirsels on their newly-bounded moorlands. The monastery probably traded in such sheep products as tallow for candles, and parchment for manuscripts. (Some scriptoriums were lucrative publishing houses.)

Stealing a sheep brought hanging as penalty. We may shudder at such an extreme punishment, but in that much more sparsely populated and unfenced countryside, sheep-stealing, particularly at night, was easy and prevalent. As cultivation spread, wild game became scarce. The people had to be taught by a deterrent law to breed animals for eating, not to hunt them. Sheep stealing was then a crime against the community.

The massive, often beautiful, buildings that attested to monastic wealth are now in ruins: but 'Sheep may safely graze' – and corn grows.

Messengers

There was no general system for carrying news and information, but Henry of Huntingdon gives a graphic description of royal messengers rushing across the island from every direction with news of the Danish landings all round the coast. Allowing for journalistic reporting, the arrival of several runners from different directions 'all on the same day' argues a large mobile intelligence force.

> When he cam to the broken brig
> He raised his bow and swam
> And when he cam to the green grass growing
> He loosed his shoes and ran
> And when he cam to the castle gate
> He let not to clap nor call
> But bent his bow against his breast
> and lightly leapt the wall.

Messengers were trained runners, and travelled swiftly; most feudal lords used them and the sovereign kept a team at government expense. The majority, who travelled inland, were chosen for loyalty and fleetness of foot, while those sent abroad would be somewhat educated to cope with a foreign language. (This royal service continues today, only now with folios and diplomatic bags.)

The ordinary mediaeval messenger probably had little education, but much stamina and ability to cope with difficulties. He ran almost naked so, for lack of pockets, he carried his sealed and packed message in a short split cane. This kept it clean and served as a visible badge of his office. None might hinder such a messenger; there were heavy penalties if he was delayed, and reprisals if he was killed. He had certain rights, being free to short-cut over growing corn and to claim hospitalities.

It would be natural to pick for this job a chap who knew the lie of the land: a youngster, seen to be fleet of foot, 'a likely lad', could be picked out for training much as today a promising footballer could be spotted. In the fen district a runner would carry a long ash pole and develop the pole-jump (aiming for length, not height) to cross the wide dykes and marshes. One very urgent runner, definitely from the land, was the warrior's runner, who carried the fiery brand to light the beacons en route to proclaim war.

Larger packages and non-portables (such as hounds) went by horse delivery, usually in bags called 'boysters' slung across below the saddle, so they could not be removed without first dislodging the rider, and they were in shape exactly like bolsters.

The lean, long-legged messenger no longer worked on the land, but he certainly covered it. By daylight he would probably use the swiftest open way, but if he carried secret information, or notes from a trader, or valuables, he would be likely to run aside from the main tracks and find lodging in some isolated shelter, with simple people: where a simple explanation would satisfy simple minds and where he could get a small amount of plain food and even smaller amount of sleep less noticeably.

THE RUNNING OF A LARGE HOUSEHOLD

Every feodary knoweth his station
And his place of service.
Andrew Borde (late 14th century)

For good or bad, the feudal system formed a mixed mass of peoples into units. Lordling squire, household servant, labourer paying rent of service, slave, disbanded mercenary, almost independent small-holder, completely free man, vagabond, malefactor, poacher – all belonged to their own feudal system. The Wardcorne was the reliable man on top of the castle who kept watch in all directions and announced arrivals, by blowing his horn. This would sound over the courtyard and grounds; and he would have also his relays of young pages, or reliable grooms, to take the full message to the correct quarter.

In mediaeval days 'grooms' meant trained servants working in their various departments: the grooms of the pantry, the reliable ones who attended to the gold and silver plate arranged on the sideboard, those who attended to the livery cupboard (a cupboard with pierced openwork in the doors where light refreshments could be kept or a dish stored for a latecomer). The cellarer had his own department and his own workers. There were also the waiters in hall (as well as the pages in training) and the waiters between kitchen and hall – the latter being commis waiters who were not allowed to serve the table, only to serve the waiters waiting on the table (there was special leave for a commis waiter, if he saw a guest in difficulties and no correct waiter available, to step in – but he had to do it very respectfully).

These few details show the exquisite finish characteristic of a mediaeval household, whose prestige reflected far across the mediaeval fields to the distant huts of workers who belonged to it. Further afield some labourer would watch the feudal entourage when it travelled from one district to another, because the land had to supply everything needed; and some things needed to complete the economy of the estate were only obtainable in certain districts. At intervals the lord himself, with accountants, scribes and all essential personnel, would visit the works to supervise, and to 'see the local managers' about reconstructions and so on. Feudal society moved round pretty often, riding from Ely to Cornwall, Kent to Northumberland, Lincoln to Chester, generally using main routes (kept open by workers of these far-flung settlements) but under stress cutting across country at speeds which compare very well with a modern convoy.

Here is how a typical Seneschal – or overseer – thought things should be run:

The *seneschal* ought on visiting the manors to inquire about wrongdoing, and trespass done in parks, ponds, warrens, conygarths and dove houses.

Office of wagoners. To keep the horses and curry them and load and carry that they be not overloaded or overworked . . . and he must know how to mend his harness and the gear of his wagon. The bailiff ought to see how many times the wagoners can go in a day to carry marl or manure, or hay or corn, or timber or firewood without great stress; and as many times as they can go . . . the wagoner must answer for . . . at the end of the week.

Each wagoner shall sleep every night with his horses and so shall the oxherds sleep in the same way with their oxen.

The *swineherd* ought to be on manors where swine can be . . . kept in the forest or woods or waste or marshes [note the distinction] and if the swine can be kept with litter sustenance from the grange during hard frost, then must a pigsty be made in marsh or wood. When the sows have farrowed, let them be driven with the feeble swine to the manors and kept with leavings as long as the bad weather lasts. [Pigs kept and *fed* don't pay.]

The *ploughmen* ought to be men of intelligence and ought to know how to sow, and how to repair and mend broken ploughs and harrows and to till the land well and crop it rightly, and how to yoke and drive oxen without beating and hurting them, and they ought to forage them well and look after the forage that it be not stolen nor carried off, and they must not carry fires into the byres for a light, or to warm themselves, nor light unless it be in a lantern for great need and peril.

The shepherd ought to find good pledges to answer for his doings and for faithful service, although he be companion to the miller, and he must cover his fold and mend it within and without and repair and make hurdles, and ought to sleep in the fold, he and his dog.

No shepherd ought to leave his sheep to go to fairs, or markets, or wrestling matches, or wakes, or to the tavern, without asking leave or putting a good keeper in his place.

Let all the lord's sheep be marked with one mark and let no ewes be milked after the feast of our Lady. [He is responsible for the life of the sheep at lambing time; and] three times a year let the sheep be inspected by men who know their business and the daft picked out and sold . . . [It is bad to let the sheep after Lammas] eat the web of the rime, and the little white snails, from which they will sicken and die.

The hayward ought to be an active and sharp man for early and late; he must go round and keep the woods, corn and meadows, and . . . sow the lands and be over the ploughers and harrowers at each time of sowing, and make the tenants come in and do the work they ought to do [in the fields], and in haytime he ought to be over the mowers, the making and the carrying, and in August assemble the reapers and ought to keep tally of all the seed, book work, customs, and labour throughout the year.

The dairy maid ought to be faithful and of good repute and keep herself clean, she ought to know well how to make cheese and salt cheese, and she ought to save and keep the vessels of the dairy, that it need not be necessary to buy new ones every year. And she ought to know [i.e. make a note of] the day when she begins to make cheese [in the early spring] and when she begins to make two cheeses a day [in summer] and how much weight.

(Adapted from *Seneschaucie*, an anonymous treatise on Country Life, dating from not later than the reign of Edward I.)

Plants and Herbs

In March and in April from morning till night
In sowing and seeding good huswives delight.
To have her a garden, or other like spot,
To trim up the house and to furnish the pot.

Thomas Tusser (1524–1580)

When they were new, castles stood up as clean and uncompromising as office blocks. Manors and farms were set about by pig styes, sheep pens, cow byres, privies and muck heaps. The labourers' housing had only to be firm and dry, not ornamental. Picturesque cottages with hollyhocks bumping the windows and creepers on the walls are of the nineteenth century: they are not shown in any early manuscripts.

In castles pot plants seem to have been popular, often restrictively trained on sticks in the modern fashion, but mediaeval people usually kept their gardens away from their dwellings. Castles usually put them beyond the moat, and farms set them apart, frequently fencing them about to keep them in their place and to keep out animals. Utility was considered more than beauty.

They enjoyed a great variety of wild flowers, far more than we have today: the whole land foamed with blossom. Pastures quivered with cowslips, marigolds floated molten gold over the marshes, lilies of the valley flowed through the woods, 'ladies smocks all silver white, filled the meadows with delight'. Hedges were few before the sixteenth century, but the whitethorn (whose black bark made a mediaeval ink), hawthorn and rowan, spread freely. Ferns – many now rare, or lost – fell in green fountains over the rocks. Even forty years ago the silk-soft blue corn cockle grew in clouds along canals, with bullrush, reed mace, musk, meadowsweet and mallow, and many other flowers and bulbs grew plentifully wild. Some may have been planted by 'escapists', for even a single plant will rapidly spread over a wide area, if left undisturbed in suitable soil, and in mediaeval England they were not disturbed.

The herb garden of today often grows the plants arranged with 'old-world charm' but in the mediaeval period such garths were made for use only. Labourers and country folk collected the plants they wanted for use direct from the wild, besides many that were collected for trade purposes, as so many of the names suggest – soapwort, tanners root, butchers broom, dyers whin, and so on. The 'lavender ribbons' of the sixteenth and seventeenth centuries were still dyed with mixtures of blackberry and bilberry.

Both culinary and medical herbs were in regular use, and odd plants still surviving wild will often indicate to the research walker localities where they were used for particular purposes: for example, by old hostels. In 'horse power' days, the commonest accidents would be broken collar bones, fractures, concussion, saddle sores, stiffness, rheumatism, pneumonia and the usual traveller's tummy upsets. Around the sites of hostels, then, you would expect to find wild comfrey called 'boneset' in Scotland and used instead of plaster of Paris for setting bones, horse radish (which, mixed with grease, makes a good embrocation), balm for sores, hoarhound (taken with honey for coughs), plants for plasters, and rushes for scouring. Around farms and dairies you would find nettles for rennet, and docks for nettle stings. By the river, the yellow iris, the traveller's fleur-de-lis, often indicated a ford upstream, for iris roots grow in shallow water and being broken off by the trampling of travellers, the roots would drift *downstream*.

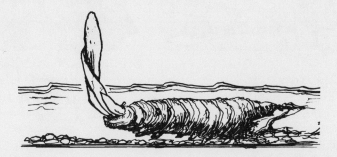

Broken pieces of the iris rhizome float downstream. New root buds develop forward, as if deliberately trying to get a grip against the pull of the current so as to remain in shallow water where the plant can grow.

Many plant seeds were carried long distances in the dung dropped by horses. These plants sometimes determine the routes of old tracks across the hills. If the seed falls in suitable soil and finds a sheltered position it may form huge clumps, and re-seed downwind for miles: groves of foxgloves are a good example of what seed dispersal can do. The foxglove leaves, taken at flowering time, are most potent for medical use, but we found no record of its use in mediaeval times, though it may have been tried.

The wild yellow snapdragon, the wallflower, and many garden flowers were 'wildings', also the strawberry and the raspberry and other fruits.

The curative content of many plants is now prepared synthetically. Our wise old gardener commented: 'There's too much haphazard taking of medicine these days, just because it's cheap. All plants, when they take their food from the soil, are bound to take the minerals in the soil, and that mineral varies with different plants. Watercress, now, took up a lot of iron, and broom and gorse they took up sulphur, so you used the plant itself, if you wanted iron or sulphur. Now chemists are so clever they get the mineral out of the soil direct but ...' (a thoughtful pause) 'as we are animals, and plants come between us and the minerals, it does seem sense to let the vegetables digest the minerals before we use them.'

(See also Appendixes.)

Huts

Our independent man made his home with whatever materials were available locally; his national traditions (if any) were sublimated to local

(1) Ruins of a boulder-built hut set into the side of a hill. The long rock on the ground at the right extended into the hut, forming a low shelf. The boulders were so large that only five were needed for the entire height; the top ones at the back were probably rolled down into position from above. The original roof of birch boughs thatched with heather had perished and been replaced by reed from an adjoining lake (Bala). The author found it in the 1920s; by 1950 it had been demolished completely. Many other similar boulder-built cottages were then still inhabited; a few remain. (2) The black and white house. Where old ships' timbers were used they were usually dark, and tar dressing was later used as a preservative. The filling between the timbers was usually wattle and daub, but when this broke away the spaces were frequently filled in with brick. Sometimes there was a cruck structure, but as a rule the timbers used were squared, or dressed by an adze; the scoop marks of this tool gave a surface quite distinct from that of sawn or split wood. (3) The erroneously-named 'mud hut' was a studied mixture of selected earths, sand and binding materials, thoroughly blended and packed and rammed into solid walls between wood supports which were removed as the wall dried. The texture was constant, so that windows and doors could be cut where they were wanted. The cob mixture had to be kept dry, so deep thatch with overhanging eaves was used for roofing. (4) Cruck construction needed well-grown forest trees to split into pairs; the ridge pole and roof rested on these, not on the walls – which could be wattle and daub, plastered, or stone, according to locality. The crossed crucks supporting the roof were usually bracked across.

conditions. Thus men from mountainous countries would choose mountainous localities. (You may find for instance Scandinavian stone work on a moor in the North Riding.) Foresters used timber, and fen men reeds – the *only common* denominator was the man's own measurement: a man can crawl into a low hut, but he *must* have six feet to lie down in.

Convenience and custom produced round huts (the diameter was established by the height of the man in charge, and his dependents would fit around the curves); corbel structure eliminated the central support – huts of this sort are found in Western Ireland and in districts with whaling and perhaps therefore igloo influences; some were long used as sheds where fish oil was extracted and inland they seem to have turned into pig sties. The illustrations are the most likely squared types built by our independent countryman.

Expert archaeological knowledge is needed for research on hut circles, but the intelligent pedestrian walking across country can often find mediaeval dwellings of a very early date. The building will be near a spring for a supply of water, and the stone foundations half-buried in later growth can usually be identified by measurements – six feet interior length – there should be a narrow entrance, and with luck a firemarked or split stone. The walker will probably be following some old trackway, utilising a pass or avoiding a marsh.

Housing in Trade Settlements

In the country were many trade settlements, their exact positions depending on some local material, such as clay, mineral ores, chalk, salt, flint, slate, timber, or building stone. The roads to these works and the workers' dwellings would be muddy, dusty or rocky, depending on the location and management. The settlements were usually the property of a feudal owner who visited them, perhaps once a year, to supervise their output. This was one of the reasons for scattered portions of a feudal system. Between headquarters and the 'production plant' would be a 'communication and delivery' service, probably by slow ox wain that might take a month or more on the way. These industrial settlements reflected the owner's character in their housing – which housing, perforce, depended on available material.

Clay, tile and pottery settlements used brick, and made paths with flawed tiles. The quarrymen built with stone and slate. Timber workers usually only got small wood, for the large wood was needed in the heavy stone construction of castles. (When you stand within the empty walls of a ruined castle with grass on the floor, fern on the walls, and open sky above, count the squared holes set in rows where the old floor joists fitted and work out how many square miles of forest was cleared around that castle to build its floors.)

In swamp and reed settlements there would be a compromise between wattle and daub, pisé, and unbaked brick. Timber was too valuable to use for firing bricks for cheap housing; and the saying that one 'can't make bricks without straw' comes from the need to incorporate straw with the clay to produce a self-firing brick. Unbaked bricks leave only mounds of earth to mark their presence. Huts varied with the local building material: but any type of hut had to be six foot long, for a man to lie down; and about six foot high for him to stand up. He also wanted warmth and light and cooked food. (A fire outside was all right in good weather, but there was usually a fire indoors.) The fire might be set in the centre of the hut, against a wall or in a corner.

Castles were dreadfully draughty, but huts were not. The ground inside a hut was dug out as the walls were raised, so that the floor would be below ground level. The doorstep was a step down. An extra log or plank might be placed across the bottom of the door in bad weather, as riverside people use flood boards. The fire's place would be either a small sunken pit, or a raised hearthstone, depending on the fuel used. Any window opening would be small and deep set, and thus easily blocked by a shoved-in sack of bracken or earth.

The gable ends of mediaeval cottages often show round holes at the top; the wind would blow in at one end and out the other. This draught, combined with rising heat (and smoke) from the fire was used to dry meat and fish – and wet clothes. Later mss and better housing show complicated erections like birdcages; even later there are windows set in the roof space.

Feudal Service

The feudal payments in days of work for special tasks were part of estate management. Much of this was later commuted to cash payments though during the plague, or in bad seasons, the owner would try to return to the enforced service and the labourers would demand goods, instead of the money which could not buy food. Out of these grew the peppercorn rents of later reigns. The peppercorn, being valuable, and extremely light, was in many cases only the token used to ensure a regular, yearly visit from the tenant. Many such rents had other important purposes. One peppercorn rent had to be brought from South Wales overland to Canterbury 'by eight white oxen'. The oxen were the essential part of this rent, since to maintain such a service, herds of oxen must be kept (and these could be used to feed troops if the king needed to invade Ireland hurriedly). The oxen were to be white to distinguish them from the black Welsh breeds and thus they were easily identified.

Good clay for pottery on an estate, local rents of dry fuel for the kilns or bark for tanning work, or beeswax used for metal castings, would all lead to an auxiliary local industry (in the case of the beeswax, the washing of the combs would provide for an extra potent mead brew). Hundreds of such relics of feudal service exist today.

Sex

> Bitwixe a wyf that is of heigh degree,
> If of hir body dishonest she be,
> And a povre wenche, other than this –
> If it so be, they werke bothe amis –
> But that the gentile, in estaat above,
> She shal be cleped his lady, as in love;
> She shal be cleped his wenche, or his lemman.
>
> Geoffrey Chaucer (1340?–1400)

The feudal lord, away on the battlefield, would, if wise, leave behind a wife bred in the same tradition as himself, who would be able to carry on the estate in his absence; though to carry on his 'lineage' during long absences was more difficult, and period chivalry filled contemporary literature with tedious romances of unrewarded devotion. (Religious restrictions have always been conveniently elastic.) A natural son was usually accepted and a mixture of robustious common stock was sometimes welcome. In mediaeval times, if the father was a creditable man, it might be advantageous to be his bastard.

The right of the feudal lord to claim the maidenhead of dependents if he so wished is thought of with horror, but at that time the custom was accepted and had its kindly uses. Daughters had very little legal status and could be forcibly bartered by their parents. Direct personal appeal to the lord was a saving grace in the feudal system, though it was a risk, for if the appeal was lost there could be reprisals. But if the accepted feeling was that 'the case was right', a wise overlord would have the sense to take action (and so prevent what in a factory today would be called 'industrial unrest'). For women and girls the procedure of direct appeal was difficult, but this marriage custom did give the overlord the opportunity of contact with the female members of his estate. Even if the girl lacked his language he could judge from her condition how things fared among the women workers. In common reason no man, clean and continent, would want to bed with a succession of grubby, flea-bitten, uncooperatives. If her body attracted him sufficiently to have her brought in and cleaned up, was the girl herself likely to resent it? At this date there was no disgrace attached. She was conforming to a custom generally understood and accepted. Probably for every unwilling girl there would be a hundred experienced wenches not one penny the worse. And for every lord who behaved like a licentious tup, there must have been ordinary decent men who observed the custom for the insight it gave them, and to keep the goodwill of the women.

It is impossible to formulate the ever-changing attitudes of any past period. Mediaeval centuries came to accept the leman as a pleasurable necessity, but all mediaeval amatory arrangements were most complicated – and adaptable.

Proxy marriages had very definite procedures. Tactful Froissart said that the proxy 'lyen by her a-bede curtesely, according to the custome in such matters requyred'. In some cases they were to be bedded with a sword between them; in other cases the sheet or blanket was a stipulated barrier.

LAW

> For that only is called thyne,
> That thou doest hold (it) of thy King
> So doth thy tennaunt holde of thee
> And is allowed a lyving
> As well as thou, in his degree.
> If thou, therefore, would not thy King
> Should take of thee more than his due
> Why wilt thou bate the livynge
> Of thy tenaunt and cause him rue?
>
> Way to Wealth, Robert Crowley (1518?–1588)

Labourers do not bother about a law till it blocks their way – when it has to be circumvented. If nothing happens, they do so again, and again, till it is accepted as inevitable. Thus common law was made by the labourers.

Men working together on a job sort themselves out to fit the work, tall men doing the high-up tasks, and short men the lower; and stronger and weaker men, clever and stupid, sort themselves out – rough justice being done to shirkers. The feudal system employed overseers who were themselves employed to arrange the work and see it correctly done. In a dispute between different sets of workers each overseer would defend his own, and if the overseers could not settle it, it would have to come before the feudal lord who employed them. Every feudal lord was a judge in his own right for his own people, and in the case of strife in his household he would give judgment before the household – in the Hall. But for people living in remote parts of the feudal estate, workers, probably arriving overnight, on donkeys, or afoot (punctuality was a mediaeval difficulty), their feudal lord would hold his court in the 'court yard'. This was an important issue in Magna Carta, for the common people as much as for the feudal lords (the King himself was a feudal lord and had his own Crown court), because it gave the labourer the right to be *judged by his own lord*; that is, among his own people in his own district, and by an employer who knew the district and could understand his language.

Mediaeval England was still inhabited by a mixture of peoples, mainly Saxon and Norman, but descendants of other foreign invaders and settlers still kept their own old national customs and spoke their own language. What we now call dialect is the ghost of very localised languages, dependent upon the land itself for many of its nouns. For example, on a feudal estate in the West Riding both lord and labourer would know the difference between a beck and a gill; while Wiltshire men would know that what they called a winter bourne ran dry in summer.

For a court (yard) case, the feudal lord would probably have a legal adviser on hand and the Seneschal who knew the estate, and the work and the 'cases' would be sorted out and those with similar difficulties would be heard at the same time. Serious cases would have to be allotted to special hearings.

Let us suppose the 'forestry men' had come to blows with the 'swineherds', who had been belabouring well-grown trees to shake down mast and acorns for the swine – the swineherds often made this an excuse to break the boughs with clubs and billhooks, to obtain free firewood. The forestry men did right to protect their trees, but the swineherds were backed up by the local householders, who had the *right* to collect firewood. Rights of free fuel were part payment for service, but the rumour had gone round that 'those swineherds had been stealing and selling their local firewood to outsiders'. After palaver, the feudal lord ruled that the householders might continue to collect their fire wood by hook or crook (the official weed hook, and sheep crook, that proved they were genuine sheep herds or field workers employed on the estate). With these they could hook down and pull out the dead branches – which were better removed – but there was to be no *cutting*. He commended the foresters 'for their care of the timber', and assured the local householders of their full legal fuel supply.

This imaginary court case is chosen because we still use the term 'by hook or by crook'.

Every feudal lord made his ruling according to the law of the *land* – thus the land and its workers gradually produced most of our common law.

Where estates adjoined, usage overlapped; and the feudal lords had to get together to ensure fair unity in the common laws, and bring to order any feudal lord who did not respect them. Again, we can only explain by an over-simplified example: picture the scene: lords from very varied districts sorted their problems (over lubricatory drinks). 'Is the penalty for sheep stealing excessive?' One lord says no, pointing out that he is trying to breed sheep which can bite close on short turf on land too poor for cattle, and one lost ram (stolen for mutton) spoilt a whole lambing season. Another landlord, from a rocky peak district, submitted it was not twolegged thieves, but four-legged ones who took his sheep, and was the first paying enough for wolf heads?

There were outbreaks of destruction by wolves during severe winters and a reward was often offered to encourage extermination. This extract (though Irish) could have applied to Scotland, or Wales, or the remoter mountains of England, at this date (1656):

'For the better destroying of wolves, which of later years have much increased in many parts, it is ordered and declared that the officers in chief or any two or more of the justices of peace in the several and respective precincts of the nation do consider and use and execute all good ways and means for the destroying of wolves . . . and to employ such person or persons and to appoint such days and times for hunting the wolf as they shall judge fitting and necessary. It is further ordered that all person or persons that shall take, kill or destroy any wolf, making it appear before any one or more of the said officers commanding . . . within the precincts where such wolf is or shall be taken that he or they have taken or destroyed such wolf and to that end shall bring forth the head of the wolf so taken before the said officers, who being well satisfied with the evidence . . . that such person or persons have taken or destroyed or caused to be taken or destroyed such wolf or wolves that such person or persons shall have and receive for such wolf or wolves so taken and destroyed (for which they shall bring proof as aforesaid) the sums of monies hereafter following, viz: for every bitch wolf £6, for every dog wolf £5, for every cub which preyeth for himself 40/-, for every suckling cub 10/- and no wolf after the last of September until 10th January shall be accounted a young wolf.'

(Abridged from four long pages of regulations to ensure that wolves are properly destroyed and such person or persons duly rewarded for doing so.)

The feudal lords' interchanges and discussions covered far more districts than the local courts and far more subjects. One thing they were usually agreed about: the rapacity of the ecclesiastical estates: 'Those sainted monks with their devilish fish traps are the ruin of river fishing! Our poor chaps can't get even enough common salmon to last them through the winter!'

Forest Laws

> He set a mikle deer frith,
> And he laid laws therewith,
> That whoso so slew hart or hind
> Him should man then blinden.
> He forbade to slay the harts,
> And so eke the wild boars,
> So well loved he the high deer
> As if he their father were.
> Eke he set by the hares
> That they might freely fare.
> His rich men mourned it
> And the poor men wailed it
> But he was so firmly wrought
> That he recked of all nought.

Political rhyme on William the Conqueror

Forests are usually thought of as hunting preserves for kings, and the underlying causes of the forest laws are as little understood today as they were when instigated. On the south coast there was the problem of invasion: the forest would impede this (the mediaeval army travelled mostly on foot) as a way could not be cleared rapidly except by fire (in dry weather). Another consideration was the increase of population in London and other cities, whose meat supply was often sold to them by those who lived in the forest, as was the wood fuel to cook it with. The forest supported – directly and indirectly – considerable communities. But both fuel and game were rapidly diminishing and neither could be replaced rapidly: these were government considerations.

An ejected labourer was turned out of his house and driven away from the forest from which he had got his fuel and meat; and his family would starve, 'And a hare, jugged in an earthen pot, buried in hot wood ashes – a whole meaty hare, blood and bones, with a few wild plums or crab apples to give a tang to the gravy – would have fed his whole family and . . . he was turned out and it was not fair . . .'.

Stocks and Pillories

your purpos'd low correction
Is such as basest and contemned'st wretches
For pilferings and most common trespasses
Are punish'd with
                    King Lear, William Shakespeare (1564–1616)

The stocks were very uncomfortable for the culprit, and very convenient for the magistrate. Stocks had the convenience of a 'remand in custody', and showed openly that all malefactors were securely dealt with. It was left to the general public to endorse or mitigate the punishment. No wonder villages kept stocks handy. They were cheap to run (a strongly built pair of stocks with a good lock lasted a century) and as a common form of local law enforcement they were very adaptable and ignoble. The pillory was far more serious – and dangerous – but again the severeness of the punishment depended upon the reaction of public opinion against the crime, or in favour of the victim.

Slaves

Domesday book notes the existence of slaves, but by the beginning of the fourteenth century this class has disappeared, probably because of the increasing power of the king and the law. It was useful to own a slave's life and limbs, but a lord would not wish to have to answer for his slave's crimes. The coming of Christianity bettered the slave's lot even before the Conquest, preaching 'We are all God's bondmen, and so he will judge us, as we judge those over whom we have authority'.

Early English and Saxon slaves seem to have been personal acquisitions or inherited estate property; there were also penal slaves, people enslaved as a punishment for certain specific crimes, or because of inability to pay fines and compensations they had incurred. It was not unknown, in times of great hardship, for men to sell their children or other relations into slavery.

In war important conquered foes might be kept for ransome, but often the alternatives were 'be slain', 'escape' or be 'taken into slavery'. After a skirmish the conqueror might drive off the survivors as he drove off the sheep and oxen as spoils of war, choosing the best for himself and letting his followers take and slay the less profitable. Thus he might acquire some good new slave workers. If he required good work (from oxen or men) they must be well fed; if when fed they would not work they were beaten. Both oxen and men were his property: a slave was a chattel, and would fetch the same price as eight oxen. The branding of slaves was like marking cattle; in some cases iron slave rings were rivetted on. Sometimes, where the owner was a ruler of especial renown, the slave might enjoy his reflected prestige; but what most slaves must have really desired was to be signed off, for the law recognised no property rights for a slave, and his children would also be slaves. While a freed slave was not quite on the same level as a man who was free born, anyone who could remember freedom would have welcomed manumission.

It is easier to make a slave than to release a slave. The first generation would keep their initiative and remember their past freedom; their sons, born into slavery, would *know* of that freedom; but by the next generation they will have forgotten any other existence. Once dependency is accepted it is very difficult to eradicate it. (This was well seen in the Americas, and in the Caribbean where the pathetic plea of legally released slaves was very often 'but now we belong to no one'. 'No one tells us what to do.' 'We are left all alone . . . and no one minds if our little ones die.' For previously the birthrate among slaves was much encouraged.)

The breeding of slave labour involved special arrangements between the owners. Just as a stock farmer, breeding for beef, may sell a cow in calf to another farmer who wants her for milk, and bargain that the calf, when dropped, should be returned to his own pedigree herd, so, when the pregnant woman slave was sold, the same arrangements were customary. A period for weaning was stipulated, and arrangements for return transport were considered in the terms of the sale. (It is said St Brigid (453?–523?) was sold while in her mother's womb and returned in this way, and that by her skill and diligence she later bought her own mother out of slavery.)

Male slaves, of good strong breeding, likely to produce males, were well valued and usually retained by their fortunate owners, who might arrange in their wills for them to be set free.

Among the slaves themselves developed many social layers. House slaves might be overworked and ill-treated by the heartless underlings they served; others might become valued and loved retainers whose position in the household could be far better than some overworked free hirelings. A good wet-nurse or a gentle girl slave might become a capable 'mother's help' and live to be 'this old nurse'.

THE ESCAPISTS

None shall leave his district for extra harvest work save the hill people (Wales, Scotland and Pennines). They may go and serve in Southern countries freely.

A law to control labour, 1399

England was largely feudal, and the members of the feudal systems are
fairly well accounted for, but on the fringes existed people whose life and
work are still unrecorded. All over the land they came and went, as
varied and unpredictable as a crop of coloured fungus on a tree stump; a
stump that remained firmly rooted in the earth of mediaeval England.
There are signs of these people all over the land; some in villages
abandoned because they became befouled (a usage common in all primitive
communities) – many of these are known, and air surveyors are still
discovering more. Some of these escapists may have been from the
breaking up of feudal ownership; others the debris of war. Some could
have been disbanded foreign mercenaries.

Chronicle keepers account for them by abstraction. They are the
'survivors who fled', the 'remnant who took to the woods' or were 'driven
off after the battle'. The reports are so continuous one feels those woods
were becoming pretty populous; are Shakespeare's Dukes in the Forest of
Arden their literary descendents? During the fourteenth century when
plague devastated whole settlements, labour grew scarce and owners of
estates raked in workers from the very margins of their property. Hurried
laws were made to prevent labour moving from one district to another, but
that could not prevent these marginal tenants from hurriedly clearing off.
And conscientious indeed would be the landowner who made too careful
enquiries as to where his labour came from. England in the fourteenth
century was largely rough scrub and forest, open mountains and wide,
inaccessible marshes. Once escaped, fugitives could hide as unknown, and
with luck, unmolested, as any other wild animal. During the wars and
famines the chronicles describe 'ungathered harvests' and 'abandoned
animals', so these fugitives might acquire a lost sheep, a piglet, or catch
some stray hens to produce eggs. This catching and domesticating from the
wild is mentioned by Giraldus Cambrensis (c. 1200) thus: 'A wild sow;
which had been suckled by a bitch famous for her nose, became, on
growing up, so wonderfully active in the pursuit [tracking] of wild
animals, that in the faculty of scent she was greatly superior to dogs.'

Existence was precarious but not impossible. In the wild were small
game, and abundant fuel; shelter was possible in caves or quickly built reed
and wattle huts. Remember they were all tough, experienced men, and the
basic materials for existence – food, wood and water – were plentiful.
After a time some escapists might become attached to rural communities,
coming first as strangers, willing to barter wild game for the agriculturists'
corn; for corn would be their main lack. These escapists were from very
varied backgrounds: therefore they had very varied knowledge. Survival
taught them to use every edible herb or berry. Starvation had taught them
to dig pig nuts, catch fish in the shallows and to rob wild bees for honey:
they learnt the use of the wax of bog myrtle, of many herbs and probably of

narcotic fungus. (Today we can trace foreign influences all over England by the different types of fungus relished.) They were protected by their remoteness. They were too poor, too far from trade routes, to fear pillage. Most of the materials they needed were free. In their isolation they might have avoided the thraldom of the mediaeval church, and in preserving their bodies they learnt a sturdy independence.

Yet their escape was no joyous adventure. Sometimes it was through work, early and hard, that freedom was won; and the small wattle hut, the hearthstone, and one iron pot, had been paid for by the loss of youth and strength. Sometimes, old parents or the young wife had died, starving. Bad weather, and misfortunes came, and left a broken man alone, who hated the spring and the patch of sprouting corn that had grown too late to save the little son he had longed for. Soon his animals would wander away, the hardy goats survive wild, the pinioned poultry perish. Hawk, stoat and fox would scavenge. Then the rain would melt the hut back to a mound of mud, and the forest close in over a lost small-holding.

His uncut corn shed, the plants the woman had set would fight and spread with a stronger will to live than the hands which had planted them. But the escapists who survived were a tough people who bred and increased. They no longer desired involvement in the herd. Their character was the inevitable consequence of their freedom (as were the tough brown babies who sprawled over the warm wood ashes on the earthen floor).

Hermits

All wars produce a backwash of weary men seeking solitude and peace, and mediaeval wars made many hermits. Not professional hermits, seeking discomfort in deserts, but simple tired men who built themselves serviceable huts by some spring of fresh water, and lived as best they could on small snared game and the plants which necessity had taught them to use. A fire of sticks, a blanket or goatskins, a bed of dried fern: then corn and bread would be their first need. As strangers they would be regarded with hostile curiosity, but their tales of travel and their news would cause interest and gradually they would find a place on the fringe of their communities. In many cases their acquired medical knowledge seems to have been an asset. In a period of cut and thrust warfare warriors knew more of human anatomy than did the restricted medical men; also their experience overseas among other peasants would have taught them the value of many healing herbs. The spring of fresh water for cleansing would do much for lice-infested or dirt-encrusted cases. The herbs would be well boiled in water to be carried away for continued treatment; and the boiling ensured that the water was sterile. Fomentation and sensibly applied splints and bandages helped. After the hermit died, his spring would still be used and probably hundreds of the Holy Wells all over the land were originally just the drinking water of some recluse, but later dedicated to a saint.

Now, his hut is only a few moss-grown stones by a mound of earth and bracken. One way to locate it is by measurement: the foundations would measure six feet one way (to take his bed) and below and around the flat stone that was his hearth there will be charcoal traces in the earth. But it may be only an old shepherd's hut; you must judge by the history, the locality, and tradition.

This redrawing from a fifteenth-century ms. shows a bachelor's hut (St Anthony's) by a stream in a forest. Note that there is a pool in the stream; this would be created artificially, to give a place where a pot could easily be filled with water. Once the bottom had settled, the water from this pool would be clearer than the swift-running surface water carrying debris.

THE MEDIAEVAL CHURCH

The Gift of Christianity

To mediaeval people Christianity gave unity. It did not remove all previous beliefs. Gods survive long and we still have Thor's day and

Woden's day and Saturn's day and swear 'By Jove!' The spirits continued, lights still bounced over the marshes, night mares rode and toothache was – and still is – the devil, but by consensus of opinion Christianity was considered reasonable, and the Christian God accepted.

The only comparable analogy is the later acceptance of the earth as round. To many this absurdity did not carry conviction but it stopped speculations which had previously seemed reasonable.

To our isolated land labourer the unity was different. The explanations of the mediaeval Church meant comfort for the little people huddled under the shadow of the new churches, but to the mountain dwellers the bells and white banners seemed small before the deep snow on the hills, and their unity was their serene security of God as life.

The simplicity of monotheistic Christianity suited the mind of isolated man, working a remote land alone. It was in the little crowded cities and busy villages that the detailed competence of the mediaeval Church was welcome. It was a heavenly encyclopaedia, with reassuring answers for everything. For example, man's basic fear, the uncertainty about where he went after death, was instantly resolved. He would go to Purgatory to be

A free redrawing from a ms. illustration of the Ars Morendi (Art of Dying), indicating the horror both of illness and of the approach of death. The patient is beset by devils, very real to the mediaeval mind; but gallstones or a stomach ulcer could be 'the devil'.

purified from venial sins, then on to Heaven; if very wicked he would go to Hell; if very good straight to Heaven; while unbaptised infants went to Limbo.

In cities craftsmen lived well. Every workshop, every guild had its own patron saint, with processions and pageants, and its own place in the cathedrals. It was the drifted debris of country workers, a generation cut off from the discipline of the land, where food or starvation depended upon themselves, who became helpless, their stunted bodies housing unoccupied minds. These became dependent upon the Church both mentally and bodily, as the outcrops of charities proved. They are those shown in manuscripts naked, with deficiency diseases, for whom it was an advantage if a dirt sore could be classed as leprous and so qualify them for accommodation in a well-kept house.

The drift from the land started early. It is *urban* beggars that figure largely in Elizabethan legislation even before the clearing of land to make way for larger holdings and sheep walks for the urgent wool trade.

Hand grips, rather like little stools, are shown in this redrawing from a ms. Only a complete cripple, unable to balance on crutches, would make use of such aids. (Early in this century one could see a workman whose legs had been amputated making his way along the pavements of Wigan; his knuckles were padded, and he used them just as this man uses his grips. He was probably the victim of a mining accident.)

The Church as Institution

I hold there is an infinite universe, made by Divine Power, because I esteem it unworthy of that Power, being able to create an infinite number of worlds, to create but this one . . . In this universe I place the Life by which everything lives. This Life of the body is fortified of this Divinity, this

inexplicable Power that is above all, thus in all are the thoughts of God.
Giordano Bruno, burnt 'As an impenitent heretic . . .
as one irreclaimable without remorse', Feb. 27, 1600

The serious absurdity of the mediaeval Church is incomprehensible to the modern mind, but to the mediaeval people the mediaeval Church was an international power. The growth of cities gave it a working force of people; a generation removed from the discipline of the land; these formed a mob, the power of which could be controlled by the rulers of Europe.

From early times a surprising number of men had toiled eastwards, overland, or coasting up the Mediterranean to its furthest eastern end. There, in the dust of camel caravans, drifted the old beliefs of Asia and India; also, from the North, the slow wide arcs of the nomadic tribes swept across to where the Danube made a water route to the West. Thus other ideas penetrated the simplicity of early Christianity till it was submerged under the extraneous accumulations.

Europe was then a collection of small independent states, not of large nations. The expenses of armies for the Crusades reduced these small individual states to poverty: England was taxed almost to extinction. Officially, all rewards were spiritual; and service in the crusades remitted all sin. If you died fighting, you went straight to heaven.

The Templars organised transport, much on the lines of a modern package tour. At Sidmouth today can still be seen the remains of a little chapel by the beach (now a cafe) which gave spiritual encouragement – we hope of both kinds – to those who faced a Channel crossing. Geraldus Cambrensis' account of the recruitment in Wales reads like the report of a hysterical revival meeting.

The man recruited – or commanded by his feudal owner – to this adventure, must have been able-bodied and mentally alert. If he survived to return home his knowledge of other lands and other agricultural methods would make him a live force in his neglected land – or a disillusioned hermit.

The mediaeval Church was arranged in correct feudal convention. Its angels and archangels and 'all the company of heaven' were arranged around the 'overlord with his family, mother and heir', set apart at a high table, with strong-winged messengers and musicians in attendance (harps and all the various instruments that appeared in the minstrel gallery can still be studied in cathedral galleries). The 'bord clothes' of linen, spread over the high table, were draped and overlapped exactly as high altars are still dressed – the front cloth that hid the legs of the diners and kept off the draught was the heaviest, and was later elaborately decorated.

Feudal and pontifical precedence were similar; churches were often part of, and subsidised by, the feudal estate, and the Church became a major

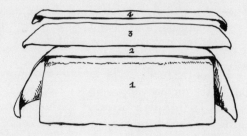

The table on the raised dais was covered in an elaborate manner: (1) A frontal, which might be richly decorated, was secured across the top of the table. It hung down to the floor, hiding the legs of the diners and keeping out draughts. (2) A long cloth, the width of the top of the table, was laid so that it would hang down at both ends. (3) Next came a covering cloth on top, large enough to hang down a hand's breadth all round and thus cover the joins between the first two cloths. (4) Finally a narrow draw cloth was laid; it went along in front of the diners, and on it stood bread, saucers, and so on. This could be withdrawn after the messy part of the meal, leaving all clear for its social ending. We still speak of 'drawing the cloth', and formal banquets still end with dessert fruits, sweetmeats and wine upon polished mahogany.

educational influence on our labourer. To people unable to read or write, the paintings on the church wall told vivid stories and they were enjoyed thoroughly. The paint was kissed off the blessed saints so frequently that the artist was kept lucratively employed replacing it; and any picture, no matter how absurd, was believed 'because the artist must have seen it to be able to paint it'.

Baptism was to some reminiscent of the rites of older worship and this rite, giving a soul 'for man only', was perplexing. In emergency anyone, and any water, could be used; but the *words* must be exact. There was a grim story of a midwife who, seeing a baby about to die, baptised it, but in her agitation used the words 'St John' instead of 'Holy Trinity' – 'thereby was a soul lost'; the child could not go to heaven! This story was to be read out in all churches as a grim warning.

The ordinary peasant's life was hard, and the brutality he used to humans, putting out eyes, cutting off hands and feet, and slaughter in battle, was extended to beasts – who the Church declared had no souls. But he kept a deep belief in the mutability of the Life force itself. From this arose complexities best explained by an example vouched for by many of the authorities of the period. Giraldus Cambrensis writes of this in about 1185:

In Ireland a travelling monk, by his small camp fire, was approached by a wolf, who explained that he and his wife were turned into wolves. 'But now,' explained the wolf, 'my wife lies sick in a cave nearby, and asks the last sacraments.' The wolf knew the monk carried a little case of holy things around his neck. The priest was reluctant (perhaps the wolf showed his teeth), but he gave the she-wolf that holy thing, and 'had her contented to die'. Afterwards the he-wolf held the 'wake' with the monk until morning. There was much argument about the monk's right to give the last sacrament to a brute beast, but would not the beast be a woman when dead? The religious argument finally reached Rome for it was, as the Bishop said, 'a highly debatable point'.

Giraldus Cambrensis also tells the story of an archer who shot a bird and put it in his cooking pot. He replenished the fire three times; but at midnight when he took out the bird it was as raw and tough as when it went in. A priest seeing this exclaimed: 'Alas! That such a thing should befall! It was one of St Colman's holy birds.' The miserable archer soon afterward expired.

A natural explanation is that, as hunters know, meat cooked immediately after killing is tender, but if it is cooked in a state of rigor mortis it will never soften.

Miracles

Aestimabaid enim lumen dictum per reverberationem lumius cuyrisdam arei ante perediam indeficienter ardevtis in pelvi ad corpus marmorei mausolei perpolitum et planum ibidem irradia et secundum flammae ejusdem ceru scintillationem visum ad lapidem per clummas ascenddere.

. . . suggested that the light might be thrown up from the wax candles; burnt low down into their holder bowls; onto the columns above, and reflected on the polished slab of marble under the corpse.

Contemporary comment (on the tomb of St Winefred)

We who can 'consult an authority' or 'read up the subject' do not realise the mental isolation of our labourer. He was far more 'self reliant' than we suppose – and he lived with continuous inexplicable miracles.

One simple example. Our labourer in his noonday rest under a bush sees a small case – not as big as his thumbnail – split open and out comes a wet 'thing' which hangs down and begins to shake! Then, as he watches, this small thing lets down a small wet limp something that grows longer and shakes and quivers in the hot air. Before his eyes it divides and shudders open into two big wings. A complete butterfly, shining with bright colours, flies away – new born, alive! What were a hundred clumsy manmade miracles to him?

Though he accepted things he could not explain, he speculated upon them – and still does so. An excellent example in the nineteenth century is Huck Finn as he lay speculating with the slave Jim on the raft:

'We had the sky up there, all speckled with stars, and we used to lay on our backs and look up at them, and discuss about whether they was made or only just happened. Jim he allowed they was made, but I allowed they happened; I judged it would have took too long to *make* so many. Jim said the moon could 'a' *laid* them; well, that looked kind of reasonable, so I didn't say nothing against it, because I've seen a frog lay most as many, so of course it could be done.'

Like our labourer, Huck thought *with his own knowledge* of the earth. He'd seen one small female frog, after mating with an even smaller male, fill a large pond with iridescent globes of jelly, each with one black spot of life in it. It *seemed impossible, but was a fact!*

Mediaeval people believed in earthly paradise, because travellers had been there and they brought back stones – rather as twentieth-century astronauts have brought back moon-dust. The mediaeval people themselves had not handled the stones, but those who had done so said they were more beautiful than any stones on earth. Wonderful, transparent, coloured stones, that had been washed down in the rivers that flowed from paradise.

Mediaeval people also knew about birds of paradise.The birds could never have trodden earth for they had no feet, and their bellies were full of seeds and spices of plants which never grew on earth. In this they were not absurdly credulous, for the birds had come from the East disembowelled, with their feet removed, and stuffed with spices to preserve them.

During the Dark Ages our countryman utilised 'Roman remains' as handy quarries for building material, as his mediaeval contemporaries used derelict castles. According to Henry of Huntingdon,there was no stone large enough to make a coffin for St Etheldreda, Abbot of Ely, so they went to Grantchester, a nearer source of supply, 'where by a ruined wall they found a beautifully finished marble sarcophagus' which fitted miraculously. Bede, himself an historian, makes no historical acknowledgment, considered it providential.

Sometimes the labourer's belief was tactful diplomacy, more often it

was a half-contemptuous amusement that made him reluctant to argue
with a superior so obviously ignorant or gullible. (An attitude that
survives today.) Examples crop up of many forms of miraculous light
which a labourer would know from long experience were the result of
natural causes. For example, a wagon containing saints' bones was drawn
to the monastic church, where it was left outside overnight with the men
who had helped pull it on guarding it. And 'all night a holy light from
heaven shone on those bones'. Now those labourers must have known
phosphorus. They used it on old wood to shine out paths in the dark. They
could rub it up with their thumbnail. To them it would be no different on a
dead fish from on a dead saint, but the learned priest said it was 'a miracle',
so who were they to contradict? (Anyhow, they were paid by the
monastery, and it behoved them to uphold its prestige.)

Reliques

Thanne have I in latoun a sholder-boon
Which that was of an hooly Jewes shepe.
'Goode men', I seye, 'taak of my wordes keep;
If that this boon be wasshe in any welle,
If cow, or calf, or sheep, or oxe swelle
That any worm hath ete, or worm ystonge,
Taak water of that welle and wassh his tonge,
And it is hool anon; and forthermoore
Of pokkes and of scabbe, and every soore
Shal every sheep be hool that of this welle
Drinketh a draughte.
                 The Pardoner's Prologue, Geoffrey Chaucer (1340–1400)

Bone-barter became an important part of the economy of the mediaeval
Church. The remains of saints were venerated, and dug up, and their poor
bones shared out among churches, cathedrals and shrines on a spiritual
commercial basis. The devout venerated and believed, and reliques
attracted pilgrims (the pilgrim was a type of mediaeval tourist – and
valuable). There might be open fighting for possession of some weary old
man's fingers, which had long since folded over their last prayer.

Remains of saints are still venerated:

'Blessed Oliver Plunkett, that most holy and dismembered of
churchmen ... after years of splendid isolation ... the former Primate's
head has been joined to his left femur, shoulder blade and two ribs.... The
great man's head ... bathed in curious green light stares impassively at
visitors. ... But according to church sources ... his remains will still be
widely scattered, even more than they were when he was hanged, drawn,

and quartered at Tyburn in 1681, on a trumped-up charge of treason . . .
exposed the day after his death.' (*Guardian* 1975)

It was perhaps by its serious absurdity that the crack began in the
structure of the mediaeval Church?

Our basic labourer, independent and earth-taught, knew bodies came of
the earth and returned to the earth – it could be the spirit of life only which
escaped back to the God it came from.

THE WORK
OF THE YEAR

The poems which open each month's work are selected from
Thomas Tusser: His Good Points of Husbandry,
edited by Dorothy Hartley (Country Life, 1931).
Unattributed verses in the same style are by the same author.
Tusser may seem to a modern reader to be performing
his tasks rather early in the year;
his January 1st would fall when we would expect January 11th,
for the calendar was not reformed
in England until 1752.

JANUARY

When Christmas is ended, bid feasting adieu,
go play the good husband, thy stock to renew.
Be mindful of rearing, in hope of a gain,
dame profit shall give thee reward for thy pain.

Who breaketh up, timely, his fallow or ley,
sets forward his husbandry, many a way:
This tilth in a tilture, well forward doth bring,
not only thy tillage, but all other thing.

Some breaking up ley, soweth oats to begin,
to suck out the moisture, so sower therein;
Yet oats with her sucking a peeler is found,
both ill to the master, and worse to some ground.

Land arable, driven or worn to the proof,
it craveth some rest for thy profit's behoof:
With oats ye may sow it, the sooner to grass,
more soon to be pasture, to bring it to pass

In ridding of pasture, with turfs that lie by,
fill every hole up as close as a die:
The labour is little, the profit is gay,
whatever the loitering labourers say.

Lay dirt upon heaps, fair yard to be seen,
if frost will abide it, to field with it clean.
In winter a fallow, some love to bestow,
where pease for the pot, they intend for to sow.

From Christmas, till May be well entered in,
some cattle ware faint, and look poorly and thin:
And chiefly when prime grass at first doth appear,
then most is the danger of all the whole year.

Be greedy in spending, and careless to save,
and shortly be needy, and ready to crave,
Be wilful to kill, and unskilfull to store,
and look for no foizon, I tell thee before.

NEW YEAR

Plough Monday, the next after Twelfthtide be past
biddeth out with the Plough; the worst husband is last.

EGALLY the farming year begins in March, being the easiest month for a transition between outgoing and incoming workers. But country people know that 'before Christmas' and 'after Christmas' are definite periods. In the autumn stock is sold, supplies bought in, storehouses filled, alterations made within the house, the window shutters put up, extra blankets given out, the woodshed filled, and arrangements made for good lighting. After Christmas is the time to prepare for the longer spring days: we start therefore at the beginning of the year with the farmer's most basic necessities: his plough and his fields.

Plough Monday, the first farming feast of the New Year, probably dates as early as the plough itself. The tradition continues most strongly in the Midlands where arable land is flat and plough furrows long; it would be less celebrated among mountains where little, crooked, tilted fields remained hand tilled. Between Nottingham and Loughborough, from 1920 to 1930, Plough Monday was kept on all the farms. For weeks previously, the lads who led the horses, trainee ploughmen, used to curry favour by doing odd jobs and giving small services to the farms, with 'You'll remember this on Plough Monday?' The local innkeeper would book a room with a good fire and the grown men stumped up for drinks. Collected gifts would be birds, joints, ham, eggs, and butter for cakes which the innkeeper's wife would cook for them.

On Plough Monday night at dusk, the lads blacked their faces, turned their coats inside out, and went round the farms and big houses, dragging an old ploughshare and demanding 'largesses for the ploughboys'. If the Gaffer paid up well, they would scratch a line across the drive to show he had been called upon, and he would not be troubled again; but if the household was mean and did not subscribe, the lads would fairly plough up the ground before the door so that it was a sea of mud for weeks, treading dirt into the house and causing endless trouble. They usually collected enough money to pay the innkeeper and have an excellent hot supper! (And no boss expected 'they lads' to be working next morning.)

That was Plough Monday up to 1930. The custom died out when tractors and cultivators displaced the horse-drawn plough.

In the early and mediaeval periods the real winter began after Christmas. The salt and dried meat of winter was varied by a pigeon pie or a rabbit; or (through early breeding of a sow) by a roast sucking-pig. The lack of winter greens was serious: dried peas and parsnips would be used up and the very last of the cheese. Outside work depended on the weather. During frost, dung from the stalled cattle would be carted to the fields, but when the ground was too sticky the heaps cluttered up the farm's yard. Wood-cutting went on, and jobs such as clearing ditches, though there were few hedgerows before the Enclosures.

Lambing and calving start; sows are breeding:

> Of one sow together, rear few above five,
> and those of the fairest and likeliest to thrive.
> Ungelt, of the best keep a couple for store,
> one boar pig, and sow pig, that sucketh before.

A very knowledgeable note, for the porkling that goes to the front teat gets most milk.

> Serve rye-straw out first, then wheat-straw, and pease,
> then oat-straw, then barley, then hay if ye please:
> But serve them with hay, while the straw stover last,
> then love they no straw, they had rather to fast.

This verse, set in December by Tusser as a warning, shows the value of hay; in the horse-power days it was almost in the position of petrol today. Any sort of pasture was used in summer, but the mediaeval lack of winter fodder came when the heavy work of ploughing and carting was done. Oxen did most of the work, but for travel and transport the swifter horse was needed. Therefore the problems of spring feed, summer grass, and winter fodder, were serious; and they were complicated also by the different requirements of the various animals. Sheep bite close with sharp forward-set teeth. Cows have no teeth, but need to sweep in the grass with their rough tongues. Horses are more sheep-like in bite, but they cannot bite as close as sheep. Goats (those standby creatures) are capable grazers almost anywhere. Breeding animals must be kept reasonably lean while carrying, but need good food to bring forth, and a continuity of good food while in milk. Cows and sheep both produce in spring (causing combats between cowman and shepherd), while breeding mares are notoriously uncertain time-keepers. Thus the timing of the varied pasture and grazing was vital.

PASTURES AND MEADOWS

Friend, always let this be a part of thy care,
for shift of good pasture, lay pasture to spare.
So have you good feeding in bushets and leas,
and quickly safe finding of cattle at ease.

That means, if you can get feeding for the beasts in bushy land or lea land, give the better pasture more time to grow. The lea land (the word covers laid aside or fallow lands) shows the earlier tradition of three or four year 'rotation of crops' and the 'strip cultivation' of earlier centuries. A strip that had been cropped for several years was laid fallow to recover heart and, being soon covered with weeds, was cropped by the animals, who thus manured it. The 'bushets' were the rough lands on the outskirts of the forest where trees had been felled, but the stumps sprouted amongst small bushes and patches of weedy grass.

Common Pasture

This was the pasture 'common to the community', land that usually extended to the border of the forest. It was free for all, and therefore badly utilised. Besides the flocks and herds sent out under herdsmen, odd animals from everywhere invaded it. This land, properly tended and fenced off, should have been good grazing, but what was everyone's business was nobody's, and the disputes over this public ownership carried on well into the period of the later enclosures when the lands cleared either side of the highways were 'commons'. The small patches of green in our villages, with the village pond, and the ghost of the maypole, are the debris left after long agricultural arguments.

While commons were in use the herders, the sheep herds, cow herds, goat herds, swine herds, the goose girl, and all who lived all day on the common land had long rest periods when their charges also slept, for all grazing beasts keep regular hours. (A knowledgeable walker across country could set his watch by the sheep who cluster together at noonday, rouse themselves to graze again about three o'clock, and move off to their own exact curfew at dusk.) Cows, called by their hungry calves and timed by their full udders, know when it is milking time, and the clank of a pail will draw any pig within earshot. (Ever timed a hungry young pig? Till they put on weight they are one of the fastest animals for a sprint.) Herders were, in theory, responsible employees, but would often leave some small boy or girl to 'keep an eye' and slip off to the tavern. The swine herd was usually unpopular, for pigs not ringed dig and destroy pasture and are aggressive feeders. Geese were also unpopular; their dung was considered unwholesome. (A connection between water-grazing geese and liver rot in sheep may have been suspected, though liver fluke was not understood till centuries later. The life cycle of the fluke is a comparatively recent discovery; it begins in the body of the water snail among the cresses and grass, which is picked up by the sheep as they crop, and having destroyed their liver, passes out in droppings on to the grass and into the water; the modern drainage of moorland sheep walks destroys the snail, part of the cycle. See also pp. 67 and 68.)

Mountain Pasture

The hills did not become valued till Elizabeth's wool sales increased the hirsels, but (as today in afforested Wales) the hills gave parking space for beasts while the valley grass had time to grow.

The Saltings or Marsh Lands

Swine will feed on seaweed and fish refuse, and sheep can crop the grey-green grass; it gives them an iodine flavour (and made marsh mutton – served with laver sauce – very popular.) But saltings were fly beset, and only of value along wide estuaries such as the Dee estuary which was an asset to Basinwerk Abbey, and grazed by cattle.

All these varied types of 'grazing land' were known as 'pasture'.
   All pastures were gradually levelled, hollows filled and stones gathered up. Moles were an advantage, as they supplemented surface drainage and supplied top dressings of fine soil to be cast about. A rough stake could be planted in the centre of any bare patch of grass for the animals to gather

round and scratch and rub themselves; they manured that spot and made it fertile, and the stake could then be moved elsewhere. (Thus the herdsman also acted as field worker.)

How long any land remained 'pasture' varied, for when grass land was definitely cultivated, defended and cherished, it was not a 'pasture' but a 'crop of grass' – that is, a hayfield.

Another pasture (still called a 'bite') was when corn came through so early that it could be caught by a late frost. Sheep were then let in to 'bite' it down. Their droppings and light trampling are good for growing corn, and the new, rich green stuff is good for the sheep.

Water Meadows

These depended on the winter rains which raised the level of streams and rivers, and the mediaeval stone and earth dykes are still to be seen along many rivers and streams. The muddy rising water flooded over the land, and the silt settled as the water drained away. The skill was to arrange the dyke entrance and exit in such a way that a strong current could not wash away the silt, and yet enough slope had to be left for complete drainage. Often a natural 'oxbow' lake was made the basis of the irrigation channel. In the spring the fine silt brought down by the flood water sank down between the rising grass blades as a top-dressing. When the meadow was

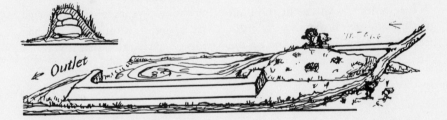

The diagram shows how water from a convenient stream can be diverted, using the natural contour of the land, to fill a square of pasture. When it later drains away at the far end a shallow layer of the silt which was carried in with the water is left to fertilise the land.

No two water meadows are alike in size or shape; some are naturally low-lying pieces of land which would be flooded every time a river or stream rose, and which only require drains to dry them out. In those artificially-formed meadows where a bank has been raised to hold the standing water, there is usually also an inlet to turn the stream on to the land. This bank is never very high. One can find examples of this kind of water meadow alongside quiet rivers; there are very good examples on the lower reaches of the Conway.

sufficiently dried out the small-footed sheep might have an early bite, otherwise a water meadow should not be trodden:

> Spare meadow at Gregory, marshes at Pasque,
> for fear of dry summer, no longer time ask.

The feast of St Gregory fell on 12 March, and from then until haytime the grass was left to grow. Water meadow banks were not high: do not confuse them with the heavier 'marsh walls' needed as defence against tidal inundation, or the smaller enclosures found by streams: these last were made for soaking hides in lime, or treating hemp and flax, or brick and daub mixing. Their position distinguishes them from the larger water meadows.

Land Meadows

When woodland has been cleared and animals pastured there, the piece may become a land meadow. But an old grass lea broken and re-ploughed for corn will be very well manured and produce a rich crop: thus the saying that 'To break a lea makes a man. To make a lea breaks a man'. With no pasture left for grazing, all stock had to be sold off, so for a year there is extra capital from the sale of the stock, and also from the sale of the rich corn crops off the broken lea (this 'makes a man'); but after that, the farmer has to start again to restore the balance between stock, corn and pasture which may take years (and to do this 'breaks' him).

(A reminder of this came to light during the war years when much rich grazing land was broken for corn. A few areas, such as Romney Marsh, had been so well tended for years and the pasturage was so rich that it was not considered wise to break it.)

Field Names

There are as many different types of land as there are different localities, nor are any two fields exactly alike. The labourer knows his fields as personalities and gives them names that endure for centuries. Today fields are often named by size – 'Long Acre', 'Ten Acre', and so on. Earlier names are more interesting, and often give a clue to past owners or history: for example 'Battle Acre', 'Martyr Bones' (that was where they upturned an old monastic burial ground), 'Bell Field' (where a church bell was cast). Field names are sometimes handed down oddly: two from a monastic foundation are amusing. The two men may have trudged together – impatient French and solid Saxon. 'How call you this field?'; 'La pluie terre.' 'And this one?'; 'La bas est sec.' And the solid Saxon linguist inscribes 'Flutter field' and 'Basket field' upon enduring parchment.

In and Out Fields

The meaning of these terms varies. In the north, where collective field-work and individual enterprise continued simultaneously, the terms 'in field' and 'out field' indicate many curiously acquired holdings. Central to the community was the 'in field', which was under continuous cultivation; if an individual wanted a piece of land of his own, then he could find a piece of ground outside the boundary of the communal land. He would have to bring it under cultivation: if it were worth clearing, as virgin soil it might be very fertile. Later this 'out field' might be assimilated in the 'in field', and the original clearer's claim to it would complicate the way in which the communal land was allocated.

The size of a field would depend on how much seed-corn a man could spare, and he would plan his work as a modern gardener plans his winter dig, so that he could keep an eye on it if at all possible, and so that he would not have to walk back across the broken surface. Hunters were free, but a man dependent upon corn had to stay where he planted his seed at least until he had harvested it, so that corn-growing developed a more stable and communal life.

Hill people, eg Celts of the mountainous west, pecked out their small fields where they could; valley people, like the Saxons who settled in East Anglia, could make larger level fields. While field size varied from area to area, they were fairly uniform in a particular locality: this is because man is uniform, and two men working from dawn to dark in similar conditions would achieve more or less the same amount of work. As a term of measurement, an acre was originally as much as a yoke of oxen could plough in a day, but the size of the acre varied according to the nature of the terrain (and perhaps according to the local breed of oxen?) A 'hide' was as much land as could be tilled with one plough in a year, and was normally a hundred acres.

Ploughing by oxen developed the straight-sided field seen in the well-known system of strip cultivation, because traction was more direct in a straight line; this had the additional advantage that areas could be more easily marked out. An attempt was made to ensure that everyone who was working the land had a share of both good and bad positions.

If the land sloped, the displaced soil would roll downhill; this tendency was particularly noticeable when only the plough was used for tilling. The slow displacement of the earth gradually levelled the field; unbroken strips would be left between the cultivated areas as paths, or wide enough to take a wagon, and gradually a terraced effect was produced. (The very small

terraces on some steep banks can be accounted for by the action of earth
worms. Darwin made a study of the relationship between the size of the
worm, the weight of the earth cast, and the angle of the bank. In some tidal
rivers, flooding produces a similar effect.)

Ponds and Water

Pits and ponds were vital for water on land used for grazing, for no
herdsman could prevent thirsty cattle from roving destructively. These old
ponds, clay pits, sand pits, marl pits, and so on, are now rapidly being
levelled out where larger fields take tractors. But in mediaeval times,
when the single-furrow plough was used, detours mattered less; the pond
in the field was not much trouble and it was very necessary for the field's
intermittent use as pasture.

Nowadays, when water is laid to the steading through pipes, we forget
the long centuries when animals were turned loose to drink at ponds. Some
years ago a firm in the Midlands – Bibby & Son, Loughborough – offered to
scoop clear old field ponds, putting the mud out on to the adjacent land. In
more than a third of the ponds they found that there had originally been a
spring of clear running water and that it was only the slow neglect of these
small watercourses that had allowed them to degenerate to muddy ponds.
The rich silt from these old ponds covered acres of land with a good top-
dressing.

'Camping'

In meadow or pasture (to grow the more fine),
let campers be camping in any of thine;
Which if you do suffer when low is the spring,
you gain to yourself a commodious thing.

Because most games wear out a field in patches, the encouragement of
'camping' is of interest. It was an early ball game (the Napoleonic Wars
may have changed the name to 'Prisoners Base'). The two 'camps' were of
unlimited number but even strength, and set at opposite ends of the field.
From one end a 'token' (later a hand ball) was flung with a shout of
challenge into the opposing camp, whose object was to field it as swiftly as
possible and hurl it back; as, while the 'token' remained in the enemy camp,
the opposing side might rush across and drag back as many 'prisoners' as
they could lay hands upon before the ball was thrown back to reverse the
challenge. The game continued until one side was depleted and the other
had secured all of them as prisoners.

Traditionally the game used a gauntlet, rather than a ball. A tough old glove, or a soft shoe, makes for a swifter game than does a ball, which takes too long to follow and retrieve. (Where a playground is near a roadway it is safer for children to use such a 'token' rather than a ball.)

It will be realised that this game did not wear out any special portion of the field, but stampeded evenly from end to end all over it, and, as originally played by bare-foot or soft-shod peasants, the firming and levelling of the land was commendable. Later, when it was played in hard shoes with a larger ball, local political feeling ran high and the intercounty contests became serious. Dutt, in his notes on East Anglia, states that in the eighteenth century three hundred men took to the field on Diss Common, between Norfolk and Suffolk, and nine deaths ensued!

Grass

The number of English grasses of fine, rounded type – as distinct from the flat-bladed – testify to the long cultivation of mediaeval meadows. The following are a few of the older grasses. The common names vary locally.

Beard grass (*Polypogon monspeliensis*)
Cat's tail (*Phleum pratense*)   Meadow Foxtail (*Alopecurus pratensis*)
Cocksfoot (*Dactylis glomerata*)   Melic grass (*Melica nutans*)
Dog's tail (*Cynosurus cristatus*)   Quaking grass (*Briza media*)
Foxtail (*Alopecurus sp.*)   Vernal grass (*Anthoxanthum odoratum*)

The *bents* are wire-like grasses whose dry stems cover the moorlands with gold and white all winter; shorter bents cover the chalk downs. Other shorter grasses make smooth green spaces between gorse and bracken. These are 'turf grass'.

Either *Agrostis gigantea*, or *A. stolonifera*, and *A. spicer-venti* were long cultivated as 'sheep bite'. *A. gigantea*, black bent, called 'mousetail', grows on the dry soil of peatish land. The *whorl grasses* were definitely grown as a pasture grass, and in parts of East Anglia the local butter and cheese were said to be flavoured by them, as the alder and rush of the Dales in spring used to flavour the Wensleydale cheese. (See p. 108.)

Later agriculturalists listed special grasses for sowing water meadows on heavy soil. These included: marsh creeping bents, meadow foxtail, darnel fescue grass, meadow fescue, tall fescue, floating sweet grass, Italian rye grass, perennial rye grass, reed grass, cat tail, rough-stalked meadow grass and greater birdsfoot trefoil.

Sheep's fescue (*Festuca ovina*) and meadow fescue (*F. pratensis*) in some districts have the suggestive name of 'floating grass'.

The corn grasses are very general. The slight predominance in any locality may indicate the previous preponderance of that type of corn in that locality, or only the change of soil and climate which made that special corn prevalent. Thus wild oats (*Avena fatua* etc.) grow on dry strong ground and in the West Riding keep their old name of 'Hapea'. The yellow wild oat, much used for fancy straw plait, was probably introduced by the French workers, and continued in East Anglia and Luton districts up to the end of the nineteenth century. Wild barley (*Hordeum murinum*) is perhaps more prevalent in the north.

On river flats there would be several 'sea grasses', but marram grass (*Ammophila arenaria*) which grows on sand is of use in reclaiming land encroached on by the sea, and salt marsh grass (*Puccinellia maritima*) is the common grass of river estuaries; it can grow for months under water and yet recover swiftly from a dry spell.

Red Darnel (*Lolium temulentum*) and rye grass (*L. perenne*) are found on clay soil. The common darnel (now rare) is a weed that so much resembles the first blades of corn that it was believed wet weather actually turned corn into darnel – in mediaeval times the dividing line between vegetables and insects and animals was easily broken. (Even today old field workers speak of lime as 'producing' certain weeds, such is its convincing effect on a mixed crop, encouraging one plant and killing another.) Darnel was also called or draik – an earlier name for lime. In the *Tournament of Tottenham* the shield of one rustic knight is 'powdered with burning draik'. A point to remember considering early natural history is the strong influence of the Classics: if darnel was the *infelix lolium* of Virgil, that would account for its being considered poisonous; for cases were seriously reported of its being ground with the bread corn or malted with barley and proving fatal, yet chemists can find no poison in darnel seeds. (See also Fungus, p. 167.)

Weeds

The change in weeds is curious. Stinking chamomile, *Anthemis cotula*, blistered the bare legs of reapers most painfully. The thistle is still with us, the vetches that 'pull downward' are listed as *Vicia hirsuta*; but now bind-weed seems to be troublesome. Cockle is now only a pleasant wayside flower, as are the pink mallow and corn marigold.

Corn marigold, *Chrysanthemum segetum*, was the cause of legislation for years. 'Searchers', or 'riders', were sent out and a fine of 3s. 4d. 'or a wether sheep' was imposed for plants left growing. Perhaps the alternative of a sheep was one of those 'loophole' clauses so common where the law had to be enforced by experts on special trades. Only someone on the spot, and knowing the land conditions, would be able to judge fairly between negligence and accident, in which case the quality of the sheep demanded might qualify the severity of the fine?

Use of Hay

There were no root crops for winter fodder, so cattle and sheep got a lean diet. Hay was kept for horses and breeding animals, this was wise. Riding horses were the farmer's only communication with markets and towns, and the draught horses and working oxen were next season's labour. Some small hay went to the milch cow and the few animals that were to be kept for the family meat supply. During snow the sheep were brought to the steading and folded, 'packed pretty tight, to keep them warm'. As today, every shepherd schemed to keep a little hay hidden against the early lambing season. The cowherd was also after special fodder for 'his breeding cows'; the competition between these continued for centuries.

LAMBING TIME

Ewes, yearly by twinning, rich masters do make,
the lamb of such twinners, for breeders go take:
For twinlings be twiggers, increase for to bring,
though some of their twigging, peccantem may sing.

Ewes were milked, and ewe-milk cheese made; but more often the milk was mixed (five ewes to one cow). The difficulty was that the sheep were sometimes herded away, and a worker had to be sent out to milk them, or else the milking ewes had to be accommodated in a pasture near the farm, and crowded pasture had to be very rich 'to fill their desire'. Otherwise the ewes did not put on weight and recover strength after lambing. Anyhow, all milking had to stop at Lammas (1 August), to give the ewes a chance to get strong before the winter and ready for the ram again in late autumn. Early lambing was an advantage, to have the ewe milk, so the shepherd began the lambing season soon after Christmas. If necessary, hovels (see p. 146) and lambing pens were erected.

Ewe-milking

'A turrible lot o' lambs'

An old Essex shepherd was very successful, his ewes dropping twins (or even occasional triplets) with seasonal regularity. When very old and bedridden he confided his secret to his Boss's young son: 'Because you be young, as tis that it would die with me, so I give it you to keep.

'In the spring, get you a stoat, a male. You know what lewd little beasts *they* be! And kill it, and put it warm into a bottle and cork it and bury it in dung-heap . . . where it's same warm as he be. No – you can't put it to stove, old woman she'll let stove out, or heat it up. No – the dung-heap stays a nice even temperature all winter, and right through summer. Then, come late autumn,' [when breeding starts] 'take you up the bottle, and there'll be some-like water in it . . . and squeeze out what's left of him and take that water and mix it with some nice warm mash of soft bread, and give it to tup before he sets to ewes – and you'll get a turrible lot o' lambs, Mas' John, a turrible lot o' lambs.'

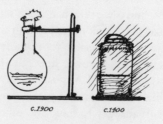

c.1900   c.1400

FEBRUARY

Go plow in the stubble, take timely this season
for sowing of vetches of beans and of peason.
Now sooner ye sow them the sooner they come
And better for household they fill up a room.

Where banks be amended, and newly up-cast,
sow mustard-seed, after a shower be past,
Where plots full of nettles be noisome to eye,
sow thereupon hemp-seed, and nettle will die.

The vines and the osiers cut, and go set,
if grape be unpleasant, a better go get.
Feed swan, and go make her up strongly a nest,
for fear of a flood, good and high is the best.

Land-meadow that yearly is spared for hay,
now fence it and spare it, and dung it ye may.
Get mole-catcher cunningly mole for to kill,
and harrow, and cast abroad every hill.

Now thresh out they barley, for malt or for seed,
for bread-corn, if need be, to serve as shall need:
If work for the thresher, ye mind for to have,
of wheat and of mestlin, unthreshed go save.

Good provender, labouring horses would have,
good hay and good plenty, plough-oxen do crave;
To hale out thy muck, and to plough up thy ground,
or else it may hinder thee many a pound.

Who slacketh his tillage, a carter to be,
for groat got abroad, at home lose shall three;
And so by his doing, he brings out of heart,
both land for the corn, and horse for the cart.

Buy quickset at market, new gather'd and small,
buy bushes or willow, to fence it withall:
Set willows to grow, in the stead of a stake,
for cattle, in summer, a shadow to make.

'REST NOT FOR TAKING
THY EASE'

FEBRUARY, fill-dyke with black or white' – the most uncertain month of the year when urgent work on the land may be hindered by bad weather. Nevertheless, there are tasks that can be undertaken around the farm, some under cover. In open weather, planting can be done at the risk of late frosts – this was the time for planning ahead, putting the land into good heart, and planting willow – which roots itself in wet ground, and was used for 'Baskets, Chayres, Hampers and other country stuffe'. The vine had been reintroduced by the Normans, and seems to have been cultivated out of doors, and we believe its juice began to replace the earlier verjuice and vinegar.

That Tusser lived on a tidal estuary accounts for his concern for the swan's nest, though Markham commented that 'To speake of the breeding of swannes is needlesse, because they can better order themselves in that business than any man can direct them'. (Swans were more common than modern ideas of Royal and Guild ownership suggest; a young cygnet was a meaty table bird.) The danger of bad weather in this month suggests the sense of keeping some corn for threshing under cover in the barn – a cheerful and warming occupation for the men.

By the end of winter, draught horses and oxen were reserved for work on the land: though high prices would be paid for heavy winter transport, that did not recompense loss of their work on the land.

KEEPING THE LAND IN GOOD HEART

The good mixed farming of this period provided plenty of animal manure, but there were curious ideas, some classical, about its application. For example, Columella, long regarded as an authority, held that the dung of 'Aquatic birds was nought', and condemned goose droppings. (This may have been an early observation of liver fluke – see p.67–8) Pig manure was also suspect. Varrow, another authority, by very natural agricultural reasoning praised horse dung for corn, since horses ate corn; and cow dung for grass. Cato recommends fern, broken straw or 'the sedge from the willow plots' to be littered under stalled cattle. Pliny recommends green manure: 'leguminous crops, dug in', 'turn up a crop of lupines before they have podded, and plough, fork, or cut them up, and bury them.' Traditionally, a dead donkey was good for a vine.

'Compass' and 'manures' were different. Compass was more like our compost, while manure usually implied the liquid from the farmyard, already well trodden into litter, and soaked up with bracken or other material. This was carted to the field, when the ground was hard during frost, and as the carts plodded slowly up and down, 'Sir Wag', the man who walked behind, hauled dung off the cart with a special fork set at an angle. Later this was spread and ploughed in. This spreading of manures was considered important. The 'privy' manure, which was mixed with wood

A lighter form of drag

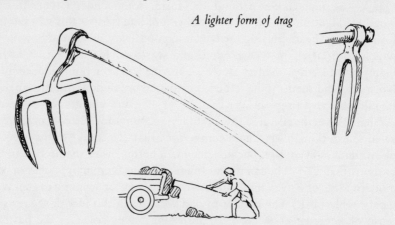

A special dung drag was used for removing manure or compass off the cart as it moved across the field. The angle of the tines allowed 'Sir Wag' to unload without having to stand on the cart, and the length of the handle meant that he was well clear of the manure as it fell (though he would have to walk forward through it).

ash, was good for corn, but rank manures were considered bad for vegetables, as it gave them 'an obnoxious and fetid odour'. (Sludge from modern sewage farms is thought objectionable for this reason.)

The attempts to keep liquid and solid manures separate caused technical difficulties in the household privy. Some of the 'underground passages' of old farms are probably the covered drains from byres and sheds. Bracken, winter's useful bedding, was less retentive of moisture than straw.

The manure on the land kept it warm through the winter, and if the following spring was mild, the wheat or barley might be up too soon, and grow too rank (what farmers call 'too forrard'). In this case, sheep might be turned on to it (see p. 55).

When milking in the field was usual, cow manure was left on the pastures. In autumn, the few cattle remaining after slaughter were taken inside and littered in fern, bracken, or reeds. The cattle sheds or byres were cleared out as soon as possible, as the ammonia given off would cause hair trouble under the beasts' bellies. Horse manure was dropped on worked fields and furrows (thus a packhorse trail later made the crop of wayside grass very valuable – a consideration after much land was enclosed). Pig manure was far less easily collected, as the swine were free-rangers; though in winter the breeding sow and the boar contributed. Sheep manure was much valued, being evenly spread and directly used, and the treading of the sheep firmed it into the soil. Sheep seem to have been hurried on to any land that needed fertilising. Bird manure, the scraping of the hen pen and the pigeon loft, was collected for its value in the laundry. It was washed and used with urine in bucking – the steeping in lye which was an important bleaching process. Spreading chalk, lime and marl sometimes helped, and sometimes hindered the improvement of the land's fertility; but this could be discovered through usage only. The seasonal supply of blood and bones from the autumn slaughter came conveniently for winter cultivation; and other waste trade products provided a form of artificial manure. The difference between immediate and slow release was appreciated, though the actual chemistry less understood.

One waste product that was not wanted on the land was goose dung: geese often grazed the same pastures as sheep did, by streams; and in these pastures the sheep often unaccountably died. The Elizabethan increase in sheep farming caused shepherds to wonder why some of the new rich pastures proved fatal to the sheep. Damp- and foot-rot, in sheep accustomed to dry barren grazing, was to be expected and could be dealt with; but these sheep died from some untraceable internal trouble. Some thoughtful shepherds advised against letting the sheep out to graze in the early-morning dew, where they might eat the small white slugs. (Goose dung would leave easily visible white and yellowish deposits in the grass, which might look a bit like slugs or snails.) For centuries it was not known why sheep grazing on this kind of pasture should die; modern research has shown that the water snail is involved in the life cycle of the liver fluke, *Fasciola hepatica*. The snail, in which the fluke spends part of its complicated life cycle, deposits its eggs in the grass; the sheep grazes there and takes in the eggs with the grass; thus the liver.fluke reaches the sheep's liver. Not only can it prove fatal, it is also capable of being transmitted back into the pasture through the sheep's dung. The water snail's eggs were invisible to a shepherd looking at his pasture; the goose dung would show up well, and so the possibility that it was the goose dung does not seem unreasonable. It is an interesting point that shepherds suspected the 'small white slugs'; these used to be collected and used in the preparation of medicine. (The mediaeval mind did not wonder why the goose was not also a victim; it was accepted that an animal would not be poisoned by its own dung.)

Artificial manures were not chemicals, used direct, as today, but the raw material which supplied those chemicals; this made it slower to become incorporated. Hillman (an agriculturalist of later date) lists marl, burnt bracken, road earth, river mud, chalk, soot, soap lees, the refuse of the tanyards, potash lees, spent charcoal, the residue of pigeon dung (soaked first to obtain washing lye), malt waste (the small sprouts from the malted grain rubbed off after drying), lime, rags, shavings and shreds of leather from the leather works, clippings of fur, coney (rabbit) skins (especially the ears), horn shavings from the horn works (the trimmings from horn spoons and drinking cups, handles of knives, and so on), hoof refuse (after they had been boiled down for glue; and therefore, presumably, calves' and pigs' trotters were used – after the cook had made jelly and brawn), 'blew clay' (this is constantly cropping up), 'urry' (wine waste, which was not to be used unless well mixed with wood ash), seaweed (wet) and the ash left after burning it, sea sand (on stiff clay this was valuable), all household refuse, including the water from the cheese press and the bucking.

Though this list was made at a later date, it covers the mediaeval 'refuse manures' that would be brought back in the 'returned empty' wains that had carried the farming products up to sell in the city. Only two may not have been used in the Middle Ages: the refuse from the malting (as most people made their own brews) and the soap makers' ash. Soap was usually made at home, but in some cities, where slaughter refuse and fish oil were available, soap-boiling traders had enough waste to be worth collecting. Some of the materials, of doubtful value as manure, would serve to lighten clay. The tanyard refuse would include the hair left in the lime after pickling hides, but this would more likely be used in the fibrous type of plaster and in the outer pargetting work that began to decorate the wood and timber buildings at the end of the mediaeval period.

Lime

Liming the land was curiously expensive, even in limestone districts, but that was not its only use. In a naval engagement off the east coast, the English boats approached the French boats downwind and by 'releasing clouds of quicklime so blinded and disabled the enemy' that they won the battle – which argues that lime happened to be available, probably shell lime, burnt with dry seaweed (which has a good potash content). Quicklime is difficult to handle, and where it touches ox or driver it burns, so it was customary to butter round the eyes of the oxen and of the men who were spreading the lime, and a very calm day was chosen for the work. When water is poured on the quicklime it boils with intense heat, and limewash was for centuries made by packing coarse waste fat in a tub of quicklime, pouring on water, and allowing the heat of the lime to dissolve and distribute the fat.

This 'limewash' is waterproof and better for outdoor use than size mediums, since gelatinous adhesives dissolve in wet, but fat does not; it probably coated the original White House in Washington; and poultry houses, cattle byres and common lodging-houses were limewashed. For preserving food on sailing voyages lime was more reliable than salt and it was customary to limewash dried ham for storage.

Lime was also used for cleaning and sweetening wooden utensils such as churns. Later, when iron was smelted with coal, the proximity of limestone rocks and coalfields was an industrial advantage.

Marl and Chalk

Chalk was a good top-dressing for clay – 'fifteen cartloads of forty bushels each was a fair dressing for one acre'. Both marl and chalk were carted on to the land *before* frost, and later broken by hand labour, using a longhandled mallet called in some districts a 'two-head', as it had a spike on one side and a hammerhead on the other. Sometimes a hand pike was used, especially when frost had followed rain, and the larger lumps had cracked. (The clods of earth from primitive ploughing had been broken in this way by generations of 'clod hoppers' – clod breakers.)

Breaking the large clods gave a finer surface tilth than could be achieved merely by using a primitive form of plough.

It was believed that lime, marl and chalk encouraged the growth of coltsfoot, one of the deepest-rooted weeds, and most difficult to eradicate. For medical use, as an expectorant for chest complaints, coltsfoot was excellent, but its broad leaves and sucker roots make it a field pest, since the smallest portion, broken and dispersed by ploughing, propagates.

Coltsfoot's flowers appear in early spring, and are followed by the leaves. The name comes from the young leaves resemblance to the rounded hoofprint of a young colt. A hot drink of coltsfoot and honey would loosen a tight cough overnight.

Burning off the Harrow

Oft it has paid to burn a barren field
Consume light stubble in the crackling flames
Whether it be that thence your land derives
Rich nourishment and hidden strength at all;
Its badness, by the burning is baked out
And useless damp expelled; or that the heat
Opens more ways and unseen pores whereby
New moisture reaches the young plants . . .

translated from a Greek agricultural treatise

'Land serves crop and crop serves land' – this was the primitive law of early strip farming. As a simple analysis, the land surface is broken to receive the seed corn, and any weed that sprouts faster than the corn does is weeded out; but later the corn must fight with the weeds. When corn and weed are removed from the land (primitively by hand cutting, in modern usage by complicated reaping machinery), this leaves the land bare, and the low weeds rampant – just as they are ready to drop their seeds. Primitive usage got rid of this weed by rough surface grazing, later by clawing the roots up by a 'tined harrow' ('The toad under the harrow knows where each tine goes.'). This harrow was dragged across the land, first one way then another, till all surface weed was loosened. After this, weed was sometimes raked together, and burnt off, or the firing off was done directly across the field, which had the effect of killing some of the weed seeds.

Then the land was turned over again to bury the ash. This burying would not have been very thorough, as early ploughs did not cut deep. Today, a deeper cut more successfully buries the weed, but still the same usage, of 'First crop, then weed, then burn off the harrow', retains the blue smoke of mediaeval days.

Paring

We can find no direct evidence of this, the removal of a top layer, in mediaeval agriculture, but include this note because it was a very old form of tillage, and the action suggests an early type of ploughing. The diagram is from sixty years ago, near Post Bridge in Devon, where they were removing the top layer of heathery soil to reach the peat below. The attitudes are similar to drawings in the Justinian manuscript.

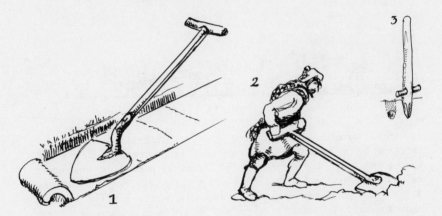

(1) A modern turf cutter, similar to one seen on Dartmoor and used for taking off the top layer of turf in the peat cuttings. (2) A faughter: it is similar in shape, but pushed from the hips and used for heavy clearing work. (3) A foot dibber: this is pushed down into the ground to make a hole, eg planting potatoes.

Forms of each of these tools seem to have been used in early cultivation before the plough.

DYKE AND HEDGE

Now sow, and go harrow (where redge ye did draw)
the seed of the bramble, with kernel and haw;
Which covered, overly, sun to shut out,
go see it be ditched, and fenced about.

The hedge is a sign of new enclosures. The mediaeval lands were changing from 'open strips', so that in the fifteenth and sixteenth centuries there were many instructions for making dykes and hedges. One idea was to twist loose straw rope incorporating seeds of oak, ash and thorn and then bury the rope where you wanted the hedge. For a dyke-and-hedge, the line

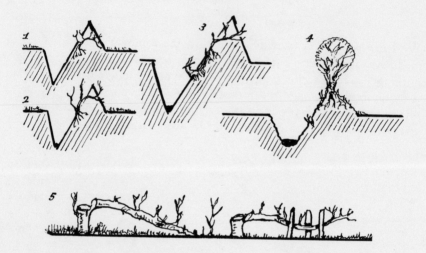

Strip fields were bounded on the long sides by the outer furrows, and on the short end by the headlands where the draught animals turned. Here would accumulate debris and stones, removed from the part of the field under cultivation. Dykes and hedges developed with the beginning of enclosures, as the system of common strip cultivation was superseded. The diagrams show an early process, from which that described in the text developed. Mediaeval gardeners were skilled grafters, and farmers too would develop layering and plashing, the use of stakes, and so on, to hold and raise plants and to maintain the flow of sap (5). The early tools used for this job were often contrived from old scythe blades, as indeed they still sometimes are. A wooden foot dibber, shown on p. 71, was used to make holes of a uniform depth for planting. An occasional tree in the run of a hedge was encouraged, as it served to stabilise the length, and gave useful noon-day shade.

(1) A ditch is dug near a bush, and soil thrown up on that side. (2) The bush continues to grow on the side of the ditch. (3) The bush is trimmed where it is too far down into the ditch. (4) Thus, the bush is found crowning the bank. (5) A hedgerow is formed by layering and trimming bushes to give a continuous line.

At the time of the Enclosure Acts, it was stipulated that enclosure must be done within the year it was granted. The hedge and its ditch had been in use for centuries; when land beyond was also hedged and ditched there was formed the curious short 'sunken roadways' which lead nowhere, and sometimes turn off at an angle and cease abruptly.

was laid across the land and marked by pegs. The ditch was then dug, the earth being flung up on to the owner's side – which accounts for the curious legal point that the ditch on the far side of a field boundary remains the property of the owner of the land on the other side of the hedge. When the ditch was sufficiently deep to drain the water from the field (the rean furrows were opened up across the headlands for this purpose), a raised bank was formed and sloped somewhat steeply, and the new hedge planted a little below the top of the bank on the ditch side. The top of the bank thus gave shelter to the young growing plants and gradually spilt down a dressing of top soil over the roots as they settled. This was most necessary where the sub-soil was strong clay. The last act was to put the grass sods, previously cut from the land before digging the ditch, back on to the bank, grass side up, and bed them firmly down. This type of dyke and hedge, on an old farm, would gradually wear down, the soil crumbling down and filling up the ditch. The reviving of such a dyke hedge was called 'water tabling'. The former depth of the ditch was refound, and a depth stick or peg marked. Then a line was cut along the bank face (on the *ditch* side) at field level, and a second line close to the base of the hedge. The grass sods between the lines were then cut out in oblong pieces and laid down on the field side of the dyke. This left the soil on the bank loose and the roots of the old hedge exposed. At this stage, thin places in the hedge could be repaired. Good soil was then dug up from the bottom of the filled-up ditch (until it was as deep as when first made) and the wet soil plastered back over the side of the bank, covering in the hedge roots, and giving again a smooth flat slope; the cut sods were pressed back into this, being wedged into the lower, slotted line, grass-side out. A good worker would often cut a second line of smaller sods from the base of the bank and finish the job by placing

Old stone land drains. (*c.1200*)

these sods, grass-side *down*, along the top of the first sods, pressing them down between the thorn roots at the top of the bank and over the cut edge of the facing sods below. This held the top edges of the sloping sides firm above, their lower edges being clipped into the ridge of the slanting cut below. Thus all was firm.

The reason for the sods being grass-side up on the side of the bank was that the grass might grow and thus bind the earth: the top sods were grass-side *down* because the hedger did not want grass to grow among the roots of the hedge.

Before commencing the work, the hedger would have plashed the old hedge, selected the new shoots he would want, and cut away and burnt the dead stumps; so that the actual hedge work was completed before the earth work started.

This reconstruction from an early manuscript illustrates how two men, with one basin and a wooden shovel, could *make* land. The fen waters now run high above the marshes they have drained. Where land did rise, it was rich and worth cultivating; the owners extended the boundaries of their small islands exactly as these men are doing. Lacking timber, tight bundles of reed laid along the margin would retain the thrown-up mud while allowing the water to drain back into the ditch which their delving had cleared. The rotting reed and consolidated mud would make it possible to walk on what had been marsh; this work carried out from both sides achieved a causeway.

The fens are very different from the rest of England: the Gough map (plate 1) shows Ely an island, best reached by water. Danes raided the country, monastic experts settled it. It was a strange impenetrable world of reeds and marshes haunted by devils and spirits, marsh lights and fevers, and owned by an undaunted people. Some of the larger islands, such as Crowland, were visited by Kings; but we study workmen who, far back in history, worked without tree or stone, lived in huts of turf and reed, and traversed that heaving mud and standing water using long leaping poles. Their land was rich in fowl and fish (eels were so plentiful that they were used as currency); there was salt on the coast for curing it, and reed for smoking it.

MARCH

White peason, both good for the pot and the purse,
by sowing too timely, prove often the worse;
Because they be tender, and hateth the cold,
prove March ere ye sow them, for being too bold.

Spare meadow at Gregory, marshes at Pasque,
for fear of dry summer no longer time ask.
Then hedge them and ditch them, bestow thereon pence,
corn, meadow, and pasture, ask alway good fence.

Sow barley in March, in April, and May,
the later in sand, and the sooner in clay.
What worser for barley, than wetness and cold?
what better to skilfull, than time to be bold?

Who soweth his barley too soon, or in rain,
of oats of thistles shall after complain:
I speak not of May-weed, of Cockle and such,
that noieth the barley, so often and much.

Let barley be harrowed, finely as dust,
then workmanly trench it, and fence it ye must.
This season well plied, set sowing an end,
and praise and pray God, a good harvest to send.

Some rolleth their barley, straight after a rain,
when first it appeareth, to level it plain:
The barley so used, the better doth grow,
and handsome ye make it, at harvest to mow.

Oats, barley, and pease, harrow after you sow;
for rye, harrow first, as already ye know:
Leave wheat little clod, for to cover the head,
that after a frost, it may out and go spread.

If clod in thy wheat, will not break with the frost,
if now ye do roll it, it quiteth the cost;
But see when ye roll it, the weather be dry,
or else it were better, unrolled to lie.

'MARCH DUST TO BE SOLD WORTH RANSOM OF GOLD.'

JANUARY may 'bid out with the plough', but February and March conditioned its usage. This is where Tusser's calendar is valuable as showing the developments in agriculture. Strip cultivation and primitive ploughing only disturbed the soil; Saxon ploughmen seem to have 'thought up' the coulter and turning bar, but their ploughs had not the ability to cut deeply enough to turn over and bury the surface. Under a thin snow or a surface frost, on the early long strips, breaking the soil surface could do little harm, and might even improve the tilth by exposing the surface to weathering. But when a plough that could turn over and bury the surface was developed, to plough in the fallen snow or frost would have made the soil cold, and unsuitable for sowing. Mediaeval seed corn was precious and broadcast sowing needed a good friable surface that would easily and *lightly* cover it in. Therefore came the saying 'March dust was worth gold' – the gold of future corn. At this time gardening work also began, and the growing of vegetable crops, of peas and beans.

CULTIVATION

'The Enemy of the Forest'

One of the mediaeval riddles in the Exeter Book of Riddles (probably eighth century) contains the lines:

> 'Nose to ground I crawl forward
> My nose is the grey enemy of the forest.'

This 'enemy' is the metal on the cutting tip of the plough. When implements were only of stone or wood, cutting heavy timber was almost impossible, even with stone axes mounted in wood. Hence, huts were then of mud, and graves of stone, even in timber country.

Ploughing for corn was most easily done by oxen. The long ox team, needed to drag the heavy wooden plough, became shorter when the plough draught was made lighter by the use of metal; but the plough used was still a single-furrow plough, steadied and directed by the ploughman and often led by a plough boy.

To turn the plough at the end of a furrow necessitated a very wide curve; leading the team for this was difficult. Therefore some fields were worked round and round, and all ploughmen tried to follow the natural soil curve. The furrows were not always arranged the longest way. The slope of the land counted more with horses than with oxen; for with oxen the draught was steady and powerful, and though impossible on hill fields, it held good on all level land. The whole field was 'laid out' before the work began, and the turning space or headland allowed for.

The plough was usually yanked out at the end of straight furrows, turned with a wide sweep, and started back again in a parallel line. Early ploughs could only work in one direction, and turn the furrow to one side. (The turn, or 'wrest' plough, in which the ploughshare could be turned over to reverse the cut, was not invented till 1700.)

View of the movement of the furrow-slice.

These two considerations – the wide turning space, and the one-sided furrow – influenced ploughing for centuries, and all innovation took account of them.

There was sometimes a ceremony for the first furrow of the year. In monastic days the abbot might stand at the end of the furrow with his cross, or the lord of the manor might hold up his sword to direct the first furrow. This first furrow left the soil to the right, on the way down: the plough turned on the headland and returned leaving the soil to the left, thus making an open furrow called a 'rean furrow'. The placing and depth of this furrow was important as it helped to drain the field. The distance between these furrows was known as a rean.

Now comes a point of interest. The distance between one rean furrow and the next was said to be governed by the turning space of an ox-plough, and of old the ploughman, making the second rean, was said to hold his long ox-whip at right angles to the plough handle and, by holding the tip directly over the first rean, cut an exactly parallel rean. That was when land was open and boundaries few. When fields became enclosed the distance from one rean to the next depended upon the number of reans possible in any one field. Once their first open furrows were cut, the plough went up one side and down the other, *between* the open furrows, making a ridge – on the same principle as they had made a furrow, only by turning the soil inwards instead of outwards. Now the field was laid out and the plough team worked up and down, round and round, steadily turning the soil into level ridges, with alternate open furrows and closed ridges which marked each rean.

Gathered-up ridges from the flat.

Twice gathered-up ridges.

I have purposely used the simple terms 'ridge' and 'furrow' as the agricultural terms vary. It will be seen at once what excellent drainage was given by these furrow and ridge lines. On sloping fields a field worker was told to take a spade and open an outlet at the end of each rean furrow across the headlands to let the water run away. It was on these headlands – sowed last and left longest uncut – that the long straw grew which was gathered to form the 'binding twists' used in reaping (see p. 176) and, because the

headlands were ploughed last, it was said of an old man working slowly
through his last years, 'he is ploughing his headlands'.

A plough mell, the short metal-headed hammer used to knock out stones that
wedged between coulter and share. A wooden mallet would not serve; the
slit between coulter and share was narrow, and a pointed metal end was
needed to dislodge an obstinate stone.

A plough sledge, for transporting a plough to the place where it was to be
used. Sometimes there were runners below, but these usually wore out; the
wood ran quite easily over rough grassland.

A plough staff was a pole with a metal cutting end; it was long enough to
be used to clear the coulter or share clear of heavy earth, or to cut through
weeds which might clog, without stopping the plough. It was not a goad,
though if long enough was probably used to prod a plodding ox.

The Harrow for Corn

At about the eleventh century a harrow seems to have joined the clod
hopper in achieving a fine tilth (probably the mallet of the clod hopper still
broke the largest lumps). But this whole operation would depend on the
quality of the soil and the weather conditions: clay or sandy, wet or dry
land.

The first harrows would be of split wood into which wood tines were
driven in staggered rows (if all a-row they might split the wood). This
harrow would probably be dragged across the land diagonally – first in one
direction and then the other. To get a flat pull the trace must have been

very long and the manuscripts usually show a horse: harrow work was a fidgety job a horse disliked! But the imperturbable Saxon ox was probably so slow that if it came on wet, the heavy harrow would sink in altogether.

The square harrow (with extra cross bars) was more efficient; the brush harrow was usually made of cut boughs threaded into a gate hurdle and used on light land. (On a remote hill farm we once saw an entire thorn tree

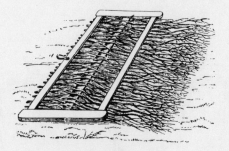

Brush harrow

hauled along by its twisted trunk.) Sometimes an extra-heavy log would be tethered on top to add weight. This brush harrow was used on grass to spread worm and mole casts. Later came the chain harrow, and much later a combination of both chain and tine harrows.

OXEN

An oxherd hight Bubulcus, and is ordained by office to keep oxen: he feedeth and nourisheth oxen, and bringeth them to leas and home again: and bindeth their feet with langhaldes and spanells and nigheth and cloggeth them while they be in pasture and leas, and yoketh and maketh them draw at the plough: and pricketh the slow with a goad, and maketh them draw even. And pleaseth them with whistling and with song, to make them bear the yoke with the better will for liking of melody of the voice. And this herd driveth and ruleth them to draw even, and teacheth them to make even furrows: and compelleth them also to tread and to thresh. And they lead them about upon corn to break the straw in threshing and treading the flour. And when the travail is done, then they unyoke them and bring them to the stall: and tie them to the stall, and feed them thereat.

Bartholomaeus Anglicus (*fl.*1230–50)

Sensible instructions observed by good ploughmen: where oxen are used, a hundred and twenty feet is a fair length for a straight pull. The oxherd should always let his oxen stop and rest at the end of every furrow, so they go the whole length in hope of this expected pause. During the pause, when they drop their heads, the herd pushed the yoke forward, so allowing their necks to cool off – they become inflamed if under constant pressure. (The type of yoke varied with locality and use.) At unyoking, the oxherd should rub and knead that part of the neck that took the weight, pulling loose the skin where it had been pressed, not allowing the damp hairs to cling. Oxen should have stopped sweating before they are fed, and then be led to water, or summoned by their own accustomed call.

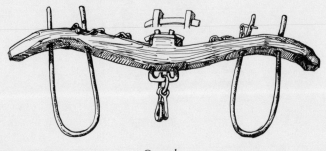

Ox yoke

Only readers who have known oxen working can understand their slow tempo. The author knew them long ago in the Transvaal, and usage there was probably exactly that of Saxon England, for the ox does not change. It is the land and the centuries that pass under his wide slow hooves.

Portage by ox-wain is slower than a man walking, so that time almost ceases to exist. An ox-wain could take months carrying a heavy load over a long distance. The splayed hoof of the ox holds well on soft surfaces; for hard travel they were shod. So, softly and surely the ox paced, placing foot ahead of foot; a man could walk alongside, ride on the cart or step off it while moving. Three miles an hour was fairly good going . . . slow . . . but sure, the ox always 'got ther' (and when he got there he stood still).

Thus was the heavy building stone and timber for castle and cathedral transported. The rough filling stone for Chichester cathedral was brought from local quarries by ox-wain. So, at the base of the columns of the west door are carved ox heads, so badly worn and defaced that Victorian restoration has developed a conventional design.

Stubborn, gentle oxen are no fools. Their minds have to be understood: some work better in pairs, others resent double yoking, and the placing of a long ox team had to be studied carefully to get a steady pace. For a long team of fourteen or sixteen, lighter animals were used who worked to a swifter step. Such a team, released to trundle an empty wagon, would swiftly thunder home through a cloud of dust, their horns raised like a storm-tossed forest.

Making the long ox chain must have been one of the earliest of the ironmaster's tasks. To it each ox was secured separately and adjusted for a level pull. When unyoked, each ox left his place in the line, and would return to it; riverside watering places were valuable, as was a watertrough, for to water the beasts singly would be very time-consuming.

The usage of oxen at the end of our period, after enclosures, is difficult. The only thing that remained unaltered was the ox. Early manuscript drawings show ox-ploughs in use. Because the early ploughs only scraped the surface of the ground (the depth of the scrape depended on the strength of the ploughman to hold down the plough), when one ox was sufficient the shape of the land was almost immaterial: but when ploughs cut deeper and required teams of oxen, then the length of the field became the ruling factor in ploughing; and the longer the team the more headland at each end of the furrow had to be allowed for turning. In some cases this seems to have turned the long, narrow strips into one central field with a smallish area given over to trees and the thrown-out stones at either end. It is surmised that the S-shaped furrows, sometimes called 'Saxon' furrows, were made to facilitate drainage, but from watching teams working we believe they may have been caused by the oxen deliberately tracing the line of least resistance to the slope – much as a cyclist will weave from side to side going up a steep hill. (The soft rounded curves still visible today on some old pastures are not ox-work, but a later eighteenth-century idea that curved shaping gave more surface and better drainage.)

The ox's sense of routine was very characteristic of the Saxon. The Norman saying, 'The ox is never woe till he to harrow go, by reason that the harrow goeth by twitches' (irregularly and not at a steady draught) is a very acute assessment of Saxon mentality.

Murrain

It is believed that the mediaeval murrain was our foot and mouth disease.

The law enforced all infected animals to be burnt, and infected heads were to be placed high on stakes around the infected district; travellers seeing such a warning must avoid the land, and no dealings were allowed with the unhappy owners. (The spreading of infection by carrion crows from these warning heads was not thought of, nor was the disinfection of shoes or clothing.) For an infected farm the laws were as strict as for a human leper; and as the leper was instructed to 'die in his hut', which was then to be burnt over him as his funeral pyre, so the animals on the land had

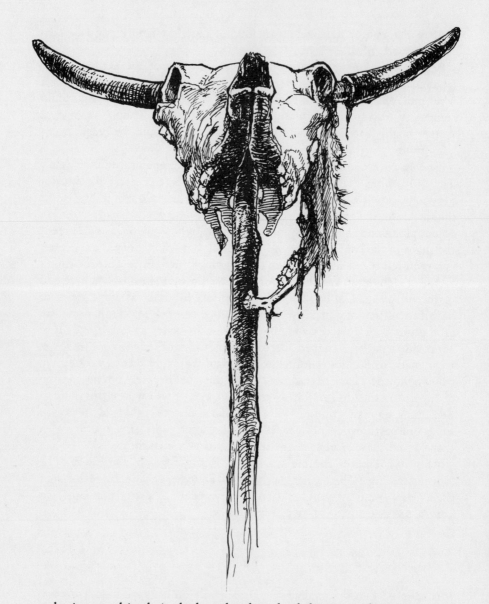

to be inpenned in their sheds and, when dead, burnt on the spot.

An outbreak of foot and mouth disease is still the most terrible fate for a farmer. One morning he may have a happy full life, a steading full of beasts, cows lowing, sheep and lambs bleating, hens cackling, his world full of happy sounds; and within forty-eight hours – nothing, no sound, no living creature, only empty desolate buildings, bare fields, and the smoke of a long burial trench. A cordon is then drawn round his lands and they lie barren, the gates sealed, and he is a broken man. Today the skulls are not set on the fences, but across his doors are pasted notices: 'Foot and Mouth', with the date.

The causes of diseases in animals were not clearly understood; an interesting record of about 1670 tells us that in November, 1581 'the Marshes of Dengie Hundred on the place called Southminster in the county of Essex there suddenly appeared an Infinate and Prodigius number of MICE, which almost covered the whole superficies of the said Marsh treading and knawing the grass by the rootes spoiling and tainting the same with their venious teeth, in such sort that the cattle that grazed thereon were struck with a Murrain, and many dyed thereof. Which Vermin by all the Policies of Man would not be destroyed, till it came to pass there there flocked together all about the same Marshes a Great number of Owls – whereby they were shortly after delivered from the vexation of the Mice . . . the like of this was about that time in Kent.'

SEEDS AND SOWING

We cannot trace grain by name, only by description. Thus, if we asked a seed merchant today for 'Runcival peas', he would be at a loss; but if asked for 'a very large pea to plant in February, or a tall variety needing heavy support', the seed merchant would probably supply us with 'Onward' or someone's 'Giant Long Pod', and this would be the closest we should get to what mediaeval people called 'Runcivals'.

A great number of plants have gone out of cultivation, while others have been retained and improved, or revived. Some corn names are still in use, and others we can guess at by their names. 'White wheat' was opaque and had a fine starch. Another type was hard, with more gluten. (It is this gluten which shows as an iridescent film lining the holes made by yeast in a well-risen loaf.) Another type, less fine, was called 'bread wheat', which made a darker loaf, though not so dark as the common mixed-grain bread.

For holy bread the finest 'flour of wheat' was used. This also made the wafers for Mass, and for centuries after the Reformation all manner of beliefs hung around this wafer. 'Manchet bread', taken in the hand and eaten, was distinguished from the 'trencher bread', which was more dense and dark, and cut into slices to serve as plates for food.

It is not likely that much white flour was used, except for pastry (flaunes), and so on. Not till rolling mills replaced grinding did bread become pure white.

An agricultural manual (Lawson, of 1850) lists nearly a hundred different types of corn, but we cannot be sure which of these types were used in early English agriculture.

Riddling Seed Corn

When farmers kept their own seed, selection was serious. The handpicking of seed required the small, skilful fingers of children and the hand-riddling of corn seems always to have been done by women. Stephens, as late as the nineteenth century, admits it was a labour he could never perform to his own satisfaction, and his description probably conformed to earlier usage. 'Riddling consists in holding the riddle with both hands a little inclined to the right and giving the corn a circular motion from right to left, accompanied by an upward jerk of the left hand, which loosens and shakes the mass of corn, bringing up all the lighter impurities to the surface' – the impurities were then thrown out. The withies of the mediaeval wooden riddle would retard the passage of corn through the meshes, the hand-picking would have to be done thoroughly, and would probably be as quick.

The Protection of Seeds

If any dressings were used, they would be mixtures of urine, lime, and perhaps sulphur, to make the seed unpalatable to mice. It should be realised that birds were probably far more numerous than nowadays and the grain

Poultry was allowed to glean – after harvest

far more lightly spaced, so that bird-scaring was a regular seasonal job.

Mediaeval manuscripts show no 'scarecrows', as we know them; the fields were smaller and labour more plentiful, so the live scarecrow with a clapper was used. Manuscripts do show miserable birds cruelly impaled or strung up.

Shelters may have been kindly provided for bad weather, or they may have been erected by the scarecrows themselves: any country lad would be capable of building a shelter for himself in the old wattle and daub days.

Sowing Broadcast

According to the variety of the corn and to the weather, sowing was done either directly after ploughing or after harrowing. When corn was harrowed *after* sowing, it could be seen to lie in neat lines, as opposed to the more random pattern of broadcast sowing.

For sowing, the field was measured out and the seed measured into sacks. These sacks were set open at either end of the reans. The sower then walked steadily down the furrow, counting his steps. He did not stride, nor force the length of his pace, but set his gait to a very smooth, steady-swinging step, and kept this step, absolutely even, throughout the field. He

The diagram shows the trajectory of seeds sown broadcast. To obtain an even distribution of seed was – then as now – dependent on soil and weather. If wind or rain came the seeds were swept down into the furrows; but the seed which fell nearest to the sower took more force from his throw and was more likely to remain static than the seed which had fallen at a greater distance; this would lie more lightly on the surface and thus have a greater tendency to roll.

guided his footfalls down two adjacent plough lines. He then computed how many steps he must take, to each handful of corn he would fling out. If he had a basket hung from his neck, he worked with both hands, casting right and left alternately. If he used a sowing cloth, he used one hand only and, as a rule, cast only to one side going up or down. The rhythm for casting might be four handfuls, two each side, to fifteen paces forward. Once the rhythm was measured, it was constant for the whole field.

The right rhythm was set for each type of corn, and for the width and depth of furrow. It was most skilled, responsible work – but often the men who did this work could neither read, write, nor count above ten. In fact they usually 'kept tally' thinking in four sets of five fingers, thus making a score. Most old agricultural 'counts' run in fours. Furthermore, as he was a skilled worker, the sower might be instructed to sow slightly more thinly on a dry portion of the field than over a damp part; and he must adjust this sowing, not by change of rhythm, but by taking slightly larger or smaller handfuls of corn. This was the skill of 'broadcast' sowing.

The grain fell against the sloping sides of the furrows and rolled to the bottom, so that the seed was somewhat 'set in lines'. Single-hand (to one side only) sowing was sometimes used where the plough furrow was very smooth and deep, in order to cast the grain against the furrow slope in such a way as to get a greater depth of soil over the seed.

If the harrowing came after the sowing, it covered the corn as it lay: if the field had been previously harrowed the corn was likely to be in less even lines. This point was important during the subsequent weeding (see pp. 125–6).

Sowing basket

Dust

Tusser advocated sowing rye 'in the dust' – that is, in dry weather. Dust is constantly mentioned in early manuscripts:

> *Bot then hyyes hervest, and hardenes hym sone,*
> *Warnes hym for the wynter to wax ful rype;*
> *He dryves wyth droght the dust for to ryse*
> *Fro the face of the folde to flyye ful hyghe.*
>   *Sir Gawayn and the Green Knyght* (late 14th century)

Droves of cattle and sheep raised clouds of dust on the bare earth, and drovers are warned to 'spread the herds' lest dust choke the end animals. The lack of hedges (which, as any motorist can see, catch low drifting dust) made a difference, and now in East Anglia the dust problem is very serious. Since the fens were drained the light silt and peat soil has a friable tilth and the flat fields, level to the coast, are scoured by the east wind. The incidence of such a wind in a dry spring, after fine harrowing, causes a dust storm, locally called 'a blow', that does thousands of pounds worth of damage, the dusty soil being lifted off the seeds and swept into the drainage dykes, which clog up. In March 1955 one farm combatted this danger by returning the land to the old 'strip' spacing: that is, the width of the fields has been reduced and the land set about with tree plantings and bush-type willows. They have also attempted to spread 'clay' over the subsoil, but unless this is extensively incorporated with the surface tilth the clay itself dries to dust and is carried off – not on to – the soil. One solution of this dust problem is to replace corn-growing with grass pasture and milk production, but the reclaimed fenland is fertile and to become 'cattle men' does not please farmers who want 'in good corn soil to brest them'.

VEGETABLES

Parsnips were probably the commonest English nep or root, but the lack of winter food gradually developed the use of other roots. The green top-growth of parsnips fed the milking cows, and sweetened and creamed the milk. Sir Francis Drake describes the New World potato as a 'sweete root that far exceedeth our English Parsnep', for the parsnip was still common usage in England up to 1700 (the foliage was fed to cows in Scotland). It seems to us extremely likely that other root crops were tried out before any definite records became obtainable.

Peas and Beans

These were definitely a field crop, as well as being grown in gardens. The whole plant was used as cattle fodder, but it was apparently also threshed for human use. There are many references to the 'small bean', the 'black bean' and the 'broad bean'; and the marginal drawings that decorate mediaeval manuscripts are our best guide to the type in use.

To go on pilgrimage with dried peas in your shoes was a refined form of torture; though we do not vouch for the salvation of the sensible monk who sang 'A little the more my feet to ease . . . I took the precaution to boil my peas.'

A single marked or coloured bean, or a special number of marked beans, in a bag was a simple way of selecting a team for some job, working a lottery, or casting a vote, so we still say 'don't care a bean'.

Dried beans are convenient counters for checking numbers; beans transferred from 'pan to poke' as a procession passed through a toll gate would indicate the number of persons attending (and the 'poke' had to be carried to headquarters for the finance department to assess how many of those persons had paid the toll).

MATHEMATICS

How much the unlettered labourer (educated only by material matters) appreciated the concepts of mathematics is unknown. Also unknown is why some men count on four fingers and a thumb, while others use the metric five. That herdsmen thought in pairs (for same reason as Noah did) is not proved. Illiterate people are capable of thinking both numerically and quantitatively. Many interesting material measures are in use today – at least until the metric system takes over completely. The stretch of a man's arrow arm was the yard, to measure how much cloth he needed for his coat; the thumb, hand breadth, and foot, remain with us. Many quantitative measures depended on how much an average man could carry, or lift (this point should be borne in mind when reading the descriptions of many of the jobs in this book). (See also pp. 281–4.) Notice, for example, the continuing uniformity of a bucket down the centuries – for the width and shape of material things must fit our hands (or heads).

The ability to 'assess numerically' is even more interesting. In a flock of sixty or more sheep a shepherd can sort out three or five, not by count, but at a glance, yet no one knows exactly how it's done. For our unlettered mediaeval labourer it was feasible to calculate very large numbers using only small units. He could use the old trick of taking a single straw from each sheaf, one bean from each sack, notch a stick as animals passed through a gate, or pick up a pebble every time his ten fingers are used and thus realise that ten sets of ten pebbles make a hundred. (Do this ten times and it's a thousand.) Some mathematical truths would be inculcated by use: he would learn, when building, the stability of the triangle, the accuracy of alternating angles; when working in clay he probably noticed conic sections, and he would use the circle for wheels, grindstones, and the occasional corn-bin or hut. (Lacking all transmitted conjectures, the mathematical possibilities of the sphere would be beyond him. At some high intellectual levels, Columbus and his mariners – with his theory of a round earth – suffered a complete lack of contemporary comprehension.)

Apparently our workman solved his problems by trial and error, but lacked the mathematical mentality to collate his findings. His calculations for wind- and water-wheels are surprisingly accurate: though trial and error may have produced the end-product, it would be used as a pattern for the future. It was all simple, sound reasoning. The nautical log was originally a floated log of wood, its passing being timed between stem and stern points of a boat. (Hydrostatically it is pleasant to think that the simple way to locate the swiftest current in a stream was to let a frog loose with a duck after it.) Mathematical minds probably cropped up unpredictably, but for centuries, and certainly for our mediaeval man, the calculating machine most in use was the tally (see also pp. 284–5).

While the labourer's methods of assessment were quantative rather than strictly numerical, it should be remembered that his educated superiors were still using Roman numerals for all calculations. This accounts for some astonishing results in mediaeval documents: the odd C for M, the addition of a few Xs were quite usual, and such discrepancies caused less comment than they would do today. The mediaeval custom of ignoring odd numbers and lumping large amounts under comprehensive terms (much as we would say 'numerous' or 'vast amounts') also varied with individuals. This makes the use of bodily measures, e.g. the foot, thumb or yard, and the working distances such as 'a day's journey' valuable.

Many rural counts went to America, were picked up by the Indians, and then in the nineteenth century were called 'Indian counts'. In England, to the writer's certain knowledge, the shepherd areas used the four-finger count as late as 1920. Assorted shepherd counts were collected by the Philological Society in 1866; and one count taught to the author by a shepherd of the West Riding was: 'eena (1), deena (2), dina (3), das (4); catiler (1), weena (2), winer (3), was (4)'. A count in Rochdale was: 'Eena (1), deina (2), pitera (3), pimp (4)', the last two words being Welsh! The explanation was that some Welsh workers crossed the border into Lancashire for employment in the smelting works, and brought their rural background with them.

APRIL

Be suer of plough to be ready at hand,
ere compass ye spread, that on hillocks did stand;
Lest drying, so lying, do make it decay,
ere over much water do wash it away.

Look now, to provide ye of meadow for hay,
if fens be undrowned, there cheapest ye may;
In fen for the bullock, for horse not so well;
count best, the best cheap, wheresoever ye dwell.

Provide ye of cow-meat, for cattle at night,
and chiefly where commons lie far out of sight;
Where cattle lie tied, without any meat,
the profit by dairy, can never be great.

Allowance of fodder, some countries do yield,
as good for the cattle as hay in the field.
Some mow up their headlands and plots among corn,
and driven to leave nothing, unmown or unshorn.

Sell bark to the tanner, ere timber ye fell,
cut low to the ground, else do ye not well.
In breaking save crooked, for mill and for ships;
and ever, in hewing, save carpenter's chips.

From April beginning, till Andrew be past,
so long with good huswife her dairy doth last;
Good milch-cow and pasture, good husbands provide,
the res'due, good huswives know best how to guide.

Ill huswife unskilful, to make her own cheese
though trusting of others, hath this for her fees:
Her milkpan and cream pot so slabber'd and sost
that butter is wanting and cheese is half lost.

Then neighbour, for God's sake, if any you see
good servant for dairy house, waine her to me.
Such master such man, and such mistress such maid,
such husband and huswife, such houses arraid.

'SWEET APRIL SHOWERS'

If April be dripping, then do I not hate,
(for him that hath little) his fallowing late;
Else otherwise, fallowing timely is best,
for saving of cattle, of plough, and the rest.

THE WORK of April, like that of March, varied according to the weather. A reasonably dry spring drained the water meadows and made manure spreading and surface cultivation easier.

April was the last spring month for work in the woods, so this was one of the busiest times of year. Though enclosures, as a political measure, were still ahead, the enclosure of home-grown timber was meritorious, as was the planting and preserving of good timber for the use of future generations.

Cutting timber to avoid waste, and skilled selection for special purposes, became increasingly important as home-grown timber grew scarcer. Shipyards and building trades had prior claim, and the owner of timber had to decide between the good selling price and his own needs. The countryman had to preserve suitable bark for tanyards, and keep a quick eye for specially shaped pieces of timber for construction purposes. Another detail that made April the last possible month for felling was cartage. Once frost was out of the ground the land became soft and cartage by ox team with a heavy load would destroy any land already in cultivation.

But the chief work of April was perhaps with cattle – the heifers and cows had calved, and the dairy-work was in full swing until 'Andrew' (30 November). At this time of year, with lengthening days and (we hope) better weather the outdoor work for the men synchronised with extra indoor work for the women. Cows were kept in the steading after the last milking. Cattle feed in two courses: first they graze, then they settle down and chew the cud. Not till this last slow process is complete are they 'full fed'. Therefore in order that they will settle down for a quiet night's sleep, a late supper of food must be given in the steading. This was a contentious dividing line between men's work in the cow-shed, and women's in the dairy.

CATTLE

Beasts that eat grass and herbs be more fat, from the beginning of spring time, to the middle of summer, and flesh is then best, for then[their] meat be good and tender ... and other beasts that eaten croppys [coppice] bows, twigs, and also branches, been good from the beginning of summer unto winter, for then bowes and branches be both ful moist and tendre, and also beasts that eat small grass and dry, be better than those that eat moist grass and herbes ... and those that eat and drink little, be better than those that eaten and drinketh much. Also beasts that bee fed in fields and in mountains be better than those that be fed at home [stall fed]. For those that be more in the mountains and in fields draw in more subtle air and dry because of rambling about ... And most lean beasts be sinewy and tough, and have little blood and little moisture, and yealdéth therefore little nourishment to a man's body. But beasts that be between fat and lean, be most profitable.

Bartholomaeus Anglicus (fl.1230–50)

The Cow Herself

Hit nis noht al for the calf that kow loweth
Ac hit is for the grene gras that in the medew groweth.

The continuity of cow covers centuries. The enclosures, which debarred her grazing rights, also developed the mailcoach roads that cleared protective space on either side (to frustrate highway robbers and footpads) and gave some space back to her. These changes went on *around* the cow, who herself remained static. As Uncle Remus remarked, 'It takes a lot to onsettle sis cow.'

The fine glossy-coated, udder-extended matrons of today do not look like the angular mediaeval cows, but mentally they remain the same. Let a score of strange cows get together anywhere and within twenty-four hours (as any farmer will agree) there will be a Boss Cow. Nothing said; a little shoving perhaps, no violent aggression, but 'the Boss Cow' becomes an established fact, and she will remain, a permanent institution (rather like Queen Victoria). Possibly, when the bellowing wild bulls faced outwards, head down and horns out, defending the herd, she was the experienced old cow who led the safe retreat, as her lineal descendant leads the way to the milking shed and all her sisters immediately rise and follow. (An angry horned cow still suckling her calf is capable of attacking an intruder and goring as fiercely as any bull.)

A cow carries for about nine months, and takes a comparatively short time to come into calf again. (A heifer who 'did not take' on her own farm might be tried out on another estate, with a different bull. If nothing 'came of it' she would be sold for beef.) Veal, condemned as 'froth' meat, was never popular in rural England. Saxons were, on the whole, good cattle men, rearing the bull calf for work and beef, and killing off only those cow calves misborn, deformed, or unlikely to thrive – a good reason for the English traditional mistrust of veal.

THE MEDIAEVAL COW

A Povre widwe, somdeel stape in age,
Was whylom dwelling in a narrow cotage
Bisode a grove, stondynge in a dale.
This wydwe, of which I telle you my tale,
Sin thilke day that she was last a wyf,
In pacience ladde a ful simple lyf.
For litel was hir catel and hir rente.
By housbondrie of swich as God hir sente
She fond hirself, and eek hir doghtren two.
Thre large sowes hadde she, and namo,
Three keen, and eek a sheep that hight Malle
Ful sooty was hire bour and eek hir halle,
In which she eet ful many a sklendre meel . . .
Milk and broun breed, in which she foond no lak,
Seynd bacoun, and somtyme an ey or tweye
For she was, as it were, a maner deye.
                                    The Nun's Priest's Tale

If the mediaeval cow was a 'one and only', she would be expected to do her share of work like the ox. If, like Chaucer's 'povre widwe' you kept three, this could allow of one going dry, and one whose calf would be sold off before the winter, and one cow in milk, in which case there might be cheese and perhaps some butter. (She was 'a maner deye' – a knowledgeable dairy-woman.)

From manuscript evidence, goats, and later ewes, were milked; of ewes 'five ewes to a cow' is given as average yield. Cows were expected to forage, and browse on broom buds, low budding trees, and the coarse grass on the common. They had a thin time until late spring, when the near-starved beasts had to be driven off the new green grass for fear of surfeit: 'first when green grass doth appear, O then is the danger of all of the yere'. Even by the sixteenth century the only fodder mentioned is parsnip tops and bruised ling.

The mediaeval cow took the bull as late as possible, in hope of there being some spring green for the calf. Instructions to 'cut down boughs and let her browse on them in the wet winter woods, and chew straw like an ox' show that she was tough. The only poor pleasure the beast got was the short time she was allowed to lick her calf and suckle it. A cow normally sleeps at nightfall, folding herself down on the warmest earth she can find,

A tie is not a tether. These light shippon ties hold the cow in place while milking is done; they are arranged loosely to let the cow swing her head up and down, but not move out of place. The tie could be quickly adjusted and released; various arrangements suit different types of building. The eleventh century shows a similar arrangement for milking in the field, using a light wooden yoke, which could easily be carried to the field, and a ground peg.

and wakes before dawn, to feed before being milked an hour or so later. She then feeds again, and settles down to chew the cud. The number of wild plants called after cows or milk are floral tributes to the mediaeval cow.

Mediaeval Breeds

The oldest, Chillingham herd, is a white, wide-horned breed, purposely maintained in a wild state. Most others are under control and the balance of the herds is maintained by weeding out and by skilled selection of the breeding beasts. The ancient black cattle of Wales are small, compact and glossy-coated animals, able to rove on the Welsh mountains with their own bulls. Their breeding stock is now under control and managed by a few intelligent farmers, so the breed is improving rapidly. Many Sussex cattle were draught oxen and indigenous to South Britain. A tradition holds that these cows were covered by imported Roman bulls. This is not proven, but if so, they take after their sires in being excellent colonists, for they have been crossed successfully with native African draught beasts. The old Devon cattle were also draught and plough beasts, and are believed to have crossed to America with the *Mayflower* settlers. They are a docile breed – such a cow as the 'Puritan Maiden Priscellia' rode upon at her wedding. Galloway is enother old breed, mentioned in the sixteenth century as 'excellent beef' and crossed to improve the milk yield.

The polled Suffolk breed of the South East is described as uncouth, heavy headed and coarse, though it fattened well and should have lost little live weight during droving; so the cattle reached London in good form. An early record (*The Tournament of Tottenham*) mentions this 'dun cow'. The use of only local bulls may account for the general uniformity, and inferiority, of the breed; but they suited the district, which covered also shipping ports, so they may have salted well.

There are many other interesting mediaeval breeds, which varied much according to their environment and perhaps also to the old national preference remembered by their breeders. So the facial uniformity of the flat-faced cattle shown in the early manuscripts is puzzling: we assume they are not realistic representations.

Bulls

Bulls breeding free are reasonably peaceable. In mediaeval times there were small herds free in the woodlands and usually only special bulls were stalled. Early herdsmen kept only enough bull calves to serve their cows and rather left it between the bulls themselves to settle by combat which was the best beast. This is so utterly different from today's selective breeding and artificial insemination that it is difficult to realise how haphazard was the arrival of a really fine breeding bull; but once he had been recognised the mediaeval cowman knew how to value him.

The insides of the testicles of the bull were of mechanical use, making a strong, long, smooth cord for fine pulley work and also for a closer binding than could be obtained by rope. The cord was suspended from the beam in the slaughter house and kept damp, while a heavy weight below stretched it out to greatest uniform length. (Later, when the first grandfather clocks were constructed, this cord was frequently used; but if at any time the weights are removed, it cockles and shrinks, making repair difficult.)

Bullocks

Bullocks for draft work were not always castrated males. Mediaevally, anything with four legs and strength was utilised for draft work, though feudal estates, especially in the lowlands, were proud possessors of excellent bullock teams; the small hut dweller had to solicit the services of a bull for his one cow, a circumstance that tended to preserve characteristic local breeds.

Calves

Calves likely that come, between Christmas and Lent,
take huswife to rear, or else after repent.
Of such as do fall, between change and the prime,
no rearing, but sell, or go kill them in time.

House calf, and go suckle it twice in a-day,
and after a while, set it water and hay:
Stake ragged to rub on, (no such as will bend)
then wean it, well tended, at fifty days' end.

The senior weaned, his younger shall teach;
both how to drink water, and hay for to reach:
More stroken and made of, when aught it doth ail,
more gentle ye make it, for yoke or the pail.

Geld bull-calf and ram-lamb, as soon as they fall,
for therein is, lightly, no danger at all.
Some spareth the t'one, for to pleasure the eye,
to have him shew greater, when butcher shall buy.

Custom varied locally, but generally the calf seems to have been left free to take the colostrum (the first 'beast milk' which nature provides to clean out the calf's intestines) until the flow of milk was established. After which the calf was gradually withdrawn, and normal hand milking in the shed took over. Calves had a supplementary diet till completely weaned, using the by-products of the dairy. As the first settlers in the New World continued this method, it corroborates that it was general Elizabethan usage, and it was thoroughly commendable for the health and stamina of the herd.

To grass with thy calves, in some meadow-plot near,
where neither their mothers may see them, nor hear:
Where water is plenty, and barth to sit warm,
and look well unto them, for taking of harm.

A cow robbed of her calf is a most unhappy mother; if she can hear it low, and feels her full udder, she will break out to find it, or if the calf is withdrawn and carted away she will follow for miles, lowing most piteously.

A 'warm barth' is any shelter where a young calf can sleep soft and warm. Tusser is also insistent upon the folly of overcrowding the pasture, and insists upon good grazing during the summer with abundance of water for all weaned stock.

'HOUSE CALF AND GO SUCKLE IT TWICE IN A DAY'

The milkmaid must, at first, feed each calf individually, because a calf can only drink by sucking with its head raised *up* to reach the teats above it. (If a calf's nose were held down in a pail of milk it would drown.) Every milkmaid had her own skill; usually she let the calf raise its head and suck milk from her fingers, gradually pouring more milk down through her cupped palm, and gently lowering her milky hand, till the calf got the idea and would suck upwards from a pail (at first raised up to the calf's level and tilted helpfully). Once one calf has started to drink, the rest soon learn.

The City Cow

There was nothing like our city supply of milk. It was heavy and its transport difficult: it was carried in wooden pails on the heads of women, for it tended to churn into butter if rhythmically jerked in pannier tubs on horseback. Milk pails floated a crossbar of wood on top to help prevent splashing. (In Africa the native water carriers use leaves the same way.)

In mediaeval cities cows were driven around and milked at the door of the customer. Later, most town families kept one cow in their stables for household use. Goats were also popular (their milk was considered better for some children) and cows welcome the presence of a goat in the shippon. Though tubercular testing was unknown, the countrywoman knew goat's milk was 'safer' before the scientists could tell her why.

It is curious that Welsh dairies preponderated in London. Fifty years ago a few cows were still kept in small sheds in London: there was such a shed set back between Euston and Hampstead Roads, next to a bakehouse that opened its oven on Sundays for local joints. There was probably a shippon there, when the large square behind was still a haymarket. (The name persists, though now blocks of flats cover the space.) Another city shippon was off Mile End Road near Aldgate pump ... by our recollection of Stepney milk fifty years ago, it seemed an appropriate position!

The House Cow

The 'house cow' has always been a point of argument between farmer and wife – especially when she has children (some mothers put great faith in always using the milk from the same cow for babies). Therefore the good husband must try to provide one cow to calve soon after Christmas, for his own household.

The milkman. In the twelfth-century ms. from which this is taken cows are shown on the left being milked, and goats on the right. This kind of churn continued in use for centuries.

THE DAIRYMAID

Fodder of any sort was in short supply after the long winter, and this gave rise to an annual contention: in spring the dairymaids were needing all available fodder for their breeding cows, simultaneously with the men wanting it for their draught beasts, working full time on the land.

The dairymaids had all the extra work with the new calves and piglets, and though they sometimes needed a man to help with the calving and the normal cleaning of byres and carting of water, the division of labour was no less contentious than the division of fodder. In early and mediaeval farming, when there was so little mechanical help available, this perennial contentious period in spring must have been very serious. One sympathises with the huswife's heartcry: 'Then neighbours, for God's sake! if any you see, Good servant for dairy house – waine her to me!'

After the calf was dropped, the dairymaid had the job of seeing that it got the first 'beast milk' or 'beastings'. Of this she would probably reserve some for family custards – as is still done today. (A gift of this 'beast milk' being sent to neighbours, the jug was emptied and returned unswilled, as it was considered unlucky to swill out the jug in case this might stop the cow producing more milk.) Then she had to wean the calf (ensuring that the calf got sufficient milk from the right mother) and collect the surplus milk for butter and cheese. She tried to see that the separated calves were kept 'where neither their mother could see them or hear', or the cows bellowed continuously and fought to reach the calves. Once the calves were self-supporting, milking could be done in the field – though this meant carrying out pails and stools and carrying the milk back to the dairy.

For centuries smallpox was so prevalent that descriptions of a beauty specially note 'unmarked by smallpox'. It was the exceptionally good complexions of the milkmaids that caused Dr Jenner to query the cause. He was told by the workers that the girls working among the cows frequently contracted cowpox through contact with their beasts and, though similar to smallpox, the discomfort was very slight and left no marks. This led Dr Jenner to vaccinate his own children and overcome the smallpox.

In the mediaeval centuries it was rare to see a cow milked by any other than a woman. The term 'dairymaid' implied milking, as well as working with butter and cheese, and so on. A 'dairyman' was one who owned a dairy and employed milkmaids. This remained true of many pastoral farms until about 1900. The modern influx of machines made many mixed farms sell off their cattle, thus creating customers for their hay and straw, and the dairy farms (much enlarged) bought this fodder from the arable farms and sold back manure. Also in the dairy of the 1900s, the mechanical 'separators' took over the skilful work of the women cream skimmers, and cooling and churning were mechanised or the milk sold direct. With the dairy work gone, it was not economical to keep a number of milkmaids only for milking hours. At one time, quite a number of older farm women used to go out 'to do the milking' morning and evening. Gradually the men, and later milking machines, took over and milkmaids died out. The coming of the bicycle also helped, as it saved time in going to work on foot, so that even before the mechanical milker came into use, men had replaced women in the milking shed.

Between milking, suckling calves, looking after piglets and making butter and cheese, the dairymaids also had to scrape all the wooden pails and tubs. Scouring was usually done in running water, using trusses of marestail or other coarse fibres, rather than stiff brushes which roughened the surface of the wood whilst it was wet and soft. Because of this roughness, hairy woollen cloth was never used in the dairy; only linen.

Mediaeval milk was probably strained through rushes or a simple hair sieve; then it had to be set in shallow tubs for the cream to rise. The tubs must be large in diameter, for cream will not rise through more than four or five inches depth. Handling wide shallow wooden tubs, when full, is impossible (try it!) so shallow stone sinks were used: we believe some of the very old shallow 'slop stones', as they were called in the Midland farms, were originally milk 'standers', being barely five inches deep and common in pasture country. The beautiful polished marble milk coolers of the nineteenth century were exactly such milk coolers, and the pride of the best Home Farms. The last example we know of was in 'The Tempests' dairy in Yorkshire.

The cream was skimmed off, (the flat side of a scallop shell made an ideal skimmer) but every dairymaid favoured her own implement.

Cream pot and paddle   Milk cooler and skimmer

Pigs

The sow having farrowed, piglets were the dairymaid's next job. They had to be cosseted, warmed, and fed on milk and any meal she could extract from the stablemen. Curiously, the boar was also considered the woman's care – rather a risky job in which probably the menfolk were involved, and early breeding was usually free-range. The piglets would range with the sow, under the care of the swineherd, till he brought them back to the dairy for extra feeding. Piglets had to be fed under supervision, otherwise the strongest would hog the lot; the runkling, or smallest, was usually cooked (roast sucking-pig was very popular in the hungry spring). We have found no early evidence of mediaeval pigs being washed (as today) because for centuries they approximated to the wild pig of the woodlands, and the swineherd rounded them up with dogs and drove them out to grub up roots and fatten on acorns and beechmast in autumn, to put on weight before the winter slaughter. Fifteenth-century pictures show clean pigs ready for slaughter, but when the metamorphosis took place is not known. (Nor does a modern pig approve having its clean cool mud forcibly removed. Like much modern animal 'care', we are apt to say 'It's good for them if it's convenient for us.')

MILK AND MILK PRODUCTS

The milk yield of the cow has been increased by selective breeding and diet, and that synchronised with the increased usage of milk. Some readers may remember the sudden change that banished the 'separator', once as common as the churn: it was a machine that spun the entire cream out of the milk by centrifugal force; out of one pipe came the thick rich cream, out of the other pipe poured the thin separated milk. Cream in those days was sold by the pint, and it was not labelled 'pure', 'sterilised' or 'processed': it was 'cream in a jug', and the residue, separated milk, was entirely fat-free, thin, and of no value unless used for some manufacturing process, or fed to pigs. In contrast, mediaeval cream was hand-skimmed, with only the surface cream removed or, as in the West Country, clotted by gentle heat in earthenware pans over slow peat fires so that skimmed milk (though disparaged) and the buttermilk, fresh from the churn, had more goodness left in it.

This preliminary explanation is necessary to appreciate how changed is the product of the placid cow.

Rennet

Wheye is the watry part of mylke, departed from the other part by Rennyng, and curdynge, for Rennynge joyneth together the partes of cheese and of butter, and departeth them from the Wheye, that is thynne and Watery.

Bartholomaeus Anglicus (*fl.* 1230–50)

Let the calf suck just before being killed. Take out the milk bag at once, and let it lie for twelve hours under stinging nettles; till red. Then wash the bag clean, with warm milk, and put in a few streakings [the last milk drawn from a cow] a beaten egg or so; twelve cloves, and mace and tie up the bag and hang it in a pot. Then boil blackthorn and burnet and marjoram in half pint of salted water, and when cool put some of this flavoured water into the bag, and let the bag soak in it. This water in which the bag lies is the rennet, and the bag can be refilled and left to soak six times, before the stomachic juice is exhausted.

An early recipe

Note the mediaeval thought behind this recipe: the newly-killed calf's stomach would be watering in expectation of the meal; and so the linings of the stomach would be full of the juices required for rennet. Then, to keep the bag active, the mediaeval cook adds fresh milk to keep the stomach *fed* (the egg is a later addition). The nettles (which she thinks will sting the blood to the outer surface of the bag) may have caused the bag to shrink slightly (but probably had little effect). This mediaeval thought, that the dead bag would go on providing rennet better if it had a meal inside it, resulted in her making the inside liquid heavier than the outside liquid, so setting up a system of osmosis through the porous bag. The result of this interplay of wrong reason for right experience is typically mediaeval.

A lactic acid, which curdles milk, can be obtained from most animal stomachs; pig rennet was used by many who had only one cow and reared the calf. Later recipes were more practical; the stomach was found to work perfectly well if plain washed and salted, and provided the bag was kept dry a portion could be cut off and soaked for use as required.

Spanish influence probably caused 'Gallion' rennet to be made from the gizzard skin of a cock – it was considered fine for light junkets. Of plants, almost any with acid juices were used: sorrel, bedstraw, nettles and many others. The interplay between the type of coagulant used, variations in milk content, in temperature, time, and methods used, makes it very difficult to standardise dairy products even today using standardised ingredients and techniques.

Whey and Buttermilk

When whole milk was hand-churned, the buttermilk left in the churn had good food value, being only slightly acid and having a pleasant aroma and 'clean' texture. (In Wales it remained a standard greeting for the traveller at any farm till churning at home ceased.) Whey was the thin liquid left after both butter content and casein had been removed in making curd for cheese, and so on.

Both whey and buttermilk were used to make a hard form of cheese. The liquid was heated in a cauldron, the solid content strained off and dried out, usually in a bag hung over the fire, where it took on a smoked flavour. This – called 'poor man's cheese' – was made in Scotland until the early 1900s, the work people getting the whey and the peat fire free, so that it cost them only their own labour. If well-made (with a little bacon fat worked into the curd) it was palatable – and no harder than the oatcake it accompanied – and it was probably one of the earliest cheeses of the poverty-stricken peasant.

The recent changes caused by motor transport in the marketing of milk made it difficult to realise the complications of ancient usage. There is the difference between affluence and poverty in the difference between rich farm buttermilk, fresh, and flecked with scraps of butter, and modern whey, poor, thin and blue, after all the goodness of the milk has been extracted.

Butter in the 1400s and 1800s

Butter is made of crayme . . . it is good to eate in the mornyng – a lytell porcyon is good for every man in the mornyng if it be newe made.

Andrew Borde

I would never desire better butter . . . than that churned every morning, from sweet cream. Such butter, on cool, new-baked oat-cake, sweetened with virgin flower honey, accompanied with a cup of hot strong coffee, mollified with crystallised sugar and fresh cream, is a breakfast worth partaking of.

H. P. Stephens

The mediaeval farm used the wooden plunge churn. The dairymaid would have to force the long handle of the plunger up and down for hours to produce butter. At first the plunger rose and sank easily; later, as the liquid changed, the plunger moved more heavily, and finally the uneven feel of loose butter lumps floating inside told the worker to cease churning, open the churn, scrape down sides and plunger, and collect the soft butter for washing and making up. The dairymaid would then feed the buttermilk to the pigs (an old connection between the dairy and pig side of farm work).

Butter-making with cream alone left milk which, though almost devoid of fat, was usable for hard cheese. Butter made from whole milk used rather more of the solid content of the milk, and was thought to make slightly more butter, but the residue of buttermilk (though appreciated by some when fresh) was mainly used for pigswill, or leather dressing.

The summer's supply of butter would be salted down for winter. Salt was added in an average of 1 oz. salt to 16 oz. butter. The butter, well drained, was *flung* down into the barrels, being 'knuckled and kneaded' down closely to avoid air holes. (This salt butter was sold to shipping.)

Camden says that 'great store of cheeses were exported to France, Spain and the Low Countries' and that, as this cheese was made from skim-milk, it kept well and was probably supplied to the Navy. Summer-sold butter was pressed into wooden bowls, which caused some districts to sell the butter in round shapes marked with the special 'token' of the farm. Parts of East Anglia had ring gauges through which rolls of butter were passed for size and then sold by the yard. Almost every locality had its own special usage.

Pliny mentions cheese soaked in thyme and vinegar. The 'sage' cheeses may have been treated in the same way, and the soaking of cheese in brine or vinegar and coating with a crust of various sorts was usual on the Continent. The smoking of cheese in nets over a pungent wood fire is still practised on the Tatra summer farms in Czechoslovakia, which are the equivalent of our mountain 'hafods' where cattle were kept through the summer while the lowland pastures were in hay. In Wales these 'hafods' continued to the nineteenth century.

Comparatively little butter is made on farms now, and regular 'cheese factories' work all the year round, which enforces a standard cheese that can be made regardless of the season. Much of the dairy work on the farm has ceased.

Cheese

After butter churning came cheese making. Early English cheeses must have been very varied, because they were made locally, flavoured by local herbage, and made by different methods according to the customs of our many different national settlers. The bacteria cultures would remain localised through the use of impregnated wooden utensils. Salt marsh and seaweed, on the coast, would affect cheese, the wet juicy grass of the valley made more milk, but on the whole the dry hill pastures gave more solid content. Skim-milk cheese is probably exactly the same as that which would have been made from an eleventh-century cow. All that was required was one iron pot, one length of coarse linen, and perhaps a little salt. The skim milk was heated in the pot, curdled, strained, and pressed till dry.

In Wensleydale, when cows were released for the first bite, the alder growing by the stream – often breaking into bud while melted snow still netted the fields – gave the special flavour to Wensleydale cheese, which could only be made to perfection in the early spring. Even today in Wensleydale they disparage winter-made cheese, calling it 'hay cheese' and opine it is 'only good enough for Lancashire folk to make welsh rabbit'.

Of Essex cheese it was said:

> Those that made me were uncivil
> They made me harder than the devil
> Knives won't cut me, fire won't light me
> Dogs bark at me, but can't bite me.

Tidal saltings and the quality of hay grown on the slightly salted water meadows probably accounted for this.

Andrew Borde gives five kinds of cheese: 'grene chese, softe cheese, harde chese and spermyse ... besyde rewene chese, the which, if it be well ordered, doth passe all other cheses, none excesse taken ...'

CHEESE PRESS

To squeeze the water out of the curd and form a solid cheese, sounds simple; to wrap the curd in a linen cloth and put a hefty stone on top works well for a small cheese (and was probably the earliest idea.) The difficulty comes in drying out the centre of any large mass, after the outside of the mass has become a firm, dry case. Early stone presses, of which quantities of many sizes and centuries still lie around the countryside, tried to combat this by arranging that the weight came down on to the top of the curd through a plunger that fitted closely into a strong cylindrical container with drain holes in the base. The great variety of these old stone presses is accounted for by the various sizes and types of cheese they were required to press.

To 'let down' the heavy stone was easy, but to lift it up again was difficult, and so some early stones were fitted with counter weights and a central screw, by which the heavy stone could be lifted up again. This 'raising screw' had to be strong and set dead centre, and often required two men (and the 'capstan action' of a long crossbar) to turn it. Also side grooves and guides were made to prevent sway and obtain a steady lift. The pressure, by direct weight, was in use for centuries. Then the screw (originally designed to lift up the stone) may have suggested providing the downward pressure by screw. Later the old stones were discarded for an iron screw press, less satisfactory because someone had to keep going in and tightening down the screw as the curd shrank. And it took another century or so to get round that!

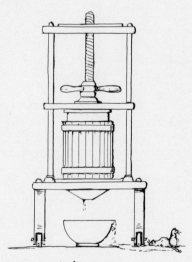

A cheese press

MAY

At Philip and Jacob, away with the lambs,
that thinkest to have any milk of their dams:
At Lammas leave milking, for fear of a thing,
lest (requiem aeternam) in winter they sing.

Five ewes to a cow, make a proof by a score,
shall double thy dairy, else trust me no more:
Yet may a good huswife that knoweth the skill,
have mixt or unmixt, at her pleasure and will.

Where houses be reeded (as houses have need),
now pare off the moss, and go beat in the reed:
The juster ye drive it, the smoother and plain,
more handsome ye make it, to shut off the rain.

Keep threshing for thresher till May be come in,
to have to be suer fresh chaff in thy bin;
And somewhat to scamble, for hog and for hen,
and work, when it raineth, for loitering men.

Be suer of hay, and of provender some,
for labouring cattle, till pasture be come.
And if ye do mind, to have nothing to sterve,
have one thing or other, for all things to serve.

Pinch never thy wennels of water or meat,
if ever ye hope for to see them good neat.
In summer-time, daily; in winter, in frost,
if cattle lack drink, they be utterly lost.

From May to mid August, an hour or two,
let Patch sleep a snatch, howsoever ye do:
Though sleeping one hour refresheth his song,
yet trust not Hob Grouthead, for sleeping too long.

In May get a weed-hook, a crotch and a glove,
and weed out such weeds, as the corn do not love.
For weeding of winter corn, now it is best;
but June is the better for weeding the rest.

'COLD MAY AND WINDY
BARN FILLETH UP FINELY'

THE FIRST TWO VERSES of the poem are the annual combat between the shepherd and the milkmaid – the former wishing to keep the lambs on the teat, and the latter wanting the ewe milk to supplement her cows' milk.

The thatched roofs, which frost, after rain, will have 'lifted' and loosened, must be beaten back, in an upwards direction, the moss removed, and repairs done. Trees begin to grow strongly, so all cutting and trimming must cease (the only exception might be the tapping of birch trees – which will run like a spigot in March – to make birch wine); a grape vine, cut late, will bleed a bucketful overnight. So 'leave cropping': that is 'stop cutting'.

Threshing depends on the weather. Fresh chaff has a dozen uses on a farm; it was even used to fill bedding for use under babies, being soft and cool: if wetted the chaff could be shaken out, the case washed, and a clean bed made ready without fuss. On days which start fine and then turn to heavy rain, the men came off the fields and loafed about idle, so threshing was always handy, and warmed them up if they were wet. The fodder problem is serious in spring; efforts must be made to keep some through the winter for the working animals, as the spring grass may be late. Weeding of autumn-sown corn can be done, but any later sowing will not be up enough to be weeded. The early peas must be planted. All is much the same today. (We do not grow flax now, though some was grown during the Second World War for parachute gear.)

In spring field draining of grass lands was done, if weather permitted – and 'keep an eye on the Bees' (now breeding). There should be enough blossom, but if the spring came cold and late, they needed some extra feeding.

SHEEP

Of the sheep is cast away nothing.
His hornes for notches; to ashes goeth his bones
To Lords great profets goeth his entire dung
His tallow also serveth plaster – more than one –
For harp strings his ropes serve each one.
Of whose head boiled whole and all
Cometh a jelly – an ointment full royal.
Black sheeps wool with fresh oil of olive
The men of Armes with charmes they prove it good
And at straight need they can well staunch blood . . .
     Argument between Sheep and Goose (Early English Text Society)

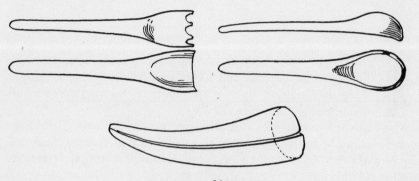

Construction of horn spoons

The Original Mediaeval Sheep

Sheep-breeding and the increasing of flocks was so intensive in the fifteenth and sixteenth centuries that the resultant breeds make it very difficult to identify the 'original mediaeval sheep'. While sheep were the main supply of all clothing, everyone kept sheep, and the type of sheep and type of wool was local, as was the clothing. This is seldom appreciated, yet the cold and rain that developed the waterproof fleece of the sheep was shared by their wet owners; and the tough, resilient, hairy wool, with a warm thick undergrowth, suited the tough, warm clothing of the locality. There is all the difference on earth between the fleeces of the ancient fierce Blackface, the clever Herdwicks, the wet Wensleydales, the Dartmoors, and the Cheviots. Then there were always isolated mountain ranges where the sheep interbred and developed into most individual and unmistakable types – for example, on the Kerry Hills, and Exmoor; also on the salt marshes and tidal grazings (for sheep, like some cattle, will browse on seaweed). There were island sheep carried about in boats, to individual islands. We can only describe a 'mediaeval sheep' as portrayed and described by her contemporary owners, but the reader must accept that there were infinite varieties.

Skull of old 'goat-horned' type of sheep

The term *merino* (denoting a particular breed of sheep) is of obscure origin. Southey informs us that 'Merino is an old Leonese title, still preserved in Portugal, though long since obsolete in the other kingdom of Spain'. Perhaps it is a mongrel diminutive of the Arabic title *mir* or *emir*, likely enough to have been formed when the two languages, Spanish and Moorish, were running into each other. It appears that the inspector of sheep-walks was called the Merino, and hence the appellation extended to the flocks under his care? It is the common opinion that merino sheep came from Spain, and some did in the end of the last century; but it appears that *fine-woolled* sheep were sent from England *to* Spain at an earlier period, for Youatt quotes from the *Chronicles of Stowe*, that 'this yere [1464] King Edward IV gave a licence to pass over certain *Cotteswolde* rams into Spain'. Other early writers give descriptions of the Spanish shepherds 'who live among their flocks till they become like sheep themselves'. These men, receiving the rams from overseas, called them 'Mare'inios'. Rogers quotes the price of rams imported at Hull – presumably for Whitby Abbey flocks, the Cistercians being good sheep farmers. (After the suppression of the monasteries some of their flocks came into private ownership, and provided wool for marketing; for though, officially, monks used the wool only for their own habits, the surplus provided a good income.) Today, Barbary and Persian sheep are tried, and Romney Marsh sheep, and other

English breeds, go to Australia, Africa and Russia. This is of interest in demonstrating the continuous *international* interest in cross breeding sheep.

Some old English sheep had a long-locked fleece and short, rather straight, horns on both ewe and ram (to be found in manuscript portrayals of the shepherds who saw the star). The heads and back of necks were dark and the fleece along the back was full of coarse hairs – old remnants of cloth show these hairs still held in the weave.

The long hairs found in the fleece of early breeds of sheep still persist in breeds in wet districts. They help to keep the animal dry; the tapering shape of the locks of wool allows water to run down to the end, where it can easily be shaken off.

The grease gland at the root of wool fibres smoothes their growth out of the skin and waterproofs them along the length. Each individual hair is encased in a covering of minute scales which lie downward (as the fine scales of a fish lie toward its tail). These scales make the hairs of the wool cling when spun, and thus a long thread can be made; smooth hairs would stay free and untwisted.

This most untechnical explanation makes understandable the difference between cloth woven from short grimp-fibred wools, and that from the long-locked type. The texture of wool imprisons air, and makes it an insulating cloth. (Wool fibres interlock rather like the plume portion of a feather; once the minute hooks on this are broken apart the plume cannot be made intact again.)

The docking of sheep's tails was not done in early times while the sheep lived on what they grazed, for then their droppings were hard and dry; it was not till sheep were fed on soft fodder that the tails became foul and induced fly and maggots; mountain sheep, grazing dry hills, still keep their long flexible tails. When young lambs suckle, their tails swing rapturously; so a shepherd inducing an orphan to suck from a bottle, shakes its tail vigorously, at the back end, to induce reflex action in front!

Mountain-grazed sheep cannot digest root fodder; even in hard winter weather they have to be supplied with dry hay (see p. 61) but most mountain 'sheep-walks' date from the seventeenth and eighteenth centuries, after enclosures.

THE OLD BLACKFACED SHEEP

Some heavy hill sheep, with long-locked waterproof fleece, are, despite their weight, nimble as goats (and the tups can be as aggressive). A Blackface will jump on to a six-foot wall with a sideways running-up jump, poise atop, all four feet neatly together, and then leap lightly down. They are still completely independent, and will cross streams and clamber over rocks, and are almost impossible to enclose.

A Leicestershire farmer we knew picked up four of them at market, drove home and set them loose in his yard, where, while he ate his tea, they ate his laundry. He then put them in the paddock, where they chased out the donkey and then went through the hedge into his garden and ate his greens. He got mad and shut them in the barn, where they sprang over the bales into the adjoining bins and ate his corn. Next day he drove them into town under a net: 'They be devils! Corn and greens have they took! They be not *sheep* – they be *devils!*'

> The mountain sheep are sweeter,
>   But the valley sheep are fatter;
> We therefore deemed it meeter
>   To carry off the latter.
>> The War-Song of Dinas Vawr,
>> Thomas Love Peacock (1785–1866)

The Hirsel

The hirsel, the herd, or the flock, all denote different groups. A flock is just a lot of sheep; a herd is a lot of sheep of the same breed; a hirsel is much larger, and more mixed, than a herd and is sometimes an entire breeding settlement.

In early centuries while sheep were few, and kept near the steading, or grazed the commons with shepherds in charge, they were 'driven out' and 'brought in' (and 'inpenned' at lambing time). After the Elizabethan wooltrade filled the hills, the sheep became independent and hardy, and each 'hirsel' had its own balance of rams and ewes and bred freely, often without benefit of shepherd, whose main job was to care for their safety, walking miles and doctoring when needed, regularly attending to foot or fly troubles on the spot. This is why his old crook was long-handled, to catch, and crooked, to hold, the slender sheep's leg (the southern crooks are of different design, and can take a neck). The mediaeval shepherd's crook, his 'tar box and scrip' continued in use for centuries.

It was (and still is) illegal to sell off a complete hirsel from any mountain, because it takes several generations of sheep to *learn* their individual 'sheepwalk', and some of the older, experienced sheep must be left to guide the newcomers, who would otherwise starve. The small narrow sheeptrails through heather (that can so easily mislead walkers) are definite sheep roadways to and from their special grazing grounds, and resting places, and dormitories. Sheep soon learn the whereabouts of the seasonal 'bite', where young reed tassels are so sweet and crisp, the later patch where the grass grows fresh; the side of the hill where the young green heather shoots are juicy; and sheep know where there is a warm slope for the spring sunshine, or out of the autumn wind; and under the one stunted tree that makes a pool of shade, they will all lie and drowse between twelve and three o'clock. Sheep are punctual animals: any old shepherd knows exactly where to find *his* sheep at any time of the day – and so does his dog. As the sun slopes down they rise again and feed diligently, so as to have a bellyful of cud to chew as they settle for the night. Those small dry alcoves. under a rock are individual sheep beds, and the long sandy scoop, warm and sheltered by the overhang of peat and heather, is used by the same sheep night after night. (If you look, you will see the wool strands and the tracks of little hooves.)

Let any adventurer benighted on the hills find such a sheep bed and, in packed oilskin, curl in tight. (When the indignant old sheep comes to bed she may try to scoop you out of it; or if you are lucky, decide to shove in on top, which will keep you warm till dawn.) In the Midlands, tramps used to 'knock up a cow' to find a warm, dry spot to doss down upon – but in the hills we use sheep.

Thirteenth-century directions for how to choose which of a flock would best stand the winter tell a shepherd to go early to the field and find the sheep upon whose fleece the rime melted soonest. These were likely to have the greatest vitality.

Sheep Stells (A Later Introduction)

Some stone circles which walkers find today on the moors were built after the wool-trade had covered the mountains with sheep. These 'stells' served

Circular stell, with hay-racks and hay-stack

as emergency protection for sheep in bad weather. You will note they are built on sloping land and have only one entrance. On closer inspection you many find marks inside the walls about three feet up, which once held wooden cribs for hay. When bad weather was expected, hay would be carried up and stacked safely in the stell. In snow, all the sheep would be driven into the nearest stell for the hay in the racks and they would be safe, comfortably fed and warm (being crowded together), and their hooves would trample the snow to water, which then drained away down the slope.

Sheep Fights

They say that tournaments were brought back by Crusader knights who watched the Eastern rams fighting. Of all animals, rams' fighting is most methodical. New flocks, mixed ewes and young rams, are soon dominated by one boss ram. When a rival challenges him, they draw apart and if, after a few preliminary butts, they decide to fight, both rams stamp; then they turn their backs, walk sedately a few yards apart, and then turn and face each other and swing their heads and stamp again before they charge – full tilt – producing a crash of skulls that usually brings them a good audience of other sheep (to stand around, but not to interfere). After each charge, each ram turns and walks back and waits to see if the rival is ready, before he charges again. They will keep this up till one of the combatants is knocked down and does not rise, when the victor walks off with the admiring ewes! That is why the prize rams at local Shows often have well-battered skulls! Young ram lambs start to practise this while still on the teat. You can see them butting each other in any spring pasture.

Sheep Marks

Sheep had two series of marks. The ancestral record of the animal was marked on the ears – thus every ewe of one breed might have a single hole punched in the right ear; if the ewe was one of twins a small nick, or other mark, might denote this. (As these marks lasted for life, the rural saying of

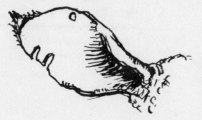

Ear mark: the single hole is the herd mark, the two notches show she was one of twins. If she continued to be a good breeder, there might be later marks.

an old family 'Their ear-marks are good' is understandable.) A temporary
mark printed on to the wool marked the ownership of the sheep, or of the
fleece. This mark used to be of red earth, the harmless oxide that exudes
under rocky outcrops on most sheepwalks. This colour (also used in mural
painting in churches) was bound by the sheep's own oily lanolin, though
later tar was used, which was soon discouraged as it stained the wool: the

Bursting iron and tar skillet

lanolin-bound red raddle had washed out easily. In this century some dark
stains, that spoilt sheepskins in their processing factory, were caused by
farmers using oil paint with a mineral ingredient that impregnated the
skin. After this cause was discovered there was no more trouble.

Marking sheep, redrawn
from a late thirteenth-
century ms. The raddle or
colour mark lasts only until
the fleece is sheared. Other
colour marks are now
sometimes used to trace
which ewes have been
mated: a harness bearing a
marker is strapped to the
ram's chest.

SHEEP DOGS

The tenth and eleventh centuries show shepherds with 'their dogs unto their girdles tied', because in early centuries when wolves stealing sheep was as common as foxes stealing poultry, the cord would jerk the drowsy shepherd awake when the silent-footed wolf aroused the dog. That shepherd dogs were used is certain, and an early Cistercian instruction bids all herdsmen use the same notes or cries for their herds, so that if one brother is away another can take over. The herd boy Watt, before he 'skips off to Bethlehem' bids his dog 'Watch well my Sheep, and Wether ring thou well thy bell.' But the early dogs do not seem to have been taught to work. This is the more remarkable as hunting dogs and hounds are shown as intelligent participants in *their* jobs. Perhaps it was not till the Elizabethan increase in the wool-trade, which covered the wide moorlands with sheep, that dogs were trained in this way.

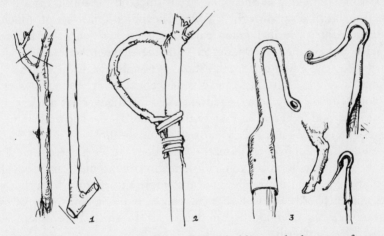

Early mss show shepherds with dogs, and often holding sticks; but apart from small bends at the top of these sticks we have found no definite 'crooks'. There are small v-shaped hooks that would come from the cutting of any bough (1); another way of making a crook would be to train the tree while it was growing (2). Metal hooks on crooks (3) are comparatively late and often of very beautiful design – the small outer curve could serve to carry a satchel or bag. These later crooks varied from large open-ended ones with short handles, which caught the sheep round the neck, to much smaller ones to catch the slender leg.

Shepherds with Trained Dogs

. . . a Sheepheard should not goe without his dogge, his sheepe hooke, a paire of sheares, and his tar box . . . and hee must teach his dog to bark when hee would

have him, to runne when he would have him and to leave running, or els hee is not a
cunning Sheepheard. The dog must learne it when he is a whelp, or else it will not
be, for it is hard to make an old dog for Sheepe.

An early Cistercian instruction

Certainly it was the practice of hill grazing that developed the speed and
skill of the sheepdog. The heavy, long-haired old English dog (so like a
sheep himself) is reliable and good in his own district, but the swift, dark
collie became most usual towards the end of the seventeenth century. The
heavy pugnacious northern rams will stand up to a dog and the dog cannot
control the ewes till the ram is defeated. So dogs were trained to 'throw'
the ram, by running alongside to shove against its shoulder, and as it turned
to butt, catching it off balance. The dog could then lead off the flock and
would later return and with a quick pull on the shoulder wool set the ram
on its feet again. (Unfortunately this prevents many of the best northern
dogs from competing at Sheepdog Trials since, in the south, for a dog to
'touch a sheep' disqualifies it.) Today Sheepdog Trials are so much an
entertainment (even in London parks and on television), that the dogs'
sagacity and complete cooperation with the shepherds are appreciated.
But the dog who does best 'at the Show' is not always the most use on the
mountain: at the Trials speed and obedience matter, whereas for working
on mountains for long hours, endurance and intelligence are more valued.
Alone – beyond sight and hearing of the shepherd – the dog must think for
himself. Once a dog has got the entire flock on the move, he usually has the
sense to hand them over to his mate (if two dogs are working together) and
then be free to gallop back to tackle a missing one; round it up if possible,
or, if it is hurt and immobile, give the single explanatory bark that will
fetch the shepherd. Tales of dogs tracking down long-lost sheep, or even
singling one out from among another flock (by smell?) are usually well
credited by shepherds.

To watch the autumn clearing of Snowdon mountain by shepherds
from adjacent farms, all with their own experienced dogs, is a deep
complete joy. At first all is quiet for an hour or two, except for an odd dog
seen leaping upon some high rock, or the distant bleat of a sheep. Then
down some shallow gulley pours a thin grey trickle of sheep, growing to a
steady moving stream, behind which the dog can be seen weaving from
side to side, keeping all moving together till the whole flock is down; a
warm pool of sheep wait on the green pasture with a circle of dogs
squatting down flat, triumphant, panting and happy, and then the men can
move in to do the sorting. There is a temporary complete unity of purpose
among the sheepdogs, and the old experienced ones – too old now for
active work – move in to approve or rebuke in canine consultation that
carries on long after, for often it is the old dog who takes over from his

winded pupil and sedately weaves behind the herd as it moves off down the road to its appointed farm.

A CAUTION TO CAR-DRIVERS

When driving sheep along the road, the dog falls behind, weaving to and fro from side to side, keeping the slow-moving mass of sheep to a steady progress. If two dogs do this, one – the swiftest – is set free to round up any escapes; or at a word, to dash far ahead to turn back the leaders before a cross-roads ahead. If a motorist *meets* sheep and has the sense to stop for a moment, the dogs will hurry the unbroken flock past his standing car in half the time otherwise wasted. Or, if the motorist wants to *pass* a flock, if he will slow down and ask the shepherd, the man will usually send his dog ahead to clear the sheep to one side, so that the car can pass through easily. On narrow country roads the sheep take the right of way since the twelfth century, just as on water sail has precedence over steam.

MUSIC AND THE SHEPHERD'S PIPE

Our road, leading us up a steep valley, we dismounted and proceeded on foot. Having reached the opposite side with considerable fatigue, the archbishop, to rest, sat down on an oak torn up by the wind, and relaxing into a pleasantry highly laudable in a person of his approved gravity, thus addressed his attendants, 'Who amongst you can now delight our wearied ears by whistling?' which is not easily done by people out of breath.

Giraldus Cambrensis (1146?–1220?)

The shepherd's pipe was most likely of plain hollow wood and had no reed fitment. The modern shrill whistle, and the more gentle modulated whistles and calls used today by shepherds (which can be heard at Trials) are descendants of older pipe music. The Cistercian instruction mentioned earlier in which shepherds are told to teach their piping to other monks who may have to take over their flocks, stipulates only the 'notes and music' (it would be inhuman to expect anyone to hand over his own pipe, he probably made it himself and was the only one who could get a sound out of it!)

Much rural music was born of boredom. Continuous repetitive movement induces rhythm, and stamping and clapping dances to music are preserved today. The gifted musician was always a rare person, and would probably evade fieldwork and be well rewarded for his skill. Other groups, who could make a cheerful noise, would beetle about and be popular. The bard held his own high position in all feudal households. Here we try to imagine the music of the landworker when he herded his beasts on the common, or worked in penfold or field. With long hours, often working alone, he would have plenty of time to practise, and he would hear and incorporate the sounds around him. Many made their own instruments, usually woodwind, for strings are better under cover, as wind and rain affect the gut.

The wooden pipes in common use were of all manner of forms; natural animal horns were adapted for use, though these were blown more as isolated blasts than for continuous music; they preceded the metal trumpets which were also variously shaped. Workers valued volume and made all manner of wooden shawms and sharamells, capable of bassoon-like bellowings.

Most rural music was pipe music and song, arranged as rounds, solos and choruses, and plain canon. Most of the rural music was composed for the open air. We are more used to enclosed sounds, and even in great halls or under high roof space, sound is retained. When the rural musician piped in his hut, that single thread of sound would be lost in the low, warm wood and thatch above him.

The tempo of music and dance depended both upon the work it derived from, and the agility of the performers, and a great deal was acrobatic. A skilled performer might be invited to show off in Hall.

Local variations in pitch have been the subject of much argument among experts. The high-pitched shrill voices of some people and the low-pitched growl of others were developed in the original native countries which had shaped their bodies before they settled in England. Immigrants, like animals, would seek out their own natural environment if possible. If impossible, there would be very slow physical adaptations down the generations. Deep forest countries confuse sounds; over open land sound carries far and the pitch changes slowly as the sound travels; grass, sand, or salt marsh contain continuous sibilant sound; calm water or rhythmic waves convey sounds very differently; and a wide open sky absorbs all sound into its own silence.

The air of this island was full of music – 'Sounds and sweet airs, that give delight and hurt not.' And there would be rounds and part-songs and choruses; and sometimes a combining of musicians; but among labourers most instruments would be hand-made to suit their owners and with very little adjustment to any definite pitch.

CATS

He is a full lecherous beast in youth, swift, pliant and merry, and leapeth and reseth on everything that is to fore him: and is led by a straw, and playeth therewith: and is a right heavy beast in age and full sleepy, and lieth slyly in wait for mice: and is aware where they be more by smell than by sight, and hunteth and reseth on them in privy places: and when he taketh a mouse, he playeth therewith, and eateth him after the play. In time of love is hard fighting for wives, and one scratcheth and rendeth the other grievously with biting and with claws. And he maketh a ruthful noise and ghastful, when one proffereth to fight with another: and unneth is hurt when he is thrown down off an high place. And when he hath a fair skin, he is as it were proud thereof, and goeth fast about: and when his skin is burnt, then he bideth at home; and is oft for his fair skin taken of the skinner, and slain and flayed.

Bartholomaeus Anglicus (*fl.* 1230–50)

Cats suffered horribly during witch hunts, which fostered or encouraged all kinds of superstition and brutality. Yet manuscripts show them about the house, playing with the spinster's twirling bobbin, and earning their living on farms. There was a certain monastic cat who played with serpents. The monks came out in spots, and accused the cat of conveying the serpent's poison. Fortunately (for the cat) it was pointed out that the serpent only played with the cat – so that any poison was delivered accidentally: as there was no 'Malaice intent', harm would not be transmitted.

However, it was advisable in the dairy to 'set trap for a mouse', for though a dog is reasonably honest, and properly ashamed if caught, any cat who will not steal must be mentally deficient – it's the first thing their mothers teach them!

WEEDING

In May get a weed-hook, a crotch and a glove,
and weed out such weeds, as the corn do not love,
For weeding of winter corn, now it is best;
but June is the better for weeding the rest.

From wheat, go and rake out the titters or tine,
if ear be not forth, it will rise again fine:
Use now in thy rye, little raking or none,
break tine from his root, and so let it alone.

Unless the corn had been harrowed, till weeding began the only rows in a cornfield were made by the seed rolling into the plough furrows. Now along these rows walks the weeder. He uses two sticks: with the first, hooked stick he plucks the weed out from among the corn stalks, and with the second, forked stick, pins the weed's head down under the fork. The weeder then steps one pace forward, placing his foot on the head of the weed, and, with this forward movement, swings the hooked stick behind

Weed hook

The weeder's feet would work along a narrow line, squashing the weeds as he went. (He would probably wear a long gown or leggings, but is shown here in a breech clout to reveal the rhythmical action along the furrow. This was perhaps very like a swinging dance.)

him, lifting the root of the weed high out of the ground, before dropping it in line. In this way each pulled up weed is shaken clear of soil, and laid with its root over the buried head of the previous weed. Thus, as the weeder goes along the line of the furrows he lays a mulch of decaying weeds alongside the roots of the corn, and forms a line between the rows at least as wide as his foot. Weeding employed a definite rhythm, and the feet of the weeder formed the lines on which much of the reaper's work depended. Thus the old lines of corn were further apart, but the corn was probably rather more closely set in the lines.

Weeding continued steadily till the workers were called away to haymaking; the only weed that was not uprooted was bindweed on corn in the ear, as pulling that out shed the corn so badly it was better to cut the stem low down and let it be threshed out later.

JUNE

Wash sheep, for the better, where water doth run,
and let him go cleanly, and dry in the sun:
Then shear him, and spare not, at two days an end,
The sooner the better, his corps will amend.

Reward not thy sheep, (when ye take off his coat,)
with twitches and patches as broad as a groat;
Let not such ungentleness happen to thine,
lest fly with her gentils, do make it to pine.

Let lambs go unclipped, till June be half worn,
the better the fleeces will grow to be shorn;
The Pye will discharge thee for pulling the rest;
the lighter the sheep is, then feedeth it best.

If meadow be forward, be mowing of some,
but mow as the makers may well overcome.
Take heed to the weather, the wind and the sky,
if danger approacheth, then cock apace cry.

Plough early till ten a'clock, then to thy hay,
in plowing and carting, so profit ye may.
By little and little thus doing ye win,
that plough shall not hinder, when harvest comes in.

Let cart be well searched, without and within,
well clowted and greased, ere hay time begin:
Thy hay being carried, though carter had sworn,
cart's bottom, well boarded, is saving of corn.

Good husbands that lay, to save all things upright,
for tumbrels and cart have a shed ready dight;
Where under, the hog, may in winter lie warm,
to stand so inclosed, as wind do no harm.

So likewise a hovell will serve for a room,
to stack on the peason, when harvest shall come;
And serve thee in winter moreover than that,
to shut up the porklings, thou mindest to fat.

THE WOOLLY SHEEP

SHEEP – or the wool from them – helped found England's prosperity (which is why the Chancellor still sits on the Woolsack). So we will devote most of this chapter to the Sheep, beginning with Tusser's instructions on how to get clean wool.

Washing Sheep

This should not be confused with modern sheep dipping. Usually some stream was dammed up to make a washing pool; one with a gravel bed, if possible; sheep were *thoroughly washed*. Foul wool and loose wool round the udder was removed and the shepherd was on hand to examine the sheep's heads and mouths and ears (and later, when shearing was done, their legs and hooves). Sheep swim well and, floating in the water, are light to turn about. When wool was important the fleeces were parted, and washing lye was used. Some skill was required in handling the strong active northern sheep (we saw one old ewe, resenting the indignity of being washed behind the ears, rear up, plant her two front feet firmly on the chest of the washer and shove him over backwards (he got *his* bath right enough!). Sometimes the workers stood in barrels in the stream, but earlier – and this was easier – they stood in the water.

A sheep when released would swim across the stream (rinsing herself handsomely) and clamber up the opposite bank, where she would stand to drip off (and be kindly consoled with a little hay). The lambs keep up a continuous outcry, and many have difficulty in again locating their mothers, and so are automatically weaned.

After washing, the shepherd keeps an eye on the sheep till the wool is completely dry and the 'yolk' (the natural grease) has penetrated back into the fibres and the sheep's skin becomes taut again.

This old method of washing changed little till the nineteenth century (after which the whiteness of a fleece was not so important). It was on Oxfordshire land that we met a shepherd whose sandy, yellow flocks were quite unwashed. He explained that now wool was being sold 'by weight'

Sheep – by Holman Hunt

and the yellow sand increased the weight. He grinned: 'First time I've been paid for dirt!' English wool in Elizabeth I's time was of the finest quality, carefully washed and expertly sheared.

Shearing

Fleece is grown afresh before each winter, and shed in summer, so shearing must be done just when the fleece is ready to be shed. The shepherd's sensitive touch can feel where the fleece is fine, close to the skin; and that is where the shearer clips off the fleece. Some old ewes may have fleece dropping loose. These were not sheared because they were near their lambing time, so the shepherd thought they 'could do with a little extra warmth and avoid handling'. Most experienced ewes take handling very placidly: it is the active tups which require strong men.

Mediaeval sheep were all hand-clipped and the pattern of the shears remains unchanged. The sheep were sorted, and the young lambs let go; ewes still suckling were done first, and rams and tups done separately. If cross-breeding was being contemplated, there would be further sorting by type. The occasional black sheep was of use, his naturally dark wool being woven into designs shading from cream through sepia to black. The opprobrious term 'black sheep' only referred to the dark markings often showing on lambs when new born. Even after a good strain was well established, occasionally one lamb would be a complete 'throw-back'. Most early breeds had long bristle-like hairs in their wool along back and neck; such hairy wool will not spin a fine thread but will weave a tough cloth, suitable for hard use. Mountain sheep were usually of this type, till superseded by Cheviots.

Shearing methods still vary locally; sheep sometimes have their legs tied, but experienced old ewes usually take it very peaceably and in hot summers register relief. If the sun is very strong the shearer may leave the wool slightly ridged to afford protection against sunburn. On salt grazing, shearers would also treat for fly as they worked, caking vulnerable parts with clay or using a 'tar' dressing. Essex sheep, and most old English breeds, kept their tails, as Welsh sheep do today. Rooks and magpies will spend hours picking over sheep for maggots, and a shepherd always carried a small box of ointment to treat fly-blow, maggot, or any broken skin on a sheep. When Stockholm tar from the shipyards replaced the older concoction of broom water, it was at first considered a slight extravagance – tar having to be bought, whereas sulphurous broom buds cost nothing – but it was 'a pity to lose a good *sheep* for a ha'pennyworth of tar'. (Perhaps it was the Elizabethan sailors about fifty years later, trading Stockholm tar to the shepherds, who began to change 'sheep' to 'ship'.)

> *A shepard on a hill he sat*
> *He had his tar box and his hat*
> *And his name was Jolly-Joly Watt.*
>   An early carol

Shepherds traditionally carried a 'scrip'. This was simply a satchel, such as workmen still use, at first probably of leather, later of woven hemp or woollen cloth.

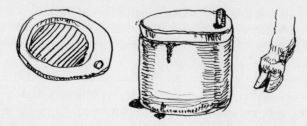

The tarbox shown here is a small wooden box, hollowed out of a misshapen piece of wood, with a lid pivoted on a wooden peg. It exactly fitted the small foot of a sheep. After the shepherd had cleaned out the cloven hoof he thrust down the foot so that the soft ointment was forced up into the cavity of the foot. This was on Rumblesmoor near Skipton- (Sheeptown) in-Craven; the shepherd was old, and so was his box, but whether it was typical of early tarboxes we do not know.

Sheep Salve

This early recipe is to 'salve poore mennes shepe that thynke tarre [tar] too costely':

> Take a shete ful of brome cropes, leaves blossomes and all and chop them very smal and sethe them in a pan with [of] rennynge water till it begyn to wax thyke like a gelly. Than take 2 pounds of shepe suet, molten, and a pottle of old pysse and as moche bryne made with salt and styr it doule and streyne it through an able cloth and washe your shepe therewith.

But: 'the beste grease that is to a shepe is to grease hym in the mouthe with good meate'.

Rooing or Pulling

Some old breeds of sheep were never sheared but 'pulled', which gave a fibre that tapered to a point at each end. This made a very fine thread.

WOOL

Ne route he theyn flockes were ameynd
bi toppes in them.
                              The Owl and the Nightingale (c. 1220)

'Ne route he' – hear the owl's beak snap in sharp contempt of the spinner who 'recked not if the soft fleece had stiff top hairs mixed in it'! The 'toppes' in this case were either the bristles growing on top of the neck and shoulders of degenerate sheep, or the pulled off locks, the soiled or torn bits of wool, that were 'laid atop' the fleece when it was rolled up.

The Rolling of Fleeces

The sheared fleece was by old custom handed over to women workers, who laid it flat, the side from next the skin upwards, removed soiled or matted wool and then folded the four leg pieces inwards. The neck wool

Rolling a fleece of wool

they dexterously pulled out, rope-wise, then from the tail end they rolled up the fleece into a neat bundle which they secured with the rope of neck wool.

The uniformity of these fleece rolls was important, as they then went to the wool-room where they were graded and packed into the woolpack. In these days of lorry collecting, the old wool-room is almost obsolete. In old farms the fleeces were laid out on a clean-swept floor in the wool-room and were collected at nightfall.

The fleeces were still live and warm. Each fleece was ivory white, and if the summer night was cold after a hot day, a mist, like the bloom on fruit, clouded the wool, and the cooling fleeces stirred slightly all night through. Most live materials have tension. The fibres of wool, in tension, are locked together like the plume of a bird's feather, and in an old wool-room you could hear the fleeces stirring; a faint sound like soft breathing.

The Woolsack

You cannot denie but that this Realme yeeldeth the most fine Wooll, the
most soft, the most strong Wooll, the most durable in Cloth, and most apte
of nature of all other to receive Die, and that no Island or any one kingdome
so small doeth yeeld so great abundance of the same: and that no Wooll is
lesse subject to mothes, or to fretting in presse, as the old Parliament robes of
Kings, & of many noble Peeres to be shewed may plainly testifie.

> *Principall Navigations, Voiages, and Discoveries of the English Nation,*
> Richard Hakluyt (1552?–1616)

The fleeces, when cold, were packed into strong sacks of statute size (such
as the Parliamentary Woolsack of today). The sack was suspended from a
beam in the barn so that it hung down to floor-level and the two wool
packers stood inside it; as the fleeces were thrown up to them, they packed
them down, skilfully footing them into the corners and treading down the
layers tightly. As the layers rose the packers presently would be treading

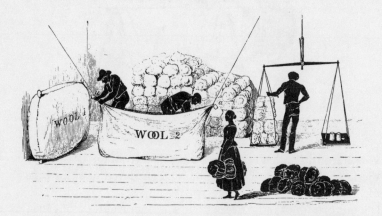

Weighing and packing wool

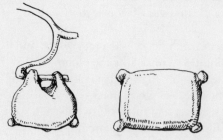

*Conventional woolsacks, carved on misericords
in Shropshire*

A fork used in fastening woolsacks

the top of a high wall of wool. As the last layer was thrown up and fixed in, they stepped out backwards along the top, sewing up the sack as they went. The woolsack was then lowered to the ground, eight 'holds' tied at the corners to make handling possible, and the woolpack was complete.

The wool was carted by wagon, covered against the damp, but ventilated against heating. A wool wain was safe on the road, as a full woolsack was too heavy and cumbersome to steal, and if a sack was slit the whole of the contents burst out. Smaller packing would have been more vulnerable. The woolsack was sold by weight, *not* by the number of fleeces in it.

A pack of wool was made up as follows:

7 lbs	= 1 clove	2 weys	= 1 sack
4 cloves	= 1 todd	12 sacks	= 4368 lbs
6 todds & ½	= 1 wey (182 lbs)	240 lbs	= 1 pack

English wool merchants were extremely wealthy and shared a great overseas trade, their merchant marks being recognised in many foreign ports.

In 1656 a law was made against trans-shipment of wool, woolfells, fuller's earth, and so on: 'They were not to lade ship or carry in any ship, barge, boat or other vessel or otherwise any wool of the growth of England or Ireland or the Dominion of Wales ... or any woollen yarn, flox, fell, Fullers earth, clay Tobacco pipe clay, or any other earth or clay which may be used in the art of Fulling.'

Wool Cloth

Most country folk grew enough wool for their own use and the early housewife was warned to see that her husband kept enough for 'his own household before he sold the rest'. Spinning was the occupation of most women, but the main weaving was usually done by men through contract exchange with some local weaver. Once the fleece was broken the product was called 'wool', and the household wool was stored till after the busy harvest, when it could be moved. On longer evenings it was combed and spun by the women until enough yarn was ready to be sent to the local weaver. If paid for by arrangement – that is, by giving part value in corn or pork and so on – the lengths and widths were fixed by mutual agreement: but if it was a professional weaving, for trade, there were definite regulations covering measurements, and the long threads of the 'setting up' had to be left on at the ends of the woven length to prove it uncut (there was constant vigilance against unscrupulous tricks in measuring).

When Elizabeth I set out to rebuild our shattered economy, it was to be

This may illustrate a curious old weave known as 'sprang', in which the warp is hung double and the front and back threads interwoven (by the figure on the left) to give a curiously elastic fabric. This is redrawn from a ms. in Trinity College, which is in its turn is a redrawing of an earlier version. The Trinity College artist seems to have been puzzled by the omission of a weaving shuttle and a supply of weft.

based on wool: so hose and cloaks were to be woollen, with linen allowed only for shifts. Wool was used in hangings and tapestries. Its use was enforced even in the grave – burial shrouds had to be of wool. This law about woollen-shrouded burial was confirmed by sailors to the north-western Russian ports where they remarked 'English wool being so plentiful, all persons are ensured of shrouds.'

Spun wool (yarn) was wound into skeins twisted as shown. If the sticks are then removed, and one end of the skein passed through the loop at the other, the skein will remain neatly twisted and not unravel.

FULLING

The woven cloth was 'fulled' under water, either by treading or beating by the waterwheel of a mill, turning a camshaft which operated a wooden drop hammer. The wet cloth then went to the 'tenting' fields.

TENTING

In the tenting field were long stakes set closely with small, angled iron hooks. These stakes were secured to the tops of high poles crossing the field like a fence. One selvedge of the wet cloth was stretched evenly along the top hooks; the lower selvedge was then pulled down and secured on to a lower set of tenting hooks driven into a heavy lower bar. This bar, swinging on the cloth, pulled it down 'full width'. The cloth was then left to dry taut and tight – upon 'tenter hooks'. The expression remains today, and in some old pieces of English flannel you can still see along the selvedge the marks of the tenter hooks. The 'tenters square' and 'fullers yard' are still common names in our old towns and villages.

All the processing of wool cloth was of as much interest to the farmer who bred sheep as milling was to the farmer who grew corn. As an agriculturalist grew the corn the trade wanted, and studied the weight of flour through the millstones, just so closely would a shepherd farmer study the amount of cloth produced by his wool. 'Trade' began in the field and pasture, for different wools were needed for different purposes. The tough, springy wool, still waterproof with its lanolin content, was best for work stockings and breeches (later so typical of men's Quaker costume; Quaker women preferred the finer, softer wool). These types of wool had to be worked out in the breeding pens, and the selection of suitable rams was one of the reasons for attending the huge annual fairs.

DYEING AND FINISHING CLOTH

How many severall colours be died is to be learned of our Diers before you depart. Then how many of those colours England doth die of her owne naturall home materials and substances, and how many not. Then to bring into this realme herbs and plants to become naturall in our soiles, that may die the rest of the colours, that presently of our owne things here growing we can not yet die, and this from all forren places.

Principall Navigations, Voiages, and Discoveries of the English Nation,
Richard Hakluyt (1552?–1616)

Small families, and that would include many who were officially employed on feudal estates, wove and finished the cloth themselves. The earliest dyeing method was to boil the wool in the largest available cauldron, with the dye stuff in a bag or at the bottom under a weighted board with holes in it. The washed wool was put in wet, and afterwards rinsed in running water and hung up to dry. Blended colours were more likely to be obtained by using different colours for weft and warp, and other tricks of weaving (which culminated in plaid patterns). Plain brown, grey, or greens were more successful than blues, though fine scarlet was treasured. Mediaeval rural colours ran to green, black and red, and yellows. From Elizabeth I's time dyes became very important, and merchants paid great attention to them, as Hakluyt demonstrates:

'A briefe Rememberance of things to be indevoured at Constantinople, and in other places in Turkie, touching our Clothing and our Dying, and things that bee incident to the same, and touching ample vent of our naturall commodities, & of the labour of our poore people withall, and of the general enriching of this Realme. . . .

'*Anile* wherewith we colour Blew to be brought into this realme by seed or roote. And the Arte of compounding the same. And also all other herbes used in dying in like manner to bee brought in. And all Trees, whose Leaves, Seedes, or Barkes, or Wood doe serve to that use, to be brought into this realme by Seed or Roote. All little Plants and Buskes serving to that use to be brought in. To learne to know all earths and minerals forren used in dying, and their naturall places, for possible the like may here by found upon sight. Also with the materials used in dying, to bring in the excellencie of the arte of dying.

'To endevour the sale of such our clothes as bee coloured with owne naturall colours as much as you can, rather then such as be coloured with forren colours.'

Mediaeval Colours

And dream of London, small and white and clean,
The clear Thames bordered by its gardens green. . . .
                    The Wanderers, William Morris (1835–1896)

The colour in a mediaeval Elizabethan farmstead is controversial. The manuscript illuminations of the fifteenth and sixteenth centuries glow with rich colour and gold; and personages of importance are resplendent. (Written descriptions of dress and tapestry are vivid and give an impression of richness.) The duns and greys of poverty are also clear and clean, the effects being obtained by decorative dilapidation. Also, landscape and plants gleam with this brilliant clarity. We must therefore realise the convention of the pigment and treatment. The brilliant colours of illuminated manuscripts were transparent water colours laid over a gleaming white gesso foundation, and gold leaf, which, being burnished, shines brilliantly, but these colours could not have been as bright on the actual dull matt cloth of garments.

Many 'natural' materials were used so; for example, linen varied from the bleached white to the soft browns and russets of hemp admixtures, and the striped and stippled effects of other mixtures. Wool was a good example of the use of natural colouring; weaving patterns utilised the lightest cream, brownish and sepia and the deep black wool of the 'black sheep' (this beautiful graded work used to be the pride of Shetland shawls and the early patterned Welsh blankets).

Certain occupations involved definite colours, for example, the Lincoln green of archers, or the white habits with black scapula of some religious orders. These colours were kept as constant as possible, and were probably the work of professional dyers.

Below are listed some prevalent heraldic colours which were the earliest and most brilliant. These were restricted in use and though traditionally of feudal origin, they continued through the tournaments and pageantry of the fifteenth and sixteenth centuries.

Argent: silver
Azure: a deep bright blue
Gules: blood red
Murrey: mulberry colour, a dark purplish red
Or: gold
Purpure: a plum colour of violet shade
Sable: black
Tonne: an orange red, or golden tan
Vert: green

All heraldic colours were opaque, flat and constant, unless something was to be represented in its natural colours, or 'proper'.

These are not country colours: for ordinary country clothes the reds, blacks, white, greens and yellows would be of natural substances, and locally made. The red raddle used for marking wool was red oxide, a mineral colour found and used in its natural state. This is a bright brick red, and sedimentary, not a transparent colour. Lime (quick lime) mixed with this gave shades of pink and was used to colour cottage walls inside and out. In some districts the clay soil itself coloured the mud and wattle huts a dull,

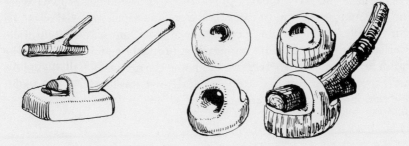

Maul is the name given to certain types of special hammers; the related muller was for grinding powder, such as pigments, on a slab. These examples of countrymen's mullers are made from carefully-shaped stones and sticks.

yellowish brown. Contrast these shades with lime white, and black glistening tar, and against a green background you have simple mediaeval effects. By obtaining refuse from the potash and sulphur hearths, a greenish grey is possible. Wood, on the whole, was little painted for country use. We believe the early linenfold panelling was often limewashed, and the new wood panelling would be light cream; limewash may have been used from the desire to lighten the walls after years had darkened the oak. (It is enlightening to study in manuscripts the fresh light stone walls, and bright new wood – it is only time that has made building stone dark and oak panelling black and gloomy.) Fifty years ago, the pink and white Irish cabin with white limewashed walls and golden straw over a brown, peaty, dry earth floor, reproduced well the colours prevalent in the fifteenth century.

Home dyeing used 'anything they could lay hands upon'. Only by experiment can one realise the infinite variety of shades obtainable from simple substances. Many colours would be arrived at accidentally: perhaps a bright transparent yellow came into use when the bee hives were washed for mead, as bee propolis (a gum the bees make to seal the hive) makes a golden stain and is solvent in soda (any bee master, after cleaning hives, will testify to propolis stain). Soot, being one of the tar products, produces another gold shade. Blackberries and bilberries stain blue and purple. The mauve ribbons of the sixteenth and seventeenth centuries were tinted with blackberry juice, and tons of Welsh blackberries used to be sold to Navy-blue merchants up to the nineteenth century. (Indigo, being from the Indian shrub Anil was, like cochineal and other foreign colours, not obtainable for ordinary use; aniline dyes only became common in the late nineteenth century.) Bistre (a brown colour) was made from extract of soot, but the finest – used by artists – was said to be direct from the entrails of a cockchafer. Saffron was grown in East Anglia, but was used chiefly for colouring foodstuffs. Many plants produced green, and blendings of dye were endless. The early 'Quaker greys' and later 'Methodist browns' were in no way 'uniform'; in most cases they were homespun material of mixed shaded wools, or the browns were obtained from tanyards. Later still the American dogwood, used by immigrants, probably matched up with the English lichen and rachan dyes (rachan being the grey lichen that gives the Harris tweeds their distinctive odour). Often what is lost from England is preserved in early colonial counterpart.

Dyestuff for Linen

Sailors were instructed to find dyestuffs for the English trade: 'In Persia there are that staine linnen cloth, it is not amisse you learne it . . . it hath bene an olde trade in England . . . but the arte is now lost. You shall find anile there ... procure the herbe ... either by seed or plant to cary into England, but leave you the making of the anile ... possibly it [the herb] groweth here already. ... In some little pot in your lodging ... make daily trials in your arte. Learne ... to fixe and make sure the colour ... and enquire the price of liquor and all other things belonging to dying. Also procure a singular good workman in the arte of Turkish carpet making: you should bring the arte into this Realme and thereby increase worke to your company.' Because (as Hakluyt points out), 'if thrums and unspun wool [that is, with the lanolin (yolk) still in it] can be dyed for carpet use, assuredly good cloth will dye even better.'

FROM SHEEPSKIN TO PARCHMENT

The preparation of parchment and vellum begins as for leather, but the finish was a specialised craft in which the mediaeval English excelled. The skin was stretched taut by lacing on to a square frame. A specially rounded knife (or 'strickle') was used to scrape the skin to a smooth, even fineness; remnants of fat and grease being extracted by repeated 'dowses' of a hot lye of soda after each scraping. When the skin was the required even texture throughout, the surface was scoured with a fine abrasive – fine sand or, we believe, powdered 'water-of-aire' stone (a fine limestone which much resembles pumice). The skins, now 'parchments', were left stretched on their frames till perfectly dry, then they were squared and dispatched to the Scriptorium. Odd lengths, or defective skins, had many uses: for covering jars (very much as we use plastic covers today), for making waterproof bags, and so on.

Sizes of Parchments

It is appropriate here to explain that the size of early manuscripts depended upon the shape of the animal that supplied the parchment. The parchment was usually sheep skin, and a 'folio' size was one skin folded in half,

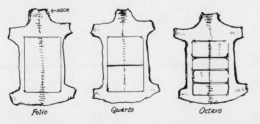

Folio   Quarto   Octavo

Parchments would be cut to avoid particularly thick or thin pieces, though these might find a use in bookbinding details (the tension of leather was well understood by generations of country people who made their own work gloves). Books were a town or community (scriptorium) trade, but the skins were sold in country markets.

'quarto' folded into four, and 'octavo' folded into eight. The outer binding was usually of heavy boards, clasped to keep the parchment from cockling. Valuable books were kept in specially-made cases and some small books, usually devotional, were so bound that the outer leather cover folded over in front and, being elongated at the top, formed a hanging bag in which the volume could be suspended from the waist or upon a cord around the neck. This special binding was called a 'chemise'.

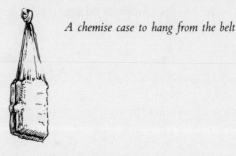

A chemise case to hang from the belt

'OF A SHEEP IS CAST AWAY NOTHING'

Horns

Sheep, goats and cattle were all horned, and each type of horn had its use. The short ridged sheep horn was used for bow ends, the ridges holding the string loop without friction, and the solid tips were used as pivots in early hinges. Horns also made knife handles, the larger inkhorns (after which the

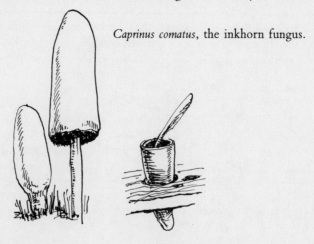

Caprinus comatus, the inkhorn fungus.

inkhorn fungus took its name) and powder-horns. Bone and horn had other uses, being carved into spoons, skewers, bobbins and, in later centuries when candles were in use, was used to outline keyholes. The curled rams' horns sometimes made elaborate drinking cups, and occasionally were used in acrobatic dancing, strapped to the feet of mediaeval entertainers who pivoted and rocked on them: a diversion probably begun at some shepherds' feast in a barn, and developed for the entertainment of the gentry. The small ends of the horns also made convenient store jars for spices and ointments.

Cattle horn was scraped thin and used in lanterns (lant*horns*), small window lights (panes), drinking cups and containers for ointments and drugs, and spoons and scoops of every description.

Everyday signals were by blown horns. The Great Horn of York is still sounded, and several other ceremonial horns survive. Echoes of the shepherd's horn died out among the Welsh mountains within living memory (as street cries today are dying out). Tinkers, pedlars, carriers, all manner of travellers, used all manner of horn blasts to announce their wares and whereabouts. The horn of the swine-gelder sounded till the eighteenth century (in fact till the cottager ceased to keep a pig). The long musical post-horn was derived from the original post boy's horn, and blown lustily when he reached the hitching post, where he awaited his fellow for delivery and exchange of mail bags. Only the finest and best-shaped horns were retained for such use; the refuse horns, and the inner honeycomb cores of the horns, went from the slaughter fields to the glue-boilers. Today the quarry horn, descendant of 'real' horns, is still used to warn of blasting – in a job where the ring of metal on stone might cause confusion, the sound of a blown horn is unmistakable. Blasting times are fairly regular, but depend a little on the work. Therefore after the charges are set the blast man blows a horn to tell all workers he is about to go around and light the time fuses. Instantly, even as the echoes of the horn hang in the air, every man puts down everything and goes direct to his allotted shelter – a low-built stone hut – where he squats down and waits, counting the numbered blasts. If a fuse fails, all must wait till the worker (at some risk) withdraws or adjusts it. But not till the horn sounds again should any man stir from the shelters. A bugle was used sometimes, but it was still called 'the horn'.

Lanolin

Lanolin was prepared from the greasy wool around the necks and udders of sheep. This wool was washed in cold water and then boiled, held down under slats at the bottom of a cauldron. After the grease had all risen to the surface of the water, the heat was withdrawn, and when the water was quite cold the grease was skimmed off as a white curd-like fat. Pliny records reheating this fat and straining it through linen, which was probably general usage: the saturated linen would make excellent bandages, and the cleared lanolin was stored in jars or bladders.

This lanolin, impregnated with vegetable oils and scents, formed the basis of most mediaeval ointments. When strongly impregnated with repeated fillings of broom buds, it made the 'yellow broom bud ointment' that was used for sheep till superseded by tar dressing. This same ointment was (to the author's knowledge) made by old women in the Yorkshire Wolds and sold to sailors whose hands were abraded by the rough, wet nets when fishing the North Sea.

Tallow

Sheep's tallow was used for tallow dips and candle making, also for greasing harness and leather. Coarse tallow was used as the lubricant of mediaeval machinery, from the working parts of the mill to hinges of doors, and the axles of the church bells.

Some early candles were dipped, like tallow dips, but more usually they were moulded. By the sixteenth century moulded candles appear to have been general (see also p. 318). Beeswax was used to harden candles, as it melts at a high temperature, but the good housewife would have her own recipe for candles for her own use.

The early missionaries in their little chapels would only use a candle when necessary. The scribe attached to a feudal estate (frequently a monk) would get his official issue of candles, according to his work and the season. Monks might carry candles between dormitory and chapel in the dark. Servants and other workers on a farm, including shepherds at lambing time, got candles for the stable lanthorns. In pre-Reformation times, the proliferation of ceremonial candles raised the price of beeswax, and made mutton fat almost unobtainable (there wasn't much of it, anyhow). The candles set around a laid-out corpse were a sensible precaution to prevent premature burial during coma – which, before medical tests and certificates, was a serious danger. They were also useful when affluent church dignitaries were laid out in state in their gold robes with jewelled clasps and rings and gold cross – though no labourer need have worried that his corpse would be robbed. The custom is excused today as symbolic and traditional, but the ballad 'Fire and sleet and candle leet and Christ receive thy saul' is for the countryfolk of moor and fell.

Candles continue on dining tables (they are still an expense at St John's College, Cambridge). Candles on cakes and Christmas candles seem to be imported customs.

Our mediaeval labourer, up at daylight and working on the land for as long as he could see, needed no candle –he went to bed.

The author's father was asked permission by an old woman to go up the church tower and scrape the black grease from the axles of the bells 'for her boy's chest'. She explained that it had to be 'well rubbed in before the fire'. She admitted it 'was just grease', like that on the axle of her husband's old grindstone, but 'from the church bells it was *stronger*'. We think this was the mediaeval tradition, for the lubricant fat given to the church would, like all gifts, be dedicated to its usage. So you would get the fat, and the blessing thrown in, though of course you risked the sacrilege involved in stealing it.

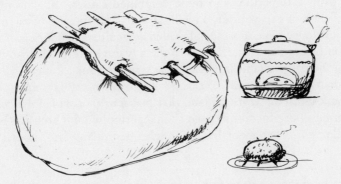

'Of a sheep is cast away nothing': the paunch could be used for cooking puddings, such as the famous haggis.

THE EFFECT OF
THE BLACK DEATH ON SHEEP FARMING

During the Black Death of 1347–50, whole families died; survivors were fortunate if they reached waste land where wild game and green fodder, or abandoned farm stocks and small uncut crops, made possible a new settlement. The Statute of Labourers (cited by some historians as an example of high-handed brutality) was, at first, an attempt to avoid widespread famine and infection, as the first Statute simply ordered the population to remain static. The law covered carpenters, masons, carters and all reconstruction workers: in fact *all* possible able-bodied men, as well as the agricultural labourers; but panic and pillage resulted, and the lack of quick communication made it impossible to control the whole country simultaneously. At that date, isolated illiterate people could not understand instructions given in the dialect of a different district.

Survivors fled wildly from the cities to the country, and from the country to pillage the cities. Parliament, itself depleted, tried to enforce restrictive laws by brutal penalties, with small effect except that of arousing bitter resentment. Communities which had moved to strange localities, and now lacked the compulsory authority of their feudal lords, welcomed freedom.

It is interesting that the attempt to enforce communal work for the good of all resulted in communal rebellion. The labourer who survived was in a strange district and could work where he would for whoever paid most. (Nor were the overlords particular to refuse such vagrant labour, being glad of any they could get.)

It is from this period, and these combined causes, that the ultimate independence of the worker, and the gradual acceptance of payment in wages developed. The shortage of skilled agricultural labour enforced the reduction of cornland, and it was to the advantage of the land-owner to turn the uncropped land into sheep pasture (and for a time to eat meat rather than bread), but the exchange was bad for the labourer, for one herdsman can do the work on land that previously occupied many hands. Wool prices were increasing, and at this period wool merchants became rich under encouragement by the Exchequer. Thus Sir Thomas More writes:

> The shepe that were wont to be so meke and tame and so smal eaten, be become so greate devourers and so wylde that they eat up and swallow downe the very men themselves. . . . For looke, in what parte of the realme doth growe the fynest and therefore the dearest wool: there noblemen and gentlemen, yea and certayn abbottes – holy men no doubt, not contenting themselves with the yearely revenues and profytes that were wont to growe to theyr forefathers and predecessours of their lands, leave no grounde for tillage; they throwe downe houses; they plucke downe townes and leave nothing standynge but only the churche to be made a shepehouse. Therefore, that one covetous and unsatiable cormorant and very plague of his natyve countrey may enclose many thousand akers of grounde together within one pale or hedge, the husbandmen be thrust oute of their owne, a els either by fraude or by violent oppression they be put out of it, or by wronges and injuries they be so weried that they be compelled to sell all. By one means or by another, by hooke or crooke, they must needs departe awaye, poore wretched soules.
>
> *History of Richard III*

HOVELS

The sun does more harm to a Cart than either Wind or Rain. However they are all three Enemies, and are easily prevented by a Cart-Shed. – Which need not cost much; for one may be made with eight Crochets, and as many

Spars. It may be covered with Bavin wood, Brakes, Furzes, or other Firing
. . . Under there a Cart is immediately out of Wind and Weather. Your Hog
(a creature extremely fearful of Wind and Rain, and to whom the heat of the
sun is pernicious) finds here Shelter and Shade and a Wheel to rub
against. . . .

Hovels are [also] very good Use to put Corn stacks, especially Pease and
Tares up on: for if there be a Dog Kennel under them and free from Damp of
the Earth, which they are very apt to draw [up they are] out of the Hogs'
reach; who will certainly undermine them if he can.

Gervase Markham (1568?–1637)

The word 'hovel' now means a poor dwelling or hut: originally it meant a
'useful shed'. The modern Dutch barns replace the many 'small hovels set
about the fields'. Hovels saved cartage, and when not used for storing a
crop, were handy for porklings. (But all bread corn should be given barn
room, to be kept safe and dry, under the eye of the farmer.)

Ling, heather, rough grass, withy bark, bracken – almost anything could
be used to thatch a small hovel. Under such a hovel near the farmhouse
would be kept fuel (for the bread oven) and sedge (for draining the
brewing vat). A small kindness would be the small, portable one put up to
shelter the hersdman or bird-scaring child. Shakespeare shelters King Lear
in a reasonably good contemporary hovel, and notes that the bedding straw
is 'short', – that is, it consists of the broken refuse from the flail.

JULY

Go muster thy servants, be captain thyself,
providing them weapon, and other like pelf:
Get bottles and wallets, keep field in the heat,
the fear is as much as the danger is great.

With tossing and raking, and setting on cocks,
grass lately in swathes, is hay for an ox:
That done, go and cart it, and have it away,
the battle is fought, ye have gotten the day.

Then down with the headlands, that groweth about,
leave never a dallop, unmown and had out;
Though grass be but thin about barley and pease,
yet picked up clean, ye shall find therein ease.

Let hay be well made or avise else avous
for moulding in goef, or of firing the house.
Lay coursist aside, for the ox and the cow,
the finest for sheep and thy gelding allow.

Wife, pluck fro thy seed hemp, the fimble hemp clean,
this looketh more yellow, the other more green
Use t'one for thy spinning, leave Mighel the t'other,
for shoe-thread and halter, for rope and such other.

Now pluck up thy flax, for the maidens to spin,
first see it dried, and timely got in:
And mow up thy brank, and away with it dry,
and house it up close, out of danger to lie.

Get grist to the mill, to have plenty in store,
lest miller lack water, as many do more
The meal the more yieldeth, if servant be true,
and miller that tolleth, take none but his due.

Pay justly thy tithes, whatever thou be,
that God may in blessing, send foison to thee:
Though curate be bad, or the parson as evil,
go not for thy tithing, thyself to the devil.

1. *This route map of 1360 shows rivers and streams because they were the routes of 1360. A traveller followed a stream up to the Pass where, almost always, low between the mountains, water lies static till wind or rain causes it to overflow down one side or the other. Therefore at this point the traveller stood and looked ahead for the next direction to steer towards. (Subsequent cartographers who drew mountains—see p. 308—showed individual skylines that could be recognized from a distance.) He then selected a stream that flowed in the right direction and followed it down. All cities have rivers leading in and out of them, and inter-city travellers soon wore trackways; some routes became known as 'Pilgrim Ways' because travellers stayed in monasteries with shrines. Many of these footworn river routes and Roman roads continue in use today.*

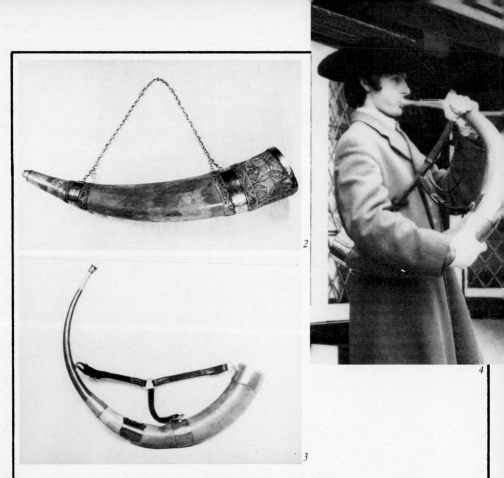

2. The Horn of Ulph, from York Minster, was traditionally presented not long before the Conquest as a visible memorial of lands also given by Ulph, an earl of Deira, to the Minster. It was carved from an elephant's tusk at Salerno, in southern Italy.

3. The Ripon horn, the same shape as that blown by a 'wardcorne' (see p. 18).

(see p. 18)

4. The hornblower of Ripon still sounds his instrument nightly.

5. Norfolk sheep were small and active, with long dark hard legs and faces. Both ram and ewe had long curved horns. They were probably an earlier breed than the Lincoln sheep.

6. *Transporting sheep to an island in the Outer Hebrides for grazing.*

7, 8 and 9. *The sheepdog has been the shepherd's friend from the fifteenth to the twentieth century.*

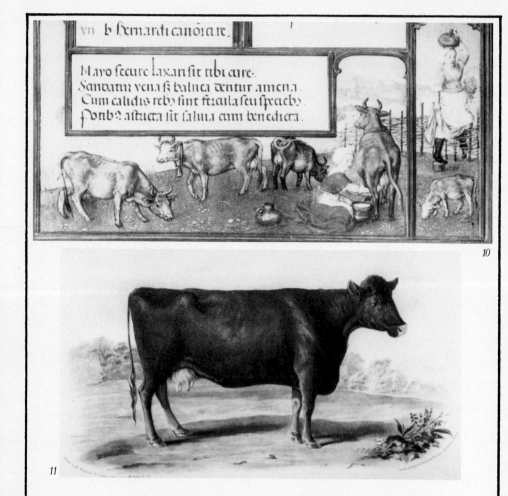

10. *A dairymaid milking in the field.*

11. *A breed of cattle common in Suffolk and East Cambridgeshire until the eighteenth century. Of a grey dun colour and 'uncouth, heavy-headed, large-boned,' it was a good milker and supplied very solid cheese. Essex beef was handy for the London market.*

12. *Muck-spreading in the twentieth century.*

13

14

13. 'Sir Wag' at work in the fifteenth century.

14. Pig-killing in the sixteenth century.

15. Making sausage skins in the early fourteenth century.

16. Salting meat in the fifteenth century.

15

16

17

17. A circular Welsh pigsty.

18. This old English sow shows her wild ancestors in thick bristle and straight hairy-switched tail. Forward-carried ears protect her eyes; mixed colouring and splayed hooves suggest shady shrubbery environment and soft soil.

18

19. The Suffolk Punch, a light dun or sorrel, with lighter mane and tail; moderate size; slow and enduring of labour; very intelligent. It was noted for ox-like impatient pulling against a fixed draught.

20. 'Come home, load bringing.'

21. An early example of horsehair weaving, carried on as a local cottage industry into the eighteenth century. Since the hairs were different lengths, they could not be set up on a loom but were woven across a linen warp. Their gloss, resilience and strength made the fabric popular for carriage and seat covers.

22. Ploughing with oxen, using a turn-wrest plough, on the Sussex Downs in the early twentieth century.

23. A Kentish plough, used only in East Kent, for loosening stubble after harvest. The broad share is different from the ordinary ploughshare shape.

21

20

22

23

24. *Harrowing and broadcast sowing.*

25. *Setting a scythe. The cutter measures from the first furrel (behind the nape) to the point (at his thumb).*

26. *A hovel.*

27. *A loaded haywain, sixteenth century.*

28. *'Tom Grouthead' catching a nap at noon.*

29. Upright barley makes a field golden brown; when the head is bent, the light lies along its beard and the whole field turns silver gold.

30. One of the oldest farm calculations was to estimate the yield by counting the grains in an average ear; one grain sown produces one ear, so the number of grains to the ear multiplied by the number of sacks of seed-corn sown should approximate the whole crop.

31. Winnowing fans were made of woven willow. The threshed grain was thrown against the wind so that the light chaff would be blown away and the clean grain caught, or the grain could be stirred as it lay on the ground and the fan flapped over it. These workers may have been selecting seed corn.

32. The shape of the winnowing fan has remained unchanged for centuries.

33. 'Thresh seed and to fanning': the corn is here being threshed by flails.

34. Flailing is still used sometimes for specially saved fine seed.

35. Thatch can be made of reed or straw and used to cover both permanent buildings and stacks which would stand for less than a year. This well-filled stackyard is near Dunmow in Essex.

36. The 63-year-old thatcher puts the finishing touches to a barn pinnacle; it is a skilled job and one in which the craftsman takes justifiable pride.

37

37. *Willow had many purposes; here it becomes a 'kiddle' for fish.*

38. *Willow was also used to make this beehive chair.*

39. *This sixteenth-century illustration shows not only the gardener and his neat beds but a host of other interesting activities in the background.*

38

39

40. Cutting a millwheel was a skilled job for a craftsman.

41. Millwheels had to be cut with special tools so that the sharp edges that cut the corn and the shallow grooves that carried the flour would work efficiently.

42. Taking up and replacing the kingpin of a millwheel was an event which probably happened no more than once in a century.

43. 'Let workman at night bring home wood or a log, let none come home empty save slut and thy dog.'

44

45

44. *Carrying home the firewood in a previous century.*

45. *An Essex hurdle-maker splitting ash hurdle poles with a reeving iron.*

46. *The saw-pit: note that it took two men to saw a trunk into planks. Laborious to produce, sawn timber was expensive.*

46

47. The Clach Eiteag, Gaelic for 'white quartzstone', now stands in the center of the village of Ardgay, in Eastern Ross. The inscription on the plaque reads: 'This stone is said to have been moved from parish to parish in former times, as it marked the site for the local market. By the eighteenth century a fair, the Feill Eiteachan, was regularly held during November, in the parish of Kincardine, for the sale of cattle and farm produce. This plaque is presented in memory of Willie Cooper, for years a devoted councillor and much loved elder of the Parish of Kincardine, October 1971.'

48

48. Women took their own place in medieval trade, riding or walking to market with whatever they had to sell.

49. This method of carrying poultry to market looks uncomfortable for the birds, if convenient for the woman.

50. Coins used in the British Isles: a Plantagenet silver penny of Edward III (1327–77); and the reverse and obverse of a Lancastrian silver groat of Henry VI (ca. 1422–7), showing the cross along which it could be divided into four pennies.

49

50

51

51. *A river boat of the eleventh century; note the cross-handled oar.*

52. *A similar boat in use in 1935.*

53. *'Merrily sang the monks of Ely, When Canute the king rowed by, "Row nearer the land, row closer in, That we may hear the monks sing."'*

52

53

54

55

54. The hoy, a sea-going boat which traded from the east coast as far as the Baltic ports, probably carried pilgrims across the Channel. Under Henry VIII the hoys were armed, and may later have helped defeat the Armada.

55. The Humber keel, a river boat, could be moored fore and aft for cargo-lading; leeboards lowered when sailing across or into a wind, to reduce leeway.

56. The Thames barge was very useful because its flat bottom allowed cargo transport across shallow water, drying out at quays and loading from horse and cart. Masts lowered for up-river travel, and the crew was small—a man and a boy.

57. The Norfolk wherry was mainly used on rivers between Lowestoft and Norwich and Yarmouth; simple gear, with no shrouds, meant that the mast lowered easily for going under bridges.

57

56

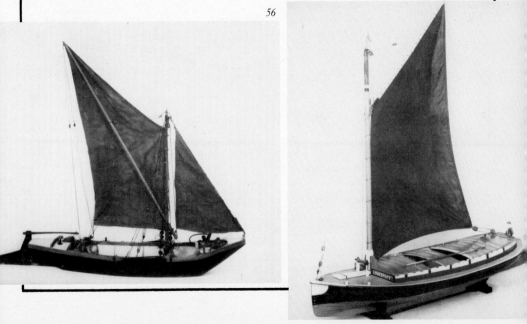

58. *Into such a hidden corner as this one in Wasdale, a strong and healthy mercenary, now bloody and concussed, might have blindly staggered seeking water. He has stumbled to the sunken ditch, rolled down, and passed out; after dark a camp follower, pillaging, finds his dazed 'corpse'. Following the stream they struggle up and away into the hills, travelling by night, sleeping by day, starving on stolen food. Up and on they go, until the stream passes a thicket at the end of the tree-line, where they dare to rest. They have wood for fire, water, and undisturbed birds and hares to snare; small fish, berries and roots for further food. With winter they roll up a few boulders from the stream to strengthen the hut they have made with wood, wattle, and mud. In time, and with the feeling of some security, they clear a little ground behind the hut—all hard manual labour then—and sow it with begged or stolen corn. It is roughly sown, but new ground gives a good yield; the years pass—there is perhaps a son, real fields and a plough.*

If any solitary wanderers read these notes, let them look where they are going, and perhaps trace other and earlier walkers, fellow escapists like themselves.

'NO TEMPEST, GOOD JULY'

HAY

THE ANIMALS were turned off the meadows in March: a few might be left on the marsh meadows till Easter, but no longer, for the grass had to be given time to grow. In June the most forward meadows were mowed, but 'only as much as may be well overcome' – that is, only as much as could be dried and carried, not left lying cut on the field. (The value of hay is shown by the instruction to cut any grass on headlands, and collect stray patches from woodlands.) July must see haymaking completed.

The field work for hay was systematic. The first day's 'cut' is left lying in swathes, which are then turned over, usually by women workers: this 'tossing' loosens heavy swathes and allows complete drying. The hay between swathe lines is then raked and left in small dollops alternately spaced down the field. The space between each row was the width of the haywain of the time. The swathes are then lifted and cocks made skilfully to ensure good ventilation, the hay slanting down and outwards to shed off dew and rain. The last forkful of hay is laid across the top, like a thatch. The size of the cocks at any one time varies with the weight of the crop and local custom.

Haymakers start work as soon as the sun has dried off the dew, and carry on until the evening dew falls. They do not go home to dinner but 'keep field in the heat'. It was the custom to allow an hour's rest and sleep at mid-day.

> From May to mid August, an hour or two,
> let Patch sleep a snatch, howsoever you do:
> Though sleeping one hour refresheth his song,
> yet trust not Hob Grouthead, for sleeping too long.

The wallets and bottles provided for field workers contained their food
and drink – barley-water, mead, light ale, or herb brews were usual, and
bread and cheese and onions in the wallet. Scythes were used to mow, and a
tub of sand and a pot of oil for the scythe hones would also be taken to the
field. The hones were dipped in the oil and then in the sand and used to
sharpen the scythes.

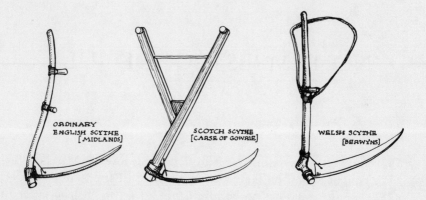

Scythes varied in every locality; old workmen usually made their own
shafts. This shows three typical types.

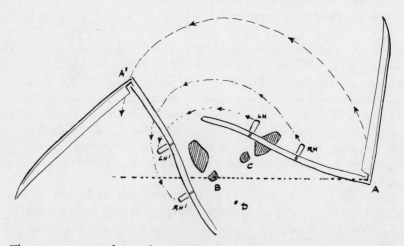

The reaper moves forward, swinging the scythe from right to left in an
almost semicircular motion; at the end of the swing the centre moves from
the left heel (B), and the scythe is drawn closer to the operator. The blade is
kept horizontal to the ground; and tendency to lift the blade is compensated
for by leaning the body forward toward the end of the stroke. The mowed
grass forms a neat swathe at the left-hand side of an experienced reaper.

The haywain was loaded as the wain passed across the field, the workers using the rake and the 'short pitchfork and the long' (the latter six or eight feet) to lift the hay to the top of the wain. (The later the period the larger the load.)

Haystacks

Hay has to be cut while still full of 'growth' – that is nourishing sap – but must be harvested dry, as damp hay close-packed heats until it takes fire. The danger of damp and heating made small stacks better than one large stack, and from illustrations in manuscripts it seems that small round stacks, after the later Scottish fashion, were favoured. Today, if a stack is 'cut' and left, it is easy to throw a waterproof tarpaulin over it. Mediaeval people did not have tarpaulins – near the coast they might perhaps borrow a ship's canvas sail, but it was simpler to make small stacks which could each be used all at once.

A stack of hay always had some foundation; it could be built upon a level flooring of stones, covered with a deep layer of still-green bracken, which does not seem to have 'risen damp' to the hay. (This quality of bracken to keep dry is an unexplained phenomenon well known to tramps.) The reasons for this bracken foundation were that through it the air could pass easily (it does not pack close like hay), and that it raised the valuable hay

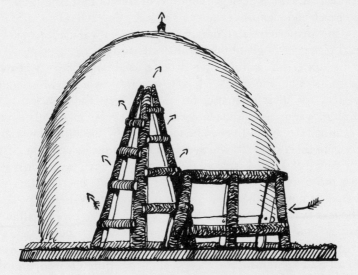

A stack centre, or fause hause. Burns refers to this in the lines 'loud skirlet a' the lassies; But her top puckle was nigh lost while kittling in the fause hause'.

several feet off the damp ground and was rat-proof – rats will not gnaw through bracken, for it, like horse tail, makes their mouths sore.)

In the wet north, stacks had wooden ventilators built into them. This 'stack centre', or 'fause hause', designed to let air into the stack centres, may also have been used in East Anglia (as French influence was felt in both regions), but we can find no proof of this. The predominance of hollow, round, straw-like grasses in mediaeval hay may have helped it to dry more thoroughly than the ribbon types now grown would do under the same circumstances.

FLAX AND HEMP

Good flax and good hemp, to have of her own,
in May a good huswife will see it be sown;
And afterwards trim it, to serve at a need,
the fimble to spin, and the karl for her seed.

Flax

Linum usitatissimum is the common flax, though there are other flax plants found wild in England. Some botanists believe *usitatissimum* to have been introduced by the Romans, others consider it native. The name means 'most used' and it has been grown for centuries in East Anglia and is found near French and Flemish settlements all over England. (The main industry is now in Northern Ireland, though some attempt was made to grow flax in several places in England during the last war.)

In the sixteenth century laws were passed enforcing its growth, the proportion being one rood of flax to every sixty acres. Most households grew flax for their own use, for sheets, shirts and smocks, and much linen cloth was used to drape tables and altars: good linen will not wear out in a century! (Its durability can be testified to by the author, who owned a home-spun sheet of 1680, which even survived the evacuation crisis and a steam laundry! Time has rendered it soft, but even now when wet it is almost too heavy to lift: when new it must have been as intractable as canvas. It is now in the Reading Rural Industries Museum.)

The flax was gathered, and the stems either set to rot in shallow water, or laid out, and water thrown over them. The latter process made a whiter flax than the steeped which became yellowish from the rotting vegetation. The stems were then beaten, the fibre cleared, and the flax 'heckled' or 'hackled' (combed) into long silky strands. These strands shone with a smooth lustre, so that it was said of a maiden's hair 'it was as smooth and fine as hackled flax'. The strands were then spun and woven.

In the mediaeval household linen was 'bucked'. That is, the linen was packed into deep barrels, with bent sticks between the folds, and a strong lye, variously made of wood ash, urine, rainwater and so on, was poured through from the top. After repeated soakings, the linen was taken out, beaten and repacked, then fresh water run through. This process was called 'leying bucks', that is, 'passing the ley through the buck'. The linen was then spread out to dry and bleach. With household linen the natural bleaching of sunlight gradually turned the sheets from cream to snow-white. For trade purposes lime was sometimes used for the bleaching.

The linen (flax) seeds, when pounded and mixed with boiling water, made the comforting 'linseed poultice' which old people will remember. The seeds, boiled, made a warm, thick, milky drink for feeding calves, which was probably one of the early 'edible oils'; though it was not until later that the oil from the seeds was combined with the dry refuse of the peat moss that had been used for packing heavy stoneware, thus beginning the useful and lucrative 'oilcake' industry.

Hemp

Fatal Hemp, which Denmark doth afford,
Doth furnish us with canvas and with cord.
Cables and sails – that winds assisting; either
We may acquaint the East and West together.

Sylvester, 1520

This refers to the import of cordage, and so on, of which Henry VIII's Navy was in short supply: a single sailing ship could use up some miles of cordage. On land, twisted straw rope secured stacks, packed carts, made beds (truckle beds), chairs and baskets, and wrapped the legs of labourers against cutting grasses or the cold. But strong hemp rope was required for binding bales for export goods, and often merchant adventurers and traders were better supplied than the Navy.

Hemp for rope was sent to the 'rope walks': many towns still retain this name for some long straight street. Rope spinning was on the whole a town trade, though small cordage for fishermen's own use was probably made locally. One of the last (now obsolete) small jobs was the spinning of Monsil ties – the numerous short strong lengths of cord used to secure the trawl nets.

HARVESTING AND DRESSING

For the harvesting and dressing of the flax and hemp crops we quote the instructions from Stephens's *Book of the Farm* (1844). Though centuries later, the old process remained completely unchanged, so the description is exact. The iron instrument Stephens described continues unaltered in willow stripping today.

Flax

When ripe, the flax should be *pulled* in this way: I use the Dutch method, by catching a few stems of the flax at a time close below the bolls, which allows the shortest of the flax to escape. With the next handful the puller draws the short flax, and keeps the short and the long each by itself, to be steeped in separate ponds. The sheaves should always be small, equal-sized, straight and even, and should never be put up in stooks or windrows, but taken to the pond the day they are pulled, or the day after at longest, especially in bright weather; for *discoloration produced by the sun on green flax will never be removed till it goes to the bleacher.* On being pulled, the plant is deprived of its bolls or seed-capsules by rippling, which consists of drawing the stems of the plant through the teeth of an iron comb 8 inches in length, set upright upon a form, across which two men sit opposite each other, and ripple their handfuls alternately, the bolls falling on a barn-sheet spread under the form. Next comes the *steeping,* a most important process. The object of steeping is to separate the outer fibre of the stem from the interior pith by disintegration. The adhesive substance between the fibre and pith is mucilage, which is the sooner dissolved the sooner the plant is steeped. The Dutch test of being sufficiently watered is certain and perfect. It is this: Try some stalks of average fineness by breaking the woody part in 2 places, about 3 inches apart, at the middle of the length; catch the wood at the lower end, and if it will pull downward freely for those 3 inches, without breaking or tearing the fibre, it is ready to be taken out. Spread the flax on the same day it is taken out, unless it happens to be heavy rain, but in any case spread the next day, for it will heat in the pile, and that heating will be destructive. Flax should be *spread even,* straight at its length, not too thick, and well shaken, so that there shall be no clots; indeed, if possible, no two stalks should adhere. Lifting, like all other operations, requires care to keep the flax straight in its length. This operation is too frequently hurried and coarsely done. If the steeping and grassing have been perfect, flax should require no fire, exposure to the sun should be sufficient; but if the weather be damp, the flax tough, then it must be fire-dried. All who can afford it should keep such flax over to the ensuing spring or summer, putting it dry into stacks, when it will work freely without fire-heat.

Hemp

The hemp, having the sexes on different plants, the entire crop comes to maturity at different times. Harvest the male plants first, they are easily known by bearing no seed. The crop is reaped by pulling up by the roots like flax; and care should be exercised not to break the stem when taking a hold of the plant near the root. When pulled, the stems should be made up in small handfuls, with the roots placed together, and tied in bundles at 3 places, 1 near each end and 1 in the middle. The bundles should be carried to the watering-pool as soon as practicable. A putrefaction ensues in the course of a few days, according to the state of the atmosphere, which has the effect of separating the fibre from the stem. About 3 weeks will be required to effect this separation entirely. As taken out of the water, the bundles should be set up against each other, to drip the water from them. Three weeks, and even 5, according to the state of the weather, will be required to make the hemp completely dry, after which it ought to be again tied into bundles, and built in a stack and thatched, ready to be sold. By the time the male plants are taken out of the pool, the female ones may be ready to be pulled. The process of pulling and bundling is the same as the male plant, with the difference that the tops are kept on the female plants, that the seed may be rippled out before the stems are ultimately bound up for the watering-pool. A first-rate man-of-war was said to require 80 tons of rough hemp to supply her with necessary tackle. Taking 40 stones on 1 acre imperial as a good crop, 4 acres are required to raise 1 ton; so that a man-of-war requires 1 year's produce of 320 acres of hemp for an outfit of cordage. Low-priced hempen cloths are a general wear for husbandmen, servants, and labouring manufacturers; the better sorts for working farmers and tradesmen in the country; and the finer sorts are preferred by gentlemen for their strength and warmth.

We have checked these 1844 directions with earlier usage, and the methods are unchanged, thus giving example of the continuity *enforced* by the materials of the land itself.

BEES

Tusser's instructions on bee-keeping are scattered through the year; a summer month, we feel, is a convenient place to bring them all together:

May
Take heed to thy bees, that are ready to swarm,
the loss thereof now, is a crown's worth of harm;
Let skilfull be ready, and diligence seene,
lest being too careless, thou losest thy beene.

September
Now burn up the bees, that ye mind for to drive,
at Midsummer drive them, and save them alive;
Place hive in good aier, set southly and warm,
and take in good season, wax, honey and swarm.

Set hive on a plank, not too low by the ground,
where herb with the flowers may compass it round;
And boards to defend it from north and north-east,
from showers and rubbish, from vermin and beast.

December
Go look to thy bees, if the hive be too light,
set water and honey, with rosemary dight;
Which set in a dish full of sticks in the hive
from danger of famine ye save them alive.

Bartholomaeus Anglicus, writing three hundred years or so before Tusser, had a view that was constant in mediaeval tradition and perhaps has not entirely disappeared:

> And in Springnye tyme they go out – for it belongeth bees to work and to travaile and none of them have leave to be idle . . . and first they make their houses and cells and children and [then] make honey thereafter and bringeth it together.

Bee-keeping was essential for many reasons. Today we think of it chiefly as producing table honey, a treat rather than a basic item of diet; but before sugarcane and slavery cheapened sugar, honey was the only easily obtained sweetening agent in general use; England produced so much she could export it. There were Honey Fairs in autumn, and bee-keepers sold wax, by weight, to city chandlers and to metal workers (the price falls after the Reformation), and the by-products of the apiary were important in many industries.

Most people kept some bees, but some kept apiaries as a main business, for the bee master was a specialised expert who understood the job, and studied 'trade requirements'. In a household, honey was used for curing hams, for preserving fruit, and in cooking many dishes (where today we use sugar). (In curing hams, the dense honey, by osmosis, extracted the lymph and allowed the salt to penetrate more swiftly. In hot weather this was an advantage; in winter, when the main salting of meat was done, the honey would be an ingredient of the liquid immersion pickles.) It was an unguent and vehicle for the pharmacy of the period, and the washing-out of the combs was the basis of mead. The propolis was a good strong dye.

The Classical Bee

> Thy Lord spake by inspiration unto the bee, saying provide thee houses in the mountains, and in the trees, and of those materials wherewith men build hives for thee. Then eat of every kind of fruit, and fly in the beaten paths of thy Lord . . .
>
> from the Koran

> Hony hyght mell, is from the air . . . and the more white and the more sweete and more pure and wyth good smell the better it is.
>
> Bartholomaeus Anglicus (*fl.*1230–50)

The direct flight of the bees (the 'beeline') through the trackless air, to and from their hives, has intrigued every generation, and honey has been used as medicine since time immemorial. The classical bee was to be found in literature all through the mediaeval period. (There was a distinction between those who studied the Classics, and those who studied the Bee.) Many classical writers had enlarged on bees: Columella, in the first century AD, reissues much of the earlier classical instruction: 'I come now to the management of Bee Hives, about which no instruction can be given with greater care than in the words of Hyginus, more ornately than by Virgil, or more elegantly than by Celsus . . .' Columella also mentions – and questions – the story of 'the beautiful Melirca' whom Jupiter changed into a bee. Virgil says that bees 'feed the King of Heaven'. Aristotle describes other bees – 'some large and globular and black and hairy, some smaller round and dusky coloured, some even smaller, nevertheless fat and broad, and some slender with pointed bodies.' Virgil most approves of the bees 'burning with gold, their bodies slatted with [stripes]? of equal size' – this may have been the Italian bee. They are 'calm in disposition', but the 'irascibility of the larger fierce bee is easily soothed by the frequent intervention of those who look after them.' All agree that 'inferior bees should not be mixed with those of high quality'. We find a description of the 'King' cell and of its singularity from the other cells: one 'expert' makes belief that 'He' is not born of a worm as are the common folk (this was written after the restoration of a monarchy made this a diplomatic point!). 'Drones may fertilize the common bee when these are turned out in Autumn' – none of this was believed by the bee master: he 'kept bees' and 'his bees kept him.'

It is typical of the later Elizabethan period that scientific minds dare to question classical dogma. The classical (and biblical) belief that bees could be generated from a dead ox – or dead lion – was not unreasonable. Those who saw swarming white maggots (looking very like the white pupae of bees) on the carcass, and observed swarms of flies and insects arising from it, knew that such metamorphosis was possible, since caterpillars became butterflies. Life was accepted as a rising process (minerals into plants, plants into seeds and seeds into insects, so as late as the seventeenth century, seeds of lavender in woollen cloth were mistaken for the larvae of the emerging clothes moths – the fact being used to demonstrate the truth of the Resurrection. The belief that hatched-out insects might emerge through the ox horns was substantiated by the structure in the interior of a horn, which is a white, brittle honeycomb of bone. Today, few people ever see the decayed carcass of an ox, and even fewer are likely to study the interior of a dried and broken horn, but in the days when these theories were held so cheerfully, both could be common country sights.

Palladius in the fourth century advises wooden or woven hives: 'Take

felures eke, or supple twiges take Ye may; but potters hives forsake.' And
Early Saxon manuscripts show hives constructed of wicker work,
plastered (exactly as their own wattle and daub houses were built). The
insides were made attractive with honey, and sweet herbs, and sticks set
across for the naturally pendant combs. Palladius tells us that hives should
be set somewhat apart, in a vale out of wind, and in the sun; shallow water
should be provided, and he adds: 'in a cold spring give the bees honey boiled
with rosemary in little wooden troughs'.

> Their hives thou set a little space asunder
> There enter, turn thou fair upon the South,
> No larger than a bee may tread thereunder
> Wicketts two or three thou make there southe
> that, if a wicket worm one hole's mouth
> Beseige or stoppe, another open be,
> And from the wicket worm – thus save the bee.
>
> To buy the bee, behold them rich and full
> To prove them by their murmured magnitude
> Or see the swarm; and carry them, if thou will
> By night, upon thy back. Then safe enclose.
> But – bring them not too far out of their air
> For change of air may put them in despaire.
>   translated from Columella

This next instruction on how to catch your bee would be reasonable to any
peasant dwelling in still afforested England: 'To find bees, watch shallow
waters where they come to drink, if they come in great numbers it's a good
bee district, mark some of the bees, and note how long they are away,
follow those that dwell nearest.'

Another dodge was to 'trap some bees in a hollow stalk of rush and,
enclosing the end with the thumb, release the bees one at a time, to follow
as they fly.' If the swarm is found in a tree, smoke the entrance and saw off
the tree above the swarm, covering it in with a wet clay cloth; then: 'saw
below the tree, and *swiftly* carry it away.' (The instruction to be quick
seems superfluous!)

The centuries-old fallacy that the bee community was 'ruled by a king'
caused wildly inaccurate speculation about breeding, and the difficulty of
observing bees working in a dark hive lasted till clear sheet glass made it
possible to observe the flat surface of a comb directly, rather than just
looking from the end. The subject is an intriguing study of traditional
beliefs holding out for centuries; perhaps because the bee masters were
usually unlettered and so did not leave their knowledge and the results of
their close observation to us.

The old bee masters could hear the faint sounds inside the hive, they could hear the noise of a battle, the killing and driving out of drones, and the chirping sound of a hungry queen. Today the microphone attached to the hive can foretell a probable swarm by the rising and falling cries of a hungry queen, clambering over the combs, pleading for the workers to feed her (who are, of purpose, starving her heavy body so that she will be able to fly out with the swarm). These are facts obtained by our modern discoveries; the old bee masters only guessed about them.

The Bee Domestic

The small native bees were black and hardy and, according to district and climate, made their hives in warm hollow trees or in sheltered sunwarmed crannies in rocks. The different breeds of bees in different localities were noted by bee masters, for 'most hives should not be trusted more than five years – unless it be some special sort of bees, which always keep themselves in heart – these bees may be kept for nine or ten years'. Today, bees are taken to orchards or heather moors for special crops. We believe of old they were frequently moved from one district to another by early experimenters. (Instructions for packing bees for transport by horse, cart, or later, railway, confirm this.)

More than most products, those of the bee proved the efficiency of the practical man: the erudite produced the theories; the unlettered labourer produced the honey. Honey was an important part of mediaeval life and its production was vital for every estate. Simple folk kept bees, collecting stocks from the wild, undertaking their management, and building colonies with hives of their own making. They may have used the honey to pay their feudal dues, but they also ran the industry, making honey and attending honey markets with apparent independence.

Much of our present knowledge of bees comes through observation hives, and the use of microscope and microphone; the old bee masters were taught by the bees (if they pleased their bees, they got honey; if not, they got stung). It is easier to explain this 'teaching method' by describing one simple process: we select that of 'taking a swarm and putting it to work'.

For the layman, who has never seen a swarm, this is worth describing. When the original home (old hole, or modern hive) becomes crowded, the bees issue out in a mass, and swarm in a warm, vibrating cluster around their queen. In this condition (as the bee master learnt by experience) they seldom sting: each individual bee, knowing it is about to travel, very sensibly packs its bags (literally, its honey bags) and these, bulging behind, make it difficult to 'work' the sting. The mass of bees then hangs (on a branch, say) waiting till the scout bees tell them where to go (very like a

mass of passengers hung up at the airport). Sometimes they move off
swiftly; sometimes they wait for hours. The bee master noted that they did
not move in rain or thunder; so *he* learnt to sprinkle water, or beat pans, to
delay them, while he got the new hive ready. (He also learnt to scent the
new hive with herbs the bees loved, and later to put down what we still call
a 'swarm sheet' directly in front of the hive entrance, and to lift the bees
down on to this.)

Meanwhile, the scout bees have been scouting round and creeping into
the new hive and darting back to report. Presently the cluster of bees stirs a
little (as does a human crowd when still uncertain), and then, when assured
the new home is desirable, the entire mass proceeds towards the entrance,
carefully inducing the queen and her court to enter first. Once the queen
has gone in, instantly, like a swift brown stream, all the bees follow!
Stragglers are rounded up in one purposeful drive; the new hive is taken
over, and at once hive routine is established. Cleaner bees penetrate every
corner so that there is no scrap of dirt left; the door keepers, and fanners
who arrange the ventilation, staff the entrance; and within, the queen and
her attendants arrange the brood chamber, and workers begin building the
wax comb.

The great change that has taken place in modern bee-keeping concerns
this wax comb: its making requires heat and time, and honey cannot be
stored till wax cells are constructed to contain it. In mediaeval times, when
the wax was almost as valued as the honey, and methods were different,
fresh comb was made by the bees each season. Nowadays, with the modern
hive, a ready-made foundation of wax is supplied, so exactly like their own
that the bees accept it and, after a cursory inspection, start to fill it straight
away. Once the comb is filled, the bees seal it and the bee master lifts out
the complete comb, cuts off the sealing cap, extracts the honey, and puts
the empty comb back again for the bees to refill ... which they do
cheerfully, and far more swiftly than if they had to begin building their
comb all over again. Thus some combs are used over again for years, till
repeated use and misshapen cells make it more economic to provide fresh.

The mediaeval bee had to make comb fresh every year, and the demand
for the wax accounts for the older brutal 'burning up the bees' at the end of
the honey harvest (and the present high price of rare bees-wax.)

One Samuel Cooke, in his *Compleat Bee Master* writes: 'Hives should be
placed facing South and East'. For large apiaries he recommends an overall
shelter, but small units are better *for the bees*. Cooke's hives or 'skeps' were
of plaited straw (skeps are used today for taking a swarm) and they stood,
and still stand, two and a half feet from the ground – as bees prefer.

Many flower gardens had shelters built into the enclosing walls to
accommodate hives (for the pleasure of hearing the sleepy drone of the
bees in a hot summer, as well as for the good of the flowers and fruit).

During the mediaeval summers, whole combs of honey could be scooped out of the hives at intervals (trusting to the bees having time to build more comb and fill it). At the end of the season, though, the early method was to kill the bees, and take out the entire honey crop, leaving only the few hives they intended to 'save alive'. This complete destruction of bees does not seem to have been general usage, for old instructions for joining small colonies under a weak 'king' to larger ones indicate careful preservation of 'tame' breeds. Without definite proof, we guess that it was only the old, unproductive colonies that were destroyed, for we have found early evidence of care in 'winter housing', and the definite statement 'that some colonies will live on for ten years'.

The shelter for a straw hive, as found in old cottage walls. These were sometimes built to take several hives in orchard or flower garden.

Deciding which hives to keep over the winter shows the close observation of the old workman. 'Stocks that do not carry out their dross (dirt) or drive out their drones in good time' are probably weak and not worth keeping, also those depleted by several swarms. The best to keep are two- or three-year-old stocks, whose hives are heavy with stored honey. In March, if necessary feed these hives with extra honey and encourage them with 'toasts of bread soaked in good strong ale, whereof they will not leave a crumb'.

Honey and Beeswax

Honey was sometimes sold loose, in the comb, but in commercial practice the comb was usually broken into deep linen sacks and hung up to drip: these drips were the best honey. The sack was then beaten and hung before the fire, when the warm honey ran out more freely: this was of slightly lower quality. The third quality of honey was produced after the sack had been pressed (under the cheese press, probably). In some places the honey was finally strained through straw, as Devon cider used to be. (This straw, pressed into bundles while warm, made excellent fire-lighters and bee smokes for clearing out hives next summer.) The empty honey-soaked comb was then put into a water bath, and the temperature raised till the wax melted and floated up. This wax 'set' solid (the dross on the under-side being scraped off, as housewives do when clarifying dripping), and it was then broken up, remelted, and poured out into moulds, according to local market usage. The old method of bee-keeping, of course, produced more wax than today's methods (see pp. 162-3).

Wax was needed to harden the mixture for candles, and melted into cloth it was used where today we should use greaseproof paper. If the cloth was wrapped around an object while it was soft and warm, it set into an airtight casing, so it was used to cover and preserve stores from damp, and for sealing bottles and jars. The serecloth of death seems to have been occasionally used when transporting corpses.

Wax was also used for furniture polishing, mould making, and for metal castings. It has a high melting temperature (bee masters soon learnt that the bees had to be very warm to make wax), so wax was used as a lubricant where friction caused heat. Sailors, tailors, leather workers – all used waxed thread. Eggs were preserved by being coated with melted wax, and unwashed beeswax was probably the earliest form of chewing-gum.

Mead

The earliest recipes for mead give no special ferment, so mycologists believe that, as the hives were made of rye straw, spores from some fungus were responsible for the original ferment, which would then develop and persist in the wooden tubs used for working the mead. By the fifteenth century there were as many forms of mead as there are of ale and beer today. There was the light mead, slightly acid, used for harvest workers; the ordinary types of table mead; the special strong meads made with pure honey; and fine metheglins flavoured with herbs and spices.

There is a kind of swish-swash, made also in Essex and dyvers other places, with honey and water which the country wives, putting some pepper and a little spice among, call Meade. Very good in myne opinion for such as love to live loose bodied – otherwise it differeth from the true Meade as chalk from cheese.

Truly, it is nothing else but the washings of the combes, when the honey is wrung out. One of the best things belonging thereto is that they spend little labour and less cost in making the same.

Description of England, William Harrison (1534–1593)

Bee Hives

According to records and manuscript drawings, the early British beekeeper used very small hives. They appear so small that today we should consider them suitable for a nucleus only – this probably accounted for the continuous swarming. Structurally they seem to have been round willow baskets, woven up from the open circle of the base, the rods being pulled inwards in the weaving to be gathered together at the top. (This conjectural construction is suggested by the basketwork calf muzzles that used to be so woven in rural areas.) These early hives were given their bee- and weather-proof finish by wool and moss packing, and clay daub (exactly like the wattle and daub construction of their bee master's own hut).

Throughout the centuries mankind – with the exception of those who built in stone – housed his bees much as he housed himself. (Though wild bees hived in caves, they do not take kindly to cold stone.) But mankind's thatch, in the form of straw or reed, made warm lightweight bee hives which were used for centuries. When it was believed that different colonies of bees used the same hive, hives were made with several entrances, but as bees hate a draught they stopped the doors they did not want. The great change in bee-keeping came when man learnt to take the honey without killing the bees. Thus a strain of bees could be kept more easily; and just as the bees educated their keeper, the keeper educated the bees: training them to make surplus honey and to store it correctly where it was wanted – in neatly finished sections. The microscope and glass inspection hive have made accurately known much that the old inarticulate bee men knew only with an instinctive understanding. This affinity between races of men and their bees was found by the Romans; they brought their Italian bees with them as part of their equipment, but employed native British bee-keepers, who then employed native bees, *who understood the British climate.*

It was change of locality rather than change of period that housed the bees in hives of straw plait in lieu of willow. The Anglo-Saxon of the reed-growing districts, and later of the corn-growing districts, made thick coiled and bound straw baskets and containers (these are still made). It was their native material, so that the round straw skep developed because of the availability of this material, rather than as a planned change of design. In the Welsh mountains the straw skep was long used for the heavy heather honey.

The circle of small round holes shown in some early manuscripts may have been derived from the structural gaps in the base of the woven hives, but it is certain that the low slit door was soon found to be much better – the round hole suggests mouse in every century!

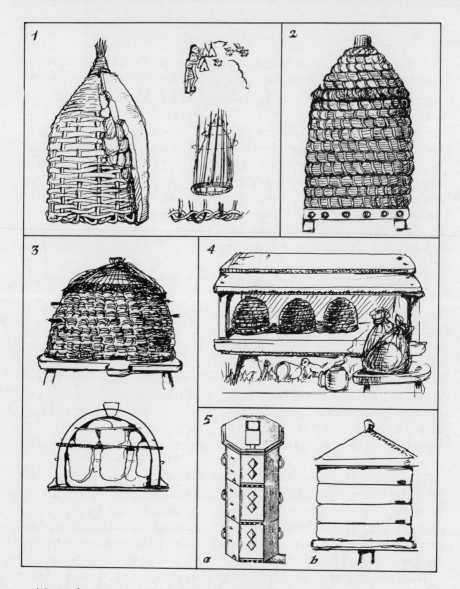

(1) Anglo-Saxon wattle and daub hives, each with only one door.

(2) Early straw hive set on wood base. There were several doors for it was believed that colonies mixed in one hive.

(3) Common straw hive, with one door. The diagram shows the rods provided for pendant combs (but the bees frequently built on to the straw walls).

(4) Straw hives grouped under shelter. One is shown sheeted, wrapped for removal.

(5) Victorian experiments. (a) Glass windows in inspection hive for study and (b) multiple door hive set up on a pole – to increase the flight range? (What the Victorian bee put up with in the architectural hive only the bee knows!)

With the coiled construction, it was easier to make a removable top than with the willow construction. (To be able to remove the lid and lift the combs would seem to have been an early development). Some instructions to loosen the end of the sticks upon which the combs hang suggest this, but it was at a much later date that the hive became an independent outer case, around removable frames. With the removable frames began the attempts to preserve the wax comb intact by draining out the honey or swinging it out by centrifugal force. Much later, the modern making of foundation comb brings us into present day bee-keeping.

These straw and wattle hives are considered the most usual, but the Hundred Years' War brought over mercenaries from many other nations who had been left stranded here. These 'escapists', as we have called them, were as likely to collect and house our native wild bees in their own way, as to collect and prepare the British plants and fungus and animals in their own native manner, and this may account for occasional unexpected drawings of wood and pottery hives.

Fungus

Furse bals Lycoperdon giganteum Pucke furze & Bulficts which in some places of England they use to Kill and smolder Bees, when they would drive the Hives & bereave the poore Bees of their meate . . .

John Gerard (1545-1612)

When used to smoke bees fungus has an instant and harmless soporific effect. The powder of puff-balls had many ordinary uses. It made a good 'tinder' to carry fire in the tinder box. It was used to staunch blood (as were spiders' webs), and for chilblains. Mediaeval surgeons used it on septic wounds, believing it encouraged the pouring out of pus, thus cleaning the wounds 'from the bottom upwards'; for they saw that if a wound healed over on top while it still contained dirt and injured tissue, there would be trouble later.

There were probably fewer of the *campestris* (field type) than of the woodland, for there were fewer fields and more woodlands.

The different peoples who settled in England were used to their own countries' fungi, and stuck to their own judgement of which were edible or poisonous. (In districts where French surnames Catell, Lacy, Voce or Voiser denote an early influx of French lace makers or refugees the Boletus (crepe) and the Bluets fetch a higher price than the field or cultivated mushroom; and rare pockets of Dutch and Scandinavian tradition use fungus their district now mistrusts.) In the hunting counties around Leicestershire and Nottingham the bulky horse mushroom is well used, but not considered as good as the more delicate pink-gilled *campestris*. In a few places the caps of the fairy ring mushroom are dried and used (often as powdered dust) and almost any type of field mushroom is considered 'safe' in ketchup! The Romans (like other settlers) brought their own ideas, for in Rome many types of fungus were considered delicacies (Claudius is reputed to have died by fungus poison) though the field mushroom seems to have been condemned by law. The reason may have been that in shape and size it resembles the poisonous death cap (*Amanita phalloides*) or the *A. Virosa* or *A. mappa* – all of which have white gills and grow in the same localities. The action of the poison is swift and painful and completely incurable, so this makes the edict against the innocent *campestris* comprehensible.

There is evidence of the popularity of the mediaeval mushroom or 'pernolle' in recipes for Kings' banquets in cities and in their value as rents (see also p. 29).

The deathcap fungus

On the Continent fungus markets still exist, and country people would sell mushrooms in local markets in the same way as they are now sold on the continent. Another smaller, sinister trade would be in drugs and poisons to the medical, magical, and mystical dealers; evidence for this extends well into later centuries. (Shakespeare's heroes and villains often pop out to pick up potions and poisons.)

Children will always sample berries or anything looking edible, and some of the small scarlet fungi growing among fallen leaves (example *Peziza aurantia*) might be nibbled with impunity; but others produced sleep, strange dreams, or delirium, and being identified (by penitents and parents) would be studied and their curious effects put to use by the country people, much in the same way as women studied and experimented with yeasts to improve their brewing. It is likely that some mysterious mediaeval 'plagues' may have been caused by unidentified fungi.

We now know that the mediaeval mystery of St Antony's fire was caused by eating corn infected by the fungus ergot, but for centuries the disease, which was classed as a form of plague, was supposed to have a supernatural origin (the burning pain was certainly a foretaste of hell fires)

The stinkhorn fungus: so named for obvious reasons

and the relics of St Antony (kept in a French church) were considered palliative. The plagues were rife on the Continent, but do not seem to have reached England till the end of the eleventh century. Ergot – the black blight – mainly affected rye; it could affect wheat but 'that loveliest corn men ete' was seldom used by labourers. They grew a fair amount of rye, as rye straw was also good for thatching – and cattle who ate diseased rye in their mixed fodder perished.

There were varied forms of 'plague': probably the restricted seasonal diet caused some, by excess of salt or lack of fresh food during the winter. In one type, fingers, arms and legs became numb and rotted off, so many cases may have been claimed as leprosy. In 1582 Lonicer recognised that disease was caused by this 'black blight' on the rye. As ergot's first discoverer, he states that the unlettered midwives had (apparently for centuries past) observed the strong muscular contractions caused by eating blighted rye, and so had been using this same black blight powder to induce the contractions in delayed, or difficult childbirth – and, probably, to cause a miscarriage when convenient.

A fungus that might have been specially sold to craftsmen, barbers or instrument-makers might be *Polyporus betulinus*, which grows on birch trees, sometimes in great quantities. It is wide, firm and white, standing out from the trunk like a dryad's saddle. It has been known by generations

of country wood-carvers as a sharpener. It would put a fine edge on any
cutting tool if it was laid flat on a work bench, or used loosely as a strop. It
is the sort of gadget that any town worker might be glad to buy. (We can
give no dates but have never found a countryman yet who did not know of
it, and had not learnt of it from his father before him.)

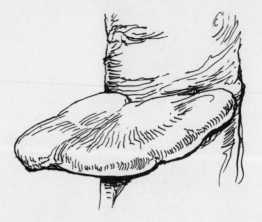

Polyporus, which grows on birch. Another common fungus is Judas ear,
which grows on elder.

> *Elder bush ever be*
> *Always bush and never tree –*
> *Since our Lord was nailed on thee.*

It is now the bane of mushroom growers.

AUGUST

Pare saffron between the two St. Mary's days,
or set, or go shift it, that knoweth the ways.
What year shall I do it, more profit to yield?
the fourth in the garden, the third in the field.

In having but forty foot, workmanly dight,
take saffron enough for a lord and a knight.
All winter time after, as practice doth teach,
what plot have ye better for linen to bleach?

To cart-gap and barn set a guide to look well,
and hoy out, (Sir Carter) the hog fro thy wheel:
Lest greedy of feeding, in following cart,
it noyeth or perisheth, spite of thy heart.

The haulm is the straw of the wheat or the rye,
which once being reaped, they mow by and by,
For fear of destroying, with cattle or rain,
the sooner ye load it, more profit ye gain.

Of barley, the longest and greenest ye find,
leave standing by dallops, till time ye do bind:
Then early in morning, while dew is thereon,
to making of bands, till the dew be all gone.

One spreadeth those bands, so in order to lie,
as barley (in swatches) may fill it thereby:
Which gathered up, with the rake and the hand,
the follower after them, bindeth in band.

No turning of peason, till carriage ye make,
nor turn in no more, than ye mind for to take:
Lest beaten with showers, so turned to dry,
by turning and tossing, they shed as they lie.

Stack pease upon hovell, abroad in the yard,
to cover it quickly let owner regard;
Lest dove and the cadow, there finding a smack,
with ill stormy weather do perish thy stack.

HARVEST

THE GATHERING of a corn harvest shows more difference between ancient and modern usage than hay. Previously there were perhaps fewer varieties of corn, but far more varied 'mixtures'.

Barley, now thought of as 'drink corn', was then used for bread. Rye was grown for bread and also used mixed. Buckwheat, which Tusser called 'brank', made a dark brown, close bread (it was used in New England up to the nineteenth century, and buckwheat cakes and maple syrup became a popular meal). Mixing of vetches and corn as a fodder crop was common.

Barley requires dry, light soil at first, as the first shoot is slender, but if it can be firmed a little later this helps the root formation. Wheat definitely does better on rough land where the clods shelter the first sprouts from the wind, and Tusser's lines are perhaps the most perfect description:

> *Leave little wheat, little clod for to cover the head*
> *that after a frost, it may go out and spread.*
>
> *If clod in thy wheat, will not break with the frost,*
> *if now ye do roll it, it quiteth the cost,*
> *But see when ye roll it, the weather be dry*
> *or else it were better, unrolled to lie.*

Mediaeval straw was left long, and later harvested with its grass and low leaves for use as fodder (stover), but growing long straw wastes the plant's strength before filling out the ear of corn – though the number of grains is already fixed. Just as rich land produces lush grass which must reach up high to reach light, so poor land grows stumpy, dry grass; the length of

straw depends upon both soil and weather conditions, and the value of
stover lies somewhere between straw and corn. To judge land by length of
straw needs the experienced eye which sees a very long blade of corn for a
'brag', i.e. 'promises well'; but it may be that the small ear of the corn that
follows 'holdeth not out'.

Rye straw made the best thatching, and was also used for what we now
call 'beehive' work – that is, a thick, soft basketry that formed excellent
warm chairs and truckle beds, as well as bee skeps and floor mats. In the
fens, reeds and rush were used for the work, but on farms rye straw was
indispensible.

'When barley hangs its head, and the oats begin to shed, and wheat
stands stiff and begins to open' were all signs noticed and understood by the
labourers. The chemistry of the soil was not understood, but the
knowledge of experience was there – for example, it was known that
legumes restore land after corn crops, and that ploughing-in a crop
enriches land that needs humus.

Once cut and stacked, the time crops should be 'left afield' varied. It
used to be thought oats should 'stand under three church bells' (about *two*

Barley or oat stook hooded

weeks) in order for the sun and wind to ripen the last green grains. Barley
was judged by the droop of his bearded head. Wheat was a very special
study, for different kinds of wheat grew on different soils. (Harvesting
peas was a special difficulty, as they shed if shaken, and if they were cut and
left to lie they started to sprout if it rained. The damp, green haulm made
them difficult to store, so it was usual to stack them out in the field, well
covered against pigeons and crows – perhaps in a hovel.)

REAPING

It is not easy to *describe* the best mode of cutting corn with the smooth-edged sickle. The body is brought low by resting on the right leg doubled under the body, while the left is stretched out to act as a stay and a balance to the whole fame. The right arm is then stretched amongst the corn, and in drawing it toward you, near to and parallel with the ground, the corn is cut, and held up with the left hand against the standing corn. A creeping advance is slowly made by the body towards the left, which brings it to rest equally on both legs, while successive cuts are made with the sickle; and the additional corn thus acquired is still gathered and supported by the left hand against the standing corn. Proceeding in cuts with the stretch of the arm, the body comes to rest on the left leg, while the right is stretched out as a balance; and this position is continued until as much corn is cut as can well be kept up by the left hand in rolling it against the standing corn, when the whole is lifted by the sickle and left hand and placed upon the band to assist in making the sheaf. Any uncut and loose straws are switched by the sickle towards the standing corn. The great aim in good reaping is to make a short and clean stubble, more straw being thereby gained to the sheaf.

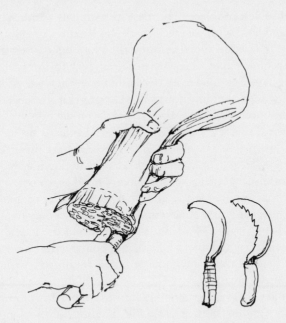

Corn cutting, reconstructed from the Justinian ms. This shows the reason for the development of the curious sickle. The corn at this date was gathered in handfuls, with the straw left for fodder.

TIES FOR SHEAVES

Now down with the grass, upon headlands about,
that groweth in shadow, so rank and so stout;
But grass upon headlands of barley and pease,
when harvest is ended, go mow if ye please.

The dollops of long strong grass that grew where oxen dropped or urinated (frequently while they rested at the turning of the headland) were cut separately to make ties for sheaves – a more urgent point in later periods when corn was cut lower, though the thirteenth century shows even the short sheaves bound up in bundles (common sense argues that it was the only way to keep the handfuls intact). Today, with binder twine available, it is rare to find anyone able to twist up the resilient green stems into ties capable of holding bundles of corn. Yet the mediaeval reapers must have made them a hundred times a day.

Bindings

Here is an unsolved problem. The early reapers cut as much corn as they could grasp and hold with a curved sickle, and manuscripts show this – and illustrations for later in the year show the small bundles of short-stalked corn piled up intact upon the wain for transport to the barn. The small bundles must have been securely tied, otherwise they would have shaken loose. When was this binding done? You have a gripful of corn stalks in one hand and the sickle in the other ... do you lay down each bundle separately, put down the sickle and use both hands to tie the binding? It would have taken hours to do so! And moreover, as the straw was still standing there was no flat place on which to lay down either handful or sickle! Early skilful weeding would leave a small space between the rows of corn, but that small track would be overgrown by reaping time. (No manuscript shows any sign of a second helper: if they worked in pairs, this would have been shown.) Possibly the reaper laid the handful across the curve of the sickle which he still held, and contrived to bind and tie with one hand. It's one of those small exasperating details that make mediaeval research so interesting

For the longer sheaves the bindings must have been very important, and many manuscripts do show clearly the binding of the longer sheaves. Stephens, in the nineteenth century, gives a detailed description of Scottish practice which seems to be reminiscent of the older sickle 'hand grip'. But whether his method of reaping does throw light on mediaeval methods of binding sheaves is uncertain.

This nineteenth-century drawing from Stephens shows the organisation of work in a corn field. (The Scots used women labourers, and the sickle had not yet been replaced by the low-cutting scythe; thus it is close to the sixteenth- or seventeenth-century harvest field.) Some workers made bands of twisted corn; the cutters laid the corn down flat; the gatherers picked up measured armfuls and laid it across the bands; the banders knotted it around the sheaves, then stood them in stooks. The work had to be carefully organised so that no particularly quick or slow worker upset the 'production line'. The balancing of sets of field workers was only one aspect of the Harvest Lord's administration.

HARVEST PROCEDURE

Thy houses and barns would be looked upon,
and all things amended, ere harvest come on:
Things thus set in order, in quiet and rest,
shall further thy harvest, and pleasure thee best.

The feudal head of an estate needed to be tough; he might, thank God, be wise and kind, but the important thing, from the workman's point of view, was that he was always visible and available.

In the early Middle Ages feudal estates called up their own dependent labourers, but this compulsory labour was gradually turning into hired labour. As we explained earlier, after the Black Death labourers migrated (illegally) and few owners of land would refuse any proffered services, and so gradually harvest help was brought in from further afield. Many city workers would still have had some experience of land work (and the seasonal nature of city markets made August a month when they could best take time off). By the fifteenth century there had evolved a temporary labour force, organised by the owner of the corn and his subordinate manager – the 'Harvest Lord'.

Harvest Help

Make suer of reapers, get harvest in hand
For corn that is ripe do but shed as it stands:

August was the accepted month for the corn harvest, but the exact week always depended on the weather, and 'getting the hay out of the way first'. (Always the seasons rule the land, and the weather rules the seasons.)

Extra hired help had to be booked beforehand. Bands of workers were collected, by an experienced leader, who served during harvest time. All were paid by the owner of the corn, and fed and housed near the work. (This custom, old as the hills, continued unchanged in Scotland till the twentieth century.) The companies of workers came from twenty to forty miles away, and many probably camped on the common.

The roving population increased mightily during the sixteenth century. One cause may have been that as temporary harvesters they found life easier in the country, where there was a better chance of 'pickings' and poaching than in the fast-growing towns, overcrowded by refugees from the Continent. They stayed on the land, and, then, moving from harvest to harvest, became the basis of the large wandering gypsy population of later centuries.

Usually the same workers came to the same fields year after year, first as children, collected in family parties from the villages, and generations of families would work on the same fields. One of the happiest sights in summer was the children, who soon banded together, usually appropriated the softest-hearted farm hand, and enjoyed the 'Harvest Holiday', sleeping soundly and needing no feather beds. Mothers who were 'bearing' or nursing babies would stay on the work site and mind the older ones – for centuries there has been a lot of common sense among country women.

A deep jar containing grease, and a small bag of sharp sand were taken to the field for sharpening tools.

The Harvest Lord

At heigh pryme Piers lete the plowe stonde
To ouersen hem hym-self; and who-so best wroughte
He shoulde be huyred thereafter whan heruest-tyme come.
                    Piers the Plowman, William Langland (1332?–1400?)

Grant harvest lord, more, by a penny or two,
to call on his fellows the better to do;
Give gloves to thy reapers, a largess to cry,
and daily to loiterers have a good eye.
                              Thomas Tusser (1524–1580)

The 'Harvest Lord' was a subordinate employee, chosen by the owner of
the corn. He would be a capable, experienced man and, if the owner was
wise, a man known to be reasonably popular and 'well thought of' and
firmly authoritative.

'Harvest Lord' was no courtesy title: he was definitely 'in charge' of the
workers; he set their positions, issued their gloves, kept strictly the rest
hour and close of work; later on he probably kept curfew over the cooking
fires. He was obviously a man with administrative capabilities. He usually
knew the land and the harvesters personally, and arranged the team work
(very much as the overseer of a hopyard, or a fruit farmer, does today).

The Harvest Lord only must give the signal to 'begin' and 'cease', for if
any workers leave before the others there will be delay in all restarting.
Workers in heavier positions must be moved to easier positions; fast, or
slow, workers must be adjusted for smooth team working. Food and drink
had to be punctual and swiftly available: the cornfield was a mediaeval
'production line' on which any one set of workers could delay a whole
field. No wonder the Harvest Lord was well paid.

The first 'break' (when they 'keep field in the heat') was from twelve
o'clock to one o'clock, and then work continued till seven o'clock. A pause

Wooden strickles: these varied in size and shape. Dipped in grease, and then
in sand, they were used as a whetstone to put a good edge on a scythe or
sickle.

of fifteen minutes was allowed twice in that time, when ale or 'a harvest
mead' was supplied. The noon sleep was taken in the field, a custom
unchanged for centuries.

The hand sickle gradually gave way to the scythe, though cutting was still done fairly high. Later in the year, after the Michaelmas goose had been fattened on the fallen corn, the straw and grass stover would be cut.

The food and drink was always carried out to the workers. In the earlier centuries the drinks would be in leather 'bottels' or wooden hoggins. The nineteenth century perhaps used more earthenware. But bread and cheese, oat cake, barley beer (and onions) belong to all centuries, for on the whole the corn changed more than the men who cut it.

'A LARGESS TO CRY'

This cry was customary when a crowd expected gifts of money from visiting nobility. It remained a strong tradition in rural areas for centuries, and today we still speak of 'three cheers' as 'being *called* for'. The Largess was 'called for' at the end of the harvest. The Harvest Lord took his stand apart, a little above his fellows, where he could watch for the farmer's coming. As soon as he sighted him, he gave the signal and all the field workers ran together, joining a rough circle. The Harvest Lord then cried 'Ah ... Har ...!' loudly three separate times, and each time the crowd picked up the 'Ah ... a ... a ... a ... Ha ...' (and bellowed it out loud and long). After these three separate 'cries' had died away, the bonus – 'Largess' – was given out. At this season every farmer was harvesting, which caused high wages, and enforced this bonus money to encourage speed. Supposing a neighbouring farmer's fields were ripe later than the fields the men were working on, the men would feel there was 'no hurry' and 'spin the work out' till they could move directly to the next contract (if they finished too soon, they would only have to hang about waiting to move across). A bonus given if they finished on time meant that if they had to wait between jobs, they had cash in hand.

Carting

Come home, lord, singing,
come home, corn bringing.
'tis merry in hall,
where beards wag all.
Once had thy desire,
pay workman his hire:
let none be beguil'd
man, woman, nor child.
Thank God ye shall,
and adieu for all.

Tusser

Hay was carted piled up high on a wain; but corn was carried in carts, or earlier, in baskets. It is a comment on the roughness of the tracks, and the value of the grain, that the fifteenth-century corn cart is lined and 'clouted with care', so that very little grain was shed in transport.

The last wain was celebrated with great rejoicing, unless it was a hopelessly wet harvest home. The last sheaf was raced for, and the cry 'A nek! A nek!' has given its name to the beautifully plaited straw and corn ornaments that often used to decorate the stacks. Once the last load of corn reached the barn there was the harvest home supper.

CARTS

The 1930 Scots cart demonstrates the basic structure of 1300. The shaft is the length of an ox, and the traction level with his shoulders and lowered head, the floor of the wain clearing the axle, and the side being adjustable for loading. All is structural. The axle height was always the main problem. In the Scots cart, the weight is fairly on the wheels, the forward pull simple, and loading position high; to get a deeper and lower floor and therefore greater carrying capacity, the wheels must be very small, and the weight trundle along close to the ground, needing a heavy upward pull, or a very long chain to replace the shaft. Elementary trial and error by our materially educated man ultimately evolved what he wanted. The experiment of dispensing with the cross-axle and attaching the wheels direct to the sides of the wain was found unsafe. All the development, from a wheeled sleigh to the cumbrous mediaeval coach, can be puzzled out in illustrations in manuscripts. Basic considerations were horse-power or ox-power and the lack of road surface. (Mediaevally, speed was less considered.)

Transporting special goods – such as mill-wheels, salt (which had to be kept dry), milk (which had to be carried smoothly, or it churned to butter), eggs, bulky bedding, heavy metal ore, as well as loose corn – caused individual problems. (All ingots of heavy metal were eventually cast to uniform size and shape, which solved other problems also.)

Gleaning

Corn carried, let such as be poor go and glean,
and after thy cattle, to mouth it up clean;
Then spare it for rowen till Michel be past,
to lengthen thy dairy, no better thou hast.

Gleaning after hand reapers was more fruitful than after modern machines:

an industrious family would collect enough corn for porridge, or to grind for bread. The early laws which had made owning a hand mill, or quern, illegal, in order to enforce grinding at the mill, later fell into disuse, and most small cottagers kept a stone quern.

There were as many types of quern as there were users; the quality of stone and the capacity for corn also varied. When constructed for use by two workers the grips would probably be made, or wear, slightly off-centre.

After gleaning, the stubble and fallen grain were worked over by the Michaelmas geese and the farm poultry; any green growth which grew up among the stubble was grazed off by the cows and close finished by the sheep.

The Harvest Supper

In harvest-time, harvest-folk, servants and all,
should make, all together, good cheer in the hall;
And fill out the black bowl of blythe to their song,
O! let them be merry all harvest-time long.

Once the last load of corn reached the barn there was the harvest supper, which would vary from elaborate feasts in the feudal hall, to monastic licence in the abbey refectory. A large farmhouse would provide roast meats, corn dressed in rich custards, and home brews hot and spiced. The parish churches – owners of glebe and collectors of special rents – adopted the tradition, and cakes and ale meetings. Even the small cottage woman storing her gleanings and counting her poultry made a special dinner for the family to mark the harvest home. This tradition still holds in most farm households, and the harvest festival in village churches is the one service everyone still attends and thoroughly enjoys. Pagan festival it might have been, Rural Produce Competition it has become, but all is to the good, for often the *best* of all that's grown goes to charity, and the flowers to hospitals.

STACK AND STORE

Comparatively few stacks are shown in manuscripts, which argues that hay stacks were not a long-term job, and that grain was too valuable to stay in stacks for long.

Threshing and winnowing were winter work, done under cover, and the corn was then stored in oak chests kept in the house or an outbuilding to be dry. The short handfuls (one could hardly call them sheaves) of the early sickle reaping seem unsuitable for stacking. They seem to have been piled into the wains, with heads methodically placed in and straw out. Barns and bins would appear to have offered better storage than stacks up to the end of the thirteenth century, but one cannot be sure. The stover (straw and grass fodder) was cut longer and later, and this would be stacked. After the fifteenth century, directions for binding the sheaves and 'keeping some threshing till later', makes the assumption that corn was stacked reasonable, though corn bins were favoured as more accessible in bad weather.

Bracken

Bracken (*Pteris aquilina*, also called 'fern' or 'brake') turns yellow in September and brown in October. Tall growing bracken covers fine grass, so if it is cut and carried, a little extra pasture is made available for grazing. Shepherds dislike bracken as on hill-grazing it is sufficiently high to hide the sheep, and encourages fly. One of the jobs to be done before harvest was in full swing was to cut enough to serve as dry grounding for stacks.

Bracken was once a valuable crop to farm and industry. Right up until the 1920s it paid the farmer to cut the bracken as litter for the steading, and the under-packing of corn- or hay-stacks. Bracken was used to deep-litter the cowshed, stable, and pig pen, it stoked the bread oven and made a tanning solution called 'brake water', which was stewed from the coarse parts and roots. Root crops were clamped with dry 'brake'. It was a good, springy and dry preservative. The surplus the farmer sold at a good price to potters and stoneware manufacturers for transport packing. In slate districts the quarries used the bracken, or heather, from the sheepwalks adjoining the quarry to pack their slate.

'Brake' also reached the city as pannier packing for small products (pack horses would not eat it and straw was too valuable to waste): garden produce was 'laid on fern', as fish is laid on seaweed. All bracken, reed waste, or trodden straw cleared out of byre and sty, was composted and ploughed in. (It is interesting that the invention of the pneumatic tyre made bracken unnecessary for the safe packing of fragile goods; far less was cut, and the bracken encroached greatly on the sheep's grazing. It is a root spreader, so deep gullies were dug to restrain its advance, but it just went down, and up the other side; and digging deep gullies cost more than cutting bracken.)

Corn Dollies

The original corn dollies (not the straw fantasies made today) were designs made by the thatcher of stacks, who set them atop his finished work as a trade mark (and so that the county could see how many stacks he had covered, and how well he had done them).

Corn Sacks

Corn for sale, or which was to be transported any distance, was carried in sacks made of hemp. The standard sack was used for land transport; for transport by water, in barges and small boats towed along rivers, or by sea, the 'ship sack' was used. This was longer than the standard sack and not filled right up, but left with a long 'neck' at the top, thus enabling the carrier to grip it firmly over his shoulder when the sack was slung on to his back, and to get it easily up the gangway and into the narrow hold or 'grannerie' of the ship.

Threshing Corn

Fettered with rings, I work intermittently
Obeying my ruler, who is also my server.
When I break into my bed, is made known by the rattle
Of the chains round my neck, set on me, by my Maker.
Often mankind, sometimes a woman, comes to awake me
When I'm heavy with sleep, in the cold of the winter.
With hot-hearted anger they rouse me, till one, hot and fiercely
Breaks the rings bound upon me –
Which pleases my ruler, my server, who then standeth idle,
He's a poor foolish fellow, who can do nothing without me.

What am I? The sweple of a flail.

Freely translated from the
Exeter Book of Riddles
(probably 8th century)

Storage arranged for corn-in-the-ear was better than that for loose grain, because it was threshed more or less as it was needed. Also, there was the feeling that as the straw dried, the small sap still in it would drain back into the grain (as gardeners let bulb leaves drain back into the bulb, before cutting them off) so grain that had been 'stored in the ear' was thought to be slightly heavier, and in some harvests this was probably correct. Porridge oats taste better fresh, and when more porridge was used, this fact was appreciated. Bread was made from more varieties of corn: if all corn was threshed at once, the wheat bin was likely to be emptied too soon, and only the poorer sorts of corn left until there was not even enough wheat left to supply the gluten to make the poorer corn into decent loaves! Mediaeval households were sensible: it was sensible to have a job of work that men could do in wet weather, to have fresh chaff for the horse, and loose, swept-up grain for the poultry and pigs to scramble for.

The threshing floor was made within the large barn, usually set between doors; in later building these opened to the top of the barn roof, so that the high-loaded wains could enter. Barns were built facing the wind and sun, so that a through draught could be obtained across the threshing floor, and a good light to see to work by. The floor would be of beaten earth, smooth and flat. Before threshing it would be 'made up' – that is, swept clean and lightly sprinkled with water to lay the dust. (There is a connection between the 'campers' who were encouraged to come and play on the grassland to stamp it firm, and the 'dances' held on the threshing floor, both offering amusement for a useful purpose.) The sheaves of corn were laid in the centre of the threshing floor, and the threshers stood round in a ring.

Small quantities might be threshed by one or two men, but a team of threshers might contain as many as eight or ten. The action was a swinging stroke that made the 'sweple', or loose end of the flail, swing around

Flails varied; that mentioned in the Exeter riddle has a chain joint for the sweple, but the more usual home-made varieties had leather joints.

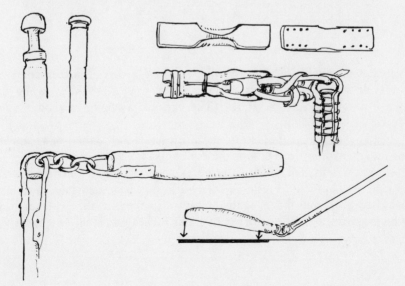

behind the head and brought the head of the staff down to the floor at the end of the stroke – thus banging the sweple down its full length across the corn: the resistance of the loose corn and the 'bounce' of the sweple made a vibratory shaking movement that loosened the corn, and shook it out, rather than beat it out, an important and much misunderstood point. (An old countryman, half excusing a 'good hiding' given to a farm lad, said : 'I didn't *beat* him, but I fair *flailed* the dust from his trousers!')

Because the corn to be threshed was piled high, the blows fell upon a deep, elastic, springing mass, and very little grain was broken under the flail; today, for agricultural seed, the hand flail is often used, as it does less damage to the delicate seed cases.

To prevent broken heads, the sweples had to be swept round in perfect time, and in perfect rhythm, rather as in bell-ringing. The leader 'called the changes', and sometimes kept time with a chant. The 'Cease flail' called all sweples down, to lie still across the sheaves – and woe betide the thresher who moved inwards, as a sweple might fall, not on the resilient

The diagram shows the arrangement of a circle of flailers; it is very similar to the ways in which bell-ringers arrange their circle.

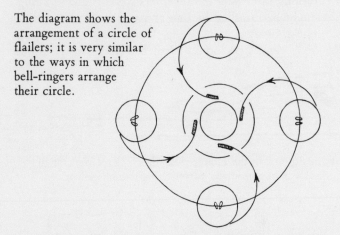

corn but across his head or sweple, cracking either. Another common threshing accident would result from the 'hinge' breaking, when the sweple might fly off the staff. (The various fastening methods varied locally and individually.)

In all the manuscript illustrations of threshers, *one man only* of a team has his mouth wide open. He was the one who called the changes.

(Pigeons were, and still are, the worst thieves of corn in the field. On the ground they actually thresh the corn with their beating wings, and stand back and peck, and thresh again. But once stacked, it is the corn bunting who is skilful: he pulls at the corn stalks inch by inch till he gets at the head.)

Winnowing

After the corn was separated from the ears by threshing, the chaff, that is the husk, was removed by winnowing or fanning. There is a large fan in Reading Museum of the type once used to 'fan' the corn (smaller fans were used to toss small quantities). The corn was also winnowed clean by casting: for this they used a casting shovel and flung the corn some distance forward against a side wind.

The setting of the barn doors facilitated the through draught required for this. The heaviest corn that fell nearest to the worker was kept for seed, and painstakingly picked over. We do not give sufficient credit to the careful old workers who have done so much, so long, to improve the quality of our corn.

Seed Corn

Once harvest dispatched, get wenches and boys,
and into the barn, afore all other toies;
Choice seed to be picked, and trimly well fy'd,
for seed may no longer from threshing abide.

As soon as the corn is safe, the next job is to select the seed corn. (Children's small fingers do this well.) Once collected, it must be cleaned and stored. Today most seed is chemically dressed to prevent mildew; in earlier centuries to find a rat-proof but *not* airtight container was important: wood was used, but since corn is apt to sweat in earthenware the leather bag, or hempen sack, seems to have been most general usage.

MILLING

When there was no law against them, the small home querns were used. Otherwise the mill ground for the whole district at a definite charge, and the miller's 'toll' (his 'thumb of gold') is constantly complained about, and the housewife is warned to 'measure before and after' sending to the mill. Mills to grind corn were contested properties. To build a mill was an expensive job, using imported stones, special timber and much skilled engineering of dykes and sluices, besides the dressing of the stones. Feudal owners often insisted on their mills being used by all their tenants and people, to recover these costs. An advantage was that the powerful mill saved hours of tedious hand-grinding; the mill owners argued that the corn was ground better, with less waste. All corn was milled with a cutting action between stones, not as today by roller pressure; stone-ground meal is of quite a different texture from the rolled.

Water-mills (over-shot or under-shot) and windmills were common; the tidal mill, worked on retained water, was most reliable, but rare. (There was a tidal mill just below Tusser's land, and a river water-mill just above it, and a windmill not far off.)

Transport to the mill was difficult, and the fees an expense, so small households went on using their own hand querns till they were made illegal. (In districts around some old privately-owned mills the number of stone querns ploughed up, or found hidden, testify to rebellion.)

The Miller

'He had a thumb of gold, pardee.'
General Prologue, Geoffrey Chaucer (1340?–1400)

The miller himself was often disliked, or mocked; an experienced miller could judge the density of his grinding, but he could also judge density and content of the corn, which varied with a wet or dry harvest and the skill used in threshing and winnowing, and he had many opportunities for sharp practice. The miller saw the corn that came to his mill, and thus became knowledgeable about the farm lands and the farmers' management of those lands. He was often the confidant of the lord or the monastery, or whoever had built the mill and was a reliable person to be consulted on the value of farms as investments. Therefore there was some cause for the labourer to consider the miller 'too much of an expert'.

The Mill

The inner working-gear of old mills is usually wooden; the wood had to withstand heavy usage, but inside it did not have to stand up to alternate wet and dry conditions, though it had to be well seasoned before building, or subsequent shrinking would loosen the fit. Apple wood was often conveniently grown into a useful curve. For lubrication they would use goose fat to sink into the timber, or perhaps a firmer mutton fat where any friction induced heat. (An old sale list has '1 Bar: gos: fa' – the barrel of goose fat kept to lubricate the gears.) The bolting-cloths that fed the corn into the hopper would be of strong linen. The grinding stones were a special care and cost to the mill, as the texture of the flour depended upon their excellence. They were adjusted for speed and feed as the varied grains required. The experienced miller estimated the type of the corn, its moisture content, its temperature, its age, if new-threshed or long-stored, and so on. He would run through a sample and try the flour with his finger and thumb, for he made his wealth by his astute calculations.

Millstones

Lands at Felstead and Great Haddow were given by William the Conqueror to the abbey of Holy Trinity at Caen – and from Caen were brought many millstones to England.

from Chichester Cathedral accounts

Some of the best millstones were imported from Caen, and were landed at the nearest quay above the mill. The stone was then drawn on a sledge downhill to the mill. Others came from millstone districts. The setting of the stone and the cutting of the flanges was done by special craftsmen (the patterns were radial, and the tool was a specially shaped 'stone adze'). It is the straight sharp edge of the stone that cuts the corn – the shallow grooves spill out the flour.

Old millstones are frequently used as the base for cider and cheese presses, or they may form the circular steps to the door of a rebuilt mill. Sometimes in old mills (as in the Abbey Mill at Llangollen) they are built into the walls, and prove that the cutting pattern remained very constant.

The Kingpin of a Mill

If it is continuously in water, wood survives reasonably well, but alternate wetting and drying destroys it. One great expense of a water mill is the kingpin, which *outside* is the axle of the wheel and wet, but *inside* engages with the grinding mechanism in dry heat. This inner end wears out first, so all kingpins are given as much extra length outside, beyond the wheel, as the balance can take: the kingpin can then be moved along to make use of an unworn part ('taken up' as a millwright called it). The balance can sometimes be helped by slightly shifting the bearing in the wall; but the adjustment cannot be much or it would move the wheel away from the direct weight of the falling water.

By good fortune we chanced to be there when our local mill was having a new kingpin fitted. The old kingpin lay on the damp grass alongside the new pin, while the shadows slid to and fro and the ducks splashed and quacked in the wheelrace below the sluice. The millwright explained to me, with care, as they made out that the date over the door of the mill was 1650, that 'It's still called the "new mill" because they shifted it from the old mill, which was further upstream, thinking they'd get a better head of

water down here. Now, naturally, they'd wait till the pin of the old mill
was worn out before they shifted her. So they'd put a new pin into this new
mill. Now the pin in this new mill wore out in me grandfather's time – and
he told my father, that when he took the pin out he found 1750 carved on it,
cut low down by the inside bearing end, so that pin must have been taken
up a good few times, seemingly. Father would be a bit of a lad when he
watched her being moved up for the last shift. It's only 1945 now, but on
account of Hitler and the way things are now, being so uncertain, we
reckon to be on the safe side, even if it is a bit previous. And we was just
calculating, the boy and me, it seems that a kingpin *should last* about a
hundred years. Of course we've only three lots of a hundred years to
reckon by, so we can't be certain, but it would seem that a hundred years be
a fair time for a kingpin to last – with steady use, that is.'

CORN PRODUCTS

Bread Corn

Make suer of bread-corn (of all other grain),
lie dry and well look'd to, for mouse and for rain;
Though fitches and pease, and such other as they,
(for pestering too much) on a hovell ye lay.

With whins or with furzes, thy hovell renew,
for turf and for sedge, for to bake and to brew;
For charcoal and sea-coal, and also for thack,
for tall-wood and billet, as yearly ye lack.

Forms of bread varied. Starting at the top table, on the dais, the feudal lord
would have white bread of wheat for eating as rolls – which the groom
who laid the table would carry round in a sling of linen and lay by each
place; or he might 'wrap up the lord's bread in a stately way' in a folded
napkin. Then there would also be a coarser bread, baked flat and sliced into
two rounds, which served as extra plates. On to these the diner would put
the pieces of food flavoured with special sauces from the 'saucer', which
perhaps his partner, who shared their one central platter, did not care for.
These extra bread plates were collected after use and passed down to the
lower tables (which is why it is still thought impolite to bite our side
bread). Lesser householders made their bread of wheat mixed with other
corn, using only enough wheat to make the bread palatable. This bread
might be in large round loaves, or smaller flattish rolls, according to the

maker and the type of oven. Cottagers who made their bread on the open hearth usually made flattish roundels, cut across so that it could be broken into four cantles. Lowest of all were the flat hard cakes that might be of oats or any sort of mixed corn. They were hard and solid; and in times of scarcity beans and bran or broken acorns were also mixed in.

Yeast to raise bread has not been proved to be used before the eighteenth century, but realising the variety of fungus moulds and yeasts that were used in brewing, and the spores that must have remained alive in the wooden bowls and troughs, it would be a queer thing if some woman did not make use of them somewhere. (The increased size of St Brigid's bread when baked was considered a miracle.) Early manuscripts show very smooth well-risen buns, so there certainly was some form of leaven in use.

Brose

We give the Scottish name, though it was a general type of cereal food and probably one of the earliest. The corn husks after threshing were put to soak in water and stirred well. After (roughly) twenty-four hours the light husks float up, and the brown flour of the grain lies at the bottom of the bowl under almost clear water. This water when boiled would thicken slightly, but the thick sediment would form a porridge. That is essential brose. Its serving with milk and honey, or salt, and so on, varied. The unboiled water, if poured into the wooden hoggings carried by shepherds, would, after some miles of mountain walking, be churned up, and infected by the bacteria or yeasts held in the wood, and become a slightly acid fermented drink. Welsh shiot was a type of brose.

Furmente

Wife, sometime this weeke if that all thing go cleare,
an ende of wheat sowing we make for this yeare,
Remember you therefore though I do it not
the Seede Cake, the Pasties, and Furmenty pot.

Furmenty was a very old and special dish made from new wheat:

Take wete and pyke it fayre and clene
and do it in a morter shene.
Bray it a lytelle; with water it spryng [sprinkle]
tyl it hulle, without blesyng.
Then wyndo it wele, nede thou most,
washe it fayre and put it in pot.
Boyle it tylle it brest [burst] *then,*
let it down, as I thee kenne.

Take new mylke, and play it up,
till it be thykkerede to sup.
Lye it up with yolkes of eyren,
and kepe it wele, lest it berne.
Coloure it with safron and salt it wele
and servys it forth, sir, at the mele;
With sugar candy thou may it dowce,
if it be served in grete lordys howse.
Take black sugur for mener menne,
beware therewith for it wylle brenne [burn].

from an early English recipe book

It is made thus in a few old farmhouses today.

Malting

The place may be so, and the skill may be such
that to make thy owne mault, it shall profit thee much.
Some drieth with straw, and some drieth with wood:
wood asketh more charge, yet is nothing so good.

Malting developed towards the end of the mediaeval period, when beer
took over from older ale and mead brews. The making of malt from barley
corn was probably a custom even while brews of ciders and honey-based
meads continued in use.

The drying Kell must be watched continuously as dried mault is very
inflammable, and mault scorched is spoilt; but it must be thoroughly dried
for it to keep well. The drying mault steam is soporific, it is almost
impossible not to become drowsy [so the worker should keep singing, to
prove she is awake and not falling asleep and letting it burn]. . . . If mault is
stored in a damp room the bowds [weevils] will breed in it and eat it.

That porklings were fattened up on the washed grain after the brewing
was done, is the origin of the term 'pig *swill*'; this was originally the swilled
malt grains – kept to fatten porkers and giving the pork a good flavour.

MASHING

The description of brewing is abridged from *Description of England* by
William Harrison, rector of Radwinter. Though published in 1577, it was
probably a traditional recipe.

Harrison's wife brews once a month for her 'owne familie'. They grind
eight bushels of malt, add half a bushel of wheat meal and half a bushel of

oatmeal, and 'so tempereth and mixeth them with the malt, that you cannot easilie discerne one from the other'. They then pour on eighty gallons of boiling water (slowly) and let it rest, without stirring; when the next eighty gallons of water is on the point of boiling she pours off the first water, and adds the second, when she puts the first 'again to the furnace'. To it 'she addeth two pounds of the best English hops and so letteth them seeth together by the space of two hours in summer' (less in winter). She reserves eight gallons of the first water in a closed vessel, which becomes yellow, 'this she calls Brack woort or charwoort she saith it addeth colour to the drinke, whereby it yieldeth not unto amber or fine gold in hew . . .' A third eighty gallons is boiled for two hours with more fresh hops (about two pounds). Finally, all three lots are mixed and half an ounce of arras and half a quarterne of an ounce of bailberries finely powdered and a handful of wheat flour and the Brack woort are added and she 'procëedeth in such usual order as common bruing requireth'.

Harrison adds that 'some instead of arras and bailberries add so much long pepper onlie, but in hir opinion and my liking it is not so good', and 'thereof we make three hoggesheads of good beere such . . . as is meet for poore men as I am to live withall, whose small maintenance (fortie pounds a yeare) may endure no deeper cut.'

> Value Malt 10/–. Wood (for Furnace) 4/–, hops at 20 pence and spice at 2 pence. Servants wages 2/6 (with meat and drink). Wearing [usage] of my vessell 20 pence? So that for my 20 shillings I have ten score gallons of beere . . .

The 'besom' or bunch of broom that was used to stir the fermenting liquor was hung up to be kept from one brew to the next. Because it was impregnated with the yeast it would start the working more quickly. Hung out to dry it was for centuries the 'bush' of an alehouse.

STRAW

For Fodder

The haulm is the straw of the wheat or the rye
which once being reaped, they mow bye and bye

For fear of destroying, with cattle or rain,
the sooner ye load it, more profit ye gain.

These four lines cover much of mediaeval harvesting. The chief difficulty of mediaeval farming was the shortage of winter fodder, so any sort was valuable. Therefore 'the straw of the wheat or the rye' was left standing; the reapers cutting off the ears of the corn, high up. After the corn had been taken the stover – the standing straw, with the weed grass that had grown among it – was cut for fodder, 'bye and bye': that is, as quickly as possible for fear of hungry cattle getting into the field, and for fear of rain, as rain would be even worse for the hollow-topped straws than it would be for grass. Wheat and rye straw are both good cattle fodder; barley straw is not, and barley was best cut low down – it was not worth leaving for stover.

For General Use

Any straw not used for fodder was used somehow in the steading. Straw, hollow, rounded and uncrushed, makes a serviceable thatch. (Threshing machines make straw useless for thatching, as the rounded straws are flattened.)

Straw rope was the basic material of much household furnishing. (The cathedral hassock is one of the few straw items remaining today.) Baskets,

hampers and beehives were of straw, and sometimes the legs of workers were straw-roped. Straw rope was also used for stacks. Short lengths of straw rope were twisted up by any farmhand as needed, but the making of long ropes was carried out in a barn (usually on a wet day, when two workers could be spared). The maker sat at one end of the barn beside a pile of 'drawn' straw (that is, straw pulled out and arranged in smooth swathes all lying in one direction). The first loop was hand-twisted; the spinner put it on to a 'throw cock', or spindle, and walked slowly back, away from the

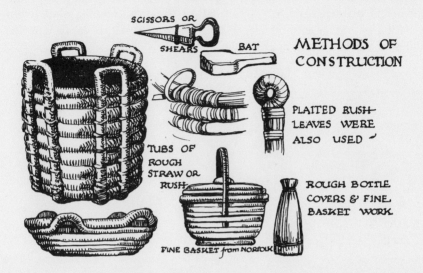

SCISSORS OR SHEARS

BAT

METHODS OF CONSTRUCTION

PLAITED RUSH LEAVES WERE ALSO USED

TUBS OF ROUGH STRAW OR RUSH

ROUGH BOTTLE COVERS & FINE BASKET WORK

FINE BASKET from NORFOLK

maker, spinning the cock round and round as fast as the maker could feed the drawn straw on to the twisted end of the growing rope. When the full length of the barn was reached, the spinner walked back, turning and winding the rope into a cone-shaped bundle as he did so.

Coils of this straw rope were made and stored against stacking time, and for many other uses. Straw rope made the trundle, or truckle, beds for instance – any shepherd or farm worker could make himself such a bed. He knelt down on the first few rounds and then, passing the coil of rope behind him and before him, made a mat, elongating it by extra turns at the ends till it was long enough to fit him. Spicks – light sharp sticks – were thrust through from side to side to hold the mat flat and on a well-made bed a 'double' around the edge made a draughtproof wall that also held in the rug or cloak that covered him. (We last saw one of these straw beds made by a shepherd who was bedding down in the lambing sheds for the season.) The same pattern, smaller and deeper, made church hassocks.

For centuries, the 'Lady in the Straw' was a woman about to give birth, as the messy part, very sensibly, took place on the straw bed, which could then be removed and burnt; after the wash-up, mother and child received congratulations in a clean bed. These straw beds were also made up for travellers and grooms – to be 'bedded down on straw' may have meant on a loose truss, but was as likely to have been a quickly-made straw bed.

Straw is an excellent non-conductor and therefore warm. Up to Victorian days (and later in the north) every feather bed had a thick straw palliasse beneath it.

Chairs were also made of straw coil. They were often called 'beehive chairs' and were the old people's special chairs. Usually they had loose covers of printed stuff, or in the hall of some old London clubs were covered by leather so their warm draught-proof structure escaped notice unless the construction was known.

SEPTEMBER

Thresh seed, and to fanning, September doth cry,
get plough to the field, and be sowing of rye:
To harrow the ridges, ere ever ye strike,
is one piece of husbandry Suffolk doth like.

Sow timely thy white wheat, sow rye in the dust,
let seed have his longing, let soil have her lust:
Let rye be partaker of Michelmas spring,
to bear out the hardness that winter doth bring.

Some mixeth to miller the rye with the wheat
temmes loaf, on his table, to have for to eat:
But sow it not mixed, to grow so on land,
lest rye tarry wheat, till it shed as it stand.

If soil do desire to have rye with the wheat,
by growing together, for safety more great;
Let white-wheat be t'one, be it dear, be it cheap,
the sooner to ripe, for the sickle to reap.

Let pasture be stored, and fenced about,
and tillage set forward, as needeth without;
Before ye do open your purse, to begin
with anything doing, for fancy within.

Provide against Michelmas, bargain to make,
for terme to give over, to keep or to take;
In doing of either, let wit bear a stroke,
for buying or selling of pig in a poke.

New farmer may enter, (as champions say,)
on all that is fallow, at Lent Lady-day:
In woodland, old farmer to that will not yield,
for losing of pasture, and feed of his field.

At Michelmas lightly, new farmer comes in,
new husbandry forceth him, new to begin;
Old farmer, still taking, the time to him given,
makes August to last, until Michelmas even.

'SEPTEMBER BLOW SOFT
TILL FRUIT BE IN LOFT'

IN THE eleventh century an air survey of England would have shown an afforested island, a few barren mountain districts above tree line, some fertile valleys, and considerable marsh, especially to the east. In the miles of dense forest were wild boars and wolves and, by the rivers, beavers. In some places near rivers were cultivated places and clusters of dwellings, built so much from the local materials – stone, willow, timber and mud – that they would seem part of the land itself. Only here and there were there towns, or cleared districts surrounding castles. In a few places broken earth or dark patches would show mines and smeltings. Observers could trace the straight Roman roads, and districts where raiders had burnt and pillaged. Earth works such as Maiden Castle, great stones such as Stonehenge and Rollright, and cleared trackways would be visible, but much of England was covered by a low scrubby growth, such as still remains in crevices on moors (Wistmans Wood on Dartmoor is an example). The dark patches of imported fir plantations are quite modern innovations.

One small point of interest would be unexpected clearings below or near high beacon sites. Beacons were the swiftest means of communication. The dry timber and brushwood needed for quick kindling were definite maintenance responsibilities in the locality, for a beacon was not built swiftly – it had to be kept always ready. The small fire towers on some old church towers stored a supply of dry fuel.

The mediaeval land-owner had three distinct types of timber: the well-grown forest trees, the smaller coppice, and the rather poor woodland resulting from previous clearing.

By the end of the mediaeval period, Tusser's notes stress the new urgent need for replanting and preserving woodlands, and the Gough Map of about 1360 already shows the extent of city and monastic building that must have cleared timber for miles around.

> First see it well fenced, ere hewers begin,
> then see it well stadled, without and within.
> Thus being preserved and husbandly done,
> shall sooner raise profit, to thee or thy son.
>
> Leave growing for stadles, the likest and best,
> though seller and buyer dispatched the rest.
> In bushes, in hedge-rows, in grove, and in wood,
> this lesson observed, is needful and good.

The word 'stadles' (probably 'standing 'uns') denotes the trees left to grow. Young woodland is to be fenced before cutting and replanting, to protect new growth. Later, in the 'new' hedges these 'standing ones' or 'stadles' were left, so that the hedger could bend them down to cross over the weak places. Often, if not so used, the tree would grow tall in the hedge.

At a later date, Samuel Cooke, a 'gardener upwards of 40 years' wrote:

> To prevent young trees being peeled by horses, rabbits and other animals, take tar which mix with any kind of grease and boil it over the fire. Then with a brush daub over the stem of the trees as high as they can reach. Do this in November it will secure trees for the whole year, it being the winter time only when creatures feed on the bark.

Some marks on trees in fifteenth-century manuscripts, however, indicate that such treatment was used earlier.

Often common grazing abutted on to woodland which had long been used for rough grazing, so to lay claim to the woodland the owner had to establish his right to the property. Long custom had allowed estate workers to gather firewood free: they might not actually cut down wood, but the shepherd with his crook, and the labourer with his weeding hook, might 'by hook or by crook', haul out dead wood, and if trees were left lying 'cut down', everyone stole freely. Open woodland, where animals had grazed too freely, was of little value for growing timber: a tree cut or damaged at an early age will never again make a clean straight trunk. Most young trees can be felled with one firm axe-stroke; the stump will then send up young sprouts, filling the woodland with bushy growth, but this will never provide large timber suitable for building. Therefore Tusser has the sympathy of every landowner when he insists that the first thing to do before felling is to fence firmly. Hewers were professionals who took over the work, and probably used local labour for the less skilled jobs (though in the age of treen, nearly every man could handle wood adequately). The actual felling was usually done with axes, and as the trunks of most trees is thicker at ground level, careless hewers often saved themselves much labour by cutting too high. (The modern Forestry Commission with its standard measurement forms tries to get round this problem.)

Tusser instructs: 'Sell bark to the tanner ere timber ye fell'. Oak and willow barks were valuable, as they produced the dark tan for leather, which gives its name to the 'tanner' and the 'tanyard'. Today, shoe-makers speak of 'willow calf' – calf tanned with salicylic acid, from the 'sally' willows – and of 'oak tan'. Whether the willow tan is more waterproof is problematic; the tradition may be mediaeval, as the properties of animals and vegetables were then firmly believed to influence their products. For example: a hare was limber, and so its fat was a good lubricant for stiff joints; and willow, standing with its feet in the water, should waterproof shoes. (See also pp. 205 and 254.)

When cutting the bark, sometimes the sap was drained to dry out the timber more quickly, a dodge to obtain clear flame and lighting for firewood in the great Hall. (All campers know that wood 'dead but on the tree' will burn, even if wet, because the sap that was in the cells has drained back into the trunk of the tree and the cells remain hollow and full of air.) Dead wood snaps with a dry crackle and burns with a clear flame, and though heat was required for the fire in the kitchen, light and brightness was chosen for the fire in the Hall.

The main flow of sap in spring being in the outer rings of a tree, directly under the bark, a round cut in March will kill any tree. (One of the ways of checking excessive growth in fruit trees, is by cutting an incomplete ring). Some trees, such as birch, if tapped in March or April, will run like a spiggot, and fill a bucket with clear sap in a very short time. This sap was used for birch wine.

ENGLISH TIMBER

It is important to realise that trees are animate. A tree, standing, is a mass of conflicting strains. A growing tree, wrongly felled, may split, cracking open along its entire length simply through wrongly released tension at the base. A tree trunk is of constantly varying pressure, and timber is capable of movement for years after it is cut.

Warping, shrinking, or 'shaking' ('shakes' is the technical term for the cracks caused by shrinking) differ in various timbers (as physical characteristics differ in breeds of animals). There are also individual differences, so that a workman must begin his knowledge of 'wood' with his knowledge of trees.

Many of our trees are imported; we list those considered 'English'.

ALDER

A tree unfortunately becoming very rare. It grew to a fair size by water, and gave most excellent waterproof wood for clogs and butter boards. (The scarlet withies bunched by streams in the north show where hundreds of alders have been cut – but alas! no new ones planted.) Alder was also the best fuel from which to make charcoal for gunpowder and was the 'early bite' that flavoured Wensleydale cheese.

ASH

A wood tough as oak, which will not splinter, and therefore used for the making of long implement handles needing tensile strength. Ash is often grown as coppice (small timber), and used for stakes and poles, cart shafts, chairs, hoops and tool handles. 'Stooled ash' is a cut-back ash, the second or third growth from the ash root, or stool. Naturally bent ash was kept for special purposes.

BEECH

A white wood (sometimes greyish), which when new cuts like cheese. For some purposes, such as kitchen use, this whiteness is good, but for handles and the like, where a dark colour is better, beech will take a very even stain. White woods, unless too soft, were liked for dairy ware and churns. Lime wood was considered the best for butter tubs.

For making tubs and barrels, wood had to be specially seasoned – sometimes soaked in cold brine before use – and withy bindings were carefully selected. Some beech was used for clog bottoms and mediaeval pattens. Country turners, who worked in the woods, would set beech blocks in the smoke of the waste fire of bark and chips that smouldered near every camp, their theory being that the acid sap of the beech is thereby changed, and the wood rendered more waterproof. Antique beech bowls and platters, however, have usually gained their waterproof durability from repeated servings of hot mutton fat

BIRCH

The mountain tree which, because it will grow in high altitudes, gets used there for everything, whether suitable or not. In the north it was the aromatic birch that gave quality to Scotch whisky distilling, and the golden excellence of the old smoked haddies and herrings was due to this resinous, aromatic wood. A bundle of pliant birch twigs was placed at the bottom of cooking pots when making soup or stews to raise the meat from sticking or burning. Birch brooms swept floors, indicated brewing, and had a pedagogic use: a 'birching' was a little harder than a 'switching'.

BOXWOOD

Though now seldom found as large trees, boxwood is very close and fine (today it fetches a good price from the instrument-makers). The earliest wood-cuts were gouged out on the side of the grain, which was a very unreliable surface, and the figuring of the wood itself can usually be seen. Mediaeval artists such as the old 'Masters of the playing cards' and those who worked with the first 'black letter' printers, were wood *cutters*. After Bewick, the *ends* of the wood blocks were used, and the craft became wood *engraving*. . . . But we digress. Mediaeval box was used for any fine work.

ELM

A curious wood, very good against continuous damp, so used for coffins, piles under bridges, quays and timber below the water line. Cart shafts, when not of ash, are sometimes elm. Elm turns very smoothly, so is good for rollers, for the dead-eyes in a ship's rigging, and the bobbins of fish nets; large table tops were often of elm, but not where wet and dry conditions alternated. In old timber yards elm trees had their bark stripped off for their better preservation. (This is of interest to us today, in the light of Dutch elm disease.) In early autumn, elm trees, often in full weight of leaf, may drop their boughs suddenly, so they say of old folk who die suddenly, 'the hale old goes as do ellum boughs'.

HOLLY

The white wood of holly is tough and fine-grained, lacking resilience. Holly cannot easily be split or broken, so it was used for tools of stress such as wedges, sweples for flails, battens for driving close the osier plaits in baskets and panniers, and so on. Because of this lack of resilience it is forbidden to use clubs or sticks of holly to drive animals. (A pig bruised in market will not 'take the salt' in curing, and a holly club, from lack of spring, bludgeons solidly, breaking the texture deeply. The 'popularity' of the old pedagogic birch, was because it stings and springs back, but does not bruise below the surface.)

HORNBEAM

The date of its introduction is uncertain. It is a very localised tree that was sought after by millers for the cogs of their wooden wheels, apple wood being another choice.

OAK

There are two kinds, *Quercus robur*, the Penduculate Oak on which the leaves have no stalk, but the acorns swing, and *Q. Petraea*, in which the leaves are stalked and the acorns stalkless. The latter, sessile, resembling chestnut, is sometimes considered inferior. Both oaks vary much according to the soil, clay soil making a tough wood, which may account for the old reputation of Essex coastal oaks for ships, and of Mildenhall oak for 'bettles' (mallets). The old oak in English architecture is a study in itself. The beams are all adze and cloven work (not sawn); pillars and posts (in barns and buildings) are used root upwards to prevent damp rising, and evenness and symmetry are got by pairing the two split halves of the same tree, or branch (hence the country saying: 'He's the splitting image' – an exact likeness). The root stump of an oak is often used by blacksmiths for an anvil base, the bark makes tanning, oak sawdust was the smoking medium for York hams, and oak galls made ink. Old oak cart-wheel spokes were often 'cut down' for use as ladder rungs. An interesting note in all mediaeval calendars is the autumn fattening of pigs by beating down the acorns and the beechmast in the woods where they were herded. Acorns are supposed to make a very hard bacon, and the description of some mediaeval bacon 'that lookes like strips of leather' does not dispute this.

POPLAR

This wood has many of the qualities of willow.

WALNUT

When it became generally used is uncertain. By the eighteenth century it was the best cabinet-makers' wood, and remains valuable. Old men affirm that the most 'beaten' trees have the hardest wood for gun stocks and the best marks for 'figured' furniture. (Perhaps it was used by the crossbow makers?) During the Napoleonic Wars the price went up and the trees came down, till England was nearly cleared of walnut trees. It is said that 'Beef steak, wife and walnut tree, the more you beat 'em, better they be,' so lads in spring go up and hack about the walnut tree till the sap runs freely. Some say that the sap attracts insects to 'set' the nuts; some, that the shaking distributes the pollen; and others that the bleeding sap induces fertility. (Elm is sometimes 'bole-trimmed' for the same reason.)

WILD CHERRY

This, like some other lovely woods, is very local in growth, and often seems in a curious way to follow Roman roads.

WILLOW

Most of the common 'sally' willows are native. Some, if left uncut, will become trees twenty feet high. The 'pollard' is this same tree, truncated at a convenient height and the rods subsequently cut each year – this is ordinary country practice. Today some market garden districts, where baskets are needed, grow willow. The common, white 'sally' willow (*Salix alba*) is a good basket willow. The goat willow has the beautiful golden catkins that children still call 'Palm', and gather for Palm Sunday. In pre-Reformation days the Corpus Christi procession was always preceded by children strewing these 'palms': even religious upheavals would not disturb this tradition. The goat willows will grow on dryish soil – hence the name – and the wood is specially tough.

The weeping willow seems to have come into England simultaneously with its portrait on the Chinese willow pattern plate. Alexander Pope is credited with growing it at Twickenham, but a more interesting willow is the old 'Kilmarnock', said to have been a 'sport' found wild in Scotland and cultivated in a nursery at Kilmarnock (the Botanical Garden at Kew took over its cultivation in the early nineteenth century).

There are other types of willow; red, golden, grey, and silver; many are now considered ornamental for gardens. But the mediaeval willow still grows 'by hedges and ditches the meadows about'.

The very springy wood was good for the making of aggressive clubs and sticks, and, as it is waterproof, for the beating paddles of the washerwoman, light boat work, waterwheel slats, and so on. It stands heat fairly well, and in old kitchens the willow bowls were used to 'set' dripping in. Willow blocks would be chosen by the wheelwright for brake blocks. Pollard willows were required to provide the rods for wattle and daub building, and wattle fencing, and all variety of woven basket work, from wain sides and panniers to 'kests' for bridge builders and market produce. Primitive river boats, coracles and light shields were of leather over a willow framework. Soaked in vinegar, the bark was used as a cure for warts. (See pp. 213–16 for other uses of willow).

YEW

The yew tree supplied wood for the English longbow – and it is poisonous.

The prevalence of yew trees in old churchyards is explained in the mediaeval rebuke by the Norfolk labourer. 'For, as often falls, broken were the churchyard walls, And the Knight's herdsman often let his beasts into the churchyard get.' With that freedom of access that was the best part of the feudal system, the labourer came to the Knight and said to him:

'Lord, your beasts go amiss
Your herd does wrong and your Knaves
To let your beasts defile our graves.'
(The Knight's assurance was somewhat vile
and this is evil in a man gentle.)
'Well are they doing right for once,
What worship should any man make
Abouten cherles bodies black?'
The bondsman assured him and said,
'Worth full well together laid
The Lord that made of earthe cherles
Of that same earthe made he earles.
Earles mighty, and lords stout
As cherles shall in earth be put.
Earles, cherles, all at one
None shall know yours from our bones.'

Naturally-shaped Timbers

Naturally-shaped wood was of value. Bending, steaming, saw scarfing, and other means of shaping wood can be used for light work; but for barns, bridges, boats, mills, or the classically shaped and carved roofs of mediaeval buildings, the timber had to be of naturally-shaped growth. Today branched, curved or knotted timber is sold cheaply: of old it was valued and stored for special purposes. Craftsmen and builders kept their eyes open for exactly the shaped piece required for their work. Michelangelo is said to have earmarked a lump of marble in the quarry because 'he saw an angel in it': so a millwright might purloin a contorted old apple tree for the sake of its subtle curves; and boat-builders ranged far and wide to serve the shipyards. Old timbers would also be purchased from the shipbreaking yards to be built into inland houses. When entering old buildings along an estuary you may still, in wet weather, smell the old ship's tar as you bump your head. Late Elizabethan houses, particularly, are full of old ships' timbers.

Cloven Wood vs. Sawn

A tree is a bundle of continuous fibres curving upwards from root to top, reinforced and knotted where they fork out into branches. These fibres are the shape of the tree, and keep their form when the tree is cloven apart along the fibres. A saw-cut will cut across some of them, thus weakening the resistance. A cloven stake will seldom be plumb straight, but it will remain unbent, strong and unbroken, when a sawn stake will warp and crack.

Symmetrical and balanced building depended upon split work. The fine Elizabethan barns, whose tall pillars and carved rafters make beautiful architecture, were matched timbers paired by splitting. When the later craze for elaborately marked and grained woods followed the Elizabethan taste for inlaid work (and later veneer work appeared), workers crossed and joined patterned woods into intricate diagonal designs.

Pegs

'... put them to work whittling woode pins.'
Piers the Plowman, William Langland (1332?–1400?)

Splitting was for building. A man would frequently build his own small house, make its very simple doors, bed, table, bench and food hatches himself. The work was pegged together with hard wood pegs. These pegs were examples of split craft; the peg of wood being halved, and halved again till the pegs were sufficiently fine. The edges were then smoothed off and the pegs dried to iron hardness before insertion in the auger holes. These pegs or pins seem to have been mass-produced, rather than made on the job by builders and carpenters doing the structural work. Pegs needed to be reasonably smooth and exceedingly dry, so that they would not shrink loose after being driven in. Some of the largest pegs, securing heavy oak beams in timber roofs, are apparently made of the same oak and may have been made from off-cuttings of the beams (some are an inch or more in diameter, and quite a foot long). These, for individual jobs, were probably individually made and driven in while on the job, but where there was much repetitive work, as in fixing long lines of panelling, the holes would all be made by the same drill, the general size of the pins would be similar, and they were probably made and dried and kept in a box, as a workman today keeps a box of special nails for a special job. Manuscripts show boxes of assorted pins, slung alongside the worker, as a man might now have a box of assorted nails to pick out the size he wanted.

The right-angled handle of this box could be hooked over the roof ridge, so that the workman would have his pegs handy as he tiled; the leather strips allowed it to be folded back into the empty box, and thus put into a pocket.

Stocking up supplies of these pegs would be an odd job for a chap unable or unwilling to do really hard work.

Beetle and Wedge

When frost will not suffer to dyke and to hedge,
then get thee a heat, with thy beetle and wedge.

A beetle is a heavy wooden mallet, and timber was split by driving in wedges of iron; it is surprising what heavy blocks of timbers can be split in this way. Blocks of stone in quarries could be split by driving in wedges of wood in line and then soaking them with water. Special double wedges were made with grooves down the centre, and a third wedge being introduced into this groove, great force could be obtained. It has been suggested that beetles may have been made from 'bog oak' such as Sir James Thornhill records finding at Dovercourt, round about 1700.

On this shore [Dovercourt] I took up a piece of oak about 5 inches long that is petrified and very heavy. We heard that it was common, but this was the only bit we could find.

Boards and Slabs

Now saw out thy timber, for board and for pale,
to have it unshaken, and ready for sale:

Save slap of thy timber, for stable and stye,
for horse and for hog, the more cleanly to lye.

The earliest way of obtaining a 'boorde' (we still use the same word to mean 'a table for meals') was by splitting the trunk of a tree. The split board was considered best for the long style of dining table in general use up to the fifteenth century. A long, straight tree-trunk was split down its entire length by wedges driven in line and forced in by rhythmical blows up and down from end to end, the musical scale mounting higher and higher until a sudden, flat drop denoted the tension broken and the tree-trunk split atwain. The halves were then laid side by side, flat side down, and the whole of the semi-circle sliced off with an adze; the worker walked slowly backwards, splitting off the wood in long thick slices. Two to four inches was not too thick for a long, narrow dining table, as two trestle-type legs were placed somewhat inwards from each end, but no central support given. If a wider table was wanted, two boards were laid side by side, secured by pins, and end pieces added across the grain. The top of the dining board was smoothed, but the adze marks are often visible underneath. The correct storage – 'bestowing' and 'stacking' – of timber was important. The wood was held apart by transverse sticks so that it dried out horizontal and flat – a warped table-top is unsightly and presents problems for diners.

'Slaps of thy timber' means the outside slabs from a tree trunk, rounded on one side and flat on the other; their shape when laid down side by side making a natural corduroy, their drainage grooves being very suitable for flooring under bracken or straw for 'horse or for hog more cleanly to lie'. Today we talk of 'slats', for the wooden grids laid on damp floors.

The Sawyer

Timber was laboriously sawn in saw pits by two men working with a long saw. In early centuries a saw pit would be specially dug on the spot and sawn planks were one of the most laborious and expensive forms of timber. For most building purposes, split tree trunk was used, roughly squared off with the adze, as can be studied along the roof tree of any old building. For wall plates on which the rafters rested, the trunk was usually split the entire length, and bedded flat side down, the top rounded side being cut to take the ends of the rafters. The rafters were usually of secondary branches, or splittings of shorter trunks, but the floor boards might be of sawn timber.

The Cooper

The cooper was a woodworker, and he probably used withy binding for his pails, buckets, milk tubs, churns, water carts, storage barrels, and drinking tubs. He also made butter casks, herring barrels, pickling kits and water

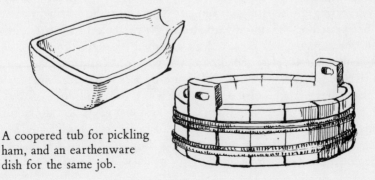

A coopered tub for pickling ham, and an earthenware dish for the same job.

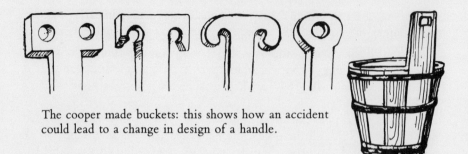

The cooper made buckets: this shows how an accident
could lead to a change in design of a handle.

carriers (these were of special pattern, rather like a modern coal hod).
Then there were the deep, two-man tubs with a long pole known as a
cowstall (often confused with the forked stick on which to rest this
transverse pole when necessary), threaded through two handles on
opposite sides of the tub rim. The cooper also made the large drinking
tankards and the small barrels called 'hoggins' for wagoners, strong
barrels for wains, specially light ones for the shepherd and walker, oval
ones for the sailor, and so on. Cooperage used both metal and wood hoops,
and found both material and employment near to the shipyards. They did
not often work away from their shops, as coopering was, and is, a most
specialised and skilful trade.

The Turner

Turning by pole lathe was for bowls, pots and mugs; and with the carving
and shaping needed for the household it was ordinary countryman's work.
The pole lathe was contrived by bending down a sapling above a primitive
lathe with two fixed ends. The cord from the top of the sapling stretched
down, wrapped twice round the pole to be turned, and was secured to a
treadle directly below the point of suspension. Foot pressure on this treadle
pulled down the cord; when the pressure was released, the sapling sprang
back, reversing the twisting movement. Therefore, the cutting tool could
only be applied on the downward stroke. Nevertheless a very continuous
turning movement was acquired by a skilled worker. Bowls, pots and
poles, and hundreds of rounded objects were, for centuries, made on this
primitive pole lathe, which is still in use by a few old craftsmen.

A point in the 'trade' turning of bowls was the 'token'; the slightly flat,
uncut piece to be found on old work. This was left to prove that the turner
had made a bowl of the largest possible diameter from his allotted wood.
For handled mugs and bowls there was a 'stop' fixed that left uncut one
portion of the wood, which would later be carved to form the handle, or

hooked end. There was not very much elaborate turning in early periods; much later, improved lathes made it become a fashionable hobby in Victorian times.

Wood Carving

Farm tools were made by the men by firelight on winter evenings. The fire was used for steaming and bending the wood, drying out pegs, and so on. In Tusser's time farmhouse furniture was simple (the inlaying of coloured woods was a new fashion from Italy, and came into rich households in the sixteenth century). Oak chests and cupboards were carved – decorated – 'at home by the fire'. That the same craftsmen decorated several pieces of furniture can be proved by pressing a small wad of plasticine into some tool mark and comparing it with another example, for the tools were usually of the carver's own make, and it was very unlikely that two tools would be exactly the same.

Today wooden spoons are thick cooking tools, but carved and polished spoons of Elizabethan times would be delicately fine, and perhaps white. Bone and horn spoons and treen all reached a perfection of finish. Unfortunately, the very fine work was the most easily broken, so we are left with more of the coarser ones. Wood and bone spoons were used with pewter bowls and platters.

(On farms the general use for centuries remained treen, but from Elizabeth's time onwards, a garnish of pewter was the pride of all good families and merchants – in Wales today such a garnish is still used for some family banquets.)

Firewood

Let workman at night bring in wood or a log
Let none come in empty save slut and thy dog.

Though most needed in winter, the supply was gathered earlier; after felling, the previous winter, the wood could be brought in by the manure carts as they returned empty in spring. For lighting in Hall, or late evening working, thin dry firewood was placed upright to give a clear flame: a thick log, laid flat, would burn slowly for a week if it was buried in wood ash. Wood to heat the stone bread oven had to be short and dry to burn quickly. Faggots, tied tightly, could be used laid flat: if set upright they were just a torch – of no use for cooking. Carpenters' chips were treasured, but everyone picked his own sticks for his special need, and many mediaeval manuscripts show countrymen bringing in firewood as they return from work – exactly as some do today.

Bavins were a form of firewood, but a 'bavin' was not solid wood, but a 'bundle' of 'firing' (that is, the bundle of light, mixed fuel that starts the fire on hearth or in bread oven till the logs take over). Bavins were the collected debris of thin twigs, material as varied as its use. Pea sticks for the 'Runcival' peas were bavins; birch boughs for besoms another form. Definitely a 'bavin' was a localised type of small wood that had many uses.

CHIPS

Tusser advises his readers: 'and ever, in hewing, save carpenter's chips.' The first reason for saving chips seems to have been the obvious domestic need to supplement the logs on the main hearth. A log fire needs a box of small dry fuel to make the little extra cooking spot so often needed. There is nothing that boils a kettle of water more swiftly than a double handful of dry sticks; and during the afternoon, when the main fire smoulders slowly, the milk for the new baby or sick animal is heated at the side of the hearthstone with small, separate kindling.

FLAMBEAUX AND TORCHES

Another use for chips was in making torches and flambeaux (torches were carried; flambeaux were usually stuck into iron holders). The wood was bound together with a mixture of tow and trimmings from the flax and hemp, and soaked in beeswax, resin, and so on. Flambeaux would light a landing stage on a foggy night, or bring some river fisherman safe to his small 'hard' from across the river. The small, cup-shaped cages set high on the top of iron firedogs are small holders for flambeaux.

With wispies and keckies and flickering rush light
To bring home the husbands that were their troth plight.
Tournament of Tottenham

Keckies, the hollow stems of umbelliferae stuffed with tow or waste flax soaked in tallow or wax, gave a smoky light. Wispies may have been bundles of straw, which would give a brighter, though short-lived, light.

Torches were made in as many and various ways for special requirements as we today select our electric torches. One small 'handy' torch has left its name in our fields; the hollow, dry stems of hemlock, cow parsley, and so on, were loosely packed with tow or waste flax and carried like a candle. These night torches were called 'Kex' or 'Keck', and children today still call the plants 'Keckies'. The rounded, velvety reed mace (now often erroneously called 'bulrush'), soaked in wax, also burned very well.

Charcoal Burners

The French and Flemish influence in East Anglia produced many household adaptations. The iron charcoal brazier so common on the Continent was probably fairly common in East Anglia, though not characteristic of England as a whole. The main uses of charcoal were in metal smelting and in the preservation of food and water onboard ship.

The 'hearths' were built in wooded districts. In Hampshire the wraiths of mist arising among the trees are still called 'colliers', as they so exactly resemble the small smoke rising from a charcoal fire. The charcoal burner lived by his hearths, tending them day and night until the earth covering could be withdrawn and the brittle, iridescent charcoal cooled ready for packing.

OSIER AND WILLOW WORK

The osier was the basis of a huge industry that made the rod men, its cultivators, important people.

We have some conception of the willow work in times if we think of it as a substitute for many modern materials, such as those used in walling or roofing, and all containers for transport. Within the house, treen (wood) formed tableware, bowls, platters, spoons, and so on. Outside, the willow and wattle fulfilled a larger need, including packhorse panniers, creels, transport baskets, wagon and cart sides, bale packings for overseas. Many of these were made to recognised standard measurements, some of which continue in the 'cran' (official measure for herrings), and, till recently, in some of the Covent Garden porters' measures.

Baskets were of any material, of every shape, for every need. But two main divisions were those made by bending and plaiting and those made by binding and coiling, the common willow being an example of the former, and coiled straw of the latter. The prevalence of the type depended on the locality; the skill in using the material depended on the worker.

Large round baskets were designed to be carried slung on a pole between two men. Store baskets in house and castle were more conveniently square:

Falstaff, of most notable girth, could pop into an ordinary Elizabethan buck basket and leave room for the laundry on top. The lover in the early Romance of Floris and Blanchefleur could conceal himself in the round basket of floor rushes carried to his lady's bower. The fishers could block whole rivers with enormous willow kiddles, and bridge-builders used

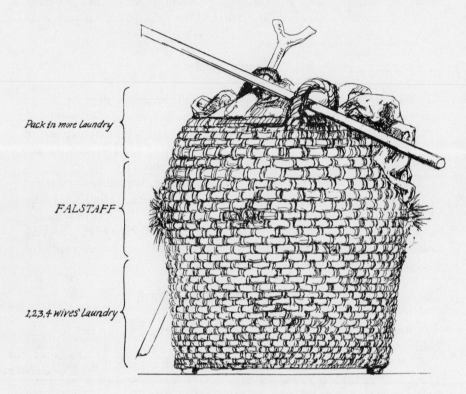

Pack in more laundry

FALSTAFF

1,2,3,4 wives' laundry

Measurement for adequate laundry basket

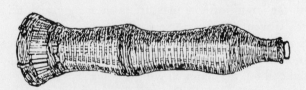

A willow kiddle for fish. We still say 'a pretty kettle of fish', but whether there is a connection is dubious.

wattle for kesh (caisson) work. Whole dwellings were built of wattle and daub. Willows were grown and cut on the spot, and the rods were seasoned in the ditch alongside the field.

Today, willows are more localised as industries, and since the draining of the fens, the reclaimed marshes of Somerset have become a chief willow-growing area. The rod men work their planted fields between the 'rhynes', and cut, prepare and sell the 'bolts' of rods. The willows are cut in spring, and if white rods are wanted, they are put to stand upright, their butt ends in water, till summer, when the bark becomes loose and can be stripped off by drawing or whipping the rod through a v-shaped slit. Some windmill sails were woven from the retted and woven strippings. They took the wind, expanding and thickening slightly with rain and, being waterproof, they withstood the weather better than any form of hemp.

Near the shipyards would be made thick 'fenders' for shipping, and the dry debris from all reed, straw, and light basket work would be worth ferrying across for burning off the bricks and tiles made, for example, in the Kentish yards at Ore and Faversham.

Brown rods were obtained by boiling the willows in their bark. This kills any willow flies, and was thought by some to make a stronger rod, but for outdoor use, and water work (or any tough strong work) the rods were used with the bark still on them.

The rods were graded by thickness first, roughly only, as some variation is useful when working; length was graded by the old well-worn method of standing the whole bundle upright in a sunk barrel and plucking the tallest handful in turn. (Today, the rod boiling is done in old long ship's boilers – the only part of the apparatus mediaeval rod men would not have had.)

The importance of willows could hardly be over-estimated, as except for the stone districts, and isolated localities, as in Devon, where the custom was to build with moulded earth (pisé), all small dwellings were of wattle and daub. Castles, fortified manors and large farms might be of stone, or local brick, but all the timber-framed houses and smaller dwellings used wattle work; and the notches and holes for the rod ends may still be seen in many timber frames that have now been filled in with brickwork.

For wattle and daub work there were two methods of insertion into the timber frame. Round auger holes were bored in the frame to receive the

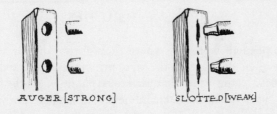

AUGER [STRONG]   SLOTTED [WEAK]

round butts of the willow (this made the stronger join); or the willow butt could be sliced with a chisel and wedged into an axe-slot in the timber. This weaker construction sometimes accounts for an entire block of wattle and daub falling out of its timber framing.

Willow is extremely tough and very elastic. Manuscript miniatures of the fourteenth century and earlier show wide inclined planes of willow hurdles up which the masons and labourers carry the heavy stone work for their cathedral building. Planks were difficult to make, metal almost unobtainable, so most of the scaffolding for heavy masonry was wattle. The brick baskets, the sides of carts, the panniers for carriers and the penfolds were also of willow. Enclosures for cattle were strongly woven between stakes, one man working on either side. Furniture seems more often to have been of woven reed or bound straw on a wood foundation, but roof linings, gates and packing cases were wicker; the cooper used it for his barrel hoops, the fisherman for his framed boat and fish traps. Hurdles of osier made trackways over swamps or pebble beaches. (These were laid down on the shingle beach at Lydd in Kent to facilitate the unloading of the fishing boats.)

When wattle was used for a wall, the interstices were first 'filled' with moss or straw, or the short hairs released from the leather in the lime vats. In some marsh localities marram grass is used to 'hold' the plaster to the willow, but not very commonly near the sea because salt, dissolving in damp, rots plaster, whereas the hair would be conveniently limed and its texture almost indestructible. The monks of Westminster arranged for a supply of home-grown willow in an 'osier hope' on the marshy spot where Westminster Hall now stands.

REEDS AND RUSHES

Reeds, when needed, were cut where they grew. The larger rushes and reeds were strewn on floors on the same principle as sand and sawdust are put down today, or the straw that used to be put down on the floor of hired coaches – both for warmth and cleanliness. On earthen floors rush covered dust or mud; on stone floors it prevented slipping. For wooden floors in upper rooms it was plaited into mats. Damp herbs were used for scouring (fleabane was very popular for this). Near Hampton Court still grow the scented rushes (that Alice found so delightful when boating with the sheep). They were probably used at the Court.

In the feudal system there would be special official rushcutters. Rushes were cut, drained and loaded into great deep baskets, carried shoulder high between two men, to be delivered to the 'rush women', who did the strewing and were supposed to clean out the old rushes before they put down the fresh. This meant lifting heavy stools and benches, and later the solidly-built tables. These had low-set stretchers to hold down the rushes which would have been pulled up into rampant tufts if there were only sharp pointed legs. The earlier trestle tables would 'take down' and be cleared away, the top boards being laid flat along the walls so that the sleepers in hall could lie on them rather than on the cold stone floor.

Small reeds were used for 'rush' lights: for these, part of the green covering of a shorter rush was stripped off (this can be done quite easily at the right time of the year) to expose the white pith, the better to soak up the wax into which they were dipped. Holders were designed that allowed them to be pulled up as they were used; and some eighteenth-century table tops still have the boxes or 'balconies' underneath, to hold replenishments from which the rushes could be pulled out, as they didn't burn long. This white pith, when delicately peeled by children or gypsies, used to be plaited into ornaments sold at country fairs. Now the little mountain sheep nibble the undisturbed green tassels.

A rushlight holder

Marram grass is a sea grass, also called matwood, and was cut and harvested for mat- and basket-making in Anglesey until recently. Its water resistance made it adequate for stack covers, until tarpaulin took over. Its great use is in holding back the drifting sand that forms high sand dunes and thus it can preserve a wind-swept coastline. In the sixteenth century Queen Elizabeth restricted destructive cutting and encouraged its cultivation.

The Thatcher

The thatcher's work began when he selected the straw or reed and superintended the cutting and transport. Rye straw was the best thatching straw. In East Anglia reeds were used. A good reed thatch lasts fifty years. 'Go beat in the reed' says Tusser, for the thatch was beaten inwards and upwards after frost or heavy rain had loosened it. River reeds were stacked till the dried leaves fell off; they were then bundled into convenient sizes and taken to the site. The thatcher would also supply withies for ties (bundles of the doubled withies split and bent into a double spring). These were called 'spics' or 'speks', and the ends were carefully sharpened. A 'cradle' was used to carry the reeds up the ladder and a flat beater to drive up the ends.

Thatch is secured differently by almost every worker and he has to adapt the work according to the type of roof. Few people realise how general was the use of thatch. Around the roofs of abbeys and churches the battlemented edges now stand up thin against the sky, but originally they were almost embedded in dark, thick thatch, of which the old line sometimes shows where the nave adjoins the central tower. Manuscript illustrations show that while stone and flint walls were being built, temporary thatching covered them to keep the mortar dry as work progressed.

OCTOBER

Now lay up thy barley-land, dry as ye can,
whenever ye sow it, so look for it than:
Get daily beforehand, be never behind,
lest winter preventing, do alter thy mind.

White wheat upon pease-etch is willing to grow,
though best upon fallow, as many do know:
But where, how, and when, ye intend to begin,
let ever the finest, be first sowen in.

Who peasecods delighteth to have with the first,
if now ye do sow them, I think it not worst;
The greener thy peason, and warmer the room,
more lusty the layer, more plenty they come.

Though plenty of acorns, the porkling to fat
not taken in season, may perish by that:
If rattling or swelling, get once to the throat,
thou losest thy porkling, a crown to a groat.

Seeth water, and plump therein plenty of sloes,
mix chalk that is dried, in powder with those:
Which so, if ye give, with the water and chalk,
thou makest the lax fro thy cow away walk.

With straw-wisp and pease-bolt, with fern and the brake,
for sparing of fuel, some brew and do bake:
And heateth their copper, for seething of grains: –
good servant rewarded refuseth no pains.

Good bread-corn and drink-corn full twenty weeks kept,
is better than new, that at harvest is reapt:
But foisty the bread-corn, and bowd-eatern malt,
for health or for profit, find noisome thou shalt.

Be suer of vergis (a gallon at least),
so good for the kitchen, so needfull for beast:
It helpeth thy cattle, so feeble and faint,
if timely such cattle, with it thou acquaint.

'OCTOBER GOOD BLAST,
TO BLOW THE HOG MAST'

SOME OF THE earliest Saxon laws concern swine, and they are also mentioned in the forest laws of the Normans. The wild swine gradually perished as forests were cleared. Charles I seems to have been the final monarch to attempt to preserve the status of the wild boar and the last were probably slaughtered by soldiers for food during the Civil War. Swine, like other wild animals, roamed the forests. They were strong-legged, slimmish foragers, with strong tusky jaws and swishing hairy tails; they were covered with bristly hair, and the tusked boars were dangerous beasts. In type they varied, according to the requirements of their district. They did not naturally take to mountains like wild goats, but they survived on swampy lands better than most creatures. Wild swine taken over on to estates became semi-domesticated and ultimately developed into the domestic pig.

The pig is one of the easiest animals to rear when caught young, and pigs were a great asset to the independent cottagers and hut-dwellers living near the edge of, or even beyond, the borders of feudal estates. The great variety of pigs today is the result of centuries of breeding, using the varied types of the original terrain. Today, certain breeds still suit certain districts for definite reasons: their ability to stand the cold, to devour an excess of soft fruit, or to survive on scanty hill land. The swine's ability to root up earth and champ the roots of weeds was probably utilised very early as a substitute for ploughing (a herd of young swine will turn over earth more thoroughly than most machines). The earliest pigs taken to America worked well as land cultivators; the woods approximated to their wild habitat. The Tamworth is the oldest pure breed of which we can be sure, and remains valuable for stamina and vitality.

The modern sow carries for four months, weans at six, and may farrow

ten or more; but, judging by records, the mediaeval sow averaged only five
or six.

While hundreds of miles of England were trackless wastes, countless
remote country folk still lived in isolation on the outskirts of this waste
land, and any peasant able to capture a couple of young suckling pigs might
rear them up in his hut and start a local stock. This catching of wild
suckling pigs is confirmed by reports from contemporary English sailors,
who naturally carried on customary methods. Hackluyt says that 'Here on
St Helena are great store of swine, very wild and fat . . . they will seldome
abide any man come neere them; except they be found asleepe, or
according to their kinde, be taken alive when layed in the mire.'

Local environments can be influential, and so can an active roving boar.
The pig, whether wild or tame, is ever a rover, and during disturbances and
wars many domesticated sows, 'if they escaped the hungry and licentious
soldiery', returned to the wilds, further complicating selective breeding.
Therefore it is unwise to be dogmatic as to the exact ancestry of any
mediaeval pig. Experts believe we had two main British types – the large,
heavy-bodied stumpy-legged type with the drooping floppy ears; and the
smaller compact pig with longer legs, sharp erect ears set high on the head,
a light skin and a pointed snout: these resemble the Norwegian pig, so may
have had early Viking forbears. Judging by their urban intelligence, the
Tantony pig (St Anthony's pig) of the mediaeval East End markets was
probably of this active type. Essex pigs are mentioned as having very fine
skins and making good porkers for the London market, and they were
the pickled pork for the Navy.

The building of the castles cleared the timber for miles around, and with
this clearing of the woodlands the wild swine diminished. There was a
difference between the wild swine, and the herds of swine kept for the
estate, although the invasions by wild boars or sows did much to retain the
stamina and character of local breeds. *Seneschaucie* states that herded swine
should be helped through the winter by waste food from the household; but
once special fodder had to be supplied, 'Pig did not pay'. Swine, like hens,
were expected to be self-supporting. In early centuries, when the wild
swine had to contend with the wild wolf, they were very different animals
from the domesticated pig.

SWINE

Fodder

To gather some mast, it shall stand thee upon,
with servant and children, ere mast be all gone;
Some left among bushes shall pleasure thy swine;
for fear of a mischief, keep acorns fro kine.

Who both by his calf and his lamb will be known,
may well kill a neat and a sheep of his own.
And he that can rear up a pig in his house,
hath cheaper his bacon, and sweeter his souse.

This word 'mast' covers beech nuts and acorns and any autumn fodder found in woodlands by enterprising swine. Acorns were the main fodder with which they fattened up in autumn. Today, acorns are considered to make flesh hard – perhaps the older swine had better digestions?

It is difficult to realise the enormous importance of mast to the Saxons. Their farming traditions, brought from the oak forests of Europe, centred around their forest-fed swine, and their ploughland oxen. There was much of the stubborn ox mentality in the Saxon. He was temperamentally ox-like – peaceful and solid on the land – and, as the Norman conquerors found, very slow to move. The rights of pannage were Saxon rights, and when the Normans closed the southern forests for game preserving they interfered with the Saxon right to feed the swine on the acorn mast, thus reducing the pigs' food and so starving the Saxon. That some penurious Saxons ate acorns, or made bread from them, is pretty certain, but it was as swine fodder that mast was essential, and the struggle over pannage laws continued until King John's reign. Without being sentimental, the Saxons felt that it was 'more than just the pigs': it was, as country people say today, 'the rights of it'.

So long as the woodlands were open, bacon was almost 'free for all', and even in towns some pigs had 'scavenger rights'. (St Anthony's pig, who went free of the market refuse, was thus 'fed by the community'). A labourer expected his winter feed 'off his own pig'. The dried pease pudding had bacon fat in it. In spring, when he unyoked his team for the middle rest, the cold boiled bacon on his oat bread expected no butter, and needed no relish but the first 'wild onion' from his garden. Crude and simple food by modern standards, but not a bad diet.

The prevalence of oak woods – until Henry VIII's navy used them up – can be realised in our place names. Oak was spelt 'eike', and acorns 'eykorne' (eike corne) and the Saxon aac or aec becomes oke, ak, ack, and later hac, haec, so that many unexpected names (like Hackney) tell of oak forests. Cows were not turned into the woods till spring, when some might crop low green leaves (and the herdsman is warned to watch that the animals do not get stuck through rearing up to reach leafy branches; it is surprising today how often hill sheep are killed in this way; a hoof slips and wedges, and there the wretched beast must hang, helpless, till exhaustion and the carrion crow finishes the horror). The swineherd also had to watch with care, for if the acorns were old and hard, young porklings could choke (the cure was a shake by the heels, or a prod down the gullet). Pignuts, fungi, truffles, and the grass beneath the fallen leaves, bark and roots were all 'mast'. The mediaeval pig was not particular as to his diet; so from the end of harvest to the first snowfall of winter the swineherd and his charges worked in the woods.

No pigs were reared in winter: once the boar had done his job his head was forfeit. Households might keep one sow under cover to provide 'sucking pig'. Otherwise, winter cold made pig-rearing a risky business, and the young swine, 'finished off' on autumn mast, were killed and salted.

An early construction with many
uses, from huts to pilchard oil works.

This pigsty reproduces the 'beehive hut' (right). Cantilever construction, with counterweights, allowed drystone buildings to be corbelled into a cone. The central roof hole might be closed with a top stone, and thatch might be added for warmth. This space could store fodder: pigs can't climb.

A good average weight for a salter was 20 stone, and four such pigs were considered 'just enough ham for the average farm family'. (This figure, quoted for New England as late as 1800, seems fairly constant.) Ham steaks replaced fresh meat, while cold boiled bacon did not require butter – there would not be much butter after Christmas.

Ring and Yoke

Where love among neighbours doth bear any stroke,
while shack time endureth, men use not to yoke;
Yet surely ringling is needful and good,
till frost do invite them to brakes in the wood.

'Shack time' was the period when trees were shaken to bring down mast. The yoke was a Y-shaped stick fastened across the pig's neck to prevent him getting through fences; but while he was among trees the yoke would be a danger. A good watchdog was justified in tackling a trespassing pig, and a torn ear and a loud squeal were the usual results. A wise dog did not tackle a boar.

More About Pigs

Helpful hints on driving pigs: carry a bag of beans and, walking ahead, drop one before the leader; the others will come trotting forward in competitive hope. Thus quite a small bag of beans will keep the pigs moving forward fairly briskly. Also, once gathered together in a round, a few beans thrown into the middle will bring all heads shoving to centre, tails out, so you can keep them from straying away for some time.

The contrariness of pig seemed to be known to Irish exporters who, when they wanted the herd to run up the gangplank, deliberately drove them away from it. Instantly they rebelled and went up it! If it is necessary to lead one pig forward, tie a string to its hind leg and pull *backwards*; the pig pulls *forward* and so goes ahead.

The greed of pigs simplified giving them medicine. Most farm animals had to be forcibly dosed, but for pigs almost any powder or solid could be embedded in an apple, to be crunched and swallowed.

The boar makes firmer flesh and flatter shoulders if he lies on a hard board. Also he takes more exercise by turning over more often. As the boar had been roving free till Michaelmas, this was important, as loss of interest and exercise could put him off his feed. It is for this reason that Tusser orders a daily 'shift' and feeding twice a day. The boar is to be looked after by the dairymaid, which suggests that he would have had a drink of whey, or buttermilk, to supplement his loss of fresh green food.

In mediaeval farming the division into ham and bacon pigs, as distinct from pork meat, must have been more by selection than special breeding. (Today's 'long-sided bacon pig', the Landrace, shows breeding's achievement.) Sucking pig was one of the first welcome meat dishes after the long winter. It was a household skill to arrange for a late lactation of a goat or cow, and the early farrowing of a sow. (Probably some pregnant woman or young mother urged her husband to arrange this.)

Slaughtering

At Hallontide, slaughter-time entereth in,
and then doth the husbandman's feasting begin:
From thence unto Shrovetide, kill now and then some,
Their offall for household the better will come.

(For Easter) at Martilmas, hang up a beef,
for stall-fed and pease-fed, play pickpurse the thief:
With that and the like, ere an grass beef come in,
thy folk shall look cheerly, when others look thin.

Here mediaeval brutality was at its worst. Cattle are hamstrung, and their heads hauled down to a block in the floor, their tails being bent up over their backs to force them (a method shown in ancient Egyptian models). This tail-twisting is one of the market-place cruelties that the modern RSPCA combats continuously. Goats and sheep had their throats cut. The house pig was usually slaughtered near the house (where tubs of water were at hand), and a capable woman attended to catch the blood as it spurted out after the pig had been 'stuck'. (The particular joint was long called the 'sticking piece'.) The butcher, who rode around to small cottages to do the killing, was called the 'pigsticker', and he brought his knives and tools and grisly spiked 'snout holder' with him. It was the custom to have ready hot boiled corn, barley, oats, and so on, on to which the blood was poured directly, so that it coagulated to make the customary black pudding mixtures. The disembowelling and cutting up was done, and the soft meat, the liver and kidneys and sweetbreads (Tusser calls it the 'froth meat'), were used at once. The intestines were prepared to make sausage skins, the bladders to contain the lard, the trotters, after the horn covering was scaled off, were (in most animals) valued, being strongly gelatinous. Calves' foot jelly was the basis of most mediaeval jelly (though some fish and seaweeds were also used).

In a few manuscripts, beasts are being stunned, or poleaxed, but mediaeval slaughtering varied in horror, some of which is still used in defiance of modern legislation.

A large community could have some fresh pork each week, and an abundance of black puddings and pies and small 'fry' for all, when the last flitch of bacon was safely in salt, and the first flitch was being smoked in the chimney. Also, till spring, there was lard for cakes and puddings, or fried bread.

Pork

Singeing methods varied and the disposal of the carcass began as soon as the pig was slaughtered, but the removal of hair and hoof were of custom done as a combined operation. The diversity of usage in this singeing job cannot all be accounted for by climate or conditions. A little may be put down to the breed of pig and length and size of bristle, but that classification does not work out in practice. For example, in the Wyre Forest they note the prevailing wind, collect straw, and with a thatcher's skill build a wigwam over the pig, butt ends of straw down and tops neatly joined. A neat truss of damp straw preserved his delicate tail and padded his ears, and the dry straw was fired and the hair was burnt off. This light ash was then dusted off and (sometimes) water splashed on. Advocates of this method affirm it shrinks the rind and firms the fat. The carcass is then disembowelled and strung up. Where pigs were long, and cottages low, we have found the pork hanging in the church porch (by permission). The custom of killing in the evening and hanging the meat overnight in a tree, while men friends were called in to have a drink and watch the body, was an old forest tradition 'to keep the wolves at bay'. In other districts the bristles are scalded and scraped off with a blunt instrument – a brass candlestick was considered excellent.

The whole bladder was used for containing lard; the skin, sliced open,

Bladders of lard

served as covering for bottles and jars. It was also one of the earliest plumber's tools: for repairs in pipes which, frequently being wooden, were likely to have an uneven bore, the bladder was partly inflated and floated down the pipe; it was then stopped and pressed out so that it expanded and blocked the bore closely. In the early years of gas pipes the plumber also used this bladder block, and a 'caul' or 'bladder', together with a 'moleskin' (for smoothing joints), were listed among plumbers' requisites.

Hog bristles were used in plaster and for all sorts of brushes, and hairs, especially long hairs from tail and snout, were apparently valued by souters for sewing leather.

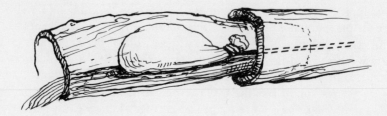

A bladder was used for repairing or making good joints in wooden pipes.

GOATS

During a plague period one writer reports that 'in the cities the corpses were buried with as little ceremony as if they had been goats', which seems to prove that goats were very common in cities. Lately there has been controversy on the early goat population, some, for lack of material evidence, practically denying their existence, and others being of the opinion that they were too common for comment.

The first goats probably arrived from the Continent with the other wild invaders; their numbers in those early centuries remain uncertain. The horned sheep drawn by artists in the Justinian manuscript are very goat-like (but then they are 'biblical subjects'). The nomadic tribes had herds of goats, and the black Bedouin tents are woven of goats' hair. It is certain that some breeds of goat were imported to England and may later have become wild. We do know that goats were carried aboard by sailors for their milk and, later, as meat. Some goats, if a voyage made unexpected calls, may have been lost or landed anywhere, even on a small island. Goats are hardy, breed early, and, we believe, they were standard 'poor man's venison' for centuries. Domestic goats were kept for milk and browsed freely. Thus a male kid would be fat, and so better meat, when early lambs were still thin. Mediaeval babies relied on goat's milk when cows' milk was not available. (That goats' milk was less liable to bacterial infection did not worry mediaeval mothers, as they did not know about bacteria.)

Goatskin made parchment and was probably used for the popular embossed and gilded leather. An imitation shagreen was made by pressure on oat grain. This craft was of Italian origin, but its product was known as

'Spanish' leather, though when the lady threw off her high-heeled shoe, 'all made of Spanish leather, oh', that shoe was probably of the softer kid which fashioned the ornate gauntleted and scented gloves so much worn in court circles. Our labourers' gloves were of tough, rough hide.

Goatskins have a long ancestry as waterbags. (In Babylonian carvings they are shown used as floats for swimmers.) Properly tanned, sometimes coated with pitch, goatskin water bags continue in use in Europe today. In England, however, our mediaeval labourer was seldom far away from water, or else he carried a hoggin. Suitably tanned (and pliant), goatskins made bagpipes, and goat hair decorated sporrans. Goat horns had many uses, and the hooves made glue. At what date the great black goat hair mats were first used under pressure to contain and strain the cider pomace is unknown. Goats were essential for some forms of witchcraft.

A few goats still wander wild on the Welsh hills, but their varied breeds prove them to have been escaped survivors of domestic goats. The continuous wars of the Middle Ages caused many domestic animals to be abandoned, or butchered by hungry soldiers. During the 1914 war, troopers brought home tales of stray cows found unmilked, and pigs being caught by gunners who had been civilian farmers, whereby some canny non-commissioned officer produced roast pork for the mess. The same thing must have happened in mediaeval times.

(Considering the reputation of an active billy goat, it is curious that his beard should provide the impressive wig of a Judge. Perhaps it put ideas into his head? But this is outside our period.)

POULTRY

Cocks

The cock was a reliable timekeeper – as Chaucer vows of noble Chaunte-cleer: 'In al the land, of crowying nas *his* peer.'

> *Wel sikerer was his crowyng in his logge,*
> *Than is a clokke, or an abbey orlogge.*
> *By nature knew he ech ascencioun*
> *Of the equynoxial in thilke toun;*
> *For when degrees fiftene weren ascended,*
> *Thanne crew he, that it mighte nat been amended.*
> (Nun's Priest's Tale)

Many animals and plants are sensitive to time; plants are named thereby:

'Jack-go-to-bed-at-noon', 'the days eye', and so on. When people lived among plants and animals they noticed this timing ('And winking Mary-buds begin To ope their golden eyes'), and used it in lieu of the watches they did not have. Tusser's observations are quite a serious study and prove very accurate:

> *Now out of the matter this lesson I had,*
> *concerning Cockcrowing what profit is had,*
> *Experience teacheth as true as a clock*
> *how Winter nightes passeth by marking the Cocke,*
> *At midnight one Cocke croweth timely, but fix*
> *with pause to his neighbour to answer betwixt.*
> *At three a clocke thicker, and then as ye knowe,*
> *like all in to mattens nere day do they crowe.*
> *At midnight, at three, and an houre ere day,*
> *cocks crow in their language, and thus do they say:*
>
> *If noise ye do here, looke al things be clere.*

The Hen Domestic

Hens were 'kept'. This statement covers the haphazard methods carried on for centuries. Hens were set upon clutches, went astray, went broody, vanished, or came back with a successful hatching, in the exasperating way common to all hens. At night they were 'called in' and enclosed against foxes, and their eggs collected in the morning. Some old birds were kept available for an unexpected meal, since, if killed, plucked and cooked before rigor mortis, they are tender and roast quickly. (When a late-night visitor arrives, and the poultry house is dark, grab the hen sleeping next to the cock; she is sure to be the fattest.)

Besides the hen house there was the smaller 'capon cote', where birds were specially fattened for the table. In *Piers Plowman*, Wrath reports 'Sister Pernell was a priest's wench . . . she had a child in the capon cote, and all the chapter knew it' – which shows that a capon cote could be a good size.

Manuscripts show pampered hens and chicks being fed by old ladies, so some were evidently treasured – others were not. They are shown being taken to market in crates and, like the wild game, sold in cities by country folk – a trade which carried on quietly in much the same way up to the 1914 war. The change of ownership of older country estates probably ended a tradition begun in mediaeval times.

EGGS

Eggs were plentiful, judging by the cookery recipes, in various ornamental dishes. In one recipe, three gold yolks are cooked, like three golden balls, in separate 'cotes' (enclosures of pastry). We wonder what pawnbroker was expected to dine that day?

There is little evidence that the 'free' hen produced fewer eggs than her immured descendant. Boorde said: 'One egg is customary; two are sufficient; more is excess', and that 'eggs hard boiled be gros meat'.

Froissart reports that large 'pipes' (crates, probably rounded and straw filled) of eggs were among the provisions brought to the quay for the French invasion of England (which did not come off); these would be 'hennes eggys', but wild birds' eggs were used all over the mediaeval countryside.

That wild birds' eggs should have been taken is natural, since there were far more wild birds in mediaeval times, and boys probably went birdnesting then as now. We know that (till lately) seagulls' eggs were harvested by cliff-climbers as a seasonal job. Eight types of egg were available up to the eighteenth century: hen, bantam, goose, duck, guinea fowl (called 'glenny'), seagull (seasonal and fishy), lapwing, plover (available today). The turkey and guinea fowl were *not* available in the Middle Ages, both being later importations; and the Barnacle Goose does not seem to have been edible, being more a controversy than a bird. It was said to be hatched from a type of egg that overhung the sea water, and when hatched it dropped down and swam off.

The 'weird egg', or 'wind egg', or 'coks eie', the soft egg laid before the shell has formed, puzzled classical naturalists. All agree that 'wyrde eggs ben unsavery' and incline to account for them by influences of the planets, and 'strong winds' which 'caused eggs to be barren'.

'Aristottle sayeth that of an egg wyth two yolkes cometh two chekyns ... the yolkes ben departed atweyne by a lytyll webbe'. Lapwings' eggs, according to Pliny, are good for 'Whytches and evyl doers and helpyth to theyr evyll deeds.' 'Aristottle' also 'sayeth that tame fowles lay eggs all summer, if they be well fed and kept warm', though some hens take two months off. Also, those that lay a lot, 'dye sone'.

Geese

Geese were pastured in flocks on the commons by gooseherds. The goose is a large methodical bird with a good brain and well-developed herd instincts. Left to themselves, they will go off each morning in a long, purposeful line to some known pasture, and there will spend the day finding food, returning at nightfall to their shed in the farmyard: they used to time their return to meet the stableman as he took corn to his horses. Very little encouragement is needed to keep a goose punctual.

After corn harvest the geese were driven out to fatten on the fallen corn in the stubble. Therefore the 'Michaelmas Goose' made the first feast of the autumn. Labourers on the farm all expected their Michaelmas Goose, and the tradition was long carried on. Perhaps the last remnant of it was found in the collieries, as many of the pits kept geese on the old shaft ponds that belonged to the colliery, and young managers and foreman all expected an 'official goose' for Christmas.

Geese were *driven* to fairs: the goose fair at Nottingham was a traditional centre for their sale. The story of 'shoeing' geese is founded on fact: they were taken from marshy lands and the last part of the way was on hard road; they were first driven over cool tar or clay and then across sand to coat their webs.

Today, under the stone stairs by the door of some old Welsh houses, there is set a goose-hole (not a dog kennel). Geese set their eggs well and were fine watchdogs to give an alarm – and attack an intruder.

The goose was a good roasting bird; his abundant goose grease never hardened, and was stored in barrels as a lubricant for all dairy and milling gear; it also waterproofed boots; and well rubbed in, it loosened a congested chest. It preserved from rust the knight's armour and the kitchen spits, and copper and brass from verdigris. It eked out the supply of firmer fats, was used in lime-washing, and was used in lieu of oil when combing wool. Later, we are assured it was rubbed over the delicate skin of a 'housed pig' to prevent sunburn (a styed pig, not herded swine).

Pigeons

The large, finely designed, stone pigeon-houses of monastic estates, castles and manors, show the importance of pigeons. Penmon Priory has a typical large, stone building. Within, the walls are a stone honeycomb – hundreds of tiered nestboxes, a flight deck near the top, and a solid stone circular staircase, on which a man standing can lift out the roosting birds. A small door, kept firmly locked, was for entrance on the ground floor.

While England was mainly uncultivated land, the pigeons would feed much of the year in the woods; but once corn was sown they became a pest, as they were most systematic thieves. Therefore the overlord's pigeon cote was a grievance to the hard-working farmer and destitution to the cottager with his small strip of bread corn.

Pigeons are small, but when fat at harvest time, are meaty birds, and handy for a quick meal (they seem to have been used rather like the modern 'chop'. The livery cupboard in the Hall was stocked ready for the unexpected traveller or some one who came in late. Feathers of pigeons were not kept (for pies the birds would be skinned, not plucked).

The wooden pigeon-cote was for small households, and can still be found now, usually hung on old farmhouse walls. Others were built on the same lines as the grander stone houses, as shown by the following instructions (the clay and straw construction would be common usage in many districts):

> A cheap and easy way of making a dove cote is to build the wall with clay mixed with straw: they may be made 4 ft or more in thickness, and while they are wet it is easy to cut holes in them with a chissel or other instrument.
>
> Of whatever materials the cote be erected it should be white – because the pigeon . . . is a cleanly bird and loves the appearance of neatness: and beside the white colour renders the building more conspicuous.

Pigeons lay two eggs, usually male and female (the 'pigeon pair').

Rock salt was given as a 'lick' to many farm animals, but not usually to birds; pigeons are an exception. At salt pans, 'cats' would be made for sale, but 'This is a common method where there are no salt works in the neighbourhood. Take a lump of earth [clay texture?] . . . and beat it up with brine, to which throw a quantity of bay salt, and a little salt petre.' The 'cat', when set firm, would be placed in the pigeon house. We have noticed some short stumps in some larger cotes – perhaps they were for the 'cat' to stand on?

Swans, Ducks and Peacocks

> Feed swan and go safely make up her nest
> for fear of a flood good and high is the best.

The long quill feathers made pens, and swansdown was collected. Cygnets were a favourite banqueting dish. Full-grown swans were not popular with cooks, for there is little fat on a swan unless it has been well fed up beforehand.

Bartholomaeus Anglicus has an interesting passage on swans:

> The swanne hygte Signus . . . is alle whyte in fethers, for noo man findyeth a black swanne. [Australia and the black swan were yet undiscovered.] The swanne syngneth swete songes with accorde of voice, & shypmen trowe that it tokenyth good, yf thei mete swannes in peryll of shippe breche . . .
>
> Whan the swane is in love, he taketh the female of te necke & drawyth her to hymwade, & joynyth his neck to y females neche as it were byndynge their neckes togeder. And after the tredynge the female smyeteth the male & fleeth hym & male bathyth hym after the tredynge. The swanne feedth of grass & rootes. He hath blacke fete, cloos & hole [webbed] & bode full able

to swymynge, & dwelleth in lakes & pondes & maketh his neste nyghe waters, upon which ben fewe stykes throwen together & syttyth on brrod & bryngyth forth byrdes & fedyth them before bryngyth them up & defendyth them with couryth [vigour] wyth wynges & bylle. And is a byrd of grete weygt & hevynesse, therefre she loveth reste & fleyth but selde. But wylde swannes fly with strong flyht with neckes streyghte forwarde & fet streghte backwards. But they ben not so fatte as tame swannes whyche ben nourished and fedd nyghe places as men anhabyte.

Ducks are shown on farm ponds, and duck and green peas were appreciated. Later, wild ducks were taken in a decoy.

Peacocks were birds of castle and manor. Colomell says 'The peahen she excuseth if a hen upon her eggs be set.' They were not 'farm birds', but were served elaborately at special feasts or celebrations.

Other Poultry Products

Giblets and legs of most poultry, being strongly gelatinous, seem to have been the basis for broth and soup squares. These were used in sailing ships till the nineteenth century, as were gizzard and crop, the latter to extract rennet, the crop from the cock being a speciality.

FEATHERS

Different sorts of feathers were stored separately in baskets or sacks. After the bread-making was finished, the clean feathers were placed in the cooling oven and left overnight to dry. They were then fit to be made into bedding, or sold. The vent feathers, or any soiled feathers, were burnt, or if in quantity worth preserving, tied below the waterwheel till washed clean; but these were never used for good bedding. Wing ends were used as small brushes. Larger wings of goose and swan swept up the corn on threshing floors. Thick quills were used to stopper bottles, to make air spiggots for casks, to act as safety valves for yeast and ale ferments, and so on. They also provided teats for young lambs and babies. Quills are still in use for pens and painting brushes – artists' brushes today are sized as 'swan', 'goose' or 'crow'. Quills were also used as floats for fishing lines.

The strong feathers of the goose flighted arrows. In a poem where sheep, horse and goose contend, 'Flight of my feathers', says the goose, ' Won the battle for the archer'. Arrow plumes had to be taken from the same wing for each arrow in order to get the air curve correct for the spin.

Because feathers are shed only at certain seasons, rapacious feather gatherers took to pulling them off the bird prematurely. The feathers and down grew again, but meanwhile the birds were part naked, cold and miserable, and their expostulating squawks appealed in vain to the unsympathetic mediaeval mind. This inhuman custom seems to have been carried by Dutch settlers into the New World, and lasted well into the nineteenth century, as is proved by this quotation from the American author of the 'Brownie' books for children.

> One said, 'Those folk can hardly thrive,
> Who pluck their poultry while alive
> For many a one, old dames have said
> Has tossed through night a restless head,
> The only sleepless one in town.
> Because, on pillows made of down,
> That cruel fingers had plucked loose
> To music of the squawking goose.'
>
> Palmer Cox (1840–1924)

The quilled flight feathers of birds were also discredited for pillows. Theoretically, being flighty, they prevented rest; practically, their sharp points pierced the pillowcase – 'They put pigeon feathers in my pillow, no wonder I could not die.'

DOWN

Down (swansdown and goosedown) always fetched a higher price than feathers. The preparation for drying down was more delicately carried out. Beds and pillows of down are specified differently, and, from the study of household inventories, we believe the 'continental' down bedcover, the Scottish duvet, was in use in mediaeval times (blankets being separately listed, and inadequate in number).

GUANO

The hen roost and dovecote were scraped with care, as the guano had many uses. It was an ingredient in the primitive gunpowder of the day, and also made ley for bucking clothes. Goose dung was not collected and was thought positively harmful: the only reason we can assign for this was the classical verdict, 'Goose dung is nought' (Palladius). It is in such details we see the old mediaeval traditions through new Elizabethan freedoms.

FEATHER BEDS

Into the water busily overboard to hale and cast. Their bags and their feather beds, and their best weeds. Their kists and their coffers and cargo and all, to lighten the ship.   (*Ms. 12th–13th century*)

O mony was the feather bed that floated on the faem
And mony were the gude lords sons that never mair came hame.
O forty miles off Aberdeen, tis fifty fathoms deep
And there lies gude Sir Patrick Spens,
With the Scots lords at his feet –

(*Sir Patrick Spens:* Ballad, 13th–14th century?)

The notes to the 1360 Gough map (detail, Plate 1) state, correctly, that the shipwrecked man 'floats on a raft'. That 'raft' was the feather bed used by all sailors from earliest times, feathers being warm, light and absolutely unsinkable. The strong, waxed, linen bed-covers were tied at each corner

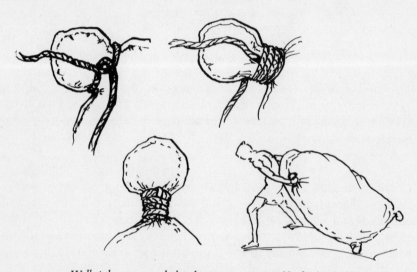

Well-tied corners made hand grips on an unwieldy feather bed

to form hand grips, as it is very difficult to get a firm hold on a feather bed – the smooth cover and resilient filling repel the fingers. When feather beds are thrown into water they float buoyantly, and even when the submerged underside is torn, or rotted away, the imprisoned feathers float upwards and keep the top cover distended, so that the mass stays afloat.

Sailors would stow the beds against the sides of the ship (as the canal boatmen used to do on the old wooden barges). The beds 'enclosed' the sleeper, who spread his day gear on top to serve as blanket and to 'dry out' overnight.

The waxing of the linen covers could be done with hot beeswax, while northern sailors used seal-fat. Today the old-fashioned huswife rubs yellow soap along the seams of her feather-proof ticks.

The torn sails of the ship in the map show a long tempest and, from the latitude, she may have been rammed by an iceberg, or rock; she is stove in just above the water line. In wooden ships the galley was set below decks, over the bilge water and stone ballast. That galleys existed we know for certain, providing 'hote malvesy, helpe for to restore' and a 'salted roste' for the seasick pilgrims to St James. The small cooking fire of wood or charcoal would be on a flat stone, and during the tempest this fire would be shut down under an iron *couvre feu* and the hatch of the very small hold would be battened down. The tossing and the partial capsize would fling the bilge water over this red-hot iron, causing an explosion that could have blown *out* the breached timber and the man and bed still asleep against it

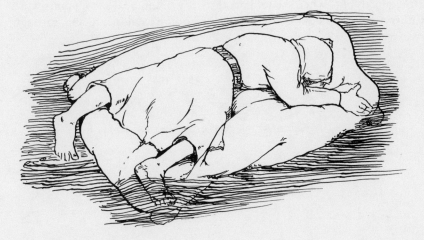

(the aperture suggests this). This is conjecture only; but it is the type of story that would be retold for centuries – and lose nothing in the telling!

The ballad of Sir Patrick Spens may have been the 1290 voyage to fetch the Maid of Norway to wed the Scots King's son. But the Maid died, when landed on Orkney. The voyage must have been before 1460, after James III made it law that no vessels were to sail north between 'St Simone & Judes day & Candlemas day'. Captain Spens, a good sailor, had demurred at undertaking the voyage so late in the winter season – and the young Maid probably died of cold and exposure, on that storm-tossed sailing boat.

Hens for Rent

The keeping of hens must have been as various in mediaeval periods as now. But small hut dwellers were more likely to 'keep a few hens just for themselves' than larger estates, who would accept hens and eggs as rental. An amusing example of this was told by an old friend near Ewenny (South

Wales). Her husband sold off a large tract of land to make three small farms; after boundaries were arranged there was a triangular depression (of awkward shape) left in the centre. After it had been unused for some years, one of the farmers asked to rent it 'as his wife wanted to keep a few hens'. The owner agreed, but waived the question of extra rent saying, 'That's all right, it's no use for anything else. Tell your wife to let me have a couple of boiling fowls when she is culling.' So for years, a pair of fowls would be brought to the house (and thanks and drinks exchanged). Her husband died and the widow sold off the whole of the land to the local Council for 'building land'. The price of the three farms was easily ascertained, but (when she told me the story) municipal accountants were still trying to work out the 'price of two boiling fowls per annum through two wars' ...

NOVEMBER

Thresh barley as yet, but as need shall require,
fresh threshed for stover, thy cattle desire;
And therefore that threshing, forbear as ye may,
till Candlemas coming, for sparing of hay.

Such wheat as ye keep, for the baker to buy,
unthreshed till March, in the sheaf let it lie;
Lest foistiness take it, if sooner ye thresh it,
although by oft turning, ye seem to refresh it.

When rain is a let, to thy doings abroad,
set threshers a threshing, to lay on good load:
Thresh clean, ye must bid them, though lesser they earn,
and looking to thrive, have an eye to thy barn.

Some pilfering thresher will walk with a staff,
will carry home corn, as it is in the chaff,
And some in his bottle of leather so great,
will carry home, daily, both barley and wheat.

Some useth to winnow, some useth to fan,
some useth to cast it, as clean as they can.
For seed go and cast it; for malting not so,
but get out the cockle, and then let it go.

All manner of straw, that is scattered in yard,
good husbandly husbands have daily regard,
In pit, full of water, the same to bestow,
where lying to rot, thereof profit may grow.

Lay compas up, handsomely, round on a hill,
to walk in thy yard, at thy pleasure and will:
More compas it maketh, and handsome the plot,
if horse-keeper, daily, forgetteth it not.

The chimney all sooty, would now be made clean,
for fear of mischances, too oftentimes seen:
Old chimney and sooty, if fier once take,
by burning and breaking, some mischief may make.

'LEAVE LATEWARDLY
REARING'

NOVEMBER brings the approach of winter, when house and outbuildings must be prepared against rough weather, and to take advantage of it. Winter frosts would rot down compass, and break up the soil: so now was the time for cleaning privies. The refuse should be removed at night, and 'buried in garden, in trenches a-low, shall make very many things better to grow.'

Chimneys, too, should be swept – constant winter fires might set a dirty chimney alight, with disastrous consequences.

Threshing was done as the grain was needed (see pp. 184–6); unthreshed corn was thought to keep better..

This was the time of year when the husbandman had to decide which of his animals he could keep through the winter. He could kill and preserve some, eat some straightaway, and sell off a surplus into the towns about.

DROVING

Along the roads. . . .
Followed by dust like smoking clouds
Scotch droves of beast, a little breed
In sweltering weary mood proceed
A patient race from Scottish hills
To fatten by our pasture rills
Lean with the wants of mountain soil
But short and stout for travels' toil
Wi cocked up horns and curling crown
And dewlap besom hanging down

Followed by slowly pacing swains
Wild to our rushy flats and plains
At whom the shepherds dog will rise
And shake himself, and in surprise
Draw back, and waffle in Affright
Barking the traveller out of sight
And mowers ore their scythes will bear
Upon their uncooth dress to stare
And shepherds as they trample bye
Leaves ore their crooks a wondering eye
In petticotes of banded plad
Wi blankets ore their shoulders slung
To camp at night the fields among . . .

John Clare (1793–1864)

Droving was not one great autumn exodus from Scotland to the South; in mediaeval times, a distributed flow of animals grazed their way across country to the markets in many cities, not only in London (where Smithfield remains as the traditional destination). Winter fodder was in short supply; so that when grazing ceased, the lord of the manor, crofter, or hut dweller decided on what animals he intended to keep and the others (whether one or a hundred) were either killed or sold off. From managers of feudal estates to labourers in huts, all attended to winter supplies as best they could. Christmas feasting gave an excuse for a good feed that used up the perishable parts of meat that could not be kept any longer (they kept meat as long as they could) and for eating the corn, beans and stores that might be going mouldy. The smoke of drying circled round the cottage rafters as urgently as on the great estates, the salt troughs spilled over, and in the low-built sheds smoking fires smouldered, day and night, tended by a drowsy old woodcutter who had brought down the oak bark from the forest, swept out the damp firewood chips from the woodshed, and fetched old reeds cleared off the hall floors. And likely enough he sloped round to the kitchen premises after the hall was cleared to get his supper (let's hope it was a good one) before he set his draught holes, and settled down to his mediaeval 'night shift' (an experienced 'smoker' was a valued man who worked day and night while the smoking was carried on).

All this work lay behind the drovers, who plodded along often with 'spares for sale'.

Droving at its peak (as portrayed by painter and poets) between the 1790s and 1890s was a way of life, and a mighty commercial enterprise; earlier it had formed the foundations for industrial enterprise based on leather, horn, glue, and soap-boiling.

Basically, droving varied with the speed of the animals, so most droves were of one sort of animal – not mixed. Also, differences in the grazing needed made it wise to let close-feeding animals (those with a low bite) follow high feeders. The pigs (which hunted coarse weed and roots) and the geese went on separate routes. The terrain could also cause problems. Water was vital and had to be easy of access and copious of supply (to prevent panic). Where the going became rough, special smiths were employed to shoe the beasts, and they had to keep up a steady supply of shoes. In other districts the routes would deviate to bypass avaricious

Droves of oxen were shod with small iron shoes. For watering, a large drove had to rest by river or lake: too small a trough could cause stampede among thirsty beasts. It is probable that mediaeval troughs resembled this Rhodesian farm trough, made from a hollowed-out tree.

landowners or pockets of outlawry. The drovers were men of substance, acting as bankers between the distant farmers and the merchants with whom they bargained. At their discretion, they were also empowered to sell cattle or sheep en route.

Though of a much later date, we give a description by Stephens (a practical farmer) of droving, for the basic facts of fodder, speed, water, rest and selection of a safe route, would have governed the smaller, earlier mediaeval droves. In early centuries, the caution required when passing through 'foreign' districts was more acute.

Being prepared for travel, sheep (or cattle) should have food early in the morning, and be started on their journey about midday in winter, and in the afternoon in summer. Let them walk gently away, and as the road is new to them, they will go too fast at first, to prevent which the drover should go before them, and let his dog bring up the rear. In a short time they will assume the proper speed, about one mile in the hour. Should the road they travel on be a green drive, the sheep will proceed nibbling their way onwards at the grass, along both sides. Before nightfall the drover should inquire of lodging for them for the night. Upon drove-roads, farms will be found at stated distances, with food and lodging for the drover and his flock at a moderate charge. The first day's journey should be a short one, not exceeding four or five miles. Allowing eight miles a-day for a winter day's

travel, and ten miles in summer for fat sheep, and knowing the distance to
the market by the destined route, the sheep should start in good time,
allowance being made for unforeseen delays, and also for one whole day's
rest near the market. The *farmer's drover* may either be his own shepherd or a
professional. As the flock know the shepherd, he makes the best drover, if he
can be spared as long away. A hired drover gets 2s.6d. a-day of wages,
besides travelling expenses; and he is intrusted with cash to pay the dues
incidental to the road and markets, such as tolls, food ferries, and market
custom. A drover of sheep should always have his dog, not a young dog (sure
to work and bark with a deal more zeal than judgment, to the irritation of
the sheep) but a knowing, cautious tyke. The drover should have a stout
crook, useful in turning a sheep disposed to break away from the rest. He
should carry provision with him, such as bread, meat, cheese, or butter, that
he may take luncheon or dinner beside his flock while resting in a quiet part
of the road, and slake his thirst in the first brook or spring he finds, or
purchase a bottle of ale at a road-side inn. Though exposed all day to the air,
and even feel cold, he should avoid drinking spirits, which only produce
temporary warmth, and for a long time after superinduce chilliness and
languor. Much rather drink ale or porter during the day, and reserve the
allowance of spirits he gives himself until the evening, when he can enjoy a
tumbler of warm toddy beside a comfortable fire, before retiring to rest for
the night. He should have a good knife, by which to remove any portion of
horn that may seem to annoy a sheep in its walk; and also a small bottle of a
mixture of tobacco-liquor and spirit of tar, with some cloth and twine, to
enable him to smear and bandage a sheep's foot, so as it may endure the
journey. He should be able to draw a little blood from a sheep in case of
sickness. Should a sheep fail on the road, he should be able to dispose of it to
the best advantage; or becoming ill, he should be able to judge whether a
drink of gruel or a handful of common salt in warm water may not recover it
so as to proceed; but rather than a lame or jaded sheep should spoil the
appearance of the lot in the market, it should be disposed of. . . .

Many dogs that live in the neighbourhood of drove-roads, and
particularly village dogs, are in the habit of looking out for sheep to worry,
at some distance from their homes. Short of sitting up all night, the principal
precaution is for the drover to go frequently through the flock with a light,
be late in retiring to rest, and up again early in the morning.

(from a report by the Scottish Board of Agriculture, 1850)

Any timetable for droving ruminants had to allow for inevitable delays, for
all ruminants need complete rest after feeding, to get value from their
fodder by chewing the cud. This, together with sleeping hours, which
depend upon the moon, made it necessary to fix distances of travel by time
as much as by conditions of terrain.

The delay caused by shoeing also varied. The shoes were needed only
over hard stony districts which heavy rain might soften, but regular
smithies holding a store of shoes were kept along definite drove stations.

As for cattle thieves, experienced cattlemen could tell by the *tracks* if cattle had been stolen. Walking cattle tracks are more even; a bullock hit across the head to turn him aside backs, splaying out the forefeet and pivoting around on his hind legs. Motor transport and cold storage have left the old drove roads a study for historians, and a problem for landowners; rail transport superseded droving, and old cattle stalls and pens can still be seen by sidings on now disused railways – the grim cattle trucks have become obsolete.

HORSES

Their bridles are not very brave, their saddles are but plaine
No bits, but snaffles all, of birch their saddles be
Much fashioned like the Scottish seats, broad flakes to keep the knee
From sweating of the horse, their panneles larger far
And broader be than ours.

On Russia, George Turberville (1540?–1610?)

Though writing on Russia, Turberville had constantly in mind what would be familiar to an English reader; thus 'snaffles all' were noticeable in contrast to the fierce curbs and bits used on mediaeval war horses, and the 'flakes' (saddle flaps) were similar to those described by Froissart as being used by the Scotch in border warfare, stiffened by thin metal plates, upon which they baked their oatcakes while travelling.

The horse varied throughout Britain. There were the high horses of the nobility; the active horse of the knight, trained to rear and strike out with spiked front feet; the 'second horse' or carrier for the page; the common 'riding horse'; the 'ambling pad'; and trains of pack horses (there were also the mules and donkeys of traders, of course). There were specially swift

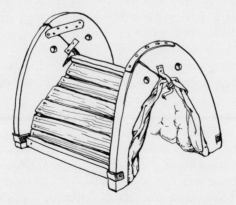

A pack saddle. The tie at the front supported the padding.

steeds for king's messengers: a certain estate in Norfolk paid rent of 'a dish of mushrooms delivered fresh for the King's breakfast in London' – this ensured the maintenance of swift horses, kept to supply the relays *en route*.

All these varied horses were the result of selective breeding for definite purposes, whereas the working horses of the countryman developed more from the type of land they lived on and the work they did: the wiry pack horse of the hill farm was utterly different from the heavy draught horse of the flat lands.

The history of the special breeds begins with the Norman Conquest. The Norman knights rode tall, handsome stallions. It was not sensible to risk a favourite mare in shipping overseas, but owing to the inadequate stabling during the subsequent campaigns (and the connivance of the 'locals') the imported stallions probably made a great many conquests among the local mares. A century later King John imported a hundred stallions from Flanders and later from Hainault. Young King Henry VIII imported lighter horses from Spain, and insisted on the nobility and clergy keeping stallions – fifteen hands was the standard. The attempted legislation on breeds lasted until Elizabeth's time: she had about 3,000 cavalry. James I started horse racing which led to horses being bred for speed, and Charles II used Turkish and Arabian imports for grace. (Chaucer's 'ambling pad' was probably of Spanish origin, as they were experts in training for this soft, easy-going gait.)

Rathegate, when travelling in England during Elizabeth I's reign reports: 'Most of the horses are low, small but very fast, and the riding horse often geldings and generally excellent, and the Queen has forbidden any horse to be exported without a licence.'

Horse travel could be comparatively swift if the horse was good and the track well known to a competent rider. A separate luggage horse meant having *two* good animals: and to travel at a gallop, the luggage had to be extremely skilfully secured or it shook loose. There were inevitable delays for tightening girths (unless the horses were in extremely hard training), and stops for fodder and water necessitated a rest, or at least a slow progress for an hour afterwards. The difference between active horsemanship on good mounts, and the plodding walk of luggage-burdened travellers was very great (though the latter was faster than ox-wain portage).

A late fifteenth- or early sixteenth-century traveller's memorandum lists equipment necessary for the journey: 'purse, dagger, cloke, nightcap, kerchief, shoehorn, boget and shoes. Spear, male, hode, halter, saddle-cloth, spurs, hat and a horse combe. Bow, arrows, sword, buckler, horne, leash, gloves, string and thy bracer. Pen, paper, ink, perchmente, reed wax, pommes, bokes thou remember. Penknife, comb, thimble, needle, thread, pointe, lest thy girth breake. Bodkin, knife, lyngel, give thy horse meate, see he be shoe'd well. Make merry, sing and thou can, take heed to thy gear that thou lose none.'

Boget: a water bag

Male: a mallet – to drive in the tether peg

Bracer: coming in the same line as bow and arrow, this may be the laced-on arm guard used in archery. Or it might be a saddle bar that braced one into the saddle to prevent an unguarded fall.

Pen, paper, etc: obviously the traveller goes to a business appointment ('paper' marks the end of the mediaeval period).

Pommes: the round bag of pumice powder used to give a surface grip for a quill pen on parchment; and this same powder could also act as the 'pomice', or ink-drying powder, in use before blotting paper.

Penknife: definitely the small sharp knife used for cutting pens, as another larger knife is also taken.

Points: strong leather ties (like boot-laces) which upheld long hose and breeches. Points were, by law, made of strongest leather and had a hundred uses.

Bodkin: sharp pointed dagger – could make a hole in a leather strap, and cut meat.

Lyngel: linen thread or string, and probably also small 'first aid' bandages of soft linen.

All very sensible. The bow and arrow may have been for sport, or for 'shooting for the pot' *en route*, as it was quite customary for an arrival at an inn to 'hand over a brace of birds, or other game' to be prepared for supper.

One does not imagine all the items were required by every rider. Their diversity, though, gives an excellent contemporary picture of a traveller setting out on horseback intending to be away for a night or so.

SADDLE BAR

In the 1960s a newspaper asked 'what was a saddle bar?' – proving how completely the dangers of horse travel have been forgotten. It was a safety device in general use for centuries. Sir Walter Scott mentioned it as an iron bar in front of a mediaeval knight to act as a brace: when he raised his arms above his head to swing the heavy sword, or even stood up in the saddle (on his specially long stirrup leathers) sword and armour made him very top-heavy.

The saddle bar was in ordinary use by work people: the last we know of was used by an old Cornish doctor doing his rounds, who would ride home so tired he'd be liable to fall asleep. He told me that it was quite customary as late as 1890 to see a countryman returning late from the market, fast asleep, slumped forward over his saddle bar while the horse plodded his

own way home. In earlier centuries, when bridle paths and roads were few
and unfrequented, any rider fallen from his horse might (if hurt) be left
helpless and undiscovered. Modern arrangements of 'being thrown clear'
were reversed: then the rider who fell with his steed might, when the horse
scrambled up, stand a chance of being carried onwards. Most mediaeval
riders appear to be well tied on.

FOOT MANTLE

The foot mantle mentioned by Chaucer was a luxury, and formed a
binding almost as secure as a saddle bar. It was used regularly against
winter cold or summer dust. A blanket is spread under the saddle, reaching
just below the stirrups. After mounting, the rider draws the back part
forward; he then folds the front part back, securing it round his waist
behind, the sides flapping back over the front of the legs. Market women
were usually so 'built up' among their baskets and panniers that they had to
be 'unpacked' before they could move at all! One Elizabethan market
woman is shown with her legs set in front of her panniers, her feet either
side of the horse's neck. Another method was to put the legs inside the
panniers and pack up around them. Long sacks of flour or meal were often
laid across the horse, front and back, the rider being wedged between
them. An old trick was a long bolster-shaped bag with a longitudinal slit in

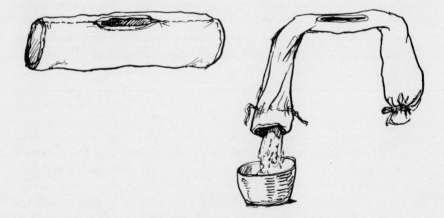

The 'boyster' was convenient for delivering loose materials.

the centre so that it formed two loosely-hung bags either side of the horse
and the only opening (the slit) lay smoothly under the saddle, which meant
that the contents could not be got at until the rider dismounted.

LITTERS AND 'COFFERS'

The litters and coffers specially made for horse transport are very interesting, some being constructed to swing between two horses (these are shown in the early manuscripts of Froissart). The section of these earlier hutches was a truncated triangle, the width at the top holding the two horses apart, the narrower base freeing the leg movement.

The Saddler

Ploughmen, carters and wagoners had to keep their harnesses in good order; it was their responsibility. The leather was regularly scraped with a sharp bone or blunt knife to remove dirt and sweat, and rubbed with goose grease and sheep's wool to keep it supple. The fashion of having leather black seems fairly recent – early manuscripts show farm leather its natural colour. (Tournament trappings were, of course, quite different.) Nor are horse brasses and decorations seen much before the end of the eighteenth century. The harness was made to order by the saddler who then, as now, sewed with the strongest flax thread and was somewhat of a tailor in fitting pillions and saddles. Boxes, slings, bags, and so on, were made to order. With leather plentiful and saddlers willing, one did not 'pack into *a* bag', one arranged what one intended to take, and the saddler made the bag to fit the luggage. Only examination of sixteenth and seventeenth-century examples can do justice to the skill of saddlers where they worked in connection with the armourers – from the earliest 'mail' armour (which was secured in overlapping scales on to specially dressed leather) to chain mail and the soft leather padding needed under plate armour. Today the modern saddler, even when hand stitching, uses a 'borkel', which gives far

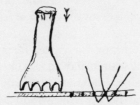

A borkel, used in saddlery to mark the position of the holes for stitching.

fewer stitches to the inch than the mediaeval workers' gauges which resemble a fine tooth comb. The quilted leather was padded with wool for softness, and boiled leather made hard and resilient enough to bounce back an arrow. This was skilled trade work, but our ordinary land labourer had skill enough to make, fit, and repair his own horse and ox tackle – and he also found time to decorate it.

The Smiths

The agricultural labourer did not have much metal to deal with: farm tools were mostly made of wood, just faced with metal where possible. The shoeing smith probably did this job as a side-line, together with any other

*A metal-tipped spade,
redrawn from an early ms.*

metalwork required. He was one of the first workers to 'work on contract', undertaking all the shoeing 'for the year'. Other small jobs might be included, but in the horse and oxen days the shoeing smithy was rather like a good modern garage. Along drove roads, where cattle came off soft land to a stony passage a special drovers' smithy might shoe a hundred oxen at a time – old drove routes show their positions. (Near Clun in Shropshire a cache of old ox shoes was found, obviously made and stored ahead ready for use.) In some cases the old tree stump that once based the anvil survives.

Travelling smiths went around outlying farms; they took their own tackle with them (and some seem to have contracted for the farmer's 'spare hide, for their bellows'). Sometimes the smith brought his own 'blower', as well as his own trained 'striker', or he would borrow farm lads and so recruit apprentices.

Large estates and farms would always have their own traditional smithy, where the labourers' billhooks, sickles and sythes were made, to suit local need.

Few realise how many different smiths existed for different jobs. The 'quarry smith' was a specialist who knew how to temper his picks and jumpers to his special stone: on the skill of this smith the output depended, for by an error in the temper of the metalwork, the quarry could be brought to a standstill through broken tools. Such breaks were also considerably dangerous for the workers. The temperature of the weather was also important – a hard frost made work impossible.

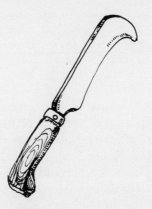

Warlike halberds, some with tassels to catch drips of blood, may have been studied by the countryman; but he made his own tools to suit himself. The agricultural labourer still uses a billhook shaped to deal with the wild growth of his own district. Even now wholesale manufacturers have to make as many designs as there are counties; and the workman still adapts them to suit himself.

The smith was employed by the cartwright and wagon-builder of later date to make and shrink the metal rims on to the wheels, and to provide the metal fittings necessary.

A small and pleasant craft (probably known even to mediaeval smiths) was to remove styes from the eyes of children. The little ones were sent to ask him to do it, and he'd say, 'Just wait till I've done this horseshoe', and the child would push close to watch, close to the heat and the steam, and blink hard, every time the great hammer came down with a bang – till in half an hour the smith would wipe his hands, and look, and smile (for the stye had burst and wept itself away).

Butcher and skinner and forester all obtained their tools from smiths. (All the labourer wanted was his dinner knife, and something to use it on!)

Finger Fern

Mediaeval people quoted from the classics to show up their knowledge, or to save the trouble of trying something out for themselves. This example in the translation of *De Rusticanus* by Sylvestris is of special interest:

And finger fern, which being given to swine,
Doth make their tripes dissolve away in fine
And horses, treading on moonwort with their hollow heels,
At night go bare-foot home.

Their master, wondering where their shoes begone?
Oh moonwort! Tell us where thou hidest the smith.
Hammer and pincers thou unshoest them with
Since the best farrier cannot set a shoe
So firm, but thou canst shortly it undo.

This was copied by every botanist thereafter, until Anne Pratt, of the nineteenth century, writes that 'the Earl of Essex lost a battle in Devon because his horses were tethered overnight on White Down and lost their shoes from finger fern.' Finger fern is a single soft frond, growing in marshy places, and could not harm anything. Moonwort is quite different: a tough, daisy-like plant growing on stony ground, it was apt to entangle in early horse-shoe nails, for the nails were not then sunk into the shoe, but spiked out. A mediaeval farrier was likely to find moonwort, or similar tough low-growing plants entangled in a loose shoe.

The real explanation for the horses tethered on White Down was probably that they were given nosebags of corn, which they shook, spilling corn. Mice gleaning would cause the horses to stamp, and possibly the shoe-nails would be caught by the moonwort growing on the stony ground. (Or, perhaps the shoes were removed by a skilful spy?) It certainly could not have been finger fern.

The Tinker and Odd Job Man

The tinker carried a small outfit for all manner of metal work. He is pictured in every century and (like most itinerant craftsmen) seems to be prosperous, till the end of the nineteenth century, when too many 'escapees' from the industrial revolution stole or bought a few tools and became tramp workers. The gypsy tribe, though, have ever been excellent smiths and tinkers. Such a 'regular' worker would call at definite times, and work would be laid aside till he arrived.

Metal facing was one of his odd jobs. Twelfth- and thirteenth-century spades were of wood with a small metal edge only. The fork for dung and implements like the eel spear were usually 'made to order' by the smith and hafted with wood by the worker. This 'marriage' between metal and wood is very important.

HORSEHAIR

When most long-distance transport was by horsepower (oxen being too slow for anything but extremely heavy draught), horsehair was freely available and used for an enormous number of things: hair sieves, the bows for stringed instruments, hair mats used for draining cider, and for curled hair mattresses (still used in old-fashioned households). The horsehair cloth, in plain, black weave, covering old chairs is now of 'antique' value, but the old damask-patterned, coloured haircloth went out early in the last century. Horsehair cloth was always narrow width. As hair was only long enough to cross one width, three workers were required, the weaver and two others, one standing at each end, who caught the shuttle, dexterously inserted a hair, thin top to thick tail (as with willow weaving) and shot it back to be refilled again at the other end. The cloth, which was woven damp, was hot pressed and glazed to a polished finish. Haircord varied from strong thick plaited cord to fine threads used in delicate instrument work.

For the bow and arrow, fine strong horsehair was used to bind the notches (made of sheep's horn) on to the ends of the bow; and loops could be worked with it at the end of the bowstring for unslinging. It was also used to secure the plume of the feathered arrows. The expression to 'draw a bead' when shooting is a reminder that the sights of the early crossbows were beads threaded on horsehair. The most vile use of these threads was to twist gins to catch the feet of small birds, the hair itself being almost invisible on the trees.

The Victorian vogue for human hair designs in jewellery was only the artistic end of what had been a serious commercial industry. It was from the spinning of ropes and fishing lines that curled-hair padding was derived. The hair was corded and spun on a throw cock exactly as straw ropes were made. The hair was twisted till the length was writhing tight, then the two ends were brought together and the twist 'ran up' to form a double cord. This cord was twisted, and doubled again, and again, until a short thick wad of twisted hair resulted. This was boiled in a dye vat (copperas gave a handsome, uniform black to the vari-coloured hairs). The wad was then dried in heat under pressure. When absolutely dry, the wad of hair was sliced across into short lengths, the released hairs springing back resiliently. This was the usual 'curled hair' filling for bedding, saddle, window seating, and so on. (Also, being light, it padded fashionable breeches.) Collars for working horses were usually filled with rush or straw plait. Sieves were made of long white tail-hairs, sewn over parchment, stretched and secured by hoops of bent wood, tension being obtained by expanding the hoops slightly after setting the hairs.

The hair of oxen, neats and goats was less valuable and was often classed with the refuse hair from the lime vats after the hides were withdrawn. This befouled hair still contained grease, so that the Upholsterers Guild of Elizabethan times affirmed that 'When warmed by the heat of a man's body it engendered a stink so pestilential that many were destroyed thereby.' Elizabethan legislation prohibited its use. Sieves made of the horse hair were called *tamise*: we keep the word today in the 'tammy cloth' used by cooks for straining jellies, and so on.

LEATHER AND TANNING

Country people either cured the leather after killing their own beasts or, if they did not do their own slaughtering and sold 'on the hoof', they might ask for the hide to be returned or arrange for it to go to the tanner's. Large establishments with estates kept their own lime vats and employed their own workers. The vats for a castle or large feudal holding would be away and *below* the main buildings, near the slaughter pens and the lowest stretches of the main running water supply, and near pits where offal could be disposed of (if they were good agriculturalists, the offal would be incorporated in the accumulated farmyard manure and spread on the fields in the hard frost of winter).

The vats varied – one measured by the author was almost twelve feet square – and were constructed like a small water meadow slightly sunk, the earth being used to raise a retaining dyke wall round it; the base had to be trodden flat and water from an adjacent stream flooded in. The lime was brought and renewed according to the number of hides to be soaked. The hides were laid in the lime vat spread flat, hair side down, and left to soak. The effect was to inflate the hair cells and so release the hair, and as the hides were stirred and changed, the loosened hair accumulated in the vat. When all the hair was removed from the skins they were taken out and scraped to remove the soft subcutaneous fat, which the lime had bleached white, and the residue of lime and hair would be scooped out and sold for plastering. The skins were then rinsed and the process of tanning carried out according to the use of the skins – whether they were to be thick for heavy, stiff working, or scraped down and rubbed and softened.

The bark for tanning – oak, willow, beech, and so on – was sometimes packed in with the leather. We have seen leather so tanned in Keswick, where the bark strippings from making the willow sculls, and the chippings of bark from split oak strips, were turned direct into the tanner's vat adjoining the bentwood workshops. Sometimes a stone roller was trundled over the bark, roughly pounding it. Afterwards the tan was soaked and beaten to a thick ooze in which the leather was immersed. A curious method of 'tanning under pressure' was called 'bagging'. In this process the leather was folded and rough sewn (with a double folding seam) into a bag; this was filled with the wet tan and allowed to drip, or be pressed out, through the pores of the leather. (The same arrangement was sometimes used in dye working, but immersion was the most probable early method.)

The dressing mixtures used varied locally, and also according to the weather and the finish required. Methods varied: one recipe gives 'half an ounce [each?] of whyte coperose and alome and salt-peter'. On farms it seems probable that refuse from the verjuice and cider presses would provide an acid at the right time (in the late autumn). Also 'soar milk' and ferments of rye would cause chemical action in the pores of the skin to raise and expand the texture. These later dressings released any deep hairs, so completing the main stripping performed in the lime vats. (Packing the skins damp in warmth, to putrefy, also had this effect, but was very unpleasant, unreliable, and condemned for household use.)

After the acid, an alkaline dressing was used to 'bate' (abate) the action, and the list of dressings is extraordinarily revolting: hen and pig dung were used, and for a form of 'Morocco leather' dog's dung was used. Simple fillings were soft litharges variously made of soap and boiled meal. Bran was used in rubbing and suppling, and a thin size made by boiling the leather trimmings or hoof parings gave a polished surface.

For centuries the dressing of leather remained an important job in any large community, and there were independent tanyards attached to the droving depots where animals were slaughtered.

The resolving of a herd of cattle into 'products' can be studied along the river in almost any old town. First the cattle pens, then the slaughter yards, then the tanyards, then the horn works and last, farthest downriver, the soap and glue-boiling yards. These were the trade yards, but most farms which slaughtered cattle for their own food had a small pit for the pelts. All large estates dressed their own leather. The lime vat can sometimes be traced outside old estates, with remnants of a hut near it. In some cases (we traced one near Northampton) centuries of using lime have altered the surrounding pasture. The tan vat would be arranged near running water, the shape varying rather more than the lime vats; it might be quite a deep pit where the skins could lie flat with the tan material packed between the layers. Different tans were used for different purposes, and there would be workmen's huts and stores for the tan.

Mediaeval people used all manner of leather for covering screens, chairs and coffers, and making belts, pouches and gloves, but comparatively little has survived, for the embossing and staining made the leather fragile. But the designs survived to influence the early inlays that begin in subsequent centuries to decorate wooden furniture.

Genuine buff leather came from the wild Russian bull, and Henry VIII's Russian Trading Company was obliged to import numbers of these hides for army use, as buff leather well scalded and polished was bullet-proof and sword-proof. An army regiment has retained the name of 'the Buffs'.

The soft sheep leather that knights wore under their armour to prevent chafing was sometimes quilted and padded and was what today we should call chamois leather. The dark, hard breastplates of polished leather that would stop an arrow or from which a stone shot would bounce back was cuir bouilli (boiled leather) and made a fine defence armour. Between that and a dainty scented lady's glove, a gold and jewelled belt and a neat small purse, there was every type of leather on the market.

DECEMBER

The housing of cattle, while winter doth hold,
Is good for all such as are feeble and old:
It saveth much compas, and many a sleep,
and spareth the pasture for walk of thy sheep.

Give cattle their fodder in plot dry and warm,
and count them for miring, or other like harm:
Young colts with thy wennels together go serve,
lest lurched by others, they happen to sterve.

For charges so little, much quiet is won,
if strongly and handsomely all things be done:
But use to untackle them once in a day,
to rub and to lick them, to drink and to play.

Serve rye-straw out first, then wheat-straw and pease,
then oat-straw and barley, then hay if ye please:
But serve them with hay, while the straw stover last,
They will eat no more straw, they had rather to fast!

Get grindstone and whetstone for tool that is dull,
or often be letted, and fret belly-full:
A wheel-barrow also be ready to have,
at hand of thy servant, the compas to save.

Both salt fish and ling fish (if any ye have),
through shifting and drying, from rotting go save,
Lest winter with moistness do make it relent,
and put it in hazard, before it be spent.

Broom faggot is best to dry haberden on,
lay board upon ladder, if faggots be gone:
for breaking (in turning) have very good eye,
and blame not the wind, so the weather be dry.

Go look to thy bees, if the hive be too light,
set water and honey, with rosemary dight;
Which set in a dish full of sticks in the hive,
from danger of famine ye save them alive.

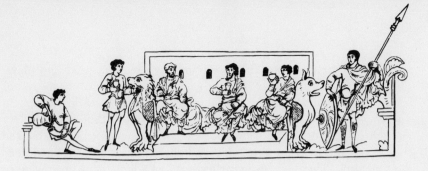

'O DIRTY DECEMBER,
FOR CHRISTMAS REMEMBER'

TUSSER'S VERSES show the household of a comfortable, prosperous, hard-working farmer toward the end of the sixteenth century. Since he left us his advice we can form a good idea of how he lived throughout the year; it is more difficult to get a picture of humbler people in their home life. By December, the work of the year was almost over: cattle had to be looked to, of course, and routine tasks done, but there was less done on the land itself. It seems as good a time of year as any to think about the people who populated it.

THE HOUSEHOLDERS

Then comes the Tax Collector, full of pomp and boast
Give me silver, it is written on my tablet as thow knowest –
More than my true tax he takes before he goest
And then . . . demands my chicken for his dinner, roast . . .

a political song

Few erudite historians were likely to enter many huts. The tax collector does not give them a bad name: disparaging remarks come from benighted travellers refuging in a hut when lost on a wet night; they report dark, damp, flea-bitten misery. The very uniformity of the remarks arouses distrust, because if all the hundreds of huts had been so bad, the inhabitants would have ceased to exist! But from some huts came men of brains and brawn, who built bridges, made mills, dug dykes and worked out engineering problems. They made lively, humorous wood carvings just for fun, and impudent caricatures of their bosses – often on the very stones provided by their bosses. They sang and cavorted and produced plays. They were humans, who'd drink with a mate and beat a wife – at the risk of being well beaten back, for not all women were meek and downtrodden. There were the bridge-builders whose 'wives went forth to wit how they wrought? four score in a flock! a fair sight' and brought excellently cooked cheese and bread and chickens; cleanly dight in white cloths, to encourage their menfolk. There is also an earlier story, in which the women went to collect the battered contestants after a 'battachomyomachy'.

> By wickes and kexis and flikering rush light
> They fetched home the husbands that were their troth plight.
> Some wives brought harrows thin husbands home to fetch
> Some brought whole doors, & some brought a hetch
> Some brought flat hurdles & some brought a cretch
> And some brought wheel barrows.
>
> Tournament of Tottenham (late 14th century)

These women, sound, strong and capable, took their fair share of farm and field work, and surely could cook and clean a hut and feed their families, so there is no valid reason to think cottage life was always uncomfortable and squalid.

Children

> Good huswives take paine, and do count it good luck,
> To make their own brests their own child to give suk.
> Though wrauling and rocking be noysome so near,
> Yet lost by ill nursing is worser to hear.
>
> We find it not spoken, so often for naught,
> that children were better unborne than untaught.
> Some cockneis with cocking are made very fooles,
> fit neither to prentice for plough or for schooles.
>
> Teach child to ask blessing, serve God and to church:
> then blesse as a mother; else blesse him with burch;
> Thou huswife thus doing, what further shal nede
> but all men to call thee good mother in dede.
>
> Tusser (1573)

Babies

She 'wrapped him in swaddling clothes and laid him in a manger'.

Infant mortality was high, and many mothers died who would have survived under modern conditions. While the astrologically educated poets (male) ascribed all variations, both physical and mental, to the influence of the planets, the earth-educated woman realised the variations in seasonal diet were likely to be responsible. By experience and observation, they noted the effect on physical and mental developments which were also observed in an idealised way in early mediaeval times. For example a woman born under Venus should have:

> Pretty mouth to sing a song, eyebrows delicate and long,
> Bodies made for bodies' bliss, sweet smooth faces, warm to kiss,
> Loving music, well can they, upon the lute or tabor play.
> Swift in love and swift in quarrel, and deliciously immoral.
>
> from a mediaeval *Hausbuch*

This is almost a clinical description of a certain physical type, with pearly teeth, fair skin and soft hair. Saturn's type, on the contrary, shows thickened bones and slow wits:

> Saturn's child is dull, grey, hard and cold.
> Cadaverous, with eyes deep set, whose tough skin grows coarse beard
> Thick and ridged their ugly teeth, within a widened mouth . . .

Birth control must have been difficult (ornate chastity belts belong to social circles where lineage was a consideration). Our working woman probably made her own attempts of which she left little record. We cannot know just how much the mediaeval midwife learnt from observation about pre-natal influences which male astrologers attributed to the influence of the planets, but she would note that a child conceived in autumn and carried through the dark months of sparse diet when there was no meat, nor milk, nor eggs, or green food, was likely to be a poor baby at birth; but if it survived it would have the good spring and summer foods, and sunshine and warmth for its first year of growth. Whereas a baby conceived in spring and carried through the summer months was likely to be a fine bonny baby at birth, but to lose badly during its first winter. Seeing this, they may well have noted the results of variations in diet during pregnancy, the extra *salt* of winter dried meat, for they advise the mother to get a goat to kiddle late, to provide a late supply of milk, and to keep some beast alive to be slaughtered as late as possible. They were always anxious to satisfy any special food whim of a pregnant woman, considering it important to her welfare.

In short, the sensible woman put things down to earthly causes, not heavenly ones.

A Good Nurse

She feedeth the child when it is an hungered, and pleaseth the child with
whispering and songs when it shall sleep, and swatheth it in sweet clothes,
and righteth and stretcheth out its limbs, and bindeth them together with
cradlebands, to keep and save the child that it have no miscrooked limbs.

De Proprietatibus Rerum, Bartholomaeus Anglicus (fl. 1230–50)

HOUSING

The animal instincts to eat a good meal, for a mother to feed her young, and
for a man to hunt, are basic facts, and at all levels the quality of a household
varies more according to its owners than to its period or position. There can
exist a squalid, mismanaged manor house, a poverty-stricken war-worn
castle, and a miserable hut. To describe any of them could be as misleading
as describing the reverse. One can only give the basic materials available,
and let the 'owners' use them.

As we study the man of the land, living on the land, building for himself,
we will report him first.

The best comment upon hut construction comes from Froissart; his
report was made outside Edinburgh in 1385: 'For though the Englysshemen
brinne our houses, we care lytell therefore; we shall make them agayne
chepe ynough: we are but thre dayes to make them agayne; if we maye
geate foure or fyve stakes, and bowes to cover them.'

Defoe attests to this basic ability as late as 1665; writing of the plague, he
describes how London men were still capable of housing themselves in the
countryside much as their ancestors had done: 'They made troughs to sleep
in, padded them with leaves, and cut up tent cloth to make covers; when a
gift of straw came, it was to them like a feather bed. One of them, a
carpenter, in a few days built a shed and later a house, with rafters and
roof, and an upper floor where they lodged warm. It was thatched and the
walls made of earth were thick [presumably wattle and daub]. Against the
earth wall at one end they made a chimney, and with a deal of trouble fitted
it with a funnel, to carry off the smoak.' These later 'escapists' went to the
markets as they were 'chiefly put to it for bread. They had no querns,
therefore they ate the corn that was given to them parched [presumably
beaten down] and some constructed a hearth with a hollow so that they
could bake bread'. He adds: 'Several families of the poorer sort built huts in
the forest', and 'Several of these families encamped for good and all and
resolved to move no more.'

This 'resolve' shows that by 1665 some working people had begun to
realise that they were better off in the country than in town, and that in spite of the

rebellion against the new 'enclosures', England was not yet too crowded for them to live *on* the land and *off* the land, as their forebears had done.

The Structure of Early Huts (and Cottages)

There was no hard and fast rule, because so many different peoples brought their traditional ideas and adapted them to local materials. The dwellings seem to have been rectangular in wooded districts, where timber was available, and circular in reed and clay localities. The basic measurement was Man's – six feet to lie to sleep, and a central height of seven feet where possible. The difficulty in constructing with wattle and daub lay in finding timber for doorposts and steady posts to support the wattle weaving. As the osiers were woven the interstices were rammed full of dry moss, or wool and hair, or anything that would 'hold' the clay and mud when it was 'thrown' at the wall, and pressed into it. (See also p. 216.) As the walls rose, the outsides were rough plastered, upwards till the wall was complete and the roof set on, the final plastering being smoothed downwards to ground level.

Within, the same work was done, but the floor was often dug down somewhat, the displaced earth being piled up against the inside wall to form a low ledge or narrow seat, in some places made wide to form a raised bed. This gave rather more headroom in the hut and the step down stopped the 'draught along the floor'.

Though we deal with huts and cottages, it's convenient to collate their lighting and heating with houses and halls, because the same fuel was used in both.

For light, a high flame is needed, and for heat, red glowing coals, therefore in the Great Hall the fire dogs stand tall and logs are upended against them to catch the draught and throw up a flame. In the hut, the owner props up two dry logs, or builds a pointed wigwam of three sticks to make light, or lays them flat to cook on. (The rule 'one log won't burn, two may burn, three must' is common campers' lore.)

In a well-equipped cottage in a well-wooded district they might arrange a back slope of logs that would slide down slowly as the lower ones burnt

One won't, two will, three must. For slow cooking the fire is banked up.

through. (Later, sloping fire backs were used.) Cooking fires were best enclosed, and the hut woman arranged stones or damp wood to form wells of hot red ash over which to do her simple cooking; later they had iron stands of different heights to support their pots and pans.

Pots and Pans

In a hut or cottage the iron cauldron was so important that it became a status symbol and a family inheritance. The earliest did not have legs but

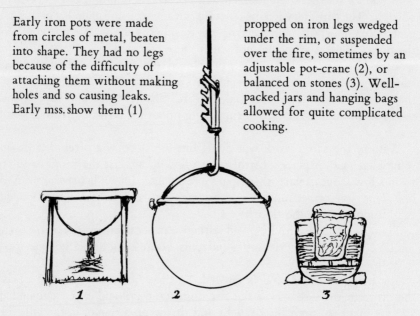

Early iron pots were made from circles of metal, beaten into shape. They had no legs because of the difficulty of attaching them without making holes and so causing leaks. Early mss. show them (1)

propped on iron legs wedged under the rim, or suspended over the fire, sometimes by an adjustable pot-crane (2), or balanced on stones (3). Well-packed jars and hanging bags allowed for quite complicated cooking.

1   *2*   *3*

balanced precariously on three stones or adjusted logs. They held boiling water in which bags of food could be cooked, or, resting on a piece of flat wood, earthenware jars could stand and contain things to be stewed. Over wood, simmering rather than quick boiling is usual (often to the preservation of food values). Flat bake pans of iron were common. It is

A Welsh 'planc' for baking oatcake. Made of iron, it is approximately sixteen inches in diameter and a quarter-inch thick.

described how in the Scots wars of the fourteenth century the Scottish riders would remove the small flat metal plates from their saddles, set them over a little fire of sticks and on them bake oat cakes (from the store of meal they kept in linen bags mixed with bourne water). The static hut dweller could even more simply use the hot hearthstone direct. 'Pans' of metal or even pottery were few – wooden bowls were more common and less easily broken. It is possible to heat a drink in a wooden bowl by dropping a hot stone into it, or by stirring with a burning stick – or a red hot poker.

The comparative *weights* of metal and pottery ware, compared with wood, altered arrangements in both hut and Hall. In castles can be seen the huge built-in boiler cauldrons, static, with fire holes scooped out down below (keeping them low for convenience in lifting the water pails that kept them filled). The hut cauldron, if unsupported, stood on the floor and there is a record of an interesting case in which a baby was scalded to death. The husband was judged responsible – the argument being that the cauldron was too heavy for the woman to lift.

Doors and Windows

The door posts were the most important and durable part of the building. Often they were used to record the family's number and might be retained by the owners, when moved from feudal property, The lowness of the door was economic and defensive. An intruder creeping in bent double, head first, was very easily decapitated.

In stone buildings windows were often slits; where the walls were solid wattle and daub they did not exist, and the low earthen hut was pretty dark, lit only by the central fire cooking the evening meal or providing warmth in cold and stormy weather. When there *were* windows in cottages they would be small, and blocked when necessary with shutter or sack. They could be filled with waxed cloth or plates of thin horn. Contemporary travellers in Russia reported that they used talc for windows:

> They cut it very thinne, and sow it with a thread,
> In pretie order, like to panes,
> No other glass, good faith, doth give a better light
> And sure the rock is nothing rich, the cost is very slight.

Till the eighteenth century thin horn remained in use for stable lanterns, as it was not easily broken when carried about. The early glass for cottages needed to be set in mullions because the pieces were so small. The early molten glass was whorled and spun out into a circle, so that it graded off from the thick central points to the perimeter. The outer, thinner portion

was the best glass, the inner the thickest. (All show the wave of the spin.)
The central nub where it was broken was of the least value and was sold off
cheap for cottage use. This is what we now term 'bottle glass' and
consider 'decorative'.

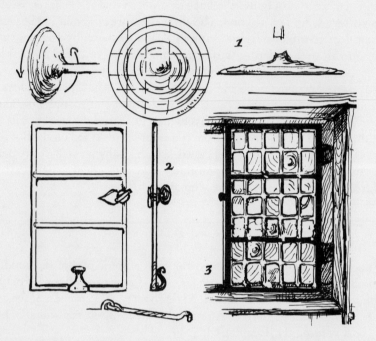

Plate glass was expensive, and not made in quantity until the nineteenth
century. Before then glass was spun (1) and when cool cut into panes. (Early
Victorian glass shows the slightly distorted effect of the wave.) Small pieces
of glass were cheaper, but presented problems. A frame, and its fastenings
(2), were of no use unless they could be filled with glass. The small squared
pieces of glass were leaded together (3) and the limp lead and glass wired to
iron supports, holding it firm to the frame.

Chimneys

Sir, he made a chimney in my father's house and the bricks are alive at this
day to testify it.

Henry VI

These were built into and on to castles and mansions long before the
cottager ran one up outside. Early chimneys were complicated jobs. Some
localities had corner fireplaces. Quite early, the one central fire, which
was used for boiling, was considered insufficient for baking, and so

enclosed ovens were developed. A space was cleared on the hot hearthstone, and the bread or pie was set on it and covered with an iron pot. (These iron pots were used in Devon till recently. Speaking of their use, the cottager said, 'If 'tes pies, I put her under her on a dish, but if she be a loaf I set her down naked.') Usually the new baking place was built outside. Later, this bakeoven was built on one side of the main fire, and a boiler built on the other side, thus giving the kitchen a 'range' of three fireplaces all in one, for the logs from the central wood fire were used to heat the other two when required.

Soot depended on the type of fuel used. Light woods and brushwood made light ash and light soot. Firs made an inflammable soot and gave a

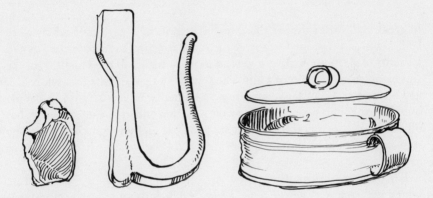

The warm chimney kept tinder dry in its box. On the left and middle are a flint and steel for striking a light to ignite the tinder, which was usually prepared from partially charred linen or the Male Agarick, a form of puffball.

blackish tarry deposit, which when scraped off had several uses. White woods have a light soot, but their ash was valuable for making washing lye or (with added fats) a type of soap. Cottage chimneys, when short and easily accessible, were swept with a holly bush pushed from below. (Or a hen dropped down from the top cleared a short chimney very quickly. Most householders had their own methods.)

In some later households a 'shoot' dropped the soot down to the shed where the soap-boiling was done.

Floors

In huts and cottages there would be the trodden earth, levelled during the hut construction. Once this has dried out hard, and been subject to repeated sweeping, it ceases to be dusty and acquires a smooth texture. (In African huts we have found black floors given a hard surface by the use of ox blood. We have never been able to find evidence of this being used in these islands, but so primitive a custom might go unremarked – it would only be used by the people whose contemporary home life was not studied.) Rush and straw strewing is noted in halls and houses, but in small huts around open fires such loose straw would be dangerous even if they could afford it. Bracken was thrown down as bedding for man and beast. Bracken does burn, but not so swiftly.

Sleeping

In great Halls after dinner the thick boards of the long trestle tables were laid down on the stone floor near the walls for the grooms and guards and servants to sleep upon. There was no more hardship in the bundle of brake and blanket on the floor of a hut. The squared huts and cottages usually also had a wooden ladder leading up to an open ledge under the roof. A couple of hides, or rough woven cloth, made a curtain and gave some privacy, but otherwise the sleepers aloft could see and hear all that went on below. The step-ladder could be drawn up for safety after the children had been sent to bed.

For owners of draughty castles the 'night gown' was the thick wrap, which was removed before getting into bed; in huts, one kept on clothing if cold; or discarded it if warm – or amorous. It is very probable that the straw or brake in the hut was twisted and woven into the thick mat or 'truckle bed' which was used for centuries to supplement sleeping accommodation in most households and inns.

straw rope

spicks

bed

The truckle or trundle bed was usually of straw rope or plait, formed like a mat and held flat by spicks (long wooden spikes) thrust through the plait. The edge was finished with two or three raised rows, kept upright by shorter spicks thrust down into the mat below. This edge kept off the draught and held in the bedclothes.

THE CONTRAST – TOWN AND COUNTRY

The Cottage in the Town

Pitiful it is to read the cottage woman's woe
Charged with a crew of children
And with a landlord's rent.
In the narrow room carding, combing, clouting,
Washing, rubbing and winding, and peeling rushes.
Ashamed to beg, ashamed to let the neighbours know.
                    Piers the Plowman, William Langland (1332?–1400?)

Langland's cottage is an example of the expanding town that completely altered the lives of erstwhile country folk. The same disruption occurred during the later Industrial Revolution. If you cut any plant from its roots it dies of starvation. So for the poor in the mediaeval slum, 'bread and thin ale for them are a banquet, a farthings worth of mussels or cockles were a feast for them'. But we study the household still well-rooted in the land, remote, independent and isolated, or paying work rent in return for their modicum of communal protection. So contrast Langland's description of:

The Cottage in the Country

I have no penny, pullets for to buy
No, neither goose nor pig, but only two green cheeses
A few curds, a little cream, and a haver cake.
And two loaves of beans and bran, baked for my little ones.
And by my soul I say, I have no salt bacon, nor a cook boy collops to make
But I have parsley, cabbage, leeks and a cow and a calf.
And a mare to draw the dung afield while the drought lasteth.

'For my little ones' – herein lies the basic side of history.

'HUSBANDLY FURNITURE'

Yokes, forks, and such other, let bailiff spy out,
and gather the same, as he walketh about;
And after, at leisure, let this be his hire
To beath them, and trim them, at home by the fire.

The fire was necessary not only for light to see by, but because heat and steam were used in making wood tools, for wood is curved by steaming and bending while wet. Metal rims were shrunk on to wooden bowls and tools, exactly as metal tyres were shrunk on to wooden wheels (by making the metal red-hot for expansion and contracting it on to the wood with cold water.) Pegs of wood must be dried till they are firm as iron before being driven into holes, for if they dried and shrank afterwards, they would drop out. One reason for the extra length of pegs sticking out of old pegged rafters was that if they were inserted in damp weather they could be checked again, to see if hot sun on the roof or heating from below had shrunk them. Wooden bowls in daily use had to be waterproofed with grease, or beeswax. The cracked side of a wooden bowl can be repaired by soaking the opposite side till the crack closes, when the crack can be secured by a metal band closing it, or it can be sewn up with wire. Trenchers and other flat wooden articles are repaired by wedges tapped down into the wood for a close fit; a quick dip into boiling water will often straighten a bent handle.

As the worker whittled and sliced, the wood shavings lit the room with dancing flames. Cups of iron raised high over some fire dogs could hold a bright burning brand lifted out of the fire to give extra light. These iron cups were sometimes used by cooks to finish off something in a small pan at eye level, but their main use was to hold a little extra lighting, close to the fire (where a candle would melt).

Wood was used for many things in the house and about the farm – beds, stools, benches, boxes of every description – a four-foot square cornbin, a carved and locked box (that probably also held family bible and papers, quills and ink well) – the shepherd's wooden tarbox which he hung on his staff, the child's doll, the rope spindle, the crow clapper, and the leather-hinged salt hopper.

> A good Husband will alwaies have his Forkes and Rakes made ready in the winter before; and they should be got between Michaelmas and Martilmas. When the husband sitteth by the fire and hath nothing to doe, then may he make them readie, and toothe the Rakes with dry wilhie wood, and bore the holes with his wimble both above and under, and drive the teeth upward fast and hard, and then wedge them above with dry wood of oake, for that is hard, and will drive and never come out . . .
>
> Have a care that the Rake and the Forke lye upright in thine hand; for if the one end of thy Rake or the side of thy Forke hang downward then they be neither handsome nor easie to work with.
>
> *Booke of Husbandrie*, attributed to Sir Anthony Fitzherbert (1470–1538)

NOMENCLATURE OF TOOLS

Notwithstanding I have give them those names as most familiar unto mee,

yet in other Countries I know they have other names, which I am assured are
not so farr different, but by these the simplest may conceave my meaning.
Booke of Husbandrie

The local names of tools remain unchanged for centuries, and where a
stranger comes from another locality he will need to adopt an entirely new
vocabulary, use it daily for weeks, and instantly change back again to his
own local names when he returns home. So long as the earth needs tools,
tools will remain in use. Some of the words are probably onomatopoeic.

A long-handled narrow scoop, used to scrape up the wet stones and mud
from the bottom of a drain, was called a 'scruppet' (that is, 'scrape-up-
n'out'). Whether a 'beetle' was once a 'beat 'um' is controversial; recently
a paviour in Tottenham Court Road told me he'd always called it a beetle,
but 'here in London the men calls her a "beadle"' (we know it was also
called a 'bithel'). From Abingdon comes the 'pickoys', or the 'pyke, as sum
men says'. Some names survived the disappearance of the old usage which
gave rise to them. The old quarry hands used to call the blasting fuse the
'reed', as a hollow reed of straw filled with gunpowder was their original
fuse tool. Language experts have a field of research here.

Tusser's farmland was on the bank of the Stour estuary, so readers may
find Suffolk words in his list of 'husbandly furniture'.

> *Barn-locked, Gofe-ladder, short pitchfork, and long,*
> *flail, straw fork, and rake, with a fan that is strong;*
> *Wing, cartnave and bushel, peck, strike ready hand,*
> *get casting shouel, broom, and a sack with a band.*
>
> *A stable well planked, with key and with lock,*
> *walls strongly well lined, to bear off a knock;*
> *A rack and a manger, good litter and hay,*
> *sweet chaff, and some provender, every day.*
>
> *A pitch-fork, a dung-fork, sieve, skep, and a bin,*
> *a broom, and a pail, to put water therein;*
> *A hand-barrow, wheel-barrow, shovel, and spade,*
> *a curry-comb, mane-comb, and whip for a jade.*
>
> *A buttrice, and pincers, a hammer and nail,*
> *and apern, and scissars for head and for tail,*
> *Whole bridle and saddle, whitleather, and awl*
> *with collars and harness, for thiller and all.*
>
> *A pannell and wanty, pack-saddle, and ped,*
> *a line to fetch litter, and halters for head;*
> *With crotchets and pins, to hang trinkets thereon,*
> *and stable fast chained, that nothing be gone.*

Strong axle-treed cart, that is clouted and shod,
cart-ladder and wimble, with percer and pod;
Wheel-ladder for harvest, light pitch-forks, and tough,
shave, whip-lash well knotted, and cart-rope enough.

Ten sacks, whereof every one holdeth a coom,
a pulling-hook handsome, for bushes and broom;
Light tumbrel and dung-crone, for easing (Sir Wag),
Shouel, pickax, and mattock, with bottle and bag.

A grindstone, a whetstone, a hatchet and bill,
with hammer, and English nail, sorted with skill;
A frower of iron, for cleaving of lath,
with roll for a saw-pit, good husbandry hath.

A short saw, and long saw, to cut a-two logs,
an axe, and an adze, to make trough for thy hogs;
A Dover Court beetle, and wedges with steel,
strong lever to raise up the block from the wheel.

Two ploughs and a plough-chain, two culters, three shares,
with ground clouts and side clouts for soil that sow tares
With ox-bows and ox-yokes, and other things mo,
for ox-team and horse-team in plough for to go.

A plough-beetle, plough-staff, to further the plough,
great clod to asunder that breaketh so rough;
A sled for a plough, and another for blocks,
for chimney in winter, to burn up their docks.

Sedge-collars for plough-horse, for lightness of neck,
good seed and good sower, and also seed peck;
Strong oxen and horses, well shod, and well clad,
well meated and used, for making thee glad.

A barley-rake, toothed with iron and steel,
like pair of harrows, and roller doth well;
A sling for a mother, a bow for a boy,
a whip for a carter, is hoigh de lay roy.

A brush-scythe, and grass-scythe, with ridle to stand,
a cradle for barley, with rubstone and sand;
Sharp sickle and weeding-hook, hay-fork and rake,
a meak for the pease, and to swinge up the brake.

Rakes also for barley, long toothed in hed,
and greater, like toothed, for barley so shed,
A skuttle or skreen, to rid soil from the corn,
and shearing-shears ready, for sheep to be shorn.

> *Hog yokes, and a twitcher and rings for a hog,*
> *with tar in a tar-pot, for the biting of dog;*
> *A sheep-mark, a tar-kettle, little or mitch,*
> *two pottles of tar to a pottle of pitch.*
>
> *Long ladder to hang, all along by the wall,*
> *to reach for a need, to the top of thy hall;*
> *Beam, scales, with their weights, that be scaled and true,*
> *sharp mole-spear with barbs, that the moles do so rue.*
>
> *A clavestock, and rabbetstock, carpenters crave,*
> *and seasoned timber, for pinwood to have;*
> *A jack for to saw upon, fuel for fire,*
> *for sparing of fire-wood and sticks from the mire.*
>
> *Soles, fetters, and shackles, with horse-lock and pad,*
> *a cow-house for winter, so meet to be had,*
> *A stye for a boar, and a hogscote for hog,*
> *a roost for thy hens, and a couch for thy dog.*

Flail, fan and wing: for beating out corn, winnowing and cleaning.
Cart- and wheel-ladder: possibly extensions to support hay and corn.
Coom: ten sacks = one coom = four bushels.
Tumbrel and dung crone: dung cart and hook for the man (Sir Wag) to pull down dung into the furrows as he tails along after the moving cart – now a throw to left, now to right – it *does* look as if the cart was wagging its tail. Tusser's queer names are very vivid.
Timber: Payne quotes Harrison's praise of the elms around Dover Court being good for beetles, etc, and Norden, writing nearer Tusser's date, has 'This shire seemeth not anie where altogether destitute of wood, though no where well stored.'

The country houses in the district around Holbrook have avenues of ancient oak and elm which bear out Harrison, and the comparatively high cliffs at Dover Court probably sheltered the specially good trees which Harrison and Tusser both mention.
Sedge-collars: filled with reeds rather than straw(?)
Mother: local East Anglian term for a girl (sling for a girl, bow and arrows for a boy).
Twitcher: for ringing the nose (of swine).

BASIC FOOD MATERIALS

History describes 'A Banquet for Kings' of varied and elaborate dishes, usually with imported fruits and spices and gilding. Dishes were often so elaborate that the basic materials are disguised, yet those basic materials were provided by the cottagers, the hunters and farmers. The basic fuel was the same for everybody, wood or peat, and so were the basic methods of roasting, boiling or baking. The king had foreign spices, but the countrywoman had 'spicing of leaf and bark and rote'. It was not a king but a peasant who first put mint sauce to mutton, and combined the aromas of sage and onions. Today, anyone walking over swampy moorlands can locate with his nose wild thyme, bog myrtle, dried sage, and a score of other aromatic possibilities. The 'bouquet garni' is as old as the hills.

Like the comfort of a household, the commissariat in all centuries varies by 'owners' more than 'periods'. A good housewife in her hut, living on open land could, and probably did, live better and on more healthy food than kings. She had one fire, we hope one iron pot, and a hungry family to provide for – and plenty of time to learn from her mother and from experience. Take plucking a fowl: feathers come off fairly easily; it's the small pin feathers (the ungrown toughly-encased growing quills) that are difficult to pluck out. She'd try singeing them; that might lead to encased clay cooking. Meat sticking to the bottom of the pot? Springy birch twigs under the meat cured that, and gave an unexpected pleasant aroma. The acid of wild crab apples cooked well with tough bacon. The hot peppery bite of watercress improved the herdsman's oat bread and bacon fat or cheese. A cottager who had a cow in calf was well provided during the lactation period, and goats' milk seems to have been available; the little short-horned sheep gave milk and wool.

In the hut the cooking fire had to be small, or the family would have been asphyxiated (though the smoke was drawn up to the smoke hole by skilful ventilation, managed by opening or blocking holes in the gable ends to suit the wind). This smoke also preserved and flavoured the hanging meat, and kept the flies at bay. Experience taught how to flatten down the red embers under the accumulated white-hot ash to make a level cooking base that would keep a pot simmering all night, or cook food wrapped in leaves and buried in it. Cooking in the hut was usually slow cooking: quick spit-roasting was better done out of doors, and baking done in clay ovens or stone-lined cooking holes. For a large carcass the community would probably revert to the old method of 'seething in the skin'. Fresh-killed meat, before rigor mortis has set in, is very tender, and the subcutaneous fat from the pelt lubricated the stew and made good broth.

Pottage

Good peason and leekes
Make pottage for creeks [grubbers]

Have spoonmeat enough
For cart and the plough
Good poor man's fare
Is poor man's care
And not to boast
Of rod [fish]and roast.

Pottage was a mediaeval standby. To come in tired and wet and hungry to hot soup with a hunk of oat bread and salt is to be well fed; and hot, easily assimilated broth is better than solid food when you're weary. Soup was deservedly popular until the late industrial revolution, when charity made it a symbol of poverty (and some of the charitable soups do sound pretty thin). Mediaeval pottage was good food value. It had a laudable ancestry, both Saxon and Norman, perhaps because it denoted the ownership of a metal cooking pot, for such a cauldron was expensive to buy, and needed a good-sized fire to keep it simmering.

Coarse pottery is reasonably fireproof on a wood fire, so if there was no iron cauldron, pottage could be made in a pot (to the dietetic advantage that all the vitamins weren't boiled out of it). A common mediaeval pottage was chopped up kale leaves or parsnip leaves – in fact, almost any green leaves – stewed to a pulp and added to the oatmeal or barley porridge. This is where the mediaeval cook selected savoury leaves to give it a flavour, and added meat broth when available.

Work on the land was hard, but wholesome, and punctuated by celebrations. Let us leave Tusser with the final word.

The Farmer's Feast Days

Good huswives whom God hath enriched enough,
forget not the feasts that belong to the Plough.
The meaning is onely to joy and be glad,
for comfort with labour would sometime be had.

SHROVETIDE
At Shrovetide to shroving go thresh the fatte henne,
if blindefilde can kill it then geve it thy menne.
Maides fritters and pancakes inough see ye make,
let slutte have one pancake for companys sake.

SHEEPSHEARING
Wife make us a feast, spare fleshe neither corne,
make Wafers and cakes, for our shepe must be shorne.
At sheep shearing neighbours no other thing crave
but good chere and welcome like neighbours to have.

THE WAKE DAY

To Oven with the flawns mayd, passe not for slepe,
to-morrow thy father his wake day shal kepe;
Then trimly go daunce with what Lover ye will,
though love make you beaten, kepe Lover yet still.

HARVEST HOME

For all this good feasting yet art thou not loose
till thou give the Ploughman in harvest his goose.
Though goose go in stubble, yet passe not for that,
let goose have a goose be shee leane be shee fat.

SEED CAKE

Wife, sometime this weeke if that all thing go cleare,
and ende of what sowing we make for this yeare,
Remember you therefore though I do it not
The Seede Cake, the Pasties, and Furmenty pot.

These verses of Tusser's refer to a farm type of housekeeping, but the same causes and the same dates would be known by the labourers who worked on the farm, and by their wives, working in their own huts. Each dish depends upon the material *available at that date*. For example, furmenty was made when the new wheat was still soft and easily hulled. Black puddings marked the killing of the pig and the thick custards (made from colostrum) · were only available when a calf was born.

Christmas Husbandly Fare

Good husband and huswife, now chiefly be glad,
things handsome to have, as they ought to be had.
They both do provide, against Christmas do come,
to welcom their neighbors, good chere to have some.

Good bread and good drinke, a good fier in the hall,
brawne, pudding, and souse, and good mustarde withal.
Biefe, mutton, and Porke, and good Pies of the best,
pig, veale, goose, and capon, and turkey wel drest,
Chese, apples, and nuttes, and good Caroles to heare,
as then, in the cuntrey is counted good cheare.

What cost to good husbande, is any of this?
good householde provision onely it is:
Of other the like, I do leave out a meny,
that costeth the husband never a peny.

THE COMMERCIAL
WORLD

TRADE

HE OLD SCALE of commerce is difficult for modern thought to grasp. Today 'shopping' (note the word) is done almost daily, money being spent on many things, seen and liked, rather than planned for. It is mainly the wealthy who regularly deal direct with the specialist. They may purchase fewer goods, but these goods are often specially ordered. The 'stock size' and 'standard quality' packed goods are bought, in smaller quantities, and more frequently, by the less wealthy.

In mediaeval days wants accumulated for months, becoming definitely formulated, so that when you went to market you knew what you needed and how much of it, and bought a year's supply. In towns, workers usually sat in their shops where they displayed the goods they made, and collected special orders, but all goods were of one craft, or one material, in that one shop. Work in towns varied – in Ipswich, for example, in the late Middle Ages there were the following artisans: twelve tanners, five shoemakers, a parchment maker, a glover, six blacksmiths (and these would deal in small ironware goods, not doing the work of the farriers and shoeing smiths), a goldsmith, a carpenter, a coppersmith, a maker of catapults (crossbows), four dyers, two weavers (the new double-width materials required looms too large for small household weaving). No spinners are listed as all womenfolk spun thread continuously; there were never enough spinsters to keep the weavers supplied.

WEIGHTS AND MEASURES

It is to be lamented that one general measure is not in use throughout all

England, but everie market towne hath in maner a severall busshell. Such is the covetousnesse of manie clearkes of the market, that in taking view of measures they will alwaie so provide that one and the same bushell shall be either too big or too little . . . so that diverce unconscionable dealers have one measure to sell by and another to buie withall – the like is also in weights.

Description of England, William Harrison (1534–1593)

From this came the market saying 'To measure my corn by his bushel'. The stick which was drawn across the filled bushel to 'strike off any overweight' was known as a strike; it was sometimes round, sometimes flat, and that too caused controversy – a roller might press down what a flat would scrape off. The word came to denote a measure called a 'strike'

The bushel was filled with corn and the top struck off level with a stick – this gave the name of 'strike' to such measures.

(which did not always mean an official measuring tub). A 'peck' was similarly adapted; from a definite size, it became a local customary sized basket, varied between towns but constant for one place's special commodity at the time.

Some General Measures for Assorted Market Goods

Goods each had their customary measure: some of them are given here:

Barrel for butter, beer, herrings and other fish, (including salmon!) eels, tar, pitch, wines, gunpowder.

Bolle for honey and thick liquids.

Bolt for sackcloth, sailcloth and large quantities of haircloth (for straining cider?).

Cartload for hay, straw, faggots and lime, rushes (the rush in smaller
quantities was sold by the *shoulderload*, i.e. *creel*).

Chaldron for new coal, salt and quicklime, shells.

Clove for wool (see p. 135).

Cradle for breakable glass (the same word is still used today).

Diker for hurdles, tanned hides, napkins (?) sheepskins, needles (these were
also sold by specific quantities).

Dozen for candles (also sold by weight).

Ell(e) for linen and small lengths of haircloth.

Frail for soft fruits.

Firkin for smaller quantities of goods sold in barrels; fish roe.

Gallon for almost anything!

Kilderkin, Puncheon or *Tun* for ale and wines.

There were other curious measures: eels could be bought by the *stick* (they
were slung on to a stick which went through the gills). *Sow* was a term for a
large oblong mass of solidified metal, such as might be obtained from a
blast- or smelting-furnace. A *pipe* of something (wine, beer, cider, beef,
fish and so on) was a large cask with its contents; as a measure of capacity it
came to be the equivalent of half a tun – or two *hogsheads*, or four *barrels* (it
usually contained a hundred and five imperial gallons). The *pack* was used
as a measure of various commodities, including cordwood. The *stone* was
usually fourteen pounds avoirdupois – like the petra – but the first could
vary with different commodities from eight to twenty-four pounds.

There were also local measures in most districts, as settlers adapted
measures they were used to; current local usage would supply a measure
near enough to the one they had known to go by that name.

The word 'peck' stayed in use for centuries. Sometimes this
was the result of packaging or preparation. Thus a 'wash of cockles' was
the result of long experience in the size of the tub, the depth of the water

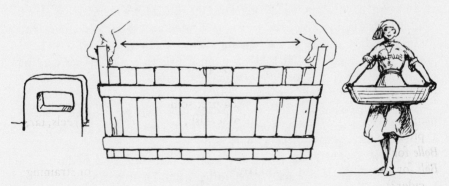

Made to measure

needed to wash off the mud or sand without the mud or sand becoming too thick in the water or filling up the tub with sediment. The number of cockles that could be lifted out clean was curiously constant, and the tub had to be emptied and the water renewed with great regularity. The punnet of raspberries or frail of strawberries may vary slightly in weight, but the punnet or the frail are accepted as measures just as is the sack of potatoes, or the cran of herrings. We still use 'adaptable' measures.

Sacks

Things dependent upon animals remain static for centuries: it is machinery that changes rapidly. The sack depended upon the man who had to haul it. The size, therefore, was dependent on man's back and, to a slight extent, upon the width of the loom, which in turn depended upon the length and strength of the weaver's arm. The sack was as much a human unit of measurement as the stool he sat upon, the bed he slept in, or the yard-long arrow of his bow.

Any membranous sac inside any animal was greatly valued in the periods before plastic bags. Woven bags required sewing to shape and netted bags would not contain corn or meal, or anything wet – a square of material with its corners tied together was a mediaeval hold-all. Some goods could be wrapped in cloth or leather and string-tied into a parcel. Today, the bladder of lard, the haggis, the sausage in all its forms are the last mediaeval form in general use. (The caul as a sailor's float is now obsolete.)

A round bundle packed upon a flat square and tied up by the corners (like Dick Whittington's handkerchief) was impossible portage for grain or powder and inconvenient for anything likely to shake loose and spill. Thus the sack was developed early, and from the sack developed sizes of handbarrow, wheelbarrow, cart and wagon. The seam of the sack was a problem for centuries. The base and side had to be firm and not split or leak; from illustrations in mediaeval mss.the rolled seam seems to have been most used. The mouth of the sack was secured according to contents and transport. If it was to be carried about, the sack was secured with hand holds which needed a flat fold-over top with two 'ears'. Where cartage or storage was static, a single central hold sufficed.

The moving of sacks varied by weight of content and strength of the man. Using two hands, a full, well-packed sack could be 'walked' along on its base with a diagonal movement. To lift it on to a man's back, two men standing either side raised it as the carrier bent forward; he reached back, gripped the top of the sack over his shoulder with one hand, and took the base weight behind his back with his other hand. To lift a sack alone he had previously to stand it on something behind him and then, leaning backwards, grip the two top corners (you see the reason for the two holds) and bend forward to take the weight. Some men, well accustomed to the work, faced the sack with crossed arms and dextrously swung it up as they turned round.

(1) Four sacks set up handy for use, one rolled down open, with scoop and measure. The handle of the wooden measure lets it stand steady, and it could be hooked to hang over the rim of a tub.

(2) Plan of sacks stored in the corner of a granary; when needed, a whole line can be removed without disturbing the others.

(3) A loosely-filled sack, arranged with a long 'hold' so that a man could carry it on his shoulder up a gang plank, then sling it into a cargo hold.

(4) In contrast, a well-filled two-handed sack.

(5) Ways of tying sacks according to how they would be handled.

(6) A hand barrow to be carried by two men, as distinct from the wheeled barrow.

The hand-barrow had four handles; made to the measurement of the sacks piled on to it, it was carried by two men, one at each end. The wheelbarrow was a hand-barrow with a wheel inserted in place of one of the men. The curious long-shaped sack trolley developed very early: it is shown at the docks before the fourteenth century. It is still in use on railway platforms.

Stacking sacks was done systematically. Set symmetrically, the long line becomes unstable and once aslant the whole line slides down. Sacks placed diagonally were stable, and could be stacked very close.

Today the filling, tying up and stacking of sacks continues just as in the Middle Ages; and men who handle sacks handle them exactly as our rural workman did – they still use the dextrous two-handed lift to sling the load up and on to the back, while a man loading cargo still walks the plank with the weight set steadily on his back using a long grip and a loosely-filled sack. The farmer, packing sacks to be left for months safe in a barn, or set handy for use, wanted the top to roll down easily once a sack had been opened. The knots and ties and usage of sacks are the long history of agriculture.

Tallies

The tally was much used in rural areas. Forms of it, for trades dependent upon manual labour (such as quarry and cargo work, where the activity was remote from official reckoning), and where both overseer and labourer may have been unlettered, remained in use till recently. One form had a 'tag' removed from each package, and kept by the worker, being handed in for counting at the end of the job. The loading of bananas on to cargo ships still uses this tally method in some unmechanised ports. For field labour, by parties of labourers, the tally was scored across a line of sticks, each man taking his tally stick. At the end of the day's work all

brought their tallies and laid them again in line for the next score across –
this was done every day till the work was finished. It was quite impossible
for a labourer to cheat as, if he was away, he would have no score mark for
that day. Nor could he fake a mark, unless every single labourer came

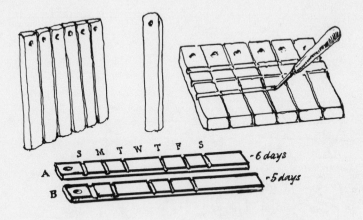

The tally was difficult to fake: the diagram explains the workings of a simple
system. If six men were employed on a job for a week, at the end of each
day's work they would all lay their tally sticks side by side to be scored
across (not cut) by the overseer. If a man failed to turn up, then his stick
would be unmarked; and unless he could get all of the other workmen to aid
and abet him he would not be able to fake the score mark. Each man would
be paid at the end of the week according to the number of days he had
worked. (Here A has worked for six days, while B has worked for only five
days.) More complicated tally systems are based on this simple system.

together and helped him; since the sticks did not lie in the same position
each day. When it was one man and one employer, only two sticks were
matched up. The labourer, unable to read, or write, could 'keep tally'.
Another simple method was to make one tally and *split it* lengthways,
across the score mark. This, used as a receipt between two people, gave
each one half exactly matching the other half.

The chirograph related to the tally, and could be used as a bond between
two people, even if one was almost illiterate. The agreement was written
twice upon a parchment which was then cut through the middle (if it were
cut through a space between the scripts the word 'chirographum' was
written in the space and cut through). Neither holder could use the
parchment independently, and the 'matching up' could be seen by a
labourer accustomed to matching up the 'scores' on a wooden tally.

Trade Marks

The common lack of literacy was combatted by sign marks, some derived
from drawings of tools, that would be recognised by other workers in the
same trade. Other sign marks developed variously, many from the owner's
initials. In trade circles these signs are analogous to the heraldic symbols
recognised by knights (and we believe caused some social friction).

Trade signs crossed national boundaries: they helped labourers
recognise goods and enabled consignees to claim what had been sent them.

The sign marks had to be simple, and bold enough to be easily

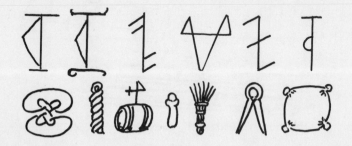

Trade or merchant marks are known to have been in use in England by the
end of the thirteenth century; it seems that they had already been in use for a
considerable time, originating in Europe and reaching England in the
normal course of trade. It is thought that runes form the basis of many of the
early marks. The top line shows some of these.

The bottom line shows more evolved marks: from left to right they are a
knot, which may have been the personal mark of the builder of the house in
Shrewsbury on which it appears; a skein of wool; a barrel, which may
denote the occupation of the unknown owner of this mark; an unidentified
small tool; a butcher's block brush, made of butcher's broom; a pair of
shears; and a woolsack.

recognised, even at a distance, by ship masters, deck hands, and dock
labourers, both at home and abroad; something that could be easily drawn
large upon large bales, and yet recognisable as the same mark when drawn
on small packages. A merchant's mark was used to indicate not only
ownership of goods, or the origin of a product, but came to stand for the
merchant's integrity, and the quality of his goods. In foreign ports they
would be recognised, and shipping companies would know whose goods
they were transporting.

The line drawings show examples based on trade tools, but other marks
derived from initials, or perhaps invented by some local carrier or trade
designer, defy analysis.

CURRENCY

Our mediaeval labourer didn't see much currency – in remote districts none at all. Exchange and barter were the basis of his working and trading. The various nationalities that came to these islands brought their own gods, own customs, own languages, and probably some of their own coins, but these coins would only be widely accepted and used among themselves, they would mean nothing to other people. In the same way the Romans brought their own gods, customs, languages and coins.

Because the Roman currency was prestigious, and the Roman occupation was well organised, abundant Roman coins may be found all over England, from the south right up to Hadrian's Wall, in comparison with native coins which are very scarce and usually localised.

Coins

I am indebted to Mr Neil Chadwick for the remarks on coins which follow.

The British tribes, mainly those south of the Thames and East Anglia (such as the Atrebates, the Coritani and the Iceni), used coins, probably not minted in Britain, but brought over by Gallic and Belgic traders. They were of gold, silver, bronze and tin. The heads of chiefs or kings (such as Cunobelin – Shakespeare's Cymbeline – and Tasciovanus), appear on the obverse of some British coins just before the Roman occupation, but they were comparatively rare. For four hundred years the Roman Imperial coin was the usual currency of Britain. The aureus and the solidus were of gold, the denarius (the origin of the 'd' for penny) and the antioninianus of silver, and the sestertius and the dupondius of bronze. Roman coinage was minted in many places, but every Roman coin bore Caesar's image and superscription, and Britons could only obtain Roman currency by working or selling to the Romans for payment. Thus, Roman money ensured the cooperation of native rulers. Roman coins were minted in Britain in the third and fourth centuries, mostly in London and Colchester, and these small silver or bronze coins are comparatively common. There is little evidence of any coinage in Britain between 450 and 600 AD, for that early period of invasions was indeed dark and confused. Even the Anglo-Saxon coinage between 600 and 800 AD, chiefly the sceat of silver and, less commonly, of bronze, is more rare than Roman coinage. Sceats bore patterns of birds and 'fantastic' animals, and, from about 800 AD, sometimes the heads of the kings of Northumbria, Mercia, Wessex, Kent and of the Archbishop of Canterbury.

From this time until the Norman Conquest, the predominant coinages were those of the kings of Wessex – Ecgberth, Alfred the Great, Edward the Elder, Ethelred the Unready, Edward the Confessor – and those of the Viking invaders, culminating in Canute (or Cnut). The silver penny, successor to the sceat, remained the principal currency in England throughout the last two and a half centuries of the Anglo-Saxon period, and through Norman and Plantagenet centuries up to the reign of Edward the Third.

There were two hundred mints throughout the country, and the pennies of these centuries are inscribed with the name of the moneyer and the mint on the reverse, which was generally also inscribed with a cross with three 'pellets' in each segment. Kings' heads appear both in profile and full face, but they were by no means a true likeness.

Until as late as the reign of James I, kings of England did not demean themselves by minting coinage of base metals, which would have to bear the king's head, and there was a phenomenal increase in the output of silver pennies from one hundred thousand to eleven million a year.

All coins throughout the centuries were issued exclusively on the king's authority, although the Archbishops of York and Canterbury might have their initials on the coins of their provinces. One of the charges brought by Henry VIII against Wolsey was that the latter dared to use a Cardinal's hat on the silver groat.

England's commercial progress in the fourteenth century, particularly in the wool trade, is reflected in the currency revolution in the reign of Edward III, in the introduction of gold coins, and the extension of the silver penny to the groat (4d.), producing the half-penny and the farthing. From Edward I to Henry VII, all silver coins bore a monotonous stylised portrait, while the splendid gold nobles (6s. 8d.) were enhanced by a halflength portrait of the king bearing sword and shield, and standing in a ship – symbolic both of England's defence against enemies, and her overseas trade.

There was another revolution in English coinage when Henry VII introduced coins bearing a true profile likeness of the king. In the later Tudor period there was a phenomenal increase in the number of denominations: in silver alone there were added the crown, the halfcrown, the testoon or shilling, the sixpence, the threepence, the pennyhalfpenny, and the three-farthing piece; and coins were now dated for the first time.

TRADES DEPENDENT ON THE LAND

As cities grew in size and importance, they provided scope for the development of specialised trades; but there was no total separation between town and country, since the materials for many of the trades that led to a city's prosperity would be supplied by the country people round about. The following list of city workers is drawn from *Coke Lorel's boke*, a satirical work of the sixteenth century, and gives examples of this transformation of country materials into trade goods: the basis of commercial industry.

The fyrst was goldesmythes and grote clyppers[1]:
Multyplyers[2] and clothe thyckers[3]:
(Called fullers everychone)
There is taylers, taverners, and drapers:
Potycaryes[4], ale-brewers, and bakers:
Mercers, fletchers[5] and sporyers;
Boke-prynters, peynters, bowers[6]:
Myllers, carters and botylemakers[7];
Waxechaundelers[8], clothers, and grocers:
Wollemen, vynteners, and flesshemongers;
Salters, jewelers, and habardashers;
Drovers[9], cokes and pulters;
Yermongers[10], pybakers, and waferers:
Fruyters, chesemongers, and mystrelles:
Tallow chaundelers[11], hostelers, and glovers:
Owchers[12], skynners, and cutlers:
Bladesmythes; fosters[13], and sadelers:
Coryers, cordwayners, and cobelers:
Grydelers, forberers[14] and webbers:
Quyltemakers[15], spermen, and armorers:
Borlers[16], tapestry-worke-makers, and dyers:
Repers, faners, and horners[17]:
Pouche-makers, below-farmes, cagesellers:
Lanterners, stryngers, grynders:
Arowe-heders, maltemen, and corne-mongers:
Balancers, tynne-casters, and skryveners:
Stacyoners, vestyment-swoers, and ymagers[18]:
Sylke-women, pursers, and garnysshers:
Table-makers, sylkedyers, and shepsters:
Goldeshears, keverchef, launds, and rebone makers[19]:
Tankerde-berers, bougemen[20], and spereplaners:
Spynsters, carders, and cappelnytters[21]:
Sargeauntes, katch-pollys[22], and somners:
Carryers, carters, and horsekeepers:
Courte-holders, bayles and honters:
Constables, hede-borowes, and katers:
Butlers, sterchers, and mustarde-makers:
Hardewaremen, mole-skers, and ratte-takers:
Bewardes, brycke-borners[23], and canel-rakers:
Potters, brome-sellers, pedelers:
Shepherds, coweherds, and swyne-kepers:

Broche-makers, glas-blowers, candelstycke-casts:
Hedgers, dykers, and mowers:
Brouderers, strayners, and carpyte-makers[24]:
Sponers, torners, and hatters:
Lyne-webbers, setters, with lyne-drapers:
Rope-makers, copersmythes, and lorymers[25]:
Brydel-bytters, blacksmythes, and ferrars:
Bokell-smythes, horseleches and goldbeters:
Fyners, plommers, and peuters:
Bedmakers, fedbedmakers, and wyre-drawers:
Founders, laten workers[26], and broche-makers
Pavyers, bell-makers, and brasyers:
Pynners, nedelers, and glassyers:
Bokeler-makers[27], dyers, and lether-sellers:
Whyte-tanners, galyers[28], and shethers:
Masones, male-makers, and merbelers:
Tylers, bryck-laters, harde-hewers:
Parys-plasterers, daubers, and lymeborners:
Carpenters, coupers, and joyners:
Pype-makers, wode-mongers, and orgyn-makers:
Coferers, carde-makers, and carvers:
Shyppe-wrightes, whele-wrights, and sowers:
Harpe-makers, leches, and upholsters:
Porters, fesyens[29], and corsers:
Parchement-makers, skynners, and plowers:
Barbers, bokebynders, and lymners:
Gonners, maryners, and shypmasters:
Chymney-swepers and costerde-mongers[30]:
Lodemen[31] and bere-brewers:
Fysshers of the sea and muskel-takers.

1 *Goldesmythes and grote clyppers*: might be legally employed in any of the 200 mints, where the round coins were stamped out of thin sheets of metal. Today, the cuttings from round tins show the same, but larger, metal netting, which may be scrapped or re-melted for use again. The clipping would not be mechanically exact, and the illegal groat clipper was the chap who sneaked small clippings from current coinage, to the detriment thereof.

2 *Multyplyers*: an old name given to those who professed to increase gold and silver by a magical formula? An alchemist's methods?

3 *Clothe theyckers, called fullers everychone*: fulling was a legal form of consolidating the weave of cloth. Less legal, impregnating it with substances such as wax, or clay, to give it weight. Later, much Devonshire clay was exported to China to thicken oriental fabrics, as well as give them a smooth surface for printing.

4 *Potycaryes*: uncertain. They may be lads, like Falstaff's, who fetched and

carried drinks to the workers; or include potters' transport.

5 *Fletchers*: in connection with spurs, may have been the skilled placing of the flight feathers on to arrows. These had to be selected with the same wing curve.

6 *Bowers*: in connection with the above, bow-makers.

7 *Botylemakers*: a glass-blowing trade. After the bottle was spun the necks were shaped in special clay furnaces.

The diagram shows how bottle necks were thrust into a small furnace (a 'boteler') and then finished off by a pair of pincers. The furnace is drawn from an heraldic catalogue.

8 *Waxechaundelers*: our country dwellers made their own household candles, but there was a great demand for candles in cities, churches and private houses; for this the country supplied wax and flax.

9 *Drovers*: the seasonal droves of cattle would remain outside the city, being purchased and brought in by local men who knew the streets. It might also refer to the important owner-drovers who would stay in the city while negotiating cash, as they acted as bankers for the country people far away, who supplied the cattle.

10 *Yermongers*: as today, the word is tied to cooking apparatus, household and farming implements, appropriate for the pie-man. At this date the ironmongers would make and cast the beautiful, elaborate wafer irons, so popular before the Reformation.

11 *Tallow chaundelers*: distinct from the wax changlers, and used the tallow from the slaughter houses.

12 *Owchers*: oswers? were rounded buckles or brooches which soon developed the pin. But by context with skinners, owser was also tanners' ooze, the thick oil-fat-water and tannin sludge pressed out of dressed skins.

13 *Fosters*: in this context probably from *fother* (Chaucer), a carrier for loads (German *Fuden*).

14 *Forberers*: the very small silver penny, cut into four segments, made farthings so minute that they were little larger than a small barleycorn, and

about the same weight. This was no currency to have loose in a bag, and we believe the fobs were the very small purses seen in ms. tied to the belt; that the small modern appendage tied to the watch chain retained the name of 'fob' suggests this.

15 *Quyltemakers*: apart from padded bedcovers, quilted padding was worn by knights under their armour. These probably supplied the armourers, as our cottage dwellers would assuredly make their own bedding from their own materials.

16 *Borlers*: bureller? A cloth finisher, in connection with tapestry works and dyeing.

17 *Repers, faners, and horners*: these, being farmers' workmen, might cover city workers still capable of returning for temporary work in the harvest fields (see p. 177).

18 *Ymagers*: the multiplicity of small religious images?

19 *Launds and rebone makers*: makers of musical instruments of the period.

20 *Bougemen*: the bouget was the leather water bag.

21 *Cappelnytters*: makers of caps or bonnets, of which there are many references in Hakluyt. Elizabeth I suggests them for trade overseas, 'as our people make them very well and need a vent'.

22 *Katch-pollys*: employed by the sergeants and summoners to secure the

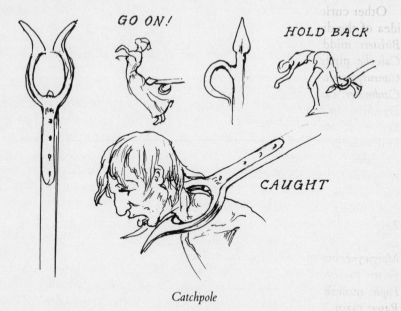

GO ON!

HOLD BACK

CAUGHT

Catchpole

offender. Those with sprung metal endings to long poles were designed to pull back the runaway (others had a pike to prod him forward).

23 *Brycke borners*. The old yellow Kentish brick of East London was self-

burnt, the clay being mixed with straw and coal dust and built into kilns fired by draughts arranged with old sails that caught and fanned the wind suitably.

24 *Carpyte-makers*: by the 16th century the long tables were often covered by carpets.

25 *Lorymers*: a strap or fastener becomes the name for a lad at a loose end.

26 *Laten*: latour, a more resilient metal than soft pewter.

27 *Bokeler*: we already have a buckle-maker, so this might be the provider of lime and other mordants used in dyeing the leather, or the making of the shield and buckler.

28 *Galyers*: a form of gumdressing, used as a stiffener for leather – we speak of a gallypot.

29 *Fesyens*: festucous means made of straw (we still have fescue grass); taken in connection with upholsterers might indicate seating of chairs or upholstery of rush and straw.

30 *Costerde-mongers*. There was a custard apple and today we have a costermonger?

31 *Lodemen*. 'Lodemenage' (Chaucer). Pilots using the lodestone or compass, perhaps the makers of compasses. River pilots follow the sequence and in some waters the guide boat is still called the 'lode-ship'.

Other curious terms dealing with trade are listed below, and give some idea of the diversity of occupations followed.

Birlsters: middlemen selling fish. Billingsgate?

Caboche: pipkin.

Caneurykestrete: candlewick makers.

Cardmaker: carding hands for wool, also made pins.

Dyssheres: in context, female dishwasher?

Dykers: ditchers.

Firmacula: fasteners.

Fripperers: old clothes dealers. Under legislation against alteration and removing trimmings before sale.

Gaunters: glovers.

Garlekhithe: garlic seller.

Lormerie: the materials for making small purses, etc.

Luti oppositores: Daubers or primitive pargetting?

Margwyne: butcher, in some special sense – its sounds as if he mangled them.

Pestre: pastry.

Pople: moleskins?

Raser: razor.

Ribinour: ribboner?

Scavengers-v-Rakyers: scavengers were in charge of clearing up streets (and markets?). Rakyers did the job.

Scrympyns: in the fur trade.

Shealds: open sheds near markets for storage of cranes and scales.

Tawyny: dressing for leather and its colour: tawny.

Teule: Tiles. Some brickwork?

Teybraces: tie braces – the beams in buildings.

Tilpynnes: tile pins, wood pegs securing tiles to roof.

Tinae: tin tubs.

Tramale: Tramel – a special trawler word.

Traventers: carts and packhorses available for hire

Verrers: Glaziers. That the glass would be small pieces inset in iron frame-work is indicated; window frames are mentioned as being torn out and used for shields in riots.

Wadmal: poor wool (wadding).

Wyndyngrodde: Winding rod – several uses – we know the thatcher's winding rod that carried the rope.

TRAVEL

ROADS

OLD ROMAN ROADS were used; but the mediaeval road was not made *for* transport and travel, but *by* transport and travel. That is, the need to go from one place to another created the road or track. The migrations between estates, undertaken regularly by feudal families, made regular cleared roads, which in a few cases were capable of taking a lumbering coach drawn by a team. Where special trade workings such as quarry, mine or pottery existed, there would be tracks worn between the works and the towns and markets. Heavy transport, such as a mill wheel, or the regular cartage of building stones for castle or cathedral, made some country roads possible for slow ox-wains. Other roads made by packhorse trains would be only narrow bridle paths for quite long distances.

All these 'roadways' had to pass near water (as vital for horse or ox as petrol is for the modern vehicle) and many tracks lay beside guiding streams. Old bridle paths appear sunken as a result of continuous use by horses, who in wet weather churned up the earth to mud; this was washed away in winter, and blown away as dust in summer, till presently there would be less a track than a running stream. Near farms or workings it paid the owners to clear out this mud, flinging it up on either side till it formed the high banks you still see in the sunken lanes of Devon.

The laws that cleared all timber and brushwood for statutory distances either side of main roads were to make them safe from ambush attacks by thieves, and this clearing was helped by the wayfarers themselves, for to cut wood and make a cooking fire was usual; the horses rested, and the packs were lifted to let the sweated hide dry off (necessary to prevent saddle sores). If there had been an aerial view, mediaeval roads would have shown as thin lines passing through wooded country, or as tracks across the hills, lines which deviated and curved to pass swamps or rocks. Only near work buildings and estates would they show as definite well-worn tracks. Huts would be set in small clearings and around them, as around farms and manors, the tracks would be well-worn. Cobbles of local stone, rounded river stones, or close-packed sea-beach pebbles, sometimes brick and tile work, made tracks to pens and sheds. It was only in towns and cities that the typical cobbled street existed, frequently with a gutter down the centre. On steep hills there would be a double line of smooth stones to take the wheels of carts, with rough cobbles in the centre to give a good firm grip for horse or ox.

Footpaths

Save saw-dust and brick-dust, and ashes so fine
for alley to walk in with neighbor of thine.
Tusser

Footpaths were made from whatever was easily available, that might otherwise have been wasted. Near shipbuilding yards, sawdust and pitch would be used – a mediaeval equivalent of asphalt. In the 1930s such paths were being made across the shingle at Lydd in Kent. After boats were tarred, the buckets would be emptied up the pathways, and repeated layers of tar, sand, or finest pebbles, had gradually raised firm paths which were immensely durable, resilient and well drained. The barrel-wheeled carts that trundled over them firmed them without cutting into them.

The Quarterstaff

I might here speak of the excessive staves which divers that travel of the waie doo carry upon their shoulders whereof some are 12 or 14 foot long besides a pike of 12 . . . No man travelleth by the waie without his sword or some such weapon except it be the Minister who commonly weareth none at all unless it be a dagger or hanger at his side.

Description of England, William Harrison (1534–93)

This 'stave' or 'quarter staff' was the standard defence of the pedestrian for centuries. The Fen Men used it to pole-vault across their dykes and marshes (they retained the grip on the pole, it being horizontal distance, not height, they needed). As a weapon it required skill, and the training was strenuous. The heavy pole could be kept whirling in front as the man advanced so that no one could reach him through its spinning circle. It could be made to whirl horizontally above the head with such force that, at a spring from the ground, the weight of the pole carried him full circle to face another direction. It could also be flung up in the air after the manner of a band leader whose raised pole can be seen far back along the following procession. (These ornate processional manoeuvres may have originated in the old quarterstaff skills.) The pole could also be suddenly thrust forward in a lunge capable of bursting a man's belly, or be brought down from above, to break his head.

OVERNIGHT ACCOMMODATION

Mediaeval Inns used by Workers

A large feudal entourage travelled on known routes and would make all arrangements ahead, perhaps with other lords who had the space and equipment, or at some monastic estate. These last would also have outside accommodation where the labourer or hapless wayfarer would be cared for: as their buildings always show a separate outside water supply, and from mention of 'brother Barabas washing the guests' blankets' and other references, there seems to have been sensible arrangements for vagabonds who arrived soaked to the skin and lousy (they would have to strip, and could hardly attend chapel naked!)

Inns, taverns, alehouses were to be found in towns and cities, and were very various. The local landowner usually owned the inn on the direct road to his estate, which is why so many inns on the outskirts of market towns are still called the 'Boult Arms' or the 'Wydkyn Arms' according to the name of the local estate. At that inn country people going to town from that district could be sure of finding their own dialect understood, and respect paid to their local usages.

The tavern in country districts was often a farm with a brewery business

---

Maps illustrate the preoccupations of the traveller. That on the following two pages, that on page 308, and the detail of the Gough map reproduced as Plate I, show how these altered. The Gough map, dating from 1360, is the earliest, and shows the importance of rivers as routes. The map on page 308 was published in 1546; here mountains are clearly shown, with an indication of passes (usually at the source of a river). Bridges are shown, though they are not very numerous: a traveller on foot or horseback needed to know how he could cross a mountain or river. There would also be ferries, though these are not shown. The map on pages 298–9 is from the coaching era; routes are depicted lineally, with an indication of terrain, but what was important to the traveller at that time was the towns through which he would pass.

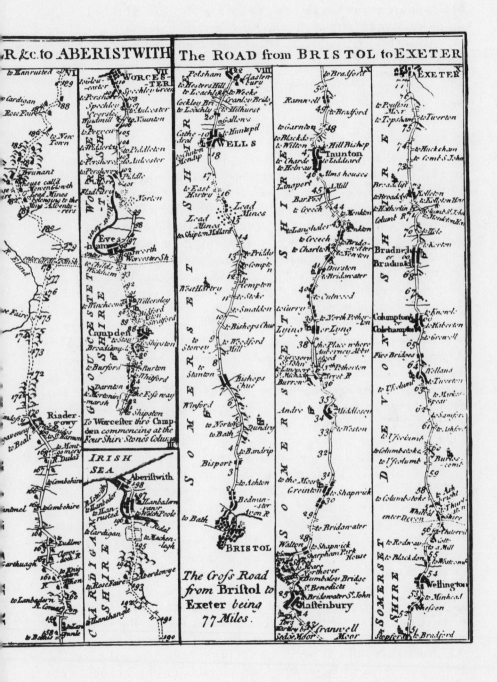

attached. That is, they made ale for sale, and took in travellers as part of the household arrangements. Thus the landlord sat at table and his own family did the cooking and serving. If many travellers arrived simultaneously they had to share beds. Gradually the family inns either degenerated into rough houses with little or no service, or developed into the fine coaching inns of the seventeenth century.

The Ferry Hostel

For the traveller following a coast road there were many small hospices kept by lay brothers attached to some religious community. These hospices usually developed in connection with the monastic farm which supplied the community with produce (and sold it to travellers and traders, so that they were a source of revenue). Monastic maps show how numerous and well placed were these hospices and, allowing for local variations in building material and situation, they were almost standardised in their equipment. The lower floor was open stabling, and a grazing paddock and smithy were available. Outside stairs led to a dormitory, probably divided by movable wooden partitions into 'stalls'. Each party of travellers appropriated a stall and settled down. Plaited 'beds' of straw or dried rush were laid down. (Blankets were carried, or perhaps hired – one reason why the long travelling cloak was so popular.) Such straw beds were used up to the eighteenth century as 'trundle' beds, to slide under the large bedsteads. They were no more hardship than a camp bed is today, and instructions for making them include a raised rim to keep out draughts, and a raised pillow of straw with 'wispes drawn out at foot and head' (see pp. 195 and 268).

For supper, boiled fowl, bacon and eggs, bread and wine and drinks could be purchased (brewing would be done on the premises).

At one end wall of the dormitory was a drain; the lay brother in charge (and perhaps a lady in charge of the lay brother?) were housed in a small cell underneath the dormitory. Travel was rough, over bad roads, and the hospice might have to deal with a broken collar bone, double pneumonia, or a miscarriage. These hospices, and most particularly those at ferry crossings, deserve more study, for they were the left luggage office and trade exchange for centuries, often maintained by a brother whose 'worldly' instincts (and perhaps previous training) had made him suitable for the job. Traders from a distance, bringing news of a 'glut of herring' or a 'scarcity of wool', would provide valuable 'market intelligence' to the monastery.

A man holding official status went around to supervise and report on outlying granges and store barns, and probably on these hostels also. Chaucer mentions such an official:

This noble monk, of which I yow devyse,
Hath of his abbot, as hym list, licence,
Bycause he was a man of heigh prudence,
And eek an officer, out for to ryde
To seen hir graunges and hire bernes wyde . . .

The Shipman's Tale

It is not realised how wide were the interests of the religious communities: they approximated to shareholding companies today, with a central administrative office, and drawing revenue from smaller subsidiary enterprises. Thus today we have the Abbey Horn Works, the Abbey Brick Works, the Abbey Tile or Timber Works, and so on: the traditional ownership is gone, but the name sticks.

SEAFARING

If ye schalle on pilgrimage go
Be not the third fellow for wele ne wo
Three oxen in plough may never well drawe
Nothing be craft nyt ne this lawe.

1460. Sloan ms.

For centuries there had been a regular 'service for pilgrims' that brought in an excellent revenue to the churches on the south and east coasts. They might provide accommodation for passengers waiting for the return boat; and provide burial for any dead still on board. (There was a tidal limit for burial at sea – for instance, Graves-end on the Thames. St Clement of Ipswich was partly responsible for this navigational convention, and during the Black Death, and the Plague, ships were discharged on the lower reaches, not being allowed to sail up river on account of infection.)

Local and Coastal Trade

By the thirteenth century coastal services were in regular use, with many across channel to Europe; there was a regular 'tourist service' of popular pilgrimages to the shrine of Compostella. This shrine issued the 'Shell' token ('How should I your true love know? . . . By his cockle hat and staff'). There were also fairly regular voyages north: in 1360 'from Lynne in Norfolk . . . it is not above a fortnights sailing with an ordinary wind and hath been of many yeeres a very common & usual trade . . . which further appeareth by the privaliges granted to the Fishermen of the town of

Blacknie by Edward IV.' This trade up the east coast to the Orkneys, called
Isles of Orcades, took leather goods of good size (the island cattle were
small) and good ropes – very necessary to a Norse seafaring people. The
trader found that they preferred to barter poultry and eggs and fish, of
which they had great store, rather than to use money, though they
understood English coin. (They also reported that the people of the isles
were very poor, ate oatcakes and drank ewes' milk. The country was void
of wood, and they burned turfs and heath. The sheep were very hardy and
small, and were carried from one small isle to another to use up the scant
grazing.)

The southern Cinque Ports were for naval defence, not trade. Naval
rejects and smugglers probably supplied seamen who took to the coastal
trade (the winds and currents between North Foreland and the Scilly Isles
were good training). There was transport from Kent to Bristol; cherry and
apple trees, for instance, were taken west to improve the cider orchards of
Devon and Hereford and Monmouth, for cider became a considerable
trade in the West Country.

During the eleventh and twelfth centuries while the Norman defensive
castles were being built, there was localised coasting trade in special
districts to bring suitable stone, often from a distance. Cathedrals, too,
imported stone: the outer stone for Chichester cathedral came by regular
service across channel from Caen. Slabs of Purbeck marble have been
found in the Stour in remains of long-vanished riverside churches and
monasteries. Hull has records of mill stones, and they were probably
imported up rivers for monastic watermills, for grindstones are very
specialised and must be transported all in one piece and cut in situ to suit
both the grain and the grinding power. Occasionally, the odd stone of a
distant quarry turns up in an old building or wall; or a single stone, split by
fire, marks the site of a long perished mud and wattle hut. Such stones may
also mark some long-forgotten transport route, having been dropped from
an unbalanced wain on its way inland.

Labourers built and used rafts and shallow draught tub boats for
transport along rivers and streams, which they kept cleared and dredged
for this purpose. These were towed along, by people or by horse or donkey,
in time wearing out riverside trackways. Centuries later when canal
transport, towed by a line of donkeys, or a horse, used long,
shallow, draught barges, the bargees lived on board in cramped cosy
comfort as they had done in huts (or caravans), and carried on their own
traditions with mediaeval independence. They adapted to their own
individual taste the traditional decorations of castles and bright coloured
flowers, using their old skills of handwork in clothing, bedding and
pottery, and reared families of tough illiterate children.

Inland Waterways

Rural workers early arranged portage by water for their heavy goods, such as stone or slate – lighter goods went by pack trail. Quite small streams were cleared for this, and thus streams were joined to rivers, and rivers to estuaries, where the inland craft could join boats carrying cargo along the coast. The design of the vessels varied according to where they would sail.

Two men could clear a stream using no more than a pick and an iron bar; the build-up of the current as they cleared a length would make the job progressively easier. In lowland areas, where the stream tended to spread, they would deepen the bed, or raise embankments, or even dig a detour. Experience gained in engineering water meadows (see page 55) helped them; and a tow-path was automatically constructed as they worked. This could be used either by man or pony, for even before the major construction of canals in the eighteenth and nineteenth centuries cargoes were helped on their voyage by horse power. With canals, man also designed the waterway – engineering long tanks by essentially the same methods as the rural labourer had used to adapt a natural waterway.

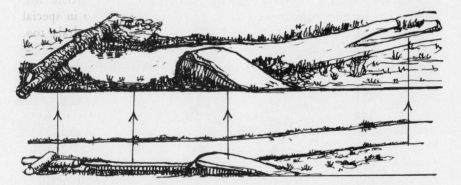

The small island mid-stream is dug out, and the soil used to block the shallow spread of water lower down. The stone jutting into the stream is turned aside, the fallen tree cut up and used in the blocking embankment. The cleared stream itself assists the work, which can be carried out by a couple of men with a lever bar to turn the stone, shovels, and a small raft. They then have a clear run for hauling loads by water.

The principle of towing a boat or barge is that the water passing between the bow and the bank pushes the barge out from the bank. (How far depends on the distance the barge is from the bank to start with, and both its own speed and that of the current.) The more direct a pull can be given to the boat, the less is the resistance, and thus the lighter the tow. To get a direct pull requires a long tow-rope: exactly how long and the position of the tow-post are dependent upon many considerations, such as the weight and position of cargo, the speed at which the towing is done, and the line of the tow-path. With modern barges, sailing on specially constructed canals, this could be standardised; but our rural engineer towing his cargo as best he could along streams and rivers learned – and transmitted – infinite adaptability.

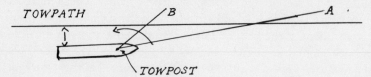

If the boat is towed from A, a much more direct line of pull is achieved than with a shorter tow-line as in B, which would tend to bring the nose of the boat sharply in toward the bank.

Early mediaeval portages probably used log rollers when available, as an aid to traversing difficult terrain. Fen men, poling their craft through the shallow waters and reed beds, were a law unto themselves. The countryside supplied no natural stone, and thus they could not construct hard causeways for towpaths – but they exported cargoes of corn, reed and enough eels to pay for the portage of stone for the building of Ely cathedral.

Overseas Trade

> *Qaint he was and right hardy*
> *An ingenious man and fey*
> *That first made ship on sea to fare*
> *To be turned with the wind he knows not where*
> *Lands to seek that he knew not*
> *Nor witherward he should be brought.*
>   Early English Text Society publication

Sadly, as early as 795 there are records of 'trade restrictions' and 'unworthy competition', between Offa, King of Mercia, and the King of France, whose 'mindes were so alienated, that bearing hauty stomacks, on both parts, even the mutuall traffique of their Marchants was prohibited'.

But on the whole it was adventurous discovery, rather than enrichment by trade, which produced mariners. St Brendan's 'isles of the Blest' (materialised as the Canaries or the West Indies) were very early discovered and some trade done.

Although mediaeval boats, from the earliest crusading period, were passenger boats rather than traders, they did stow in essential cargoes. (One Froissart ms shows how they removed sections of a ship's side to walk in horses, with their heavy metal armour. That full armour was some-times worn on deck is shown in one sad report of a young knight who, to prove his agility, leapt onto the gunwale; his foot slipped on the wet wood and he shot overboard – to sink instantly while 'the ship sailed on'.)

The early ships of war had high 'castles' raised prow and stern from which to cast down shot and stones, but by the sixteenth century when tactics had changed to swift manoeuvring and ramming low by the water line, the construction was different. There are comparatively few accounts of cargo boats built for trade only; the great overseas development was during the sixteenth and seventeenth centuries.

Elizabeth I retained a feudal concern for her people; she also knew that women enjoyed rich appearances, fine dresses and shows as much as she did herself. She knew the needs of her poor people and appreciated their skills, hence the common sense in these instructions to her traders and the kindly consideration for her lowest workers:

'If you can find . . . a vent [sale] for the Cappes called in Barbarie Bonettos colorados, which is our red Scottish cap, without brims [tam o' shanter]. You should do your country much good foras a sacke of wooll turned into fine Devonshire kersies doth set many more people in worke, then a sacke spunne for broad cloth in a grosser threed, so a sacke of wooll turned into those Bonets doth set many more poore people on worke, then a sacke turned into Kersies, by reason of the knitting . . . And by the vent of our knit hose of Woollen yarne, Woorsted yarne, and of Linnen thred, great benefit to our people may arise . . . and knitwares may be couched in small roome . . . [for] these things our people are growen apt, and by indevour may be drawen to great trade.'

Elizabeth also kept an eye on agriculture, and encouraged it during a period of enclosures and wool production: 'Saffron, the best of the universal world, groweth in this realm, and is a thing requiring much labour of diverse sorts, and setteth the people on worke plentifully.' She must have seen the saffron crocus growing and had been told of the delicate work of collecting the stamens of the flower as well as the cultivation of the plant itself. (See also Saffron, pp. 354–5.)

Numerous small trades, completely mediaeval in content, continued under Elizabeth. Trade notes such as these show us her concern. In one letter she deals with the 'making of Oile of seeds of a herbe (Egyptian) . . . If this herbe will prosper in oure country, our merchants may easily bring of it' and gives the urgent instruction to find somewhere to sell the 'Cappes called in Barbarie Bonettos'. Even the poor women knitters are become manufacturers of trade goods. With the expansion of trade, our island had become too small to supply large quantities of bulky material; it must turn to industry and manufacture. There is the same change in plants and herbs: saffron was to be gathered and processed in Saffron Walden, in Wales and Herefordshire, and the land workers are to see the 'Soile be manured, and in that way the land workers would be employed'.

There were other instructions: 'For the future vent of our commodities take with you frizadoes, motlies, bristow friezes, Spanish blankets, baies of all colours, specially with stamel, worsteds, carels, saies, woadmols, flanels, rash, etc., felts of divers colours.' This represents a great advancement on the simple mediaeval cloths with their gentle vegetable dyes. A list of items traders were to try and sell shows how special trades developed from the earlier mediaeval beginnings: there were night caps, neck ties, garters of several kinds, girdles 'especially wastegirdles' with gilt buckles (a fashionable development), gloves, knit and leather – mediaeval country-folk had made for centuries their own leather working gloves – perfumed gloves, such as Chaucer would have commended, 'velvet shooes and pantoufles to be sent this time for show', purses, a garnish of pewter – in which English craftsmen excelled, making bottles, flagons, spoons and many other things of this new pewter. Other products which seemed of interest to exporters included – 'looking glasses for women, great and faire', spectacles, hower glasses, combes of ivory, boxwood and horn, linen, handkerchiefs, glazen eyes to ride with against dust (our modern goggles), knives, needles, buttons, boxes with weights, for weighing gold to show people our right weights and measures to impress them of our settled government, and the several silver coins of our English money 'which is a thing that shall in silence speake to wise men more then you imagine'. And from the English mechanic, 'locks, keys, hinges, bolts, haspes, of excellent workmanship, of these you must have great regard'.

Of greater interest to the worker are materials such as brimstone, and minerals used in casting, such as antimony. Tinder boxes with steel, flint and matches and tinder, 'the matches to be made of juniper to avoid the offence of brimstone'. Candles, of wax, to light by the use of brimstone (and how they did it we don't know!) Bellowes, a pot of cast iron, for that is a 'natural commodity of this realm'. It had ceased to be the expensive status symbol in the mediaeval cottage and was in general use. The traders were also to take common knives for barter by the men.

The same list mentions red ochre 'because we have great mines of it'. This was the red earth used to mark the sheep's fleece, for it would wash off without staining the skin. It was popular in the Middle Ages for much rough colouring, and continued as the 'red raddle' in use on red brick floors for centuries. A small curious item was 'black coney skins', probably from specially-bred rabbits.

By Elizabeth's day England had truly become an exporting manufacturing nation.

SHIPBUILDING

England inherited many types of boat, from the Northern long serpent to the squat Dutch boat that was used in the fenlands. The traditional squat Dutch eel boats remained in the Thames for centuries: they had two fins, one either side, which they let down (like legs) to stand steady when they grounded on the mud. The most typical mediaeval boat was an open wooden tub steered by an oar, with one square sail fixed to a short mast which could be lifted out bodily and laid down flat, or raised and lowered by thick ropes. On the west coast of Ireland there were broad-bosomed boats to breast the Atlantic swells, and the long, light curraghs, originally of stretched leather and willow. For the lively Welsh rivers the squared coracle was made with the same materials.

Though shipbuilding from earliest times employed numbers of our countrymen, perhaps even more were employed in finding the timber, for the ships depended much upon the natural shape of the wood. We think of wood as straight planks and baulks, but for millwrights and shipbuilders it was the natural curve of the wood which was needed; timber that could be split with the grain into two symmetrical pieces was valued, for wood grown into shape will never warp. This was used also in barn and house building, so that the sides would match. Usually boats were small, but a few ships were built with raised decks, and 'castles' fore and aft. Under the castles were small enclosures, and the galley was set low down on a slab of stone just above the ballast and bilge water.

Ipswich, by reason of its timber and tidal basin, was a mediaeval 'shipyard' for London, with Dovercourt and Harwich as 'shipyard ports'. As indication of the extent of this trade, the list for the year 1572 gives:

Ipswich (ships built)	100 tons	5
	50 tons	12
	20 tons	10
Under 10 tons		11

In 1576 Ipswich built one ship of 160 tons and two of 120 tons. (These are very large ships for the period and would clear a good sized tract of timber for boarding, beside the specially searched-for trees with naturally curved boughs, for the ribbing and stern.) Between 1580 and 1582 eight ships of 100 tons were built, and a London coppersmith called Olyff Burre himself built two ships of 150 tons each in the Orwell (not actually in the Ipswich basin but perhaps at Pinmill, where the river has a deeper channel: did he use the local copperas deposits?)

This very brief outline of the work of one small district gives a fair idea of the way shipping had developed. We think of the Elizabethan shipping as Spanish Armada boats, and later 'The World Empassed', but much must have been developed, and many shipwrights trained, in much earlier centuries.

(See notes at foot of page 297.)

MARKETS AND FAIRS

TO MARKET

When harvest is ended, take shipping or ride,
ling, salt-fish, and herring, for Lent to provide:
To buy it at first, as it cometh to rode,
shall pay for thy charges, thou spendest abroad.

Chuse skilfully salt-fish, not burnt at the stone,
buy such as be good, or else let it alone:
Get home that is bought, and go stack it up dry,
with pease-straw between it, the safer to lie.

This lesson is learned, by riding about,
the prices of victuals, the year throughout:
Both what to be selling, and what to refraine,
and what to be buying, to bring in again.

As oft as ye bargain, for better or worse,
to buy it the cheaper, have chinks in thy purse.
Touch kept is commended, yet credit to keep,
is pay and dispatch him, ere ever ye sleep.

Thy market dispatched, turn home again round,
lest gaping for penny thou losest a pound,
Provide for thy wife, or else look to be shent,
good milch cow for winter, another for Lent.

In travelling homeward, buy forty good crones,
and fat up the bodies of those seely bones:
Leave milking, and dry up old Mulley the cow;
the crooked and aged, to fatting put now.

MEDIAEVAL MARKETS were temporary townships, covering wide spaces and occupying and disorganising entire districts. They were lucrative for the estates upon which they were held, and also for the adjacent towns.

To visualise how people converged upon the market, consider the layout of the public houses and inns in any market town and remember how different, in dialect, were the country folk surrounding that town. All would approach directly from their own district. The inn facing them on arrival would be their natural stopping place, where they would be likely to meet people they knew.

The influx of 'foreigners', people who would have different dialects (and possibly different morals and diets), accounts for the arrangements needed for a large market. A special Court was set up, with interpreters, officials for weights and measures, and legal advice laid on for the country people who came in wagon, ox cart or, mainly, on foot (wherefore the Market Court was called Pied Poudré – the Court of Dusty Feet).

At these Courts a country lad, who could understand the dialects and was good at figures, could get his chance to leave the land and by displaying his talents enter the commercial world.

The market was also a type of 'employment bureau', where arrangements could be made to hire a craftsman's skills. For instance, the carpenter would have a shop, but the carpenter himself came to work in

your own home, on the spot, which is why pieces of furniture in different farmhouses frequently show the same tool marks, since he carried his tools with him, and pieces were made, altered, remade and sometimes built in. Pieces resembling each other, in different parts of the country, indicate the radius of a certain craftsman's work. Later, portrait painters and inside decorators went around in much the same way. Dressmakers, and tailors and upholsterers came, and were given rooms and facilities. These specialists lived in the house while they were employed, being given a special workroom, and members of the household were told off to go and assist them if possible. This was specially the case for upholsterers, and bedding and clothing workers, where an expert could utilise less trained hands to do the routine stitching of long sheet seams which, by hand, took hours to sew. The dressmaker was the last of these visiting experts: she continued to visit large private houses till Victorian days. (Her modern version now helps out in hospital linen rooms, or sometimes contracts for boarding school bedding during school holidays.)

The water supply for a market or fair had to be good and was 'laid on' through wooden pipes or open conduits running along the line of the stalls; the stalls had to be set in fixed lines with passages between, and places for fires made (and fuel provided). Latrines were dug and lime purchased and the 'deposit of manure' increased the value of the land. Cut reeds and old straw, cleft timber and stones were laid to improve roads and prevent heavy loads blocking the entrances to the market. Food and drink stalls were specially arranged. Special beer was brewed and special bread baked and on the appointed day the market was proclaimed open! A formal speech was made; we reproduce a typical example for a fair:

'All Keep the Peace!

'No manner of persons may make any congregate or affrays among themselves whereby the peace of the Fair be broken.

'All unsealed wine, ale, bere, must be sold by measure, by the gallon, pottle, quart or pint. Bakers bread must be wholesome for a man's body.

'No manner of cook, pie maker, or huckster to sell, or put for sale any manner of victual but be good and wholesome.

'No manner of persons may buy or sell but with true weights and measures sealed according to statute.

'No one may make attachment, or summons of executions, but the Owner of the Fair.

'No person within the Fair presume to break Lords Day by buying or selling. No sitting, tippling and drinking in any tavern, ale house, or cooks house, nor do anything to break the peace thereof.

'And any person soever who finds themselves grieved, injured or wronged by any manner of persons in this Fair they are to come with complaint before the Steward of the Fair and no one else.

'Therefore now, at this Noon, begin in God's name and the King's and God send everyman luck and this Fair a good continuance.'

The Fair ended at sunset and the Marshall of the Fair had to ride through it and proclaim that every trader *forthwith* shut his stall.

Local Markets

Both Saxon and Norman custom established what can only be described as 'casual markets' – not great seasonal markets, but local affairs, caused by the periodic clearance of surplus goods from a local manor, or stock from a large farm. (These would be similar to the 'farm sales' or the 'private house sales' of today.) There would also be continuous sales at shrines, and at regular meeting places, such as the well by a town gate, or by a church or market cross. These sales seem to have been arrangements made among the local inhabitants, but *regular* markets had to be fixed at certain times in certain districts to sell off some special product – for example, the Honey Fairs still held in Wales and the Horse Fairs in the North. By law (how closely enforced is uncertain) all markets had to be over five miles apart. Twenty miles was a fair day's walk – ten miles in and ten out – and at three miles an hour all could get *in* and *out* before dark.

A list of the products sold at these local markets is also a list of the local industries.

A sidelight on the arrangements for these local markets can still be seen in one Scottish village, Ardgay, where a large lump of white quartz is carefully preserved, because for centuries it was used 'to pin down' the spot where the next market should be held. The white stone was conspicuous and individual, and weighed several tons, so that many strong men were required to transport it. Many strong men had to agree, then, as to the site of the next market. (We gather they had to be strong enough to overcome any opposition by other strong men.) The matter being decided, the strong men heaved up that market stone and transported it, by sleigh or cart or trundle, to the site decided upon. (There cannot have been too much opposition by the populace, or they could not have done this: thus it was an excellent executive expression of public opinion. Mediaeval people were very good at that sort of thing.)

Some Laws concerning Markets

Markets had special laws governing the disposal of unsold goods. If the owner of the goods had asked someone to sell them for him, he could claim them back *before* the market closed: but after that they belonged to the stall owner (this law carries on today).

There were other laws – all notably stern, for a rowdy market was difficult to control.

If any market was kept open after time its grant was withdrawn, and if anyone sold market goods after the market was closed they paid twice the value of those goods in an instant fine. (This law had loopholes, and caused much grumbling by local shopkeepers. It was probably designed to prevent market goods not being fair samples of regular stock.)

Finally: anyone robbing booths or stealing goods at Market was to be beheaded.

He who takes what is not his'n
If he's cotched he goes to prison.

Directions for Drovers, Badgers, Butchers, Inn holders, and Tanners, etc

A Drover here means the business head – one who buys cattle in one place and dispatches them to another to sell – not the man who walks and drives the herd. A Badger is one who buys corn or victuals in one place and carries them to another. The need for London to have regular and reliable supplies of food at a reasonable price led to the creation of regulations such as that a drover or badger must be 'a Married Man, and a Householder, Thirty years and upwards, & Licensed, under Penalty of Five Pounds. Also he must have dwelt three years in the County selling in open Fair or Market for the Provision of Houses ... There must give Bond, not to *Forestall*, nor to buy corn out of Fair or Market ... Traders in Butter & Cheese prohibited in open sessions from buying ... (unless they are Free-men of London)'.

There are regulations governing who could buy what, to protect the interests of each separate craft: 'None shall Ingross Oak bark, under Penalty of Forfeiting it. So of Hides, coming to Market. Nor buy, except of the Owner of the Beast, to be spent [i.e. used] in his House.'

There were also restrictions on barley and oats made up into oat- and barley-meal, and so on. Other regulations, too long to quote in detail, applied to the wine and victuals of Inn Keepers, to dried fish and other foods, eg: 'Fish, brought by Persons dwelling within a mile of the sea; also oyls, & Foreign victuals, (fish & salt fish excepted).'

'All Bread called Horse-Bread [i.e. a loaf of mixed corn, or bread made from *Faba vulgaris*, a field bean used for horses, but also baked into bread] must be of a lawful & sufficient size, according to the Price of Corn, as in the Neighbouring Markets at that time [but] An Inn holder, or Ostler, in a Throw-fare Town Corporate or Market Town, being a Baker, & one that hath been Apprentice thereto seven years, may make Horse-Bread within his House [qualified by "There being no Common Baker at hand" to do the job].'

The needs of one craft led to regulations affecting others: 'A Butcher also using the Craft & Mystery of a Tanner, loseth for every day 6s. 8d. A Butcher that Gasheth, slaughtereth or cutteth the Hide of an Ox, or Deer, or Bull, or Cow, so that it is impaired loseth 10d., or that Wetteth or Watereth any Hides (unless in June, July, or August) or putteth to sale any putrefied or rotten Hides; for everyone of them loseth 3s. 4d. . . .

'A Tanner, using, also the Mystery of a Shoo-Maker, Currier, Butcher, or any other Artificer, Using, cutting or Working in Leather, loseth the Hides & Skins tanned.'

Forestalling

A forestaller was defined as 'a Party who buys, or contracts, for any Victuals or Wares before they come to the Fair, Market, or Port, or moveth any Party to Enhaunce the Price, & not to bring such Wares to the Market . . .' There were fixed penalties for such an offence: 'The Party being convicted before Justices of the Peace . . . by the Examination of two Witnesses . . . shall lose the Goods, & be Imprisoned two months, without Bail or Mainprise; for second offence, lose double the value of the goods, imprisoned six months & for the third, lose the goods & stand in the Pillory & be imprisoned during the King's Pleasure.'

Forestalling – buying up goods before they reached the market, so as to resell at a higher price – was a crime, since it interfered both with supply and prices; 'supply and demand' fixed 'market values'. There are many examples of regulations forbidding it: 'None shall Forestall any Hides coming to a Fair or Market, except such as Kill for the Provision of their own House. None may buy, or contract, or bespeak, any rough Hides or calve-skins but only a Tanner or Tawer of Leather, except Salt Hides, for the Necessary use of Ships, on penalty of 6s. 8d. [shipping was vital for trade and defence]. None may buy Tanned Leathers or Wrought, but such as will convert them into made wares; except Necks, spreads of Sadles & Girdles [i.e. odd waste, or pieces or of awkward texture. The necks of oxen were likely to have been galled by the yoke; also in shape necks are difficult bits] . . . A Tanner putting to sale any Insufficient Leather not thoroughly Wrought & Tanned, or not well dryed; and the same to be so found by the Tryers appointed, loseth so much as is Insufficient.'

The Middleman

There was strong feeling against the middleman:

'see how most places . . . are pestered with purveiours [purveyors], who take up egs, butter, cheese, pigs, capons, hens, chickens, hogs, bakon, etc in one market . . . and suffer their wives to sele the same in another, or to pulters of London . . . In like sort, the buttermen travell in such wise that they come to mens houses for their butter faster than they can make it. It is almost incredible to see how the price of butter is augmented. Whereas, when the owners [i.e. farmers] were forced to bring it to market, and fewer of these butter buiers were stirring, our butter was scarclie woorth 18 pence the gallon, that now is 3s. 4d. or perhaps 5s. Whereby I gather that the maintenance of a superfluous number of dealers [in most trades, 'tillage', or farming always excepted] is one of the greatest causes why the prices of things become excessive, for one of them doo commonlie use to out bid the other.'

Contemporary comment

Social Prestige in the Market

Fate hath but small distinction set
Betwixt the counter and the coronet.
The True-Born Englishman, Daniel Defoe (1660–1731)

The 'oppressive feudal system' has never been completely eradicated from rural England – because the 'oppressed' insist on retaining it! – The 'gentry's' distaste for trade was matched by the traders' disapproval of their engaging in it. A contemporary comment runs:

'As of old . . . one ancient ladie, which maketh great gaine by selling yeerelie hir husbands venison to the cookes, and another of no less name, will not sticke to ride to market to see her butter sold . . . [had] infinite scoffes and mackes, even of the poorest pazents of the countrie, who thinks them as odious matters, in ladies and women of such countenance, to sell their venison and their butter' . . . [This was as infra dig as for] 'an earle to seele his oxen, sheepe and lambs,(whether they be readie for the butcher or not,) or to sell his wove unto the clothier, or keep a tan-house, or deale with such like affaires as belong not to men of honor, but rather the farmers and grafters . . . so to degenerate from true nobilitie and betake themselves to husbandrie.'

Stourbridge Fair

At Bartlemew tide, or at Sturbridge Fair,
buy that as is needful, thy house to repair.
Then sell to thy profit, both butter and cheese,
who buyeth it sooner, the more he shall leese.

Tusser

Stourbridge (Sturbich) Fair was an autumn cattle fair. Stourbridge lies between Chesterton and Cambridge. The brook Sture watered and partly drained the fields where the huge mediaeval fair was held in September. King John is said to have started it by the grant of a fair for the upkeep of the hospital for lepers; it came under the jurisdiction of the University of Cambridge. It was one of the largest fairs in Europe. The land was divided into streets of booths and whole districts surrounding the actual fairground were portioned off for the various drovers and traders to lodge upon.

Street Names

The small stalls of the little street markets of London are very similar to mediaeval stalls (and small shops regularly put out a stall in front, extending the window down to the pavement in the same mediaeval fashion). Certain goods could only be sold in certain places and at certain times on certain days, and that was complicated by the ruling that insisted on people selling similar goods all at one place. This ruling gives us the names of our streets: 'Butchers Row', 'Cockspur Street', 'Wood Street', 'Bread Street', 'Petty Cury', 'Poultry', and so on.

Traffic Problems

Parking in town was a mediaeval problem. The streets were narrow, and traffic moved at different speeds – there were swift riders, singly or in parties, ordinary horse-drawn carts of assorted sizes, and the slow, solid bullock carts, swaying, and moving at walking pace or less. There were regulations as to unloading for special goods, like straw or hay that might blow about, and sand that might spill. These goods hazards were nothing to the trouble of rubbish dumps, children playing in the streets, drunks and stray animals – the worst was probably the pig. Only the tantony pig, a privileged porker wearing a small bell, and belonging to St Anthony's Hospital, was officially *allowed* free range – other animals just took it.

Parking time was much disputed. People came in, and left their horses to be shod while they turned into the local for a snack and drink. Then there would be: 'Please sir, would you come and shift your horses. There's an ox wagon can't get past.' The shoeing smith had special troubles, and was forced to keep a paddock behind the smithy (and there would not be parking room there sometimes). There would be traffic hold-ups, a hay wain upset, or brewer's wain with a hogshead rolled off and split. There were overhead signs to be dodged – which were sometimes knocked down and blocked up the road. On steep hills wagons used drags to lock the wheels; these were usually slung behind the vehicle and were used for centuries. On a slope, the wheels of a stationary wagon might be wedged by blocks. An extra trace horse was used outside towns on extremely steep hills (by mailcoach times these were so well trained they could be hitched on to the travelling coach and released without pause or delay). Packhorse trains would not usually come into towns: picture a long line of perhaps twenty mules tied nose to tail, winding their devious ways around corners and involving packages and pedestrians in a crowded mediaeval city. They would be unloaded outside in sections, and the goods brought in by porters.

Returned Empties

There were special restrictions on the wagons returning from market: firstly, the drivers were *not* to rattle back home in reckless speed with their empty carts – there were definite speed restrictions. Economically, few would want to return empty – there were tenders for return journeys and wagons that had come in heavily loaded with country products would take back the refuse and debris left after the material had been processed in town, to use as an early form of artificial manure (see p. 68).

Timber debris would be contracted for by soap boilers and glue makers and chandlers and all the other stinking trades that adjoined the shipyards down river (industry was *stream-lined*). Smaller adze chips and sawdust (especially if redolent of tar) would make well-flavoured smoking for the fish curing sheds. Again – it is difficult to assess 'waste trade products' but to go up in smoke would be the ultimate end of timber.

The amount of material that came into a city was so much larger than what went out that cities now are risen high over their original foundations. Where there were steps up into the cathedral, now you step down into it, and it takes excavators and diggers to reach back to Roman remains in cities.

COMMODITIES

Bark

BARK WAS REMOVED before felling the tree, and broken and packed and sold to the tan yards. Oak bark and willow were (and still are) the best tans for waterproof shoe leather. The bark was beaten and soaked in tanpits and the leather immersed in the tannin.

It was the salicylic acid this contained which was of value to the tanner. ('Tan willow calf' is still advertised in the best shoemaking trades.) Sacks of 'Bark for the Tanners' were a marketable commodity and fetched a reasonable price. (See also *Timber*, pp. 201–213.)

Candles

To the chandler the countryman might sell surplus beeswax to help stiffen the mixture of tallow and fat – each chandler had his own mixtures, and would obtain most fats from the nearest slaughter yards. (In sending the beast to town 'on the hoof' the countryman supplied all the material in bulk.) The chandler might purchase his wicks direct from some flax workers. They need not be in long fibres, but must be unbroken and well plaited, neither too tight nor too loose, and adapted to the density of the candle. The common tallow dip, and lanthorn candles, were home-produced, as were the rush lights. (Church candles were a special department and caused controversy.)

The chandlers' candles would be for use in houses and workshops, and when ordered in bulk for special customers were timed with care to burn for exactly so long (candles were often official issue to employees, and part of their board and wages contracts).

Candles were usually lighted from the fire, or one from another; once a solitary candle had blown out in a room without fire, it was difficult to relight. To blow out any candle wasted wax, pinching it out broke the brittle, charred wick, and beating the wick pressed it down into the melted wax. So the small extinguisher came into use fairly early, earlier than the elaborate snuffers and other gadgets that caught the drips.

Cement

Great quantitie of clay being washt by ye power of ye waves into ye sea before petrification, makes the shore itself . . . Some being perfectly hard rock. Of this stone, ye churches are built, Dovercourt which is the mother church of Harwich and ye streets are paved with it.

Description of England, William Harrison (1534–1593)

The Romans dredged for our large river mussels for the sake of their pearls. One of their quays is still traceable on the Conway River. Ordinary sea mussels were a palatable and popular food, and likely to be plentiful and plump in the silted estuaries below mediaeval cities (see also list, p. 290). The burnt shells were also a valuable source of lime for many industries. Massive encrustations of smaller shells would supply fodder for mediaeval poultry and the broken shells would still be available for lime.

Cement and mortar materials were always contracted for, rather than marketed. Roman cement, which in some cases remains like a hard honeycomb after the bricks have crumbled, is still something of a mystery. London had an interesting supply of 'cemment stones' that were dredged up from the mud of the Stour estuary – these stones can still be seen in the estuary. They are packed together in flattened layers as if some giant had trodden on a huge grey honeycomb. These may have been used by the Romans for making cement – they were sometimes known as Roman stones. Cardinal Wolsey used this stone for cement for his college at Ipswich, and it was used in Framlingham Castle and elsewhere.

The stones were broken up and burnt in kilns, and when baked the cement was sifted and packed in dry-baked barrels, to be used with a mixture of sand. We believe this early process used sawdust and ash in the burning (as at the old brick works at Oare and Faversham across the water in Kent). The somewhat illicit collecting of these stones for cement was a flourishing trade. The cliffs at Harwich and down the Stour estuary were mined till the owners took action against the cement workers. They then 'dredged for the stone' or even 'worked at night stealing it'. (One report describes the hunting of Roman stone as a scene of pillage.) As late as 1812 the Thames Board of Ordinance built a cement mill at Harwich, and in fifty years this mill had depleted the banks, and employed a small fleet of cutter-rigged smacks to dredge the sea bottom for the stones. The supply being exhausted, the earliest Essex firms closed down, but the cement trade continues in the district and wherever else where suitable material is found, the historical interest being that the trade now depends more on quality of the material than its proximity to the building it is wanted for.

Mediaeval builders used the nearest good supply, rather than the best. This was a matter of transport as, lacking waterproofing materials, large supplies were a risk; cement, like salt, was perishable. It would have had to be transported by ox wain or coastal shipping: an open wain coming into a town could have suffered stringent traffic control on account of the dust; or if the cement got damp the value would be impaired, or destroyed. Contrast these considerations with today when often whole sackfuls of cement are dumped into position, sometimes still in the sacks – not being hand-woven and laborously sewn they are dispensable. Mediaeval cement had to be trodden, or laboriously turned and mixed with shovels (as it still is for small jobs). Early builders used lime, sawdust, ash, and so on, to slow up or hasten the setting, but when you see a modern ponderous, rotund cement mixer (rotating steadily upon its own transport lorry) squat contentedly on building sites (under the placid eye of one competent driver) think back a few centuries . . . because you are seeing the mixing of history.

Copper

We have mentioned on p. 308 the name of Olyff Burre as 'a rich coppersmith' – rich enough to build ships. A multitude of all manner of copper and brass skillets and copper-banded cooper work and special shipyard requirements made copper an important industry in certain localities. Around Copperas Bay on the Stour loose copperas stones (an outcrop from some under-water strata?) were collected. This was an industry in the fifteenth century, and as late as 1696 there were two working 'copperas houses' in the district. The by-products of the industry are constantly mentioned by contemporaries.

Cloth

Cloth had to be kept dry, and this was often the first stall to be settled in the Cloth Market or Market Hall. In remote districts the country workers carried out the entire process, spinning, weaving and finishing the cloth from their own wool or flax. This continued into the eighteenth century in some places. (Sixty or seventy years ago it was still going on in parts of north-west Ireland. For knitting, women sometimes spun from a distaff, considering this to produce rather more soft a thread than the wheel, which was large and whirled continuously. Several cabins spun, and in one was a loom on which cloth was set up as the spinners in turn were ready.)

At a very early date the weaver became a separate worker. (In 1939, in Joyce's country, my host was taking an ass-load of spun wool across the bog to the cabin of the weaver, expecting to bring back the previous consignment which the weaver would have completed.) The loose endthreads would be left on the woven length, to prove the completeness of the work done: but the spinners cut off and used these threads themselves: whence began the later commercial ruling that formed the

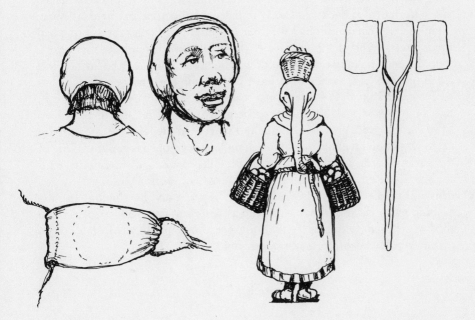

Headdresses were customarily worn: the liripipe could be made of linen or wool, while the cap would have been of linen.

basis of legislation for centuries. When cloth was sold by the bale of definite length and weight these end threads were a guarantee of the length of the weaver's work; if a cloth was deficient in length these ends were cut off and the cloth could not be sold in the cloth market – hence the development of Fent shops, where such goods could be sold. In the woollen towns of Yorkshire the Fent market dealt with all odd lengths, left overs from contracts, or trial bits or misprints, of many different lengths and goods. (The Fent is no longer a disgrace, but probably a bargain.)The saying 'to give an inch . . . ' is a cloth term: when the yardstick came into use the dealer was by law permitted to put his thumb down to mark the end of it, before he cut off or carried on – then the dealers took to putting down not their inch-wide thumb but the palm of their hand . . . and that was an ell.

Corn

'Stock and staple' are the terms given to types of corn sales. 'Staple', or 'sample', is when the farmer brings samples of his corn and books the order, which he delivers *where required* and collects the payment. 'Stock' is when he takes the corn in sacks and sells it direct, collecting payment at once. 'Staple' saves cartage in bad weather (an important consideration on bad roads); moreover, if the buyer sees the farmer has brought heavy sacks a long distance he may try to beat down the price, knowing the farmer will let all go cheaply, rather than have to cart the corn home again.

The earlier the date the less corn reached the markets, because while all the country was agricultural everyone grew their own corn for their own animals, and precious few had much to spare. On the larger estates, where there was good level land and ploughing had developed from a breaking of the surface with wooden single-line ploughs to a deeper furrowing with the metal-nosed plough (later with a turn-over action), more corn was grown, but the fields still required clod hopping and harrowing, and the reaping methods were very wasteful, although to compensate for this the shed corn made valuable fodder for geese and poultry. (Today, a hen couldn't get a beakful off a modern field.)

Fish

The fish market was supplied by fishing fleets, and the tradition of Scotch herring workers on the East coast is as old as dried stockfish; which is exactly the same as that sold today. Then, it was dried hanging on ladders slung out on a windy roof; it was staple diet on shipboard, and a large white flap of it hung at the yard-arm served as a 'Blue Peter' to show a ship well-provisioned for sailing.

The preparing of salted, smoked and dried meat and fish for winter was important. Certain woods 'smoke' with distinctive flavours: oak chips and sawdust gave York hams their flavour. The picric acid preparations (now painted on) of herrings attempted to copy the salty ship-building timber used to give kippers their zest. The smoke of the hut fire that fumigated the dried meat hung around the smoke hole was probably very mixed, but any

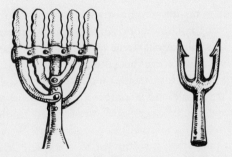

Fish spears were of various kinds, and were used either to spear individual
fish or were prodded into the bottom at random. That on the left is a gaff
type of iron with a central shaft; and that on the right is an eel spear of the
type used on 'hard' bottoms. It is an early type of wrought iron with flanges
bolted to a central shaft (the waved edge was produced by hammer action on
the flanges).

special flavour might be noted and used for special purposes. To a late date,
smoking of fish was done in pits where a smoke fire of seaweed and
driftwood smouldered and the fish hung above the pits.

Hay

Not much hay was marketed in mediaeval England – it was too precious; it
depended much on water meadows, and was needed by their owners.
Froissart reports that in West Yorkshire and on the Pennine Hills the land
seemed poor, but 'all the time he was there, a penny bought the same
amount of fodder, whether sold to knight or knave'. (A tribute to the
northern honesty, and also to the wide river valleys; there were abbeys
and the monks were good husbandmen.)

Hay production developed as horses replaced oxen. Oxen were fed on
corn *straw*, and small work horses got mixed straw and weedy grass, while
the tough little shelties and pack donkeys cropped turf close as sheep. It was
the heavy horses introduced by the Normans that needed hay and corn. In
1327 the members of an expedition towards Scotland (with transport
wagons) starved in misery for lack of any fodder: 'they were without brede
wyne candel lyght foder or forage, neither for horse or man . . . and yet
besides . . . it never ceased to rayne the hoole weeke . . . whereby theyre
saddels and pannels and countresyngles [countless things] were all rottyn
and broken . . . [and the horses had sore backs] and they had nothying to
mak fyre withall but greene bowes the wiche wolde not burne because of
the rayne'. This indicates the great importance of hay; small highland
ponies could scrape a mouthful from the moorland, but the carthorse type

of beast, needed to take the weight of an armoured knight, required hay.
What passed as hay for land-working animals was the grass allowed to
grow up among the stalks of cut corn, which was harvested as 'stover' (see
page 173). Therefore there were special sales for precious hay into cities, or
such towns where the grazing outside on common or in wild woodland was
insufficient. Donkey, mule and packhorse trains, like drover herds, chose
routes and seasons where it was possible to graze overnight. On the whole
there was very little hay available in open markets. What there was was
sold in regulated quantities: a statute of William and Mary for 1693 laid
down that a truss of dry hay should weigh 56 lbs, but of new hay (hay sold
between June and August) 60 lbs. A load was 38 truss.

Horn

The horn trade was comparatively large, for horns were much used (think
of it as a forerunner of plastics). Many types of container, small pocket
boxes to large caskets, were made of horn. Horn drinking cups were often
elaborately ornamented and lidded. Of the daily drinking horns, the best
had round bases of horn, and others had wood bottoms. Spoons were of
horn – everybody used them. Long-bows were tipped with horn, using the
natural grooves of the small sheep's horn to catch the loop of the bow
string. There was also the ink horn of the scribe, the comb for the hair
(though it was advised to 'comb the head with an ivory comb, nothing
recreates the memory more') – and a lucrative trade in 'Unicorn horn',
which was so reliable a guard against poison that the nobility kept a
drinking horn to test with. Some of the long writhed horns that remain as
'treasures' in cathedrals were, in their period, very costly and important
gifts to the Church. (It was a mediaeval belief that when the unicorn
stopped to drink, he dipped his horn into the water to test it.)

Ink

By Tusser's date, liquid ink had become a sales product, though specialists
still made their own. An early mediaeval ink was made from blackthorn
bark, which was macerated in rain water till the black powdery deposit
formed a thick deposit at the bottom. The water was then strained off and
the black residue was dried, mixed with various gums, and ground down.
(The gums exuding from cherry and apple bark were used.) Other inks
were made from oak galls. Most of the early scriptorium inks had their
special recipes and these inks have remained clear for centuries. The thick
printing ink used for Tusser's first edition would probably have been oil-

bound, and in some cases the oil has permeated through the paper, causing a blurred shadow on the reversed folio, though this may be due to pressure, or the temperature of storage conditions. (A copy of Bartholomaeus Anglicus in the British Museum of the same date as a copy in the Cape Town Library, is less clear than the Dutch copy.)

Moles

'Get mole catcher cunningly mole for to kill' – the farmer Tusser, at his 'enclosure period', wants level fields; while strip cultivation continued the mole did small harm and his workings helped to drain and break up the rough furrows and big clods. Their tiny, soft skins were too small for use by workers, who had plenty of larger game, but there may have been a sale for the skins to city workers, because from time immemorial the curious mole fur, which is capable of lying smooth in either direction, has been used by lead workers and other metal experts, and is still used by modern plumbers when smoothing soldered joins, though the 'piece of moleskin' in the plumber's tool-bag is now often a synthetic substitute.

Musical Instruments

The array of musical instruments (usually being played by angels) in our cathedral carvings, proves the skill of the craftsman, who, being a master of his craft, would go out to find and select his own material for himself rather than rely on anything brought in to the market. He might ask some countryman to 'keep an eye' for certain fine woods or fine horn or white horsehair or leather, suitable for some special piece of work on hand. (Countrymen have always been adept at making pipes and whistles out of suitable wood, so could understand the requirements of the instrument makers.) But the instrument makers would be able to supply a musical countryman with a treasure better than he could make for himself (let's hope he enjoyed it at home by the fire).

Mustard

Maids, mustard-seed gather, for being too ripe,
and weather it well, ere ye give it a stripe:
Then dress it, and lay it in soller up sweet,
lest foistiness make it, for table unmeet.
                                                            Tusser

Before spices were imported, any fragrant native plant was treasured. Settlers would recognise a plant which also grew in their native lands; some settlers would bring in new ones, which either perished or became 'wild'. Sometimes the foreign name stuck; for example our wild comfrey was for centuries called Saracen's root, from the belief that it was brought to England by the Crusaders.

Probably most people used the various charlocks: a weed in early corn crops, its early growth made welcome 'spring greens' after the winter salt meat and dried beans. Today, we also welcome our winter salads of quick-growing mustard and cress. (The cress seed should be sown two days before the mustard.) None of the charlocks have the flavour of the true mustard plant, the seeds of which were pounded for use with the pungent husk still intact, making what is now called French mustard.

In some mediaeval recipes, the 'mustard' poured into the 'saucer' under brawn or other food seems to have been a mustard-flavoured white sauce. The admixture of horseradish is also an ancient usage. During the period

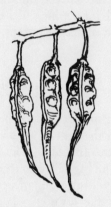

Mustard seed (enlarged) in pod and husk

when travel depended upon horseback transport this seems to have pre-dated 'Elliman's Embrocation' as a warming lubricant; horseradish is one of the plants often surviving wild near old travellers' hostels and monasteries.

Mustard does not seem to have been a definite field crop before the fourteenth century, though all households grew enough for themselves. A tiresome crop to harvest, its seeds mature and shed at a touch. The women folk probably gathered it whole into linen bags or their aprons, and carried it indoors, direct, where it was not threshed but the bags beaten with light canes. Tusser bids the girls 'give it a stripe'. The small seeds were sifted out by hand after blowing off the chaff, perhaps using the fireside bellows?

Essex (Tusser's country) probably grew mustard for the London markets. Later it became a commercial product in East Anglia. It was the difficulty of harvesting and processing the seed which tended to make mustard become an early monopoly product.

Needles

One of the goods on sale at the market would be a selection of fine sewing needles. Stowe mentions 'A negro from Spain' who made these in 1545. They were expensive and were probably sold 'encased'. The term 'needle case' precedes the Victorian needle book.

Physick (and Poisons)

Several veterinary cures are obviously the aftermath of long mediaeval medical muddles: one-third classical tradition, one-third religious invention and one-third plain common sense and experience. Mediaeval people had a genius for getting hold of the wrong end of the right stick. Some of the medical ideas were thoroughly sound, though seemingly fantastic. Here is one simple example: 'To learn the chances of a feverish patient, tie violets round his wrist and note how swiftly they wither.' Lacking a clinical thermometer, this was quite a reasonable guide. Violets are chosen as being simple flowers, not complicated by leaves growing on the stalks, and all violets are liable to wither at about the same rate, under the same heat conditions (though any similar flower could be used in the same way). Symptoms that any experienced GP notes automatically, such as the position in which a patient lies, his rate of breathing, discharge and smells, probably carried information to the gifted mediaeval man as directly as they do today.

Surgery was performed on animals without anaesthetic; for human beings various drugs were tried, as also the more successful plain knockout.

Medicinal plants (see Appendix 1) were used for their special medical contents or, as with comfrey, for bone-setting. Limestone and some chalky marble stones were used, much as we use milk of magnesia: some early alabaster effigies may have lost their noses and toes to cure a sick cow! These and many other country goods were demanded by patients (and sometimes doctors). The dried, rounded dung of the hare was said to have been used as a pessary (the shape does seem right). Measurements used were vague: a pugil was a pinch, and a manipolus a handful.

In connection with the 'medical trade' it is fair to mention distilling, for crude stills were used very early, and for obtaining essences the distillers must have purchased quantities of herbs and other country material, and the special fuels for use with the apparatus. How much the alchemist added to the work of the medical man will never be known.

Again Tusser provides the steady peg for the assessment of values. Distilling *was* done, and even in the late seventeenth century became popular, but it was not much done by ordinary country-folk. It required a specially-built still, and that implied extra space, which small houses lacked; it required the individual attention of one person; and, above all, it took time, which the workers could not spare. Brewing drinks of various kinds was as routine as cooking food, but distilling remained a specialist job. Exactly when and where the Scottish and Irish illicit still began is 'non proven'. At times the alchemist seems to have been involved. Chaucer's description of the explosion in the Alchemist's laboratory (one worker thinks it was caused by using the wrong fuel) sounds more like a primitive still than a forge. And though the experiments were 'mercurial' the accusation of the special timber used does suggest that more than the rural mine's products, and groat clippings, etc., may have been imported from the country, as solvents.

The distilling of scents and essences belonged to the new leisured class. From the detailed descriptions, it appears that men enjoyed inventing and contructing elaborate stills (though 'done to please the wife' was implied) and the publishing of their excellent working frustrated their masculine rivals. By the end of the seventeenth century and well into the eighteenth century, the wives had taken over and employed a stillroom maid (to clear up?).

Potash

The potash industry was one of the basic trades of any community. Household washing and bucking used ley and soap, and many families made their own from their own wood ash. But trade soap and potash made a 'waste trade product' between the leather dressers (who supplied the fat) and the potash burners. All these trades worked downstream near the banks of the estuary. The leather dressers, and soap boilers, were instructed to do so by law, but the potash burners did so because they were also scavengers, collecting the driftweed (which was rich in mineral salts) and rubbish from the tide marks: they also burnt refuse and gleanings from the common lands – old thatch, broken straw, and so on.

The potash burners lived in small huts by their hearths, much as in the woods, charcoal burners lived near their hearths. Records show that they bought wood ash from local houses and smithies to sell to the soap boilers. (Among soap boilers it was illegal to steal another soap boiler's 'ashencarrys', that is, to entice away another man's refuse collector.) The ash refuse was collected and packed into a barrel, filled up with soft water, stirred and drained off, the process being repeated till the water had dissolved out all soluble salts. The solid contents of the barrel were then tilted out and sold for manure or cheap earthenware; but first the water had to be evaporated off by boiling, or more often soaked up in clean straw, which was then spread out to dry and burnt off on an open flat hearth.

The black crystalline deposit left under this last burning was 'black potash', and was sold in sackfuls to the refiners, who turned it into white pearl ash. The ordinary black potash was used for many trades. A special 'Red Essex' potash, mentioned in old records, may have had some oxide, or even some of the Essex red clay, held in suspension in the water.

Gradually the importing of foreign potash and the general burning of coal had killed the small, local potash trades, and people bought soda and ready-made soap for their cleaning. Some emigrants, though, carried the knowledge to the New World and made soap for themselves 'as they used to do in England'.

The washed ash manure from the potash workers could not have been rich in soluble salts, but would have some value, and because of this we claim that Tusser was one of the early users of 'artificial fertilisers'.

Pottery

Mediaeval pottery was an important trading commodity, varying from district to district, being adapted to local fuel and fireplaces; the different clays of different areas also gave rise to local variations. Not until the nineteenth century, when canals and road transport superseded the packhorse, did the thousands of small potteries all over England close down. In earlier periods few households bought pottery from further than fifty miles away. The china (and glass) of cities were expensive transported specialities, but the heavyweight country pottery (in constant demand) made the local potter as much one of the community as the local smith. And each potter had to be a specialist.

Clay, flints and chalks, and other materials now transported, were used on the spot (probably the primitive camshaft used for stamping ore was adapted, or flints may have been pulverised in fires lit on the beach and quenched with sea water, as they broke field stones in Ireland). The local clay was the main colour factor. For example, Essex pottery was a dullish clay, decorated with a white strip of malm from the Thames estuary. Chalk was fetched from the Downs, and glaze was variously coloured by refuse from the copperas and lead workings. There was great variety, as there were many localities. The Devon reddish pot with cream glaze is an example of a surviving ancient style.

Over wood fires most pottery would be sufficiently fireproof, but it is
noteworthy that pastry, which needed the hottest fire, was usually made in
a raised, or coffer, shape (now used for pork pies) as this was self-
supporting. Earthenware dishes could withstand the heat necessary to cook
custards and milk dishes, however.

The local potter adapted his ware to local requirements. For centuries
wine-making districts specialised in wine jars and ferment pots, all slightly
different in shape. The size of local joints or poultry set the size for stewing
pots. Dairy districts wanted milk-skimming pans, skimmers and cream
pots. There were salting troughs, though curing usually used wood, and
wooden cheese vessels were valuable in preserving bacteria culture.
Pickling and preserving pots varied, as did honey pots (both for working
and preserving), grease jars, and the gally pots of glue boilers and painters.
Pottery was as intimately connected with its locality as architecture was.

While horse transport lasted, twenty-five miles was a fair distribution
radius – out with the heavy load, and back next day with a lighter
commodity. Twelve miles out and twelve back was the limit for heavy
stoneware pots. (In mediaeval times drainpipes were usually of wood, but
later pipes were made in brickyards.)

The pedlars of pots used carts, or packhorses on bridle paths. The gypsies
carried on this transport of pots right through to the last century, and
'throw outs' and 'rejects' accumulated in markets because common pots
were country products, and were traded into cities rather than carried out
of them. Fern (bracken) was used as packing for pots, as heather was for
slates.

Poultry

The trade in geese and poultry was very definitely seasonal. Poultry, unless
specially fattened up or as capons, were not specially favoured, but in an
illustration we find that the *leg* of a chicken is shown on the platter
prepared for an invalid. At table in Hall pages were taught how to slit the
meat of the leg upwards to the top, letting the pieces stand out in a whorl
easy to bite off, and to wipe the bone end 'handle' before handing it over.

Many old markets have degenerated into Fairs. A typical 'Goose Fair'
still exists in Nottingham. Originally droves of geese set out on their long
slow way to city markets. They were the 'Michaelmas geese' – the plump
results of gleaning and fattening in the corn fields of a rich agricultural
district. As soon as the corn was cut and carried the geese moved on to the
land, hence the position of the 'goose fairs' was related to that of the corn
markets. There was often a small stone 'goose hole' built by the cottage
door, under the outside stone steps that led up to the corn loft.

Rabbits and Game

The locality of the market would decide on the amount of game for sale. Hare usually counted as game, but in the wilds, or remote from estates or Royal ownership, anything wild was hunted freely, and would be carried to town to be sold or bartered. Wild rabbits (as distinct from conies, which were especially cultivated) are included in lists of market goods. That the skins were used is known, but the fur seems to have been a separate trade: the short hairs and soft underfur from the pelts were usable for making felt. Rabbit skins would be treated in vats similarly to other skins. That process would leave a deposit of matted waste that may have been used for stuffing small articles, or in forms of quilting and stubb work. The stirring and working in the vats would have the effect of matting and consolidating short woolly rabbit hairs. They were probably used in the hat trades, which flourished at the end of the liripipe period, and went out of production finally with the last change in top hat production.

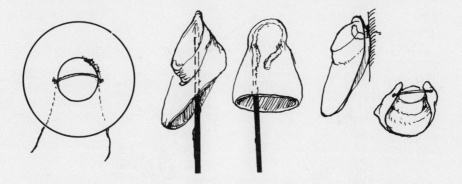

The diagram shows how many of the complicated hats worn by workmen were not specially designed: a soaking wet felt hat hung up on a pointed stake, a shepherd's crook, or a peg on a wall, would take on a characteristic shape. The Wife of Bath wore a hat 'as brood as is a bokeler or a targe': the strings would tie it safe in a wind, and the rim would sport her shrine tokens.

All felt fabrics prove tractable under tension. It was used for wrapping edged metal, as in some forms of armour; and the wooden cases of manuscripts, whose covers were often embellished with precious metals and jewels, were sometimes lined with felt.

Felt-makers used wool; early felt sometimes incorporated the long strong hairs of early breeds of sheep. Hatters used rabbit fur: we believe this was done comparatively early, since market prices for rabbit skins returned empty from the market quote heads, skins and ears separate. (Andrew Young, at a much later date, writes of the sale of skins being a commercial asset to the owners of warrens.)

Rabbit skins being light, the vats could be small, and we surmise the work was done in towns where the felt maker worked. An indication of this is that quantities of rabbits, for food, were sent to town, and the 'returned empty' loads list included only rabbit *skins* (not pelts), and specified that 'discarded heads and pads' be returned to the land as manure.

Scouring Materials

Sand was used before sand-paper, and long remained in use for scouring table tops, and also for stone and tiled floors. For metal, including steel armour, the horsetail (*equisetum*) was used, the coarse, whip-like growth of which incorporates particles of flint. Later, when pewter came in, it continued in use.

Near the coast, white cuttle-fish bone was an excellent abrasive, and it may have been vended inland, being a small item and light to carry. As the pack horse trails crossed the land, drovers and countrymen going to market

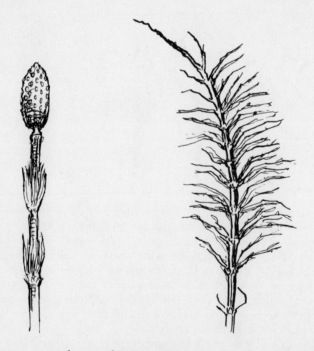

Equisetum was used as an abrasive on account of its flinty texture. It had many names: shave grass; or pewterwort when it was used to scour the pewter dishes; it was in such demand that it was imported from Holland and called Dutch grass. It was used for scouring wooden utensils, and continued to be used in Dales dairies until quite recently.

with the main loads would be likely to pick up small oddments which they knew from experience they could barter or sell for a small sum to some town worker. Today, many oddments, unobtainable elsewhere, can be tracked down in small local markets which carry on this very long tradition.

Tallow

Beside making dips, tallow was also the vehicle for many lubricants and abrasives. Whereas today's boatyard uses 'waterproof' sandpaper, previously a sand-impregnated tallow did the job. Tallow was also the source of the thick grease for metal bearings, and the resultant 'black

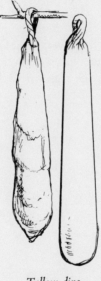

Tallow dips

grease' had special value since it was supposed to contain some of the strength derived from the metal. (See p.145.) Tallow was also used to waterproof winter boots and shoes. While sheep remained 'thin mutton' tallow was comparatively expensive.

Timber

In the first section of this study we wrote of the river of history flowing at various speeds in different places, sometimes in tempests and floods bursting powerfully into new channels. Yet earlier, upstream, a sheltered pool might stand still, barely stirring.

The sixteenth and seventeenth centuries show such a swift flood that it is difficult to connect them with the twelfth and thirteenth centuries. Near the end of the sixteenth century Tusser (a reliable timekeeper) advises the householder to buy his firewood before the cold weather raises the price – his great-grandfather probably had all the wood he needed free for the fetching. But Tusser says: 'now the woods be nigh gone'. So timber cannot be classed as a market commodity: shipyards and others would pay almost any price for exactly what they wanted – if they could find it.

A century later, when some of these 'new Elizabethan ships' were old and broken up, their timbers again fetched good prices for building the houses in the rapidly developing trade town. Timber was in demand for ship-building and metal smelting (coal had not yet come into common use), so that though there was much bargaining and buying and selling of timber, it was more often contracted for some special purpose than traded in the open market. The new merchants wanted it for their heavily-timbered and panelled houses; shipbuilders hunted their timber with no regard to transport if they could find the right growths (see p. 206).

APPENDIXES

COMMONLY USED WILD
AND CULTIVATED PLANTS

Gardeners and botanists may find the following list of interest.

(The word 'officinale' or 'official' derives from *Officina*, the monastery dispensary, where were kept the drugs and herbs for official use in the infirmary. Later apothecaries used the word for their store rooms, and by the end of the seventeenth century the word was in use to denote a herb that was officially recognised. For example: *Symphytum officinale* was for many years officially listed in the British Pharmacopoeia.)

ALKANET (*Anchusa officinalis*)
The source of colouring matter used for cheeses, to make them golden red. It is now a very rare wild flower, though the plants continue in some localities. Old cheese farms frequently have a clump gone 'wild' in the garden. The rich blue flowers of the Dropmore Anchusa which is now a popular plant in the herbaceous border belong to a cultivated version.

BROOM (*Sarothamnus scoparius*)
This surely takes its name from its usage, as it has been used for centuries for sweeping the hearth or bread oven. The birch besom was used for the cobbled yard, but for ordinary household floors, sanded, or the dust below the rushes, broom was used tied into bundles and hatchet-trimmed to a firm surface. Split or shredded wood was also formed for small stiff brushes, but not till the seventeenth and eighteenth centuries do we find the new 'wail bone' broom. Broom was also bruised for cattle fodder, using a flail action, or a beetle.

BUCKRAMS (Ransoms or Bear's garlic) (*Allium Ursinum*)
The common wild white garlic that grows in woodlands. Mediaeval people ate it green with cheese, and with cold boiled bacon. As the first green vegetable of spring and eaten raw it certainly promoted good health. A much later generation took the distilled oil in brandy medicinally. A Dutch family in the Transvaal imputed their superb health to eating onions

or garlic overnight and breathing the dawn wind. The plant grows like a green carpet in some districts so that the cows' milk is tainted by it.

CALAMINT (or Wild basil) (*Calamintha officinalis*)

This looks at first glance like a small pink-flowered dead nettle. Its scent is aromatic. It used to be brewed into a strong 'tea' and drunk hot to loosen a chest cold. Syrup of Calamint is still sold as a cough mixture by some old-fashioned chemists.

CARAWAY (*Carum carvi*)

Now listed as one of the rare wild plants, or as an 'escape', it seems to have been common and popular in 1400. A 'seed cake' is made with caraway seeds. The pungent leaves were sometimes used as a salad, and the root was also eaten (as a medicine?). Later, from the seventeenth century onwards, as sugar became cheaper, quantities of 'caraway comfits' were made.

COLTSFOOT (*Tussilago farfara*)

Tussis means 'cough' and the plant is still in use as a soothing decoction for the chest, and as 'coltsfoot candy' and lozenges, etc. Dioxorides mentions the smoke from its dried burning leaves being sucked into the lungs to alleviate pain and it is quite probable that dried herbs were used in this way before Sir Walter Raleigh introduced tobacco. Today, the dried leaves, variously pickled and blended, form the basis of home-made tobaccos. The white seed-head was a convenient size to be soaked in saltpetre and used as tinder. Coltsfoot's small golden flowers are welcome as one of the earliest signs of spring, but the plant is a bad agricultural weed.

COMFREY (*Symphytum officinale*)

This plant, or a close relative, has recently been advertised as 'New Russian Cumphrey', and used for pig fodder. Yet mediaeval people used it, and it was listed as a wound wort and used in the setting of broken bones, hence its Scottish name of 'boneset'. A herbal of the sixteenth century states that the root juice makes new healing growth, is good for blood spitting and 'for those bursten within'. The name 'Saracen's root' suggests it was brought over by Crusaders from Eastern medical hospitals. As a bone setter, the large hollow-crowned root was pounded up raw, when it reduces to a mucilaginous mass (rather like mashed swede). The juice was used to wash the wound (if there was a compound fracture) and then the pulp was partly drained through a linen cloth and packed round the straightened bone as it lay in a wooden trough splint – exactly as a surgeon today uses plaster. It was actually used recently for plastic surgery as having certain advantages over plaster (it sets slowly, with no heat and no warping). Masses of comfrey grow around the site of old monasteries, fords, hospices and landing places, anywhere that travellers' broken bones might be expected. It is frequently found with horseradish, which was used as embrocation for sprains or rheumatism.

A note on the plant appeared in 1912 by R. J. Gibson, M.A., F.Z.A., of Liverpool. And a booklet in 1936 by J. MacAlister, M.D., who with A. W. Titherly, isolated the substance 'allantoin' from comfrey, and established its use as a cell proliferant.

On the agricultural side the use of the plant has been continuous; a farm at Tarvin in Cheshire grew it as fodder for cattle and a farm near

Cheltenham had four acres kept for its horses. The gypsies purposely camped where the plant grew in order to feed their animals, and many country people eat the leaves as spinach in spring, or make a tea of the plant for gastric ulcers. The active element is in the roots from October to March, but during the summer it is in the growing leaves and buds.

CORIANDER (*Coriandrum sativum*)

This was extensively grown in Essex, and the wild plant is common there. The small round seeds had a hundred uses in the kitchen. The seeds are still used today to mask less pleasant flavours in medicines, and in making various curry powders and pickles, etc. In mediaeval times they may have been used in curing meat and were certainly used in spicing it.

CORN COCKLE (*Agrostemma githago*)

A silky purple flower an inch or so across with lavish green and silver foliage, is found today on field borders and canal paths. It is not now a troublesome weed, as it needs space, and modern corn grows closely. But when bread flour was stone-ground, not rolled and dressed as today, the small black seeds of the corn cockle, which were said to be poisonous, were shed at harvest time and gathered in with the grain, so that they bespeckled the flour and showed up in the bread.

DOCKS (*Rumex*)

Several of the dock family were used as pot herbs, *R. sanguineus* and sorrel being cooked together to form a blackish-green sauce, of the colour, of laver, though with a coarser texture. The broad leaves of *R. obtusifolius* were used to wrap up cheese and butter for the market (before paper became common).

FEVERFEW (*Chrysanthemum parthenium*)

This was perennial and supposed to be one of the anti-insect flowers.

FLEABANE (*Pulicaria dysenterica*)

This small yellow-flowering plant was specially gathered and burnt to exterminate fleas. Anne Pratt gives Linnaeus as authority for its use by the Russian Army whose unchanged wadded coats needed it!

FOXGLOVE (*Digitalis purpurea*)

The name is of disputed origin. A tall upright peal of tuned handbells was called a 'glauve' and the flower certainly resembles a Folks' (little people's) glauve. But Turner, a contemporary of Tusser, calls it 'Thimble flower'. Its use as a heart medicine does not seem to have been known or understood till a later date.

GERMANDER (*Teucrium scorodonia*)

A common woodland plant, small with yellow flowers and red stamens. It was used in brewing ale and is one of the ale plants that the hop supplanted. It clears the beer and gives it a dark colour and bitter flavour. Later, agriculturists regretted the use of the expensive hop 'which uses so much space and labour, when this small plant would better answer the purpose'.

GLASSWORT (*Salicornia herbacea*)

A low plant, with queer jointed cactus-like stems, a very bright pellucid green, not in the least like the opaque grey-blue samphire with which it is sometimes confused; though it can be pickled in the same way, and probably was so used. It was one of the few salt marsh plants which was lush and juicy and much liked by animals. It is extremely rich in soda and was used in the old process of glass-making.

HOUSE LEEK (*Sempervivum tectorum*)

This was called *Donderbaard* in Holland; in England it was considered a deflector of lightning. (The Irish use it on roofs today.) The fleshy leaves' crushed juice is used as an eye lotion and in parts of England is used, as is watercress juice, to soothe the irritation of lupus (a skin disease).

House leek

LADIES BEDSTRAW (*Galium verum*)

This was used for rennet and as a dye for wool.

LAMB'S LETTUCE (*Valerianella locusta*)

This has very small green leaves, tiresome to pick, and its chief virtue is its early appearance – at lambing time in March. It was dressed with oil and vinegar and was welcome after a long winter.

LEEKS (the *Allium porrum* of Linnaeus)

These were sown thickly in spring, and some were pulled and eaten as a spring onion, or cut for salad, like chives. The residue were transplanted and cultivated as today, though some growers blanched them under stones or potsherds. Leeks were the basis of many farm dishes; under 'leek' are probably included the old 'perennial onions' of the type the Welsh call 'Holtsers'.

LETTUCE (*Lactuca: L. verosa* and *L. serriola*)

Supposedly the ancestors of our garden lettuce. (When our cos has run to seed the resemblance may be traced.) The white juice of the lettuce was dried into brown cakes and used as a form of opium – it is strongly narcotic. A mediaeval 'House Book' of the early fifteenth century mentions this dried juice being given to produce sleep for surgery. When Britain produced her own drugs, quantities of *L. virosa* were grown in Forfarshire. It was used for agues and fevers.

LOVAGE (*Ligusticum scoticum*)

This was definitely a Scottish speciality and Anne Pratt in botany books of 1850 gives a very interesting suggestion that east-coast communication by sea from the north made it cultivated down south. Lovage was eaten by fasting Highlanders as a preventative of infection – 'the Shetland islanders who eat it as salad, as well as boiled, call it "'Sirenas'" – and it is 'much planted in English gardens where it groweth huge and great' (this last note is of approximately the time of the great plague). It is a sea-coast plant, and more research into its dietetic history would be rewarding.

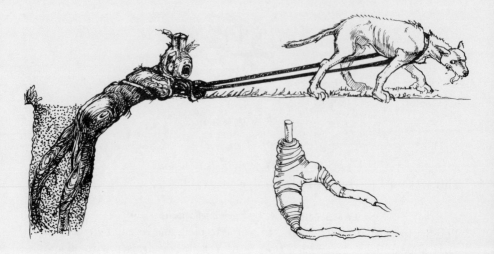

MANDRAKE (*Mandragora* sp.) was highly thought of as a masculine tonic, inducing fecundity; the origin of this may lie in Genesis 30, vv. 14–17. The common mandrake root was said to scream when torn out: it was wise to have it dragged out by a black dog. (Below) Eastern mystic reports of ginseng (*Panax* sp.), the 'two-legged man plant' may have been confused with mandrake.

MAYWEED (*Matricaria?*)

It is uncertain which of the camomile types of daisy 'mayweed' was used to indicate.

MEDLAR (*Mespilus germanica*): a slow-growing tree, with very hard and durable timber, which can live to a great age. The fruit resembles a small apple, but has very pronounced calyx-lobes. It is hard and bitter when ripe, but becomes agreeably acid when it begins to decay; this is when it is eaten.

MULLEIN (*Verbascum*)

The tall plant with the golden tapering spike rising four or five feet from its circle of grey flannel leaves is very common in parts of England. *V. blattaria* was used against cockroaches – any sort of fine plaster or dry lime setting in their narrow throats chokes these beetles and apparently the powdery 'wool' from mullein leaves was reputed to have the same effect. The great mullein *V. thapsus* had been called 'high taper' being like the tall altar candles lit for the Mass. Bullock's lungwort was another Saxon name, as the thick leaves, eaten by the plough oxen, were supposed to be good for their winter coughs. The golden flowers carried a high reputation to the New World as a valued tonic.

ORACHE (*Atriplex angostepolia*)

The old French name 'arroche' was used for *A. angostepolia*. It is common enough in most of the southern counties – like 'Good King Henry' it was boiled as greens. 'There are many dishes of meate made of them [the orache plants] while they are young.'

RAMPION (*Campanula rapuncullus*)

Apparently not native, but it was in cultivation in the fourteenth century, and valuable as one of the few root vegetables for winter use. Its white root was boiled and served as a dish with sauce or sliced and served raw. (It is interesting that this very old root is now listed as a 'new vegetable'.)

RHUBARB (*Rumex alpinus;* or possibly *aquaticus*)

Monk's rhubarb was used in monasteries' infirmaries as a standard aperient in place of the expensive imported rhubarb root. The plant, now wild, is one of those which help the field worker to trace the sites of old monastic settlements.

SAMPHIRE (*Crithmum maritimum*)

A very localised plant growing where there is a shingle beach. It is not a garden plant and is difficult to cultivate. Most people dislike its strange pungent aroma, but those who do like it develop a passion for it, and seem to revel in the scent, and even crunch it raw – it is usually pickled.

SEA HOLLY (*Eryngium maritimum*)

The deep-rooted stock of the blue sea holly was a favourite mediaeval flavouring. A Dutchman, Samuel de Groote, developed 'candied eryngo root' as a trade product, and it was sold in the local markets. It was presented to visiting royalty in 1617. The root was apparently dug, boiled, peeled and candied in strips, and sold as a sweetmeat. The water from the boiling (we found from experiment) made excellent eryngo-flavoured candy. We read of eryngo root as one of the aromatic 'chewing gums' recommended against plague infection. Unhappily, this plant and the long-horned gold poppy, and all the lovely sea-coast and shingle plants are now being destroyed under sea-front promenades.

SICKLEWORT (*Ajuga reptans*)

This plant, more often known as bugle, was supposed to be good as a staunch for cuts – some old herbals call it also 'carpenters herb'. The slightly woolly texture of the plant may have been of use.

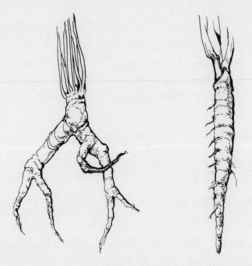

SKIRRET (*Sium sisarum*): a species of water parsnip, with white tubers which were cooked and served like salsify (the oyster plant). On the left is the original wild form, and on the right is a domesticated root.

SOPS-IN-WINE (*Dianthus plumarius* var.)

One excuse for the name is the dark wine-coloured spot in the centre. The clove pink called 'clove gillyflower' was the favourite garden flower of the period, and the name sops-in-wine came more probably from a clove-scented wine cup. (We believe it to be a compromise between the old mediaeval 'hypocras', a spiced wine, and the French sirop.) The flower seems to have been floated in this thick sweet cup, in the same manner as borage was used in a lighter cup. There is a 'wall pink', wild, that is found in the clefts of cliffs and old castles, etc., that seems to have transferred the name gillyflower to wallflower? The French muslin weavers of Paisley seem to have cultivated the pink and some of its dainty beauty is traceable in their designs.

STRAWBERRY (*Fragaria moschata*)

'Strawberries and cream are many a rural man's banquet, we have known such banquets to put men in jeopardy of their lives.'

The strawberry of the fourteenth and fifteenth centuries is well shown by miniature paintings in the old manuscripts of the period. It is a single berry, more rounded than the Alpine strawberry and larger than the wild strawberry. The hull sits high on top of the rounded end, and the stalk is comparatively long. Also it is carried high among the long-stalked leaves, not flat to the ground as the modern Royal Sovereign and double type of squared strawberries.

TOBACCO – 1573

In these daies, the taking in of the smoke of the Indian herbe called 'Tobaco' by an instrument formed like a little ladell . . . is gretlie taken up and used in England. . . . This herbe is yet not so common but that for want thereof divers do practise for the like purposes with the Nicetian called in latine Hyosciamus Lutens or the Yellow Henbane.

William Harrison (1534–1593)

WATER PARSNIP (*Sium latifolium*)

Pliny says the seed taken in wine disperses calculi, assuages hernia, removes freckles on females and scales on horses.

WILD ARUM (*Arum maculatum*)

Known also as wake-robin, lasses and lads, jack-in-the-pulpit, and many other names. *Arum maculatum* was the early basis of sallop. It is uncertain if the root of this plant was used in mediaeval times. The acid poison must be entirely washed out before the starch can be used. The earliest record we can find is where it was cropped and prepared in Dorset, before the importing of West Indian arrowroot made sallop a general soft drink for the poorer classes. (To bite a newly-dug root of *Arum maculatum* is like biting a red-hot poker!)

WILD BARLEY GRASS (*Hordeum murinum*)

This is also called swine's tail (the wild boar had a hairy swish exactly like a rope unravelling, or a wisp of barley). A note from a 1450 traveller advises riders to find an inn where it is not in the hay, as it makes horses' gums so sore that a bit cannot be used. (The bulbous buttercup will also blister the mouth.)

WORMWOOD (*Artemisia absinthium*)

According to Gerard, this 'voided worms from the guts', and the use of it to scour floors during spring cleaning was good against fleas.

PLANTS AND FLOWERS COMMONLY GROWN
IN THE LATE MEDIAEVAL PERIOD,
DRAWN FROM VARIOUS
CONTEMPORARY SOURCES

Herbs and Roots for Sallads and Sauce

Alexanders, at all times
Artichocks
Blessed Thistle, or Carduus
  Benedictus
Cucumbers, in April and Maye
Cresse, sow with lettuce in the
  spring
Endive
Mustard-seed, sow in the spring and
  at Michaelmas
Musk, in Aprill and Maye
Mintes
Purslane

Radish, and after remove them
Rampions
Rockat, in Aprill
Sage
Sorrell
Spinage, for the summer
Sea-holye
Sperage, let growe two yeares, and
  then remove
Skirrets, set these plants in March
Suckery
Tarragon
Violets

Herbs and Roots to Boil or to Butter

Beanes, set in winter
Cabbegis, sowe in March and after
  remove
Carrets
Gourdes, in May
Nauewes, sowe in June

Pompione, in Maye
Parseneps, in Winter
Roncivall pease, set in Winter
Rapes, sow in June
Turneps, in March and April

Herbs, Branches and Flowers, for Windows and Pots

Bae, sowe in January
Bachelers' buttens
Botles, blew, red and tauney
Collembines
Campions
Daffadondillies
Eglantine, or sweete-bryer
Fetherfewe

Flower amour, sowe in Maye
Flower de luce
Flower gentil, white and red
Flower nyce
Gelyflowers, red, white and
  carnations, set in spring and
  harvest in potts, pailles, or tubs, or
  for summer in bedds

Holiokes, red, white and carnations
Indian eye, sowe in Maye or set in
  slips in March
Lavender of all sorts
Lark's foot
Laus tibi
Lillium cumbalium
Lilies, red and white, sow or set in
March and September
Marigolds, double
Nigella Romana
Pauncies, or hearts-ease
Pragels, greene and yellowe
Pinkes of all sortes

Queen's gilliflowers
Rosemary
Roses of all sorts
Snap-dragons
Sopps in wine
Sweete Williams
Sweete Johns
Star of Bethelem
Star of Jerusalem
Stock gilleflowers of all sorts
Tuft gelliflowers
Velvet flowers, or Frenche marigold
Violets, yellow and white
Wall gelliflowers of all sorts

Strewing Herbs of all Sorts

Bassell, fine and busht, sowe in Maye
Bawlme, set in Marche (Balm)
Camamel
Costemary
Cowsleps (paggles)
Daisies of all sorts
Sweet fennell
Germander
Hop, set in Februarie
Lavender
Lavender spike
Lavender cotten

Marjorom, knotted, sow or set at the
  spring
Mawdelin
Peny ryall
Roses of all sorts, in January and
  September
Red myntes
Sage
Tansey
Violets
Winter savery

Seeds and Herbs for the Kitchen

Avens
Beteny
Bleete, whit or yellowe
Bloodwort
Buglas
Burnet
Burrage
Cabage, remove in June
Clarye
Coleworts
Cresses
Endive
Fenel

French mallowes
French saffron, set in August
Lang de Befe
Leekes, remove in June
Lettis, remove in Maye
Longwort
Liverwort
Marygoldes, often cut
Mercury
Mintes, at all times
Nep
Onions, from December to Marche
Orach or arach, red and white

Patience	Sommer savery
Percelye	Sorrell
Peneriall [Penny Royal?]	Spinnage
Primerose	Suckery
Poset	Siethes
Rosemary, in the spring time	Tansie
Sage, red and white	Thyme
Saffron	Violettes of all sorts

TUSSER'S GARDEN

The following verses, selected from Tusser's Calendar of 1573, give a good general idea of the late mediaeval garden.

Land falling or lying full south or south-west,
for profit by tillage, is lightly the best:
So garden with orchard and hop-yard I find,
that want the like benefit, grow out of kind.

At spring (for the summer) sow garden ye shall,
at harvest (for winter) sow not at all;
Oft digging, removing and weeding (ye see)
makes herb the more wholesome, and greater to be.

In March is good graffing, the skilful do know,
so long as the wind in the east do not blow:
From moon being changed, till past be the prime,
for graffing and cropping, is very good time.

Things graffed or planted, the greatest and least,
defend against tempest, the bird, and the beast;
Defended shall prosper, the tother is lost,
the things with the labour, the time and the cost.

Time fayer, to sow or to gather be bold,
but set or remove, when the weather is cold.
Cut all thing or gather, the moon in the wane,
but sow in encreasing, or give it his bane.

New sets, do ask watering, with pot or with dish,
new sown, do not so, if he do as I wish:
Through cunning with dibble, rake, mattock, and spade,
by line, and by level, trim garden is made.

Dig garden, stroy mallow, now may ye at ease,
and set, (as a dainty,) thy runcivall pease,
Go cut, and set roses, chuse aptly thy plot,
the roots of the youngest are best to be got.

In March at the farthest, dry season or wet,
hop-roots so well chosen, let skilfull go set.
The goeler and younger, the better I love;
well gutted and pared, the better they prove.

Stick plenty of boughs among runcival pease,
to climber thereon, and to branch at their ease;
So doing, more tender and greater they wex,
if peacock and turkey leave jobbing their bex.

Not rent off, but cut off, ripe bean with a knife,
for hindering stalk, of her vegetive life.
So gather the lowest, and leaving the top,
shall teach thee a trick, for to double thy crop.

Good huswives in summer will save their own seeds
against the next year, as occasion needs:
One seed for another, to make an exchange,
with fellowly neighbourhood, seemeth not strange.

Good fruit and good plenty doth well in the loft,
then make thee an orchard, and cherish it oft;
For plant or for stock, lay aforehand to cast,
but set, or remove it, ere Christmas be past.

If garden require it, now trench it ye may,
one trench not a yard, from another go lay;
Which being well filled with muck by and by,
go cover with mould, for a season to lie.

Foul privies are now to be cleaned and fy'd,
let night be appointed, such baggage to hide,
Which buried in garden, in trenches a-low,
Shall make very many things, better to grow.

DIVERS OBSERVATIONS ON
VARIOUS CURIOUS POINTS RELATING
TO THE CULTIVATION AND USE
OF PLANTS

Early Imported Plants

And in time of memory things have bene brought in that were not here before, as the Damaske rose by Docteur Linaker king Henry the seventh and king Henrie the eights Physician, ... the Artichowe in time of king Henry the eight, and of later time was procured out of Italy the Muske rose plant, the plumme called the Perdigwena, and two kindes more, of the Lord Cromwell after his travell, and the Abricot by a French Priest one Wolfe Fardiner to king Henry the eight: and now within these foure yeeres there have bene brought into England from Vienne in Austria divers kinds of flowers called Tulipas, and those and other procured tither a little before from Constantinaple by an excellent man called M. Carolus Clusius. And it is sayd that since we traded to Zante that the plant that beareth the Coren is also brought into this realme from then: and although it bring not fruit to perfection, yet it may serve for pleasure and for some use, like as our vines doe, which we cannot well spare, although the climat so colde will not permit us to have good wines of them. And many other things have bene brought in, that have degenerated by reason of the colde climat, some other things brought in have by negligence bene lost. The Archbishop of Canterburie Edmund Grindall, after he returned out of Germany, brought into this relame the plant of Tamariske from thence, and this plant he hath so increased that there be here thousands of them; and many people have received great health by this plant: and if of things brought in such care were had, then could not the first labour be lost. The Seed of Tobacco hath bene brought hither out of the West Indies, it groweth heere, and with the herbs many have bene eased of the reumes. &c.

Description of England, William Harrison (1534–1593)

Several Plants and their Properties and Uses

BASILL

Basill is sowen in gardens in earthen pots ... it is good for the hart and for the head. The seede cureth the infirmities of the hart, taketh away sorrowfulnesse which cometh of melancholie, and maketh a man merrie and glad.

BLEW COLUMBINE

The slender sprigs whereof bring foorth euery one one flower with fine little hollowe hornes, as it were hanging foorth, with small leaues standing upright, of the shape of little birds.

CHEERIES

The best and principall cheeries be those that are somewhat sower; those little sweete ones which be wilde and soonest ripe, be the woorst they conteine bad juice . . . they do not onely breede woormas in the belly . . . therefore in well gouerned common wealthes it is carefully provided, that they should not be sold in the markets in the plague time.

The gum of the Cheerie tree taken with wine and water is reported to helpe the stone, it may do good by making the passages slippery.

Many excellent tartes, and other pleasant meates are made with Cheeries, Sugar, and other delicate spices, whereof to write were to small purpose.

CHIUES

Chiues attenuate or make thinne, open, prouoke urine, ingender hotte and grosse vapors and are hurtfull to the eies and braine. They cause troublesome dreames.

DITTANDER

Dittander is planted in gardens, and is to be found wild also in England in sundrie places, as at Clare by Ouenden in Essex . . . it delighteth to grow in sandie and shadowie places somewhat moist.

FLAX

Linseed draweth forth from the chest corrupted flegme, and if a composition with honey be made into a cake to licke on, easeth the cough. The oil pressed out of the seed is profitable for many purposes, in physick and in surgerie, and is used of painters, picture-makers and other artificers . . . with annise . . . it defends wounded members from swelling . . . being applied very warme, evening and morning. [The linseed poultice was frequently used in Victorian times!]

FLOURE GENTLE

I thinke the pencil of the most curious painter will be at a stay when he shall come to set it down in his lively colours . . . everie leafe resembleth in colour the most faire and beautifull feather of a Parat.

HEMP

Galen writeth in his book of the faculties of simple medicines, is hard of digestion, hurtful to the stomack and head and containeth an ill juice. Matthiolus saith that the seed given to hens causeth them to lay eggs more plentifully.

HORSETAIL

Horsetail, wherewith Fletchers and Combemakers doe rubbe and polish their worke.

PINKS

There is a Wilde creeping Pinke, which groweth in our pastures neere about London . . . especially in the great field next to Detford, by the path side as you go from Redriffe to Greenewich.

PURPLE COTTON THISTLE

Whereof the greatest quantitie of downe is gathered for diuers purposes, as well by the poor to stuff pillowes, cushions and beds for want of feathers; as also bought of the rich Upholsters to mix with the feathers and downe they do sell, which deceit would be looked unto.

SCORPION GRASS

Scorpion Grasse groweth in watery places with leaves like unto checkweed, having slender stalkes and branches . . . the floures of this are light blew or watchet colour.

SWEET WILLIAM

These plants are not used either in meate or medicine, but esteemed for their beautie to deck up gardens and the bosomes of the beautiful.

THRIFT

Is found in most salt Marshes in England, as also in gardens, for the bordering up of beds and banks, for the which it serueth very fitly.

WHITE JOHNS

We have in our London gardens a kinde herof, bearing most fine and pleasant white flowers, spotted very confusedly with reddish spots.

Fruit

Palladius, a Roman writer of the fourth century, was the author of a calendar of Roman agriculture, *De Re Rustica*, which was widely read in the

Middle Ages. His description of fruit storing would apply now. Hand-pick without bruising, allowing the fruit to 'sweat', lay on open slats in an airy room free from frost (and mice), store in jars full of earth or sawdust, or honey-water – he has a curious suggestion that the 'foot stalk be dipped in pitch'. At what date the drying of fruit became a farmhouse craft is unknown. The Norfolk biffin was an early form of dried apple: the tough-skinned red apple was dried slowly in a cooling bread oven, being pressed flat as it shrank so that the completed biffin was whole, but flattish and wrinkled. The crab apple deserves special mention, being a saleable trade commodity for verjuice.

Pears were early classed as 'wardons' (superior eating pears) and 'cookers'. Wild cherries, raspberries and strawberries were eaten, as were windberries, damsons and the small wild plum and sloe. But there seems to have been little attempt to store these crops.

Almonds, walnuts and cob nuts made an early English dessert, with apples, medlars, quinces and grapes. Other fruits are to be found listed, but were imported for banquets rather than common use.

Vines

Outdoor vines must have been 'sour grapes', but so was the mediaeval verjuice. Spring planting was preferred, and layers rather than cuttings. 'To grow as he stood is a part of his pride', is direct from Virgil, who states the importance of setting plants in the direction in which they grew. Theophrastus, one of Aristotle's Greek disciples who died about 287 B.C., explained that all plants make thicker bark on the colder side, thus pushing the sap-transmitting inner bark nearer to the surface on the opposite side, where a cold wind will stop the flow. Theophrastus also recommends a moist soil for planting and the 'planting be deep'.

A strong classical influence in the cultivation of vines persisted for many years.

Cinnamon Spice

... this Sinamome tree is a small tree, and not very high, and hath leaves like to our Baie tree. In the moneth of March or Aprill, when the sappe goeth up to the toppe of the tree, then they take the Sinamom from that tree in this wise. They cut the barke of the tree round about in length from knot to knot, or from joint to joint, above and belowe, and then easilie with their handes they take it away, laying it in the Sunne to drie, and in this wise it is gathered, and yet for all this the tree dieth not, but agaynst the next yeere it will have a new barke, and that which is gathered every yeere is the best Sinamome: ...

It is interesting that this was also how English oak bark was cut for tanning.

Saffron (Crocus sativus)

It is reported at Saffronwalden that a Pilgrim purposing to do good to his country, stole an head of Saffron, and hid the same in his Palmers staffe, which he had made hollow before of purpose, and so he brought this root into this realme, with venture of his life: for if he had been taken, by the law of the countrey from whence it came, he had died for the fact.

Richard Hakluyt (1553–1616)

Saffron is said to have been introduced into Essex in the time of Edward III: Norden describes it as growing as a crop around Saffron Walden and it was very generally grown in the sixteenth and seventeenth centuries. Now saffron cakes and saffron bread are mostly made in the West Country, but the cultivation is generally believed to have begun in East Anglia. In his *Chronicles* published in 1578 Holinshed gives an account of it as an established industry:

In September, the ground is pared and all weeds removed, that nothing may anoy the flower when his time doth come to rise. The flowers are gathered in the morning before the rising of the sunne which would cause them to welke, or flitter, and the chives [stamens] being picked from the flowers, the flowers are thrown on the dung hill and the chives dryed upon little kells [kilns]. The dried Saffron is then pressed into cakes and lagged up. In a good year we gather 100 pounds of wette Saffron of an aker. Where, sinth the price of Saffron is commonly about 20 shillings in money – it is easy to see what benefit is reped by this commoditie. The first year's yield of Saffron is the best, the third year the chives is now verie leane and hungrie. After 3 years the ground [after clearing] will serve well without compass for barlie. After 20 years the land may be set [with saffron] again.

In Tusser's time these were the costs per acre for growing saffron:

Triple tillage: 13s. 4d.
Clodding: 16 pence
Taking of everie load of stones from the same: 4d.
Raising of everie quarter of heads [bulbs] 6d. and cleaning them 6d.
Rent for one acre 10s.
Laying on doong 6d. a load [this for the first year only]
Setting the heads 23s. 4d., paring 5s., picking the chives 6d. a pound weighed wet.

Harrison notes that some bulbs he carried to London 'Though unset by a space of 15 daies', yet brought forth two or three flowers apiece. He also described the later rigging of the market by commercial growers who, 'wishing rather more scarcitie, because of keeping up the price', did destroy good heads. Harrison thought highly of saffron, and he gave advice as to how it should be grown:

> warme nights, sweete dewes, jet grounds, chiefly chalky, and misty mornings are very good for saffron – but frost and cold doe kill the flowers. Would to god that my countriemen had been hereto-before more careful of this commoditie then would it no doubt have proved more beneficial to our island than our cloth or wool.
> Saffron, besides the manifold use that it hath in the kitchen and pastrie, also in our cakes at bridals, and thanksgivings of women, is very profitably mingled with those medicines which we take.
>
> *Description of England,* published in 1577

Hakluyt also wrote about the suitability of saffron-growing as an English industry:

> Saffron the best of the universall world groweth in this realme, and forasmuch as it is a thing that requireth much labour in divers sorts, and setteth the people on worke so plentifully . . . But if a vent might be found, men would in Essex about Saffronwalden and in Cambridge shire revive the trade for the benefit of the setting of the poore on work. So would they doe in Herefordshire [where it is still found] by Wales, where the best of all England is, in which place the soile yeelds the wilde Saffron commonly, which sheweth the naturall inclination of the same soile to the bearing of the right Saffron, if the soile be manured and that way employed.

TUSSER'S HOP-YARD

Whom fancy perswadeth, among other crops,
to have for his spending sufficient of hops
Must willingly follow, of choices to chuse
such lessons approved as skillful do use.

Ground gravelly, sandy, and mixed with clay
is naughty for hops any manner of way,
Or if it be mingled with rubbish and stone
for dryness and barrenness let it alone.

Chuse soil for the hop of the rottenest mould,
well dunged and wrought as a garden plot should:
Not far from the water (but not over flown),
this lesson well noted, is meet to be known.

The sun in the south, or else southly and west,
is joy to the hop as a welcomed guest.
But wind in the North, or else Northerly east,
to hop is as ill as a fray in a feast.

Meet plot for a hop-yard, once found as is told,
make thereof account, as a jewell of gold.
Now dig it, and leave it, the sun for to burn,
and afterward fence it, to serve for that turn.

The wild hop was perhaps indigenous; the cultivated hop was brought from the Low Countries during Henry VIII's reign. According to Caxton and others, 'Bere was made in England by Byere brewers, who were Flemynges and Duchemen'. It was not altogether approved, and the Royal Household was warned not to add hops or brimstone to the royal brew. The hop gives a good yellow dye and the small tender hop tops were boiled and served with butter.

Hops were first grown in clumps on small hillocks into which the poles were thrust (later the poles were pickled in creosote to prevent rot). Tusser also suggests the hop might grow freely over fences and bushes. Kilns do not seem to have been used: a draughty loft and loosely-woven sacks hung around the central household chimney was the housewife's drying store for centuries.

Turkies, herisies, hops and beer
All came to England in one year.

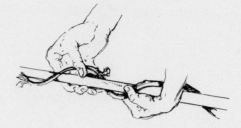

Bending a hop shoot to the pole. The last word on hops must go to Borde, writing around 1452: 'Ale is made of malt and water and they the whiche do put any other thing to ale than is rehersed except yeast, barme and godes good, doth sophysticat theyre ale . . .'

GLOSSARY

This Glossary is not intended to be exhaustive, but we hope it covers those terms which might puzzle or mislead. (Ch) denotes that the word appears in an extract from Chaucer, (T) from Tusser.

ALOME: alum, used in dyeing as a mordant; later it was used to adulterate bread.
ANDREW: the feast of St Andrew, 30 November.
ASCENSIOUN (Ch): the rising of a celestial body, or a degree in this rising. Before clocks were common, time had to be reckoned by the movement of the sun or stars.
AVISE ELSE AVOUS (T): be warned.

BARTLEMEW TIDE: the feast of St Bartholomew, 24 August.
BEATH: to heat unseasoned wood in order to straighten it.
BECK: a northern word for a brook or mountain stream.
BEENE (T): bees.
BO(O)RD: a board; the 'bord clothes' were the table cloths covering the board set on trestles which formed the dining table. Thus 'bed and board' means bed and main meals; a 'bord penny' was a rental.
BORDARS: villeins of the lowest rank, who rendered menial service in return for a cottage (held at the will of the lord).
BOWD: weevil (kinds of beetle which infest stored cereals etc.)
BRAKES: clumps of bushes, brushwood or briars; thickets.
BRAVE: showy.
BRINNE: burn.
BUCKING: a laundry term, covering the steeping of clothes, linen and so on, in lye.
BUSKES: bushes.
BUTTRICE (T): a tool for paring hooves.

CADOW (T): jackdaw.
CATEL (Ch): property.
CHAMPION (T): unenclosed land, and the farmers of it.
CHANGE (T): 'between change and the prime' refers to phases of the moon (the calves were born three days after the full moon).
CHINKS IN THY PURSE (T): ready money.
CLOWTED (T): clouted, that is nailed and patched up so that there are no holes.
COCKLE: a weed, corn cockle, which grew in cornfields and was definitely *not* wanted.

COMPASS: a form of manure.

COPEROSE: zinc sulphate.

COPPERAS: the sulphates, naturally occurring, of copper, iron and zinc (blue, white and green copperas).

COTTARS: peasants who lived in cottages belonging to a farm, as a sort of out-servants.

CRONES (T): old ewes.

CROTCH (T): a hooked or forked stick.

DOWCE: sweeten.

EQUYNOXIAL (Ch): the equinoctial circle: a great circle of the heavens in the plane of the earth's equator. According to the old astronomical reckoning this made a complete daily revolution, so that fifteen degrees would pass or 'ascend' every hour. It was believed that cocks crowed exactly on the hour.

EY (Ch): egg. The plural is 'eyren'.

FIMBLE: the female hemp plant.

FOIZ(S)ON (T): plenty, a good harvest.

GENTILS (T): 'gentles', maggots.

GILL: a narrow mountain stream, often in a deep wooded ravine.

GILSLAND: a district of moors with gullies of gills (or 'ghylls') of water.

GLEBE: a portion of land that was part of a clergyman's benefice.

GOEF (T): a 'mow' of hay.

GREGORY: the feast of St Gregory, 13 February.

HABERDEN: dried or salted cod, or possibly haddock.

HACKLING: the combing out of flax.

HALLONTIDE: All Saint's Day, 1 November.

HEIGH PRYME: about 9 a.m. (A rough translation of the whole passage is: Then about nine o'clock Piers left his plough, in order to see how things were going, and to pick out the best workers to hire again at harvest time.)

HIGHT: (also spelt in other ways) to be called or named.

HIRSEL: an entire breeding settlement of sheep.

HOY OUT (T): 'hoy' was the usual expression for driving or calling pigs; by calling 'hoy' the carter is to get the pigs from under his wheels.

HYYES: approaches. (A rough translation of the passage is: But then autumn approaches, and soon grows severe, warning it (the plant) to ripen for fear of winter. It drives dust with drought, making it rise from the face of the earth to fly very high.)

INGROSS: to buy up wholesale; to buy up the whole – or as much as possible – of a commodity for the purpose of selling again at a profit in the same, or a near-by, market.

KEEN (Ch): kine, cattle.

LADY DAY: the feast of the Annunciation, 25 March. This was one of the 'quarter days', that is one of the four days throughout the year on which tenancies began and ended, and payment of rent or other quarterly charges was due. The other quarter days were Mid-summer Day (24 June), Michaelmas (29 September) and Christmas Day (25 December).

LAMMAS: 1 August.

LAX (T): a kind of diarrhoea in cattle ('scouring').

LEMAN: what we would now probably term a 'mistress'.

LET: a hindrance or obstruction.

LEY: (1) originally a dialect variant of 'lea', but now means land re-seeded for grass. The seed is sold in various grades, according to how long it is thought it will be before the field is ploughed up; thus there is seed for three-year ley, or for a five-year ley. And if it lasts that long, it can become 'permanent'. (2) a variant of 'lye', which is any strong alkaline solution, especially one used for cleaning or washing.

LIRIPIPE: a kind of headdress with a long tail. (Also known as 'liripoop'.)

LING (FISH): a fish (*Molva molva*) usually dried or salted.

LITHARGE: lead monoxide; litharge of silver is the name given to lead when it is a by-product in the production of silver.

LOGGE (Ch): a resting place (lodge).

MARTILMAS: the feast of St Martin, 11 November.

MASHING: a term used in brewing. The malt is mixed with water (or other ingredients) to produce the 'wort' or liquor which is then fermented into beer.

MEAK (T): a hook-ended spud for pulling up, not thrusting down.

MESTLIN: maslin, mixed grain – especially rye mixed with wheat.

MICHAELMAS: the feast of St Michael, one of the archangels, 29 September; a quarter-day (see *Lady Day*).

MILCH COW: a cow kept for milking.

NOI(ETH)(ANCE): trouble, nuisance, harm.

ORLOGGE (Ch): a 'horologe'; a time-piece or clock.

OX-BOW LAKE: a pond formed when by natural erosion on one side, and silting on the other, a bend in a river is separated from the main water-course. This frequently happens in meandering rivers in flat country.

PANNAGE: the right of, or payment for, the feeding of swine in a forest or wood. It can also mean the acorns, beechmast, and so on, on which the swine feed.

PARGETTING: Ornamental plaster work, in relief or indented, for the decoration of walls.

PASQUE: Easter.

PECCANTEM (T): the more usual form is 'peccavi' (I have sinned); a confession of error.

PEELER (T): a plant which robs or impoverishes the soil.

PELF (T): property or goods.

PEASE, PEASON: peas.

PHILIP AND JACOB: the feast of Saints Philip and Jacob, 1 May.

PISÉ: stiff clay or earth kneaded, or mixed with gravel, used for building. It was rammed between boards, which were then removed as it hardened.

PLASHING: the bending down and intertwining of twigs and branches, so that separate bushes form a stout hedge.

PLOUGH MONDAY: the first Monday after the feast of the Epiphany, which falls on 'Twelfth night' (6 January). Plough Monday could therefore be no earlier than 7, and no later than 14, January.

POMACE: the mass of crushed apples in the process of cider-making, either before or after the juice is pressed out.

QUITETH: rewards.

REQUIEM AETERNAM (T): eternal rest, death.

RETTING: the preparation of flax by steeping or watering; this seasons the fibres. Retting ponds were the ponds where this was done.

RINGLING (T): pigs have rings put through the cartilage of their sensitive snouts to deter them from rooting in the earth.

ROWEN (T): grass growing up among the stubble.

ST MARY DAYS: 22 July and 15 August; the first is the feast of St Mary Magdalen, the second the feast of the Assumption.

SEEDCAKE: a sweet cake flavoured with caraway seeds.

SEELY (T): silly, in the sense of innocent or harmless.

SELVEDGE: the narrow strip down the edge of a piece of woven material.

SERECLOTH: a cloth impregnated with wax, used as a waterproof covering or winding sheet (cerecloth, cerements).

SEYND (Ch): salted.

SHENT: disgraced, lost, ruined.

SHIPPON: a cow-shed, what is called in the north a 'byre'.

SHROVETIDE: The period comprising Quinquagesima Sunday (the last Sunday before Lent) and the two following days, 'Shrove' Monday and Tuesday. The word 'shrove' is connected with 'shrive', and refers to the custom of being shriven: making confession, and receiving absolution and penance, before Lent begins on Ash Wednesday.

SIKERER (Ch): certain, assured.

SLABBER'D AND SOST (T): descriptive words, meaning nastily wet and soaked.

SOAR MILK: sour milk.

SOLLER (T): the 'solar' chamber was the upper room in a large house, often used by the women for sewing and so on; Tusser means a loft.

SOUSE: a kind of pickle, especially one made with vinegar, for preserving food; also various parts of a pig, especially the feet and ears, pickled.

STAPE (Ch): advanced.

STEADING: the farmstead.

SUCKING PIG: a piglet killed before it is weaned. It made a tasty and tender dish.

SUER (T): sure.

TALC: probably mica.

TEMMES LOAF (T): a loaf made from mixed wheat and rye, with the bran removed.

THILKE (Ch): that.

THILLER (T): harness for a trace horse.

THRUMS: short pieces of waste thread or yarn.

TINE (T): a wild vetch that grasps other plants with its tendrils.

TITTERS (T): a troublesome weed, probably a vetch.

TREEN: things made from wood.

TWIGGERS (T): probably Tusser is thinking of the sheep as branching out?

VENT: sale.

VERJUICE: the acid juice of crab-apples or other sour fruit, pressed out; Tusser's 'vergis'.

VILLEIN: a peasant occupier or cultivator entirely subject to a lord, or attached to a manor.

WAKE: a watch held over the dead, before burial, with lamentation or merry-making according to custom.

WAKE DAY (T): Wake weeks, in the north and in the west midlands, are still observed. They began as the celebration of the feast of the patron saint of the local church, then were attached to some particular Sunday and the days following, as an occasion for feasting and jollity. It is possible that this is related.

WENNELS (T): young animals (eg calves, colts) that have been weaned.

WITHY: willow. Withies are bindings made from the flexible twigs or small branches of the willow.

WIMBLE: an auger or gimlet.

INDEX

References in *italic* indicate an illustration or the caption to it. There may be additional information in the text on the same page. References in **bold** indicate an illustration in the plate section.